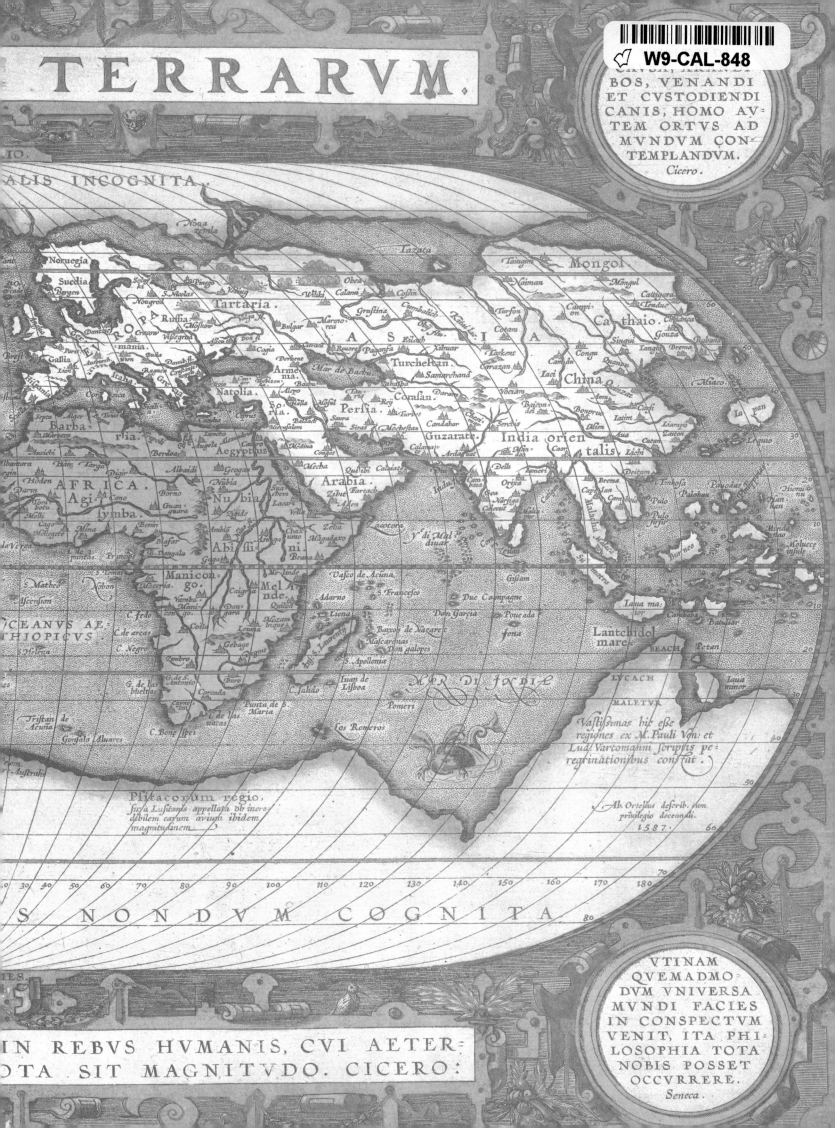

Cultural Atlas of
AUSTRALIA,
NEW ZEALAND
AND THE
SOUTH PACIFIC

Senior Editor and Project Manager
 Susan Kennedy
Art Editor Chris Munday
Design Adrian Hodgkins
Picture Editor Linda Proud
Picture Managers Jo Rapley, Martin Anderson
Cartographic Manager Richard Watts
Senior Cartographic Editor Polly Senior
Cartographic Editor Tim Williams
Editorial Assistant Marian Dreier
Index Ann Barrett
Production Clive Sparling
Typesetting Brian Blackmore

AN ANDROMEDA BOOK

Planned and produced by
Andromeda Oxford Limited
11–15 The Vineyard, Abingdon
Oxfordshire, England OX14 3PX

For information contact:

Facts On File, Inc.,
11 Penn Plaza,
New York, NY 10001

Library of Congress Cataloging-in-Publication Data

Nile, Richard.
    Cultural atlas of Australia, New Zealand, and the
    South Pacific / Richard Nile and Christian Clerk.
        p.   cm.
    Includes bibliographical references and index.
    ISBN 0–8160–3083–9
    1. Australia--Civilization. 2. New Zealand--Civilization.
    3. Oceania--Civilization. I. Clerk, Christian. II. Title.
DU107.N55 1996
990--dc20   96–1456

Facts On File books are available at special discounts
when purchased in bulk quantities for businesses,
associations, institutions or sales promotions. Please
call our Special Sales Department in New York at
212/967–8800 or 800/322–8755.

Origination by Eray Scan, Singapore

Printed in Spain by Fournier Artes
Gráficas, S.A., Vitoria

10 9 8 7 6 5 4 3 2 1

Endpapers: *Typus Orbis Terrarum* by Abraham Ortelius,
Antwerp 1570; British Library
Prelim pictures: 2–3 *Balgo Hills* Manuel Mudjidell;
4–5 *Three Snakes Dreaming* Old Mick Gill; 6 *Water
Dreaming* Clifford Possum. Rebecca Hossack Gallery

Cultural Atlas of

AUSTRALIA, NEW ZEALAND AND THE SOUTH PACIFIC

Richard Nile
and Christian Clerk

Facts On File, Inc.

AN INFOBASE HOLDINGS COMPANY

CONTENTS

Special Features

List of Maps

PREFACE

The scope of this Atlas is a vast one. It is impossible within the confines of a single volume to do full justice to the geographical, historical and cultural complexity of a region that includes the continent of Australia, the landmasses of New Guinea and New Zealand, and the many thousands of islands of the South Pacific. Within this physically diverse region there are enormous contrasts of human experience and society. The Aboriginal peoples of Australia are perhaps the oldest continuous civilization on Earth, dating back possibly as much as 140,000 years, while eastern Polynesia was the final part of the world to be colonized by humankind. The Maori settlement of New Zealand (Aotearoa) took place only about 1,000 years ago.

The Pacific was the last area of the world to have contact with Europeans. Their arrival, less than 500 years ago, was to have profound and often catastrophic consequences for the indigenous peoples. At the time of their first incursion into the Pacific, Europeans had greater understanding of the movements of the stars and the planets in the heavens than they did of the Earth's geography. That did not dampen their enthusiasm for speculation about the other side of the globe. Travelers' tales told of exotic beasts and plants and of people who lived in a world that was upside down. Map-makers drew imaginary coastlines and filled in the empty spaces of the land with mountain ranges, deserts and rivers. Belief in the existence of a great south land of vast riches dominated European thinking about the Pacific for generations: it was only with the great voyages of exploration at the end of the 18th century that this myth was finally put to rest.

European art and literature represented the peoples of the Pacific as, on the one hand, brute savages, the missing link between apes and humans, on the other as the happy and innocent inhabitants of the original Garden of Eden. One aim of the Atlas is to show how these popular imaginings continue to reverberate, influencing attitudes to the region today. In tourist brochures and movies, the islands are still exoticized as places of love and adventure, while Australia is depicted as the oldest and most remote of the world's continents. Yet the Pacific region is at the center of current global concerns. In the decades since World War II, former colonial ties have given place to new international trading partnerships, particularly with the countries of Asia and with the United States. Interregional organizations such as the South Pacific Forum bring the countries of the Pacific together to exchange ideas and form common political ground on issues of mutual concern. The use of the Pacific as a testground for nuclear weapons by outside colonial powers has made all the Pacific peoples particularly conscious of threats to their unique and fragile environments. Climate change and global warming imperil the very existence of the low-lying islands of the Pacific; they are bringing prolonged drought to some parts of the Australian continent, and increasing the incidence and violence of cyclonic storms in others.

The *Cultural Atlas of Australia, New Zealand and the South Pacific* begins its broad survey of the rich cultural traditions of the region with the arrival of the first peoples in Australia between 140,000 and 60,000 years ago. The earliest known site in Melanesia has been dated back to 40,000 years ago, and occupation may have begun much earlier. About 6,000 years ago a new population, the Austronesians, began to move into Melanesia. They were the ancestors of the Polynesians, seafarers who by about 1000 BC had settled the island triangle of Fiji, Samoa and Tonga and in the next 2,000 years peopled the furthest corners of the eastern Pacific from Hawaii to Easter Island and New Zealand. European colonization brought lasting change to the Pacific. It persistently undervalued and ignored the diverse and complex cultures of Pacific societies. Since the 1960s, there has been a strong reassertion of indigenous cultural identities and traditions.

The white settler societies that became established in Australia and New Zealand during the late 18th century and throughout the 19th century displaced the indigenous peoples from their custodial lands and caused whole societies to break up. The colonization of Australia by the British as a penal settlement was a unique event in human history. Its convict and pioneer past shaped the nation's founding myths and still influences its cultural identity. In recent years there has been a revitalization of cultural identity among the Aboriginal and Maori peoples. Land rights have become a fiercely fought political issue, forcing the settler societies to ask new questions about themselves and their occupation of the land.

These and other topics are discussed in this Atlas, which is the work of two authors. Christian Clerk wrote the chapters on the pre-European contact societies of the island Pacific and on the South Pacific today. All the other chapters are by Richard Nile.

Previous page Dusk over the Isle of Pines, New Caledonia.

PART ONE
THE GEOGRAPHICAL BACKGROUND

UNITED STATES

Rio Grande

MEXICO

Mexico City

HAWAII
(United States)

HAWAIIAN RIDGE

Kauai
Oahu
Honolulu
Maui
Mauna Loa
4169
Hawaii

Johnston
(United States)

NORTH PACIFIC OCEAN

Line
Islands

Kiritimati
(Christmas Island)

Phoenix
Islands

KIRIBATI

Line
Islands

EASTERN PACIFIC RISE

TOKELAU
(New Zealand)

Line Islands

Marquesas
Islands

AMERICAN
SAMOA
(United States)

Nassau

ESTERN
SAMOA

Upolu
Apia
Pago Pago
Mata-Utu
Tutuila
Uvéa

COOK
ISLANDS
(New Zealand)

Line Islands

Society Islands

Tuamotu
Archipelago

TONGA

Vava'u
Group

Alofi
Niue

Tahiti

Papeete

FRENCH
POLYNESIA
(France)

Ha'apai
Group

NIUE
(New Zealand)

Rarotonga

Avarua

Tubuai Islands
(Austral Islands)

Iles
Gambier

PITCAIRN
GROUP
(Britain)

uku'alofa

Tongatapu
Group

AUSTRAL SEAMOUNTS

Adamstown

Pitcairn
Island

TONGA
TRENCH

Marotiri
(Iles de Bass)

Easter Island
(Isla de Pascua)
(Chile)

RMADEC
TRENCH

SOUTH PACIFIC OCEAN

Chatham
Islands
(New Zealand)

■ capital city
□ other administrative center or important city
▲ mountain summit
(height in meters)
─·─·─ international boundary

meters

4000
2000
1000
500
200
0 sea level
200
1800
3700
5500
7300
9100

scale 1: 37 870 000

0 _____ 1000km

0 _____ 800mi

170°   160°   150°   140°   130°   120°   110°   100°

OCEAN AND ISLANDS

A vast body of water

The Pacific Ocean is the single largest geographical feature on Earth. It covers an area of 165 million square kilometers – a third of the Earth's surface – and holds more than twice the volume of water that the Atlantic, the second largest ocean, does. North to south, it stretches 15,000 kilometers from the Bering Strait on the Arctic Circle to the icy waters of Antarctica – almost the full length of the Earth. At its widest point, 5° north of the Equator, it extends across 180° of latitude and spans some 20,000 kilometers from the Malaysian peninsula in the west to the coast of Colombia in the east.

The Pacific is so large that it could contain all the world's landmasses combined without displacing all its water, and there would still be room enough to accommodate a seventh continent the size of Asia. Scientists have speculated that there may have once existed a Melanesian continent that sank millions of years ago when the structure and composition of the Earth's surface underwent fundamental changes. Ancient rock formations on some of the islands of Melanesia (that is, New Guinea and its offshore archipelagos, the Solomon Islands, Vanuatu and New Caledonia) support this theory, but in the absence of further substantiating evidence it must remain a fanciful creation in the same way as the fabled Atlantis of ancient European legend.

The vast expanses of the Pacific are dotted by more than 20,000 islands – a figure that represents 80 percent of the world's total number of islands. The vast majority, however, are small, uninhabited coral atolls that scarcely rise above the surface of the ocean. Together the islands of the Pacific cover a combined land area of only 1,300,000 square kilometers: for every square kilometer of land in the Pacific there are around 130 square kilometers of ocean surface. New Guinea accounts for 70 percent of the total amount of land and New Zealand 20 percent; the remaining 10 percent is divided between the thousands of smaller islands that lie mostly in the Central and South Pacific between the Tropics of Cancer and Capricorn. The 15 or so Cook Islands, near the Pacific's geographical center, have a total land area of less than 250 square kilometers spread over more than 2 million square kilometers of ocean surface, a ratio of about 1 square meter of land to every 10 square kilometers of ocean surface. Many islands are separated from their nearest neighbors by vast expanses of ocean: Easter Island, for instance, is one of the remotest places on Earth. More than 3,500 kilometers of sea separates it from the Chilean coast of South America while Pitcairn Island, its nearest neighbor to the west, lies 2,000 kilometers away. The vast uninhabited frozen continent of Antarctica defines the Pacific Ocean's southernmost limits, while on its southwest perimeter lies the aged continent of Australia. The smallest of the Earth's continents, Australia nevertheless covers approximately 8.5 million square kilometers, more than six times the combined land area of the Pacific islands.

Below A coral beach with palm trees swaying gently in the tropical breeze provides the perennially popular image of the Pacific; this view of Upolu island in Western Samoa, with palm trees growing down almost to the water's edge, is typical. More than two-thirds of the world's species of palms are to be found in the Pacific, and palms, ranging from small shrubs to the tall coconut palms, grow on almost all of its more than 20,000 islands. The varieties that grow in the Pacific originated in Asia and were carried to the islands by ocean currents (the coconut can germinate after months of floating at sea) and by human voyagers. Coconuts, as a source of food and drink, would have been of great value to early canoe travelers, and palm products, especially copra (the dried flesh of the coconut), remain essential to the region's economy. Palms are hardy, as they need to be to withstand the Pacific's occasional violent storms as well as the persistently high levels of salt.

The Pacific "Ring of Fire"

Deep beneath the ocean's surface, three major physiographic features define the Pacific floor. The largest of these is the Central Pacific Trough. The Earth's crust at this point is between 4 and 6 kilometers deep, and the whole area is relatively featureless except in the west and center, where volcanic eruptions have thrown up thousands of now largely inactive volcanic cones that jut up as islands out of the sea. To the west of the Central Trough, the Broad Western Margin is a more complex geographical region that is characterized by sunken continental platforms extending outward from Asia and Australia, while on the eastern edge a much narrower rim reaches out from the coastlines of North and South America.

These features are the result of massive movements of the Earth's crust that have been going on for millions of years. The outer shell of the Earth consists of enormous slabs called tectonic plates, which comprise a proportion of oceanic crust or continental crust, or both, and are attached to a portion of the underlying rigid layer of the Earth's upper mantle. About 160 million years ago Antarctica, Australia, South America, India, Africa and part of Southeast Asia formed the single supercontinent of Gondwanaland. This began to fracture and break up into smaller plates that over a long period of geological time started to drift away from each other. The landmasses that were to become India and Africa broke away first, and then Australia sheared off from Antarctica, and the continents gradually assumed their present shape.

The Earth's tectonic plates are all constantly and very slowly moving in relation to each other at rates from a few millimeters to a few centimeters each year. The Indo-Australian plate is traveling in a northeasterly direction at about 7 centimeters a year, while the vast plate that carries the Pacific, which cuts across it laterally, is moving northwest. The boundary zones of the plates are areas of considerable geophysical activity, characterized by frequent earthquakes and volcanic eruptions. Where plates pull apart, the stretching weakens the Earth's crust. Magma from the Earth's core bursts through the fissure as molten rock to create extensive ridging across the ocean floor, such as the Pacific-Antarctic Ridge. Sometimes it may break the surface of the ocean to form folded mountain ranges. The two islands of New Zealand straddle the Indo-Australian and Antarctic plates. Its geological

The geology of the Pacific region
The Earth's surface, or lithosphere, is made up of several large crustal or tectonic plates. Estimated to be between 50 and 100 kilometers thick, these plates are generally stable but where they meet and collide there is great geological activity in the Pacific region, where they throw up mountain ranges and create deep oceanic trenches. Earthquakes and volcanic eruptions are a way of life to the peoples living around the Pacific rim, especially in the region of Southeast Asia and Japan where three of the Earth's large continental plates – the Pacific, the Indo-Australian and the Eurasian – meet around the smaller Philippine plate. By contrast, Australia – the exposed land area of the Indo-Australian plate – is free of volcanoes and virtually unaffected by earthquakes.

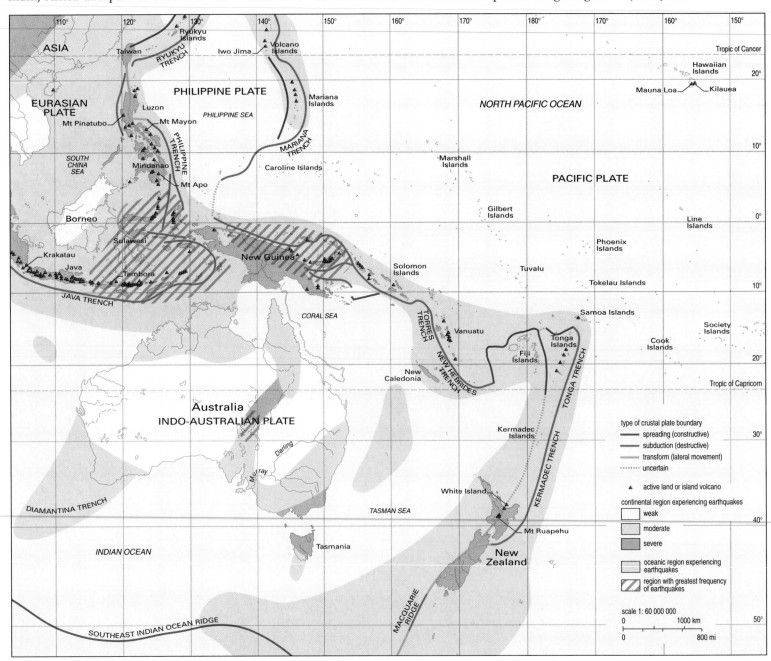

Above About 80 percent of the world's estimated 13,000 active volcanoes are to be found in the Pacific region, created by weaknesses in the Earth's crust and by movement at the junctions of the continental plates. White Island (Whakaari) in the Bay of Plenty at the northern end of New Zealand is the peak of a submerged volcano. It was named by Captain James Cook in 1769 on account of the white clouds, containing a mixture of ash, steam and gas, that billow out of its crater. It lies on the boundary of the Indo-Australian and Antarctic plates on a line that extends northward into the Kermadec and Tongan Ridges.

formation is consistent with the drag and shear of these plates as they continue to pull away from each other, creating parallel chains of high fold mountains ridging upward along the South Island.

Where two plates collide head on, one plate plunges beneath the other, throwing up mountainous ridges and volcanoes on one side and creating deep oceanic trenches on the other. In the southwestern and western Pacific, where the Pacific plate meets the Indo-Australian plate and the southeasterly-moving giant Eurasian plate, the Kermadec Trench and Ridge, the Tonga Trench and Ridge, the Yap Trench and Ridge, and the Mariana Trench and Ridge have been formed. Farther north the Japan Trench runs parallel to the islands of Japan, the Kiril Trench is matched by the Kiril Ridge and on the Pacific's northern perimeter the Aleutian Trench runs along the arc of the Aleutian Islands. Most spectacular of all is the snake-like Peru-Chile Trench, on the collision boundary between the Antarctic and South American plates, which is paralleled by the massive upfolding of the Andes. Other plates converge laterally: the North American plate, for example, is moving northwest while the adjacent

Pacific plate heads southeast. This causes upthrusting, downfolding and major fault lines such as the San Andreas Fault.

The Pacific rim or circum-Pacific belt – commonly known as the "Ring of Fire" – is the Earth's most volatile region. More volcanic eruptions and earthquakes occur here than anywhere else in the world. Most activity takes place deep beneath the surface of the ocean and appears as little more than tremors on the continental landmasses, but giant ocean waves, known as *tsunami* (a Japanese term), are caused by the shock waves from these submarine eruptions. As they travel across the surface of the ocean the *tsunami* gain in size and can cause great damage when they hit an island or coastline.

Currents and winds

The average depth of the ocean in the Pacific basin is around 4 kilometers. In the Marianas Trench, the world's deepest marine trench, it reaches a depth of more than 11 kilometers. The waters of the Pacific move in a series of complex circulations, which derive partly from the action of the wind on the surface of the

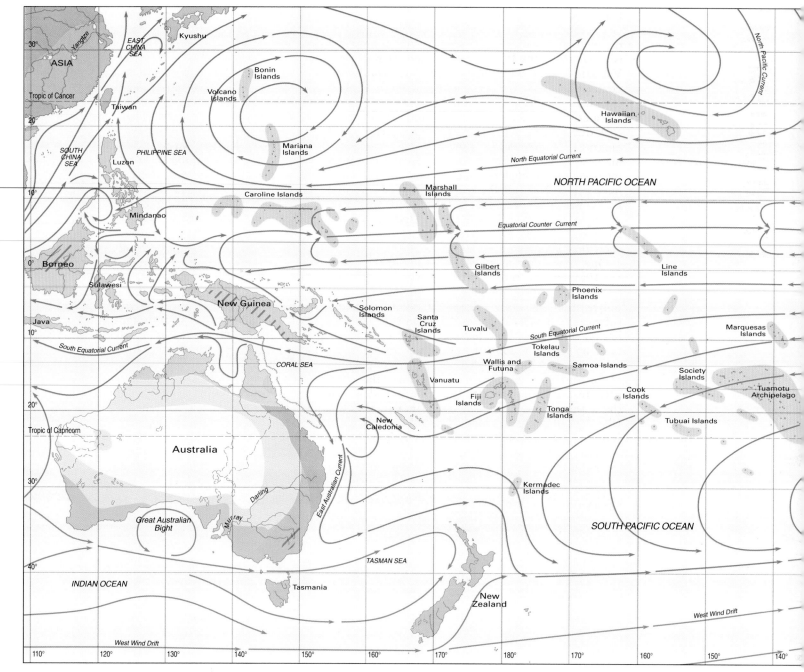

sea and partly from convective processes. In the cold seas around Antarctica prevailing westerly winds propel the flow of water eastward (the Southern Ocean Current or West Wind Drift). On reaching the continental shelf of South America it is diverted northward along the coast as the cold Peru or Humboldt Current. As it reaches the tropics the surface water warms up and is driven away from the coast by the prevailing offshore southerly trade winds. Cold subsurface water, which is rich in nutrients, rises to replace it – a process known as upwelling. The flow of water is diverted in an anticlockwise direction to form the South Equatorial Current, and a stream turns south when it reaches the New Guinea and Australian landmasses. The warm East Australia Current meets the cold waters of the Southern Ocean Current in the Tasman Sea. A similar circulation between the polar waters and the Equator takes place in the North Pacific.

The trade winds, which emanate around the Tropics of Capricorn and Cancer and converge on the Equator from the southeast and the northeast, dominate the climate of the oceanic islands. In the Intertropical Convergence Zone (ITCZ) where the winds meet, warm air rises to a height of 12 to 15 kilometers, towering cumulus clouds form and heavy rain falls. The ITCZ moves north and south of the true Equator, following the latitude where the sun is overhead at midday. Winds in this zone are generally light and variable – hence the popular designation of the "doldrums". Nevertheless, tropical storms, known as cyclones, hurricanes or typhoons, are frequent.

These intense rain-bearing depressions occur when the surface temperature of the ocean rises to 27° C. This creates an area of very low pressure, which is made to spin by the Earth's rotation. Water vapor is sucked into the vortex, creating a swirling cloud. This speeds up the rate of evaporation, more water is collected and the pressure drops still further. As the cyclone builds up winds can reach speeds of 300 kilometers per hour, cutting a narrow path of destruction, but the typhoon itself moves more slowly, and in its center (the "eye of the storm") there is a strange calm. The cyclone travels away from the Equator, and it dissipates as it reaches cooler ocean, spreading rain over a much wider area.

Currents and climate
Most of the Pacific islands fall within the Intertropical Convergence Zone between the Tropics of Cancer and Capricorn and receive rainfall all the year round. However the regular anticlockwise circulation of the southern currents and winds, which moves warm waters east–west in the tropics and cold waters west–east across the Southern Ocean, is periodically interrupted by a phenomenon known as the El Niño effect. This occurs when water temperatures in the southern South Pacific rise, and the normal pattern is reversed. Raincarrying winds blow onshore to the normally arid coast of South America, while the cessation of the easterly air currents diminishes rainfall across the Pacific, bringing severe drought to the east coast of Australia. The El Niño effect is thought to be intensifying with global warming.

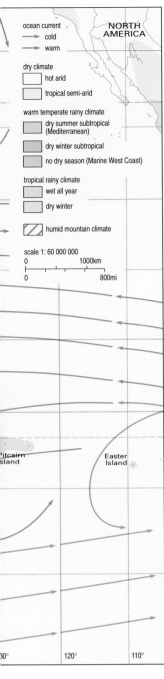

Clusters of islands

Geographers divide islands into two main types: continental and oceanic. In the South Pacific continental islands – for example, New Guinea, the Solomons and Vanuatu – lie on the margins of the Australian continental shelf, near the conjunction of the Indo-Australian and Pacific plates. These islands are made up of volcanic and ancient sedimentary and metamorphic rock that has been folded and faulted to form rugged mountain ranges, and so there is a wide range of climate, soils and vegetation. Oceanic islands rise from the ocean basin. High oceanic islands, volcanoes that have emerged out of the sea, are mountainous and rocky. Easter Island and the Samoa Islands are classic examples of the type. Low oceanic islands are usually atolls – coral reefs in the shape of a ring or horseshoe encircling a lagoon.

One theory, first formulated by Charles Darwin in the 19th century, is that an atoll began as a fringing coral reef (formed from the skeletons of tiny coral polyps) built around a volcanic island: as the island submerged, the result of subsidence, only the reef was left on the surface. Another theory is that atolls are built up from the tops of underwater volcanoes or ridges that are close enough to the surface for colonies of reef-building corals to live. Neither theory is entirely satisfactory, and atolls may be formed in both these ways. The Kwajalein Atoll in the Marshall Islands, 130 kilometers long and 30 kilometers wide, is the largest coral atoll in the world: its lagoon covers an area of 1,600 square kilometers.

The islands of the Pacific basin (often referred to collectively as Oceania) are commonly grouped into three distinct regions – Micronesia, Polynesia and Melanesia. These groupings owe their existence to supposed ethnographic differences identified in the 19th century. Micronesia lies to the east of the Philippines, mostly between the Tropic of Cancer and the Equator. Its scattered groups contain both high volcanic islands and coral atolls: Palau, for example, consists of 340 coral and volcanic islands perched on the Kyushu-Palau Ridge, and the Marshall Islands are composed of two parallel lines of coral islands and atolls set on the submerged Ralik and Ratak volcanic chains. The mountainous Marianas are a chain of volcanic peaks thrown up alongside the Mariana Trench. Guam, the largest of this group, with a land area of 541 square kilometers, is characterized by a limestone plateau in the north and volcanic hills in the south, the tallest of which, Mount Lamlan, rises to 406 meters. Yap, Truk, Pohnpei and Kosrae, the four main islands of the Federated States of Micronesia (formerly the Caroline Islands) are also high volcanic islands, but Kiribati (formerly the Gilbert Islands) consists entirely of low-lying coral atolls that extend more than 3,000 kilometers from Banaba in the west to the Line Islands in the east.

The island groups of Polynesia cover a vast triangle in the eastern Pacific extending from the Hawaiian Islands on the Tropic of Cancer to New Zealand, between 34° and 47° S, with Easter Island, just south of the Tropic of Capricorn, forming the third corner. At the center of this arrowhead are the islands of Samoa. The main islands of Savaii, Tutuila, Upolu,

Right Aitutaki in the Cook Islands archipelago is an almost complete horseshoe-shaped coral atoll sheltering a lagoon. The islets in the center and bottom of the picture are the remnants of the extinct volcanic cone, which – according to one theory of atoll-formation – has subsided below the sea, leaving only the fringing coral reef on the surface.

and the Manua island group of Ofu, Olosega and Tau are high and rugged – the tallest peak, at 1,859 meters, is Silisili on Savaii – but coral reefs are common. To their east are the Cook Islands, also formed as the result of volcanic activity. The main island of Rarotonga is 6 kilometers wide and rises to a height of just over 650 meters. The northern Cook Islands, including Penehyn, Manihiki and Rakahanga, feature atolls, reefs and sandbanks. Though straddling the Tropic of Capricorn, the climate of the Cook Islands is comparatively cool, influenced by the southeast trade winds.

Tahiti and Moorea, the two largest of the Society Islands (part of French Polynesia), are dramatic forested volcanic peaks that drop sharply to narrow coastlines. The summit of Tahiti rises to 2,241 meters and the two islands are separated by a shallow 14-kilometer channel; they are both surrounded by barrier reefs. To the south are the Austral Islands, a series of relatively low islands created by volcanic activity, and to the east a cluster of 80 islands – mostly small coral atolls – known as the Tuamotu archipelago. The largest in the group, Rangiroa, is 75 square kilometers in area. Still within French Polynesia, and farther to the northeast, are the Marquesas, a group of 14 high islands unprotected by reefs. Easter Island, a Chilean dependency on the very eastern perimeter of Polynesia, is a rocky volcanic outcrop that rises to a height of 600 meters and covers an area of 163 square kilometers. Three crater lakes nestle in the cones of its extinct volcanoes. It is sparsely vegetated with a few grasses, shrubs and trees. Easter Island's one indigenous tree, the toromiro, disappeared in the 1950s.

New Guinea and the continental islands

In the western Pacific lie the islands of Melanesia – New Guinea, New Britain and the Bismarck Archipelago, the Solomon and Santa Cruz Islands, Vanuatu (formerly the New Hebrides) and New Caledonia. Together with Fiji and Tonga (often considered part of Polynesia) they lie on the Australian continental shelf. New Guinea is less than 200 kilometers from Cape York Peninsula, Australia's northernmost point. It was formerly part of a larger Australian continent known as Sahul. Around 10,000 years ago, at the end of the last Ice Age, the narrow Torres Strait flooded and New Guinea became separated from the mainland. It is on the collision boundary between the Indo-Australian and Pacific plates, and the New Guinea highlands have been formed by the violent upthrusting and folding of the sedimentary rocks of the ocean crust. The tallest peaks of the mountain chain that runs the length of the island are between 4,500 and nearly 5,000 meters, making it the highest island in the world. The main lowland area – the Fly-Digul shelf – lies south of the central highlands, and is drained by numerous rivers. On the north side the highlands are drained by the fast-flowing Sepik river.

Rain-bearing southeasterly trade winds blow for about seven months of the year, and rainfall on the southern-facing slopes of the central highlands frequently exceeds 7,500 millimeters a year. In the highlands daytime temperatures average around 22° C,

Right The opening up of the most remote parts of Papua New Guinea to modernization is forcing its traditional hunter–gathering peoples to modify their way of life. The rainforests are cleared to build roads and airstrips, together with logging and mining encampments and permanent village settlements. This aerial view shows a village straddling a trail in the Central Province. Subsistence crops are raised in the garden plots at the village's edge, some of which have been recently cleared by burning.

but there may be frosts on slopes above 2,200 meters and snow can settle at heights of 4,000 meters. In the tropical lowlands daytime temperatures range between 30° and 32° C year-round. New Guinea supports an enormous variety of vegetation, ranging from tundra and alpine grasslands on the mountain peaks to oak, beech and pine at lower altitudes. Tropical rainforest covers the wet lowlands, with savanna in drier areas. Sago palms grow in the extensive delta swamps, and mangroves fringe the coasts. The dense forests that buffer the mountain range from the lowlands, and the rugged terrain, make the central highlands one of the most inaccessible regions in the world. In some valleys the indigenous population has only come into contact with outsiders in comparatively recent years.

East and southeast of New Guinea are the Solomons, two roughly parallel lines of exposed fold mountains, produced by volcanic activity and movements of the plates, that extend northward into New Ireland in the Bismarck Archipelago and southward through the Santa Cruz Islands into the main group of Vanuatu. The climate is hot and humid, relieved by cool winds. There is abundant year-round rainfall and the mountainous terrain is heavily wooded. Vanuatu consists of 13 main mountainous islands, linked to one another by submerged coral platforms that break the surface in several areas, and around 70 smaller islets. The highest point is Mount Tabwemaswana (1,879 meters) on Espiritu Santo, the largest island. Active volcanoes are found on Vanua Lava, Gaua, Ambrym and Tana, and there are several submerged volcanoes in the area. Earthquakes are frequent. The climate divides into a hot, wet season from November to April, with cooler, drier weather lasting from May

to October. Rainforest covers much of the islands, but in drier areas there is savanna grassland.

New Caledonia is the name of the single largest island of a group of 25 islands that include Belep and the Loyalty Islands, the Isle of Pines and a scattering of uninhabited smaller islands and islets. At just 17,000 square kilometers, the mainland (Grande Terre), as the largest island is called, accounts for almost 90 percent of the entire land area of the group. It is dominated by a rugged mountain system running northwest from Mount Humboldt to Mount Piere (1,628 meters). This ridge is rich in nickel, cobalt and chrome, which colors much of the island's soil a distinctive red. An extensive coral reef system surrounds the mainland and connects it with the Isle of Pines in the southeast and Belep in the northwest.

East of New Caledonia and Vanuatu are the Fijian and Tongan groups. Fiji's two main islands, Viti Levu and Vanua Levu, were thrown up by volcanic action, and their compact land area of some 16,000 square kilometers encompasses 30 peaks of around 1,000 meters. The highest peak is Mount Tomanivi (1,323 meters). Lying 18° south of the Equator in the subtropics, the climate is dominated by the southeastern trade winds that bring rain all year round, but particularly in February when there are also violent storms and occasional hurricanes. The Great Fijian Sea Reef surrounds the two main islands, and more than 800 islands and islets are scattered over an area in excess of 3 million square kilometers.

Tonga sits on the very edge of the Australian continental platform. It is a grouping of 169 islands in three main clusters: Tangatapu, Ha'apai, and Vava'u. The western chain consists of high islands, with several peaks over 1,000 meters and four active volcanoes.

Above The island of Hienghene – the solidified cone of a once active volcano – lies off the east coast of New Caledonia, which receives almost three times as much rain as its western side. Its spectacular rock formations are thickly vegetated, and its fertile soils offer some unusual combinations of flora.

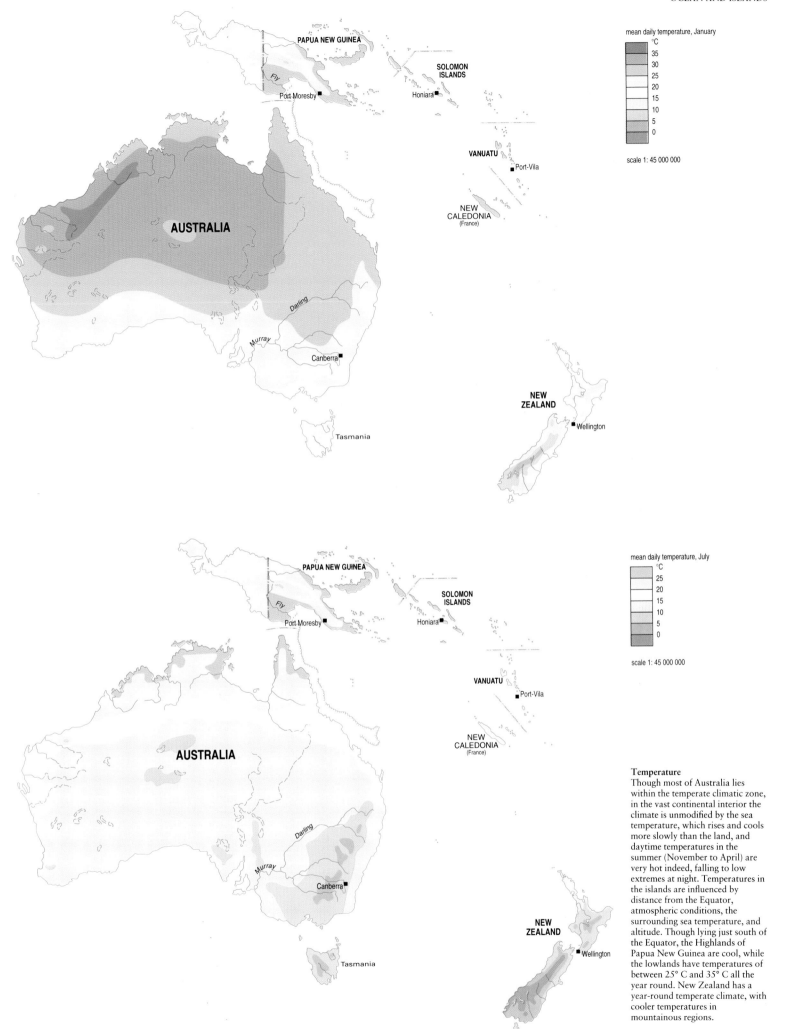

mean daily temperature, January

°C
35
30
25
20
15
10
5
0

scale 1: 45 000 000

mean daily temperature, July

°C
25
20
15
10
5
0

scale 1: 45 000 000

Temperature
Though most of Australia lies within the temperate climatic zone, in the vast continental interior the climate is unmodified by the sea temperature, which rises and cools more slowly than the land, and daytime temperatures in the summer (November to April) are very hot indeed, falling to low extremes at night. Temperatures in the islands are influenced by distance from the Equator, atmospheric conditions, the surrounding sea temperature, and altitude. Though lying just south of the Equator, the Highlands of Papua New Guinea are cool, while the lowlands have temperatures of between 25° C and 35° C all the year round. New Zealand has a year-round temperate climate, with cooler temperatures in mountainous regions.

mean precipitation, November–April

mm
- 1000
- 750
- 500
- 250
- 125

scale 1: 45 000 000

PAPUA NEW GUINEA

SOLOMON ISLANDS

Fly

Port Moresby

Honiara

VANUATU

Port-Vila

NEW CALEDONIA
(France)

AUSTRALIA

Darling

Murray

Canberra

NEW ZEALAND

Wellington

Tasmania

mean precipitation, May–October

mm
- 1000
- 750
- 500
- 250
- 125

scale 1: 45 000 000

PAPUA NEW GUINEA

SOLOMON ISLANDS

Fly

Port Moresby

Honiara

VANUATU

Port-Vila

NEW CALEDONIA
(France)

AUSTRALIA

Darling

Murray

Canberra

NEW ZEALAND

Wellington

Tasmania

Rainfall

In Papua New Guinea and tropical northern Australia there is a clear wet season, from November to April. Rainbearing monsoonal winds sweep in from equatorial regions, and there are frequent cyclones. There is less seasonal variation along the east coast, though the El Niño effect brings periodic drought. The interior remains arid throughout the year, while the southwest and the west coast of Tasmania receive most rain during the winter months (May to October), carried on the prevailing southwesterlies. Temperate New Zealand has warm, dry summers and cool, wet winters.

New Zealand

Like the highlands of New Guinea, New Zealand is the product of comparatively recent geophysical activity in which oceanic sedimentary deposits have been pushed up to form mountain ridges. In the South Island, the 500-kilometer long chain of the snow-capped and glaciated Southern Alps, which covers about two thirds of the land area, is still being thrust upward by the pulling apart of the Indo-Australian and Antarctic plates. Mount Cook (3,674 meters), in the center of the chain, is the highest mountain in New Zealand. Along the southwest coast flooded glacial valleys form deep indented fjords. East of the Alps is a narrow coastal plain – the Canterbury Plains – formed by eroded material carried down from the Alps. Covered in tussocky grass, this is the main sheep-rearing region of New Zealand.

The North Island has a greater diversity of landforms. A lower and less extensive chain of mountains and hills runs along its eastern side, and there is a central volcanic plateau surrounded by undulating foothills and plains. Volcanic ash, pumice and lava cover this plateau, which rises steeply from the crater lake of Lake Taupo, and a chain of active volcanoes extends northward to the Bay of Plenty. The plateau is the site of some of the most spectacular geothermal activity in the world, with hot springs, bubbling mud pools and geysers. These send up jets of steam at irregular intervals, created when underground water comes into contact with very hot volcanic rock. The most famous, at Pohutu, can reach heights of 30 meters, and may last for between 30 and 40 minutes. The North Island is subject to periodic earthquakes. Massive mudslides, which are also a consequence of the island's geological instability, are exacerbated by the clearance of mountain slopes for development, pastureland and agriculture.

New Zealand's weather is influenced both by the Roaring Forties and by a southwesterly Antarctic flow. In the South Island, the annual rainfall on the windward side of the Southern Alps is over 7,000 millimeters, but in the rain shadow on the eastern side it can be as little as 300 millimeters. There are four distinct seasons. The maritime influence affects temperatures, which average 15°–21° C in the summer and 4°–10° C in winter. The climate in New Zealand varies with latitude, ranging from subtropical in the north of the North Island to wet temperate in the South Island. Natural forests of broadleafs and conifers once covered two-thirds of the land area. Today only about two-fifths is forested. In the north, subtropical trees include kauri, podocarps and tree ferns. The natural vegetation of the South Island is mostly southern beech forest, together with subalpine and alpine grassland. Plentiful rain and mild temperatures have combined to give New Zealand a productive pastoral and agricultural economy.

Australia

Parts of the island continent of Australia are composed of some of the oldest rock formations on Earth. The most ancient rocks are in the west, consisting of granites and greenstones laid down between 2,500 and 3,000 million years ago at the beginning of Earth's geological history. The eastern highlands are of more recent origin, but tectonic activity and mountain building ceased between 300 and 200 million years ago. Since then Australia has been a stable landmass. It does not have active volcanoes, and it is rarely

Above Steam rises from hot springs on the Cathedral Rocks beside the boiling crater lake at Waimangu in the volcanic plateau of New Zealand's North Island. It was the site of an impressive geyser that gushed intermittently until 1917 when a particularly violent eruption created the lake. Hot springs formed by water coming into contact with hot rocks below the Earth's surface are also found on the South Island, where there are no volcanoes.

The eastern chain has been formed by the growth of coral and limestone reefs on the tops of submerged mountains. Except in areas composed largely of volcanic ash and pumice, the western islands have resisted erosion. The coral atolls, on the other hand, are in a state of perpetual change. Rain gathers in weak spots and begins to form crevices, which gradually enlarge into numerous indents and caves; at the same time, the coral reefs keep growing, regenerating the islands. The resulting complex of reefs and lagoons contains natural harbors and supports a wealth of coastal and marine resources, and it is here that most of the population live.

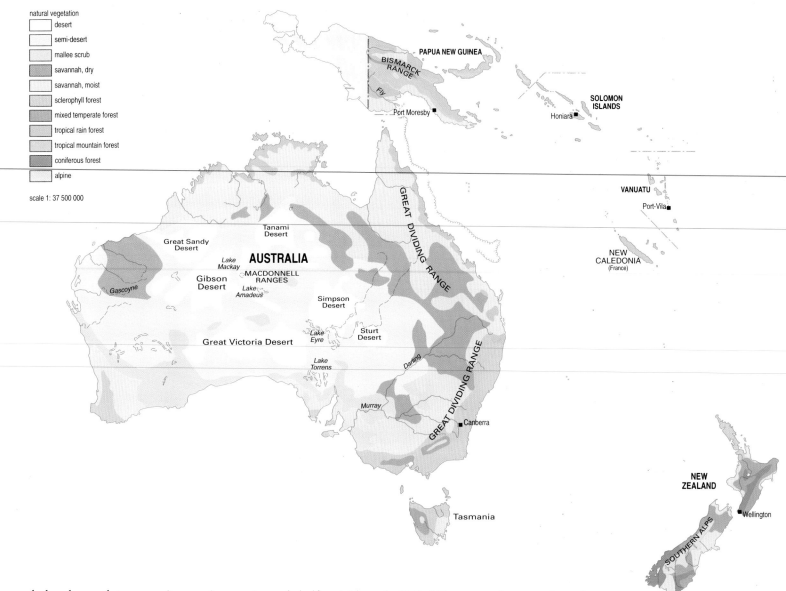

natural vegetation

- desert
- semi-desert
- mallee scrub
- savannah, dry
- savannah, moist
- sclerophyll forest
- mixed temperate forest
- tropical rain forest
- tropical mountain forest
- coniferous forest
- alpine

scale 1: 37 500 000

shaken by earth tremors; its massive continental shelf buffers it from the movements of the Earth that disturb the Ring of Fire. In the course of millions of years, Australia's long extinct volcanoes and great mountain ranges have been eroded and worn down by fierce winds and storms to small mounds, leaving little evidence of their once awesome power. The great river systems that drained the highlands have dried into creeks that flow only intermittently.

The Australian continent measures 3,700 kilometers from north to south and 4,000 kilometers from east to west, covering an area of approximately 8.5 million square kilometers. The most striking feature of Australia is its flatness. Its average elevation of 330 meters above sea level makes it the lowest of all continents. Its highest point is Mount Kosciusko (2,228 meters), which is snow-covered in winter. It lies at the southern end of the inappropriately named Great Dividing Range, a ridge of small mountain systems running the length of the east coast. In the southwest of the continent the much older Darling Escarpment undulates out of the coastal strip and subsides almost imperceptibly back into the central plateau just a few hundred kilometers to the north.

The western plateau (comprising three-fifths of Australia's land area) is a scoured plain of metamorphic and hardened sedimentary rock that stretches thousands of kilometers inland from the west coast,

rising only 230–460 meters. It opens into the great deserts of the interior, such as the Great Sandy Desert and the Great Victoria Desert – areas of sand dunes, stony deserts and salt lakes, with only occasional waterholes and river creeks. The flat monotony is broken in the north by the Kimberley plateau. Here a group of ancient mountains have crumbled into the Bungle Bungle Ranges, which crop out of the red dirt like the pot bellies of old men dozing in the sun. At the very center of Australia appear the Macdonnell Ranges (1,510 meters at their highest point) and the Musgrave Ranges (1,440 meters). Rising out of the arid plateau between them is Mount Olga (1,069 meters), and the largest monolith on Earth, Uluru (Ayers Rock) – the eerie red heart of the continent.

Australia's climate is strikingly arid. Two-thirds of the continent receives less than 500 millimeters of rain a year. Not all areas are dry, though. In the north of Australia, northwesterly monsoonal winds bear down from equatorial regions to converge with a southeasterly stream, causing cyclones between December and March. The monsoons bring in what is called "the big wet", the rainy season of the summer months – Darwin's average annual rainfall of 1,611 millimeters falls almost entirely between November and April. In winter the winds blow offshore and are so dry that they create drought conditions. In the northeast, winds blowing onshore from the Coral Sea produce locally

Vegetation
Australia and New Zealand's natural landscapes and vegetation have seen great alteration in the 200 years since European settlement – forests have been cleared and grasslands used for pastoralism and cultivation, with consequent degradation of the land. Today Papua New Guinea's forests are disappearing at an alarming rate.

Right The Bungle Bungle Ranges are part of the Purnululu National Park created in 1986. Their rounded shapes are made up of eroded sandstone deposits that are 350 million years old. They have great spiritual significance for local Aborigines, and have been protected from environmental damage because relatively few vehicles and hooved animals have passed through the region.

Animals of the Antipodes

To visitors to Australia and New Zealand, nothing is as striking as the difference and variety of the wildlife. Australia's unique range of marsupial mammals, New Zealand's flightless birds, are both the result of millions of years of separation after the breakup of Gondwanaland, when species evolved in isolation to fill every ecological niche. Something of the bewilderment that this abundance of unfamiliar animal life engendered in the first European settlers can be sensed from the lines of the poet Richard Whately who spoke of the antipodes as a place "full of contrarieties: There, beasts have mallards' bills and legs, have spurs like cocks, like hens lay eggs. There parrots walk upon the ground, and grass upon the trees is found." White settler Australia chose the kangaroo – which, with the emu, supports the national coat of arms – as the emblem of its nationhood, while the kiwi has come to represent New Zealand.

European settlement had devastating impact on this unique wildlife. Over their thousands of years' occupation of the land the Aboriginal peoples imposed some changes on the environment through the burning of grasslands and hunting. Such disturbance, however, was as nothing compared to the damage caused in the last 200 years by the widespread introduction of agriculture and the introduction of alien species such as rabbits, weasels, cats, dogs and goats, which destroy native vegetation and compete with native species. In Queensland, the cane toad, introduced as recently as the 1930s to combat a sugar cane pest, has itself become a pest. Without natural enemies, the toads multiplied rapidly, devoring countless native insect species. In New Zealand, forest clearance and the introduction of European pasture grasses have destroyed the habitats of its native flightless birds, many of which are now extinct.

Right The koala is an Australian marsupial that lives principally on eucalyptus leaves. These are low in protein and poisonous, and must be detoxified in the koala's specialized digestive system. As an adaptation to this poor diet the koala has low energy requirements. Its pattern of sleeping for up to 18 hours a day wedged in the forks of trees almost led to its extinction in the 1920s when koalas were heavily hunted for their fur. More than half a million were killed in Queensland in a few months in 1927 alone. They are now protected.

Below In the absence of predatory mammals, many species of bird in New Zealand took to living on the ground and lost the use of wings. The kiwi is a flightless nocturnal bird that forages for food with its long beak.

Left Kangaroos are the most familiar of the Australian marsupials, and carry their young in forward opening pouches. They occupy every kind of habitat, ranging from the tree kangaroos of the tropical rainforests to small rock-dwelling wallabies, but most widespread are the red and gray kangaroos that graze the open grasslands and are able to cruise at speeds of 70 kilometers an hour.

Right The platypus is a monotreme – a primitive egg-laying mammal. The female suckles her young through mammary glands on her belly, and because there are no obvious nipples, scientists initially disputed whether the platypus was a mammal or a furred reptile. An aquatic animal, it burrows its nest in the banks of creeks and lakes. Its sleek streamlined body and webbed feet are adapted for swimming and it shovels up mud with its leathery bill to scoop out its prey.

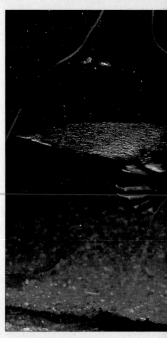

Below There are 55 species of parrot in Australia. Among the more beautiful is the rainbow lorikeet (*Trichoglossus moluccanus*). Lorikeets form into large flocks that travel considerable distances throughout eastern Australia. They live on nectar and forest fruits.

Bottom The lyrebird is found only in Australia, living in woodlands and forests. Only the males have the distinctive elaborate tail and are known for their range of calls that mimic other birds. They claim a large territory that includes the smaller territory of the female.

high rainfalls and subtropical climate in the northern half of the eastern highlands.

Over the southern two-thirds of Australia high-pressure cells are common throughout the summer months, pushing a dry easterly air flow across the continent; low pressures and rain-bearing fronts characterize the winter months, but the interior, lying in the rain shadow of the eastern highlands, remains dry. In summer the lack of cloud over the interior causes temperatures to rise to an average of 30° C, with extremes of over 38° C commonly recorded. In the extreme south, the strong westerly flow of the Roaring Forties brushes the southwest and southeast tips of Australia and strongly influences the climate of Tasmania. These areas have a Mediterranean climate with warm, dry summers and cool, wet winters. Average temperatures range between 23° C in the summer months and 11° C in winter.

Australia's expanses of desert support a vegetation of tussocky, stiff-leaved spinifex and saltbush. Fringing the deserts are areas of mallee (dwarf eucalypt) scrub and mulga (acacia) scrub. The Mediterranean climate of the south supports species-rich heathlands dominated by eucalypts and banksias, while in the north the semidesert scrub gives way to savanna grassland. Patches of tropical rainforest survive in Queensland, and Tasmania still retains areas of natural temperate rainforest.

Unique wildlife
Throughout the millions of years that Australia has been isolated from the rest of the world animal life has developed along very different lines. The landmass broke away from Gondwanaland before the rise of advanced placental mammals, and is inhabited by a unique range of animals dominated by the marsupials – pouched mammals – that diversified to fill the evolutionary niches occupied elsewhere by placental mammals. The earliest marsupials were tree-dwelling animals, similar to today's tree shrews, living off fruit and seeds. Some – such as possums and koalas – diversified to eating specialized diets of leaves; others adapted to living on the ground, including some of the possums and related bandicoots. As Australia's climate became hotter and drier, wallabies and kangaroos moved out of the forests and adapted to living on the grassland savannas. Other animals burrowed underground to survive – among them the echidnas and the duck-billed platypus. As the highlands of New Guinea were formed, the marsupials invaded this new territory. Tree kangaroos and other descendants of the the old Gondwanan forests still survive in the tropical rainforests of New Guinea and northeastern Australia. Many spectacular bird species evolved in the isolation of these mountain forests – birds of paradise, lyrebirds and bowerbirds, as well as many parrots.

New Zealand's indigenous wildlife is also unique. As the North and South Islands thrust their way upwards out of the sea the only animals able to colonize the new land were birds, bats and reptiles, which may have reached it by being swept out from their native shores on rafts of vegetation transported for long distances by ocean currents. In the absence of mammals, birds diversified to become browsers, grazers, hunters and scavengers. Many became flightless. With no ground-dwelling predators there was little need for flight, which uses a great deal of energy. Many of these flightless birds, such as the *moas*, have been hunted to extinction by humans, but the kiwi – which developed hairlike feathers and an acute sense of smell and hearing – and the kakapo, a flightless parrot, are among those that have survived.

Above More than one half of the Australian continent is desert, with an annual rainfall of less than 200 millimeters. The most common vegetation of these arid zones are a number of hardy grasses known colloquially as Mitchell grasses and spinifex, the name given to a wide variety of herbaceous plants that grow in dense clumps and are characterized by thin, sharp leaves. Very few trees grow, but Acacia shrubs such as the 200 varieties of wattle are commonplace. Yet even the driest areas abound with life, and the slightest of showers will cause dormant flower seeds to bloom, transforming the drab landscape with a dazzling, though brief, array of color.

PART TWO
THE GREAT MIGRATIONS

ABORIGINAL AUSTRALIA

Intellectual aristocrats

Humans have occupied Australia for only a fraction of its geological antiquity, but the indigenous Australians are among the oldest peoples on earth. Theirs may well be the world's oldest continuous culture; their practices, customs, beliefs and rituals reach back into remotest times. For all but the last two hundred years, the Australian Aborigines were almost completely isolated from contact with other peoples. Since then, the traditional pattern of their lives has been massively disrupted by the European colonization and settlement of Australia, beginning in the late 18th century. Throughout the 19th century it was widely expected that the Aborigines would die out as a consequence of this contact. Few Europeans at this time took much notice of Aboriginal customs, rituals and beliefs, which they viewed as little more than a transitory phase on the road to extinction.

Europeans sought to place the Aborigines within the biblical age of antiquity. By these estimates (which held sway long into the 20th century), Australia had been populated for only some 6,000 years. Today scientists estimate that Australia has supported human habitation for anywhere between 40,000 and 120,000 years. The consensus is that Aborigines have lived in Australia for at least 60,000 years. As the datelines change so, too, do estimates of the numbers of Aborigines that were living in Australia at the time of the European invasion. Early computations put the population at perhaps 40,000. The most recent research suggests a figure of over 3 million.

The largest concentration of peoples seems to have been in the country around the junction of the Murray-Darling River systems in southeastern Australia, where several large cemeteries – that is, places of ritualized and systematic burials – have been discovered. Such sites include Kow Swamp, Coobool, Poon Boon, Snaggy Bend and Roonka on the Murray river, and future excavation is likely to turn up a similar abundance of sites on the Lachlan and Darling rivers. In the early 1990s archaeological excavations uncovered what appears to be a series of major cemeteries in the Lake Victoria area – one of the most significant archaeological discoveries to have been made in late 20th-century Australia. The site appears to have been a terminus for tribes inhabiting the southeastern corner of the continent, a place of high ceremonial significance, a meeting place for trade and commerce. It has been speculated that there are tens of thousands of graves in these burial grounds alone, and the whole Murray-Darling region is now believed to have contained as many as 1 million inhabitants at the time of European contact.

Other recent archaeological studies have revealed the existence of a complex system of trade and cultural routes that spanned the continent. Thus the once widely held belief that the Aborigines were random nomads with little or no meaningful social and cultural structure is more and more discredited. In the phrase of the French anthropologist Claude Levi-

Strauss, writing in the 1960s, the Aborigines were the "intellectual aristocrats" among hunter–gatherer societies. From a very early time they had sophisticated systems of land usage and management and had developed a highly ritualized society in which daily life existed in symbiosis with the universe. They were the curators of their environment and its most sensitive conservationists.

The Lake Mungo and Kow Swamp discoveries

In the late 1960s, the skeletal remains of a young woman were excavated at a site near Lake Mungo in the west of New South Wales. Carbon 14 dating indicated that they were some 25,000 years old, making them the oldest known human remains yet discovered in Australia. The skeleton was little more than a clump of broken bones, with just two teeth and a quarter of a skull, which had been hammered into at least 175 pieces. Parts of the cranial plates had been ground into particles, and markings on the bones were further evidence that the body had been mutilated after death. Forensic investigation revealed the angles of the blows that had crushed the skull and determined that a blunt instrument, perhaps a waddi (a club-like hunting and war stick) or an ancient ax, or a heavy object such as a rock or mallee root, had been repeatedly smashed into it. The corpse had been burned then buried in a shallow grave, where it lay undisturbed for over 25 millennia. It is impossible even to begin to guess at the reasons that lay behind the woman's brutal death, but it is tempting to see in it, and in the manner in which her body was disposed of, indications that she had belonged to a structured society. Her burial in a shallow grave suggests that whoever carried out the mutilation of her body had been anxious to cover up the evidence of the deed, presupposing the existence of social rules. If, on the other hand, she had been killed as retribution for some crime she had herself committed, this too suggests the presence of customs and laws. However, the real significance of the Lake Mungo discovery was the sheer antiquity of the remains. They provided incontrovertible evidence that humans had been present on the Australian landmass for at least 25,000 years, far longer than had previously been believed.

Before it dried up about 10,000 years ago at the end of the last great ice age, Lake Mungo – today a flat, dry dust-bowl – was one of a series of lakes taking the overflow from the Willandra river, part of the Murray-Darling river system. Skeletal human remains found in this area date back at least 30,000 years. Among the many associated artifacts are ancient heating bricks made of clay to assist in cooking and tools such as scrapers. Animal skeletal remains found on and around ancient campsites suggest a human diet of fish, wallabies, emus and emu eggs, and a variety of other birds. The abundance of these finds suggests that Lake Mungo was an important site and meeting place for the ancient nomads who encamped there for several weeks, possibly even months, year after year, their gatherings marked perhaps by the performance of particular rites and ceremonies. In 1974 a complete male skeleton was uncovered in the same vicinity. He, too, was young but, unlike the first human discovery at Lake Mungo, the body had been carefully interred. It had not been mutilated or burnt; instead traces of ocher, evidence of funeral decoration, were found encrusted on the remains. The hands were neatly folded across the chest. The body had been buried with dignity, suggesting that it may have been that of a person of standing – further indication of an ordered society. The remains dated back at least 30,000 years.

As revealing as the Lake Mungo human finds are, there are limits to the conclusions that may be drawn from them. Because the span of time between their age and ours is so vast and unimaginable, it is all too easy to overlook the long interval of centuries that divides them from each other and to regard the evidence from each burial as being representative of the same era. Yet a distance of 5,000 years separates them – two and half times the period that separates the modern world from the time of Christ. The lives of these individual human beings, so remote from our own, would have been fluid and dynamic, the worlds they occupied for ever changing and reforming. It is only the great distance of time that divides us from them that makes their society seem timeless and unchanging.

Archaeologists are constantly pushing farther and farther back the date at which humans first entered Australia. Before 1968, as we have seen, people were presumed to have inhabited the Australian continent for only 6,000 years. With the first of the Lake Mungo skeletal discoveries, this leapt dramatically to 25,000 years, the second extended it even further, and by the 1980s the date had retreated to 40,000 years. Then, in the early 1990s, came the discovery of male skeletal remains at Kow Swamp on the Murray river, which are estimated to be at least 60,000 years old. Archaeologists are now beginning to talk of the Aborigines having been in Australia for as much as 100,000 or even 120,000 years.

Concealed just beneath the continent's sunburned crust is a vast museum of archaeological riches. But the science of measuring Australia's prehistoric past is very recent – the first serious excavations were not undertaken until after World War II, and even today only a handful of digs are conducted each year. They tend to be clustered in the southeastern corner of the continent, close to the major industrial cities that house the universities and laboratories that are so essential to back up with detailed scientific analysis and research the findings of those working in the field. However, in the painstaking and often unrewarding pursuit of archaeology, the breakthrough discovery can depend as much on a single chance finding as on years of academic study. Though the tempo of archaeological investigation has picked up considerably in recent years, Australia's prehistory remains largely unexplored. Who can tell what mysteries remain hidden in central Australia, which has been occupied by the Aranda peoples for tens of thousands of years? What secrets lie beneath the Pitjantjatjara territory in the northwest of South Australia? And the largest questions of all have still to be answered: where did the Aboriginal peoples originally come from? When and how did they reach Australia?

Theories and origins

In the absence of certain knowledge, there has been no lack of speculation. Early theorists, for example, conjectured that Tasmania was settled from Africa, the cradle of humanity, by intrepid navigators who crossed thousands of kilometers of open sea in flimsy boats, following the direction of the prevailing winds and currents. This romantic theory has now been discredited, but retains a following in some popular works of science. The overwhelming balance of evidence now indicates that the indigenous Tasmanian

peoples derived from the same line of descent as the mainland Australians.

The first people to reach Australia did so during the last ice age of the Pleistocene period, when the expansion of the polar icesheets locked up vast quantities of water, lowering sea levels around the world by an estimated 60 meters. Land bridges were exposed and the channels between islands became shallower. Australia formed a single landmass, Sahul, with New Guinea in the north and Tasmania in the south. The waterways separating Australia from Southeast Asia were narrower and less treacherous than they are today. In particular, the lowering of the sea waters would have shortened and shallowed the sea passages between the southernmost islands of Southeast Asia – the Celebes, Lombok, Lesser Sunda Islands and Timor – to around 16 kilometers at most. Human migration would have taken place along the long chain of islands from the Asian mainland in a process that would have occurred over a longer rather than a shorter period of time.

The widest channel – about 70 kilometers – that had to be crossed was that separating Timor from mainland Australia. The coastline would not have been visible from Timor, but the island-dwelling peoples would have been able to read the tides and the cloud formations and have realized that there was land beyond the horizon. They may even have noticed smoke from fires started by electrical storms, which would have been visible in the distance. Perhaps the first settlers were accidental migrants, fishermen whose primitive craft were swept along with the tidal currents that pulled them to the mainland. The most direct route from Timor would have brought them to a point on shore in the region of the Kimberley plateau of northwestern Australia. There is no reason, of course, to suppose that only one landing was made – that it was one chance journey that gave humanity its start in Australia.

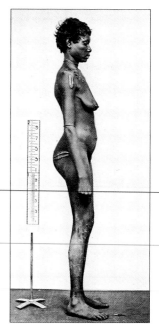

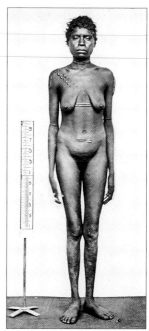

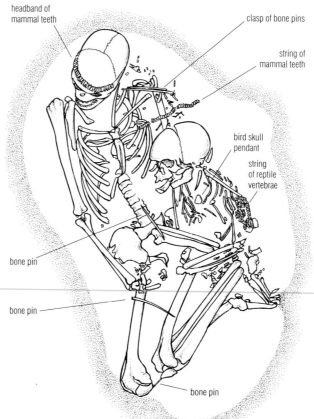

headband of
mammal teeth

clasp of bone pins

string of
mammal teeth

bird skull
pendant

string
of reptile
vertebrae

bone pin

bone pin

bone pin

Above Scientists in the 19th century believed that the Aborigines were the missing link between apes and modern man. Living specimens were precisely measured, with particular attention being paid to the shape and size of the head, while thousands of Aboriginal remains were sent to the great museums of Europe for close scientific investigation. A number of Aborigines were killed deliberately for this purpose.

Left This sketch of a burial site at Roonka in South Australia shows the 4,000-year-old skeletons of a man and a boy. The man appears to have been wrapped in a skin cloak fringed with feathers and fastened with bone pins, and both were wearing ornaments. Such indications of highly ritualized burial are evidence of an orderly society with elaborate belief systems. Similar sites nearby and at Lake Mungo indicate that ritualized burial dates back at least 40,000 years.

The early settlement of Australia
The remote ancestors of the Aborigines arrived in Australia at least 40,000 years ago – possibly even as much as 120,000 years ago – when it formed part of the larger landmass of Sahul. Australia has experienced a great many environmental changes since then as the climate grew cooler and drier, to reach peak glacial conditions around 20,000 years ago, and then warmer again. A number of theories have been developed about the subsequent spread of people from their probable point or points of entry in the north. In the 1950s J. B. Birdsell proposed that an initial colonizing band of 25 would have spread throughout the continent in just over 2,000 years: his theory, based on modern rainfall levels, is today largely discounted. Sandra Bowdler has argued that the first settlers were marine people who migrated around the coast settling close to water, while David Horton suggests that they settled woodland areas first before adapting to more arid zones. While both these theories take account of changing environmental conditions, neither entirely satisfies the available archaeological evidence.

There is a second school of thought that argues that the ancestral Aborigines crossed into Australia by the land bridge that linked it with New Guinea, having made their way into the latter from the islands of Southeast Asia. Again, this whole journey would have been accomplished over hundreds or even thousands of years. The earliest known evidence of human habitation in New Guinea dates from 26,000 years ago, and there is no way of telling which way the first migrants crossed the land bridge – it may be that they traveled eastward from the Kimberley region to what is today the Cape York Peninsula, and so north into New Guinea. At this distance in time, we can only speculate whether the ancestors of the Aborigines reached Australia by a western or an eastern route from Southeast Asia (or perhaps by both). Once established there, however, these hunters and gatherers would have traveled along the coasts and followed the courses of rivers into the interior.

In the thousands of years after the first settlement of Australia, while the land bridges and shallow waterways linking it to Southeast Asia remained, subsequent migrants would have followed the same routes, pushing earlier groups of settlers into the furthest parts of the continent. It is now believed that the Tas-

manian Aborigines were the descendants of some of the original occupants of Australia, who had retreated before the advance of the newcomers into its southeast extremity. When the land bridge between Tasmania and the mainland was flooded, they became cut off from the rest. The cultural, social and racial differences that distinguish the Nyoongars of southwest Australia from the Aborigines of the north and east are also an indication of different waves of settlement: the Nyungars have been likened to the Celts of Britain, pushed into the corners of their world by invaders.

There is an alternative theory that argues that, far from being peopled by a process of inward migration, Australia was itself a cradle of humanity. According to this view, the remote ancestors of the Aborigines developed separately and in parallel with the proto-human species in Africa, and subsequently spread northward into Asia. This line of argument has a small band of adherents, particularly among contemporary Aborigines who resent the implication that they are immigrants of however remote a period. Some tentative archaeological arguments have been put forward to suggest that such a proposition is not altogether preposterous, though the weight of evidence would seem to be against it.

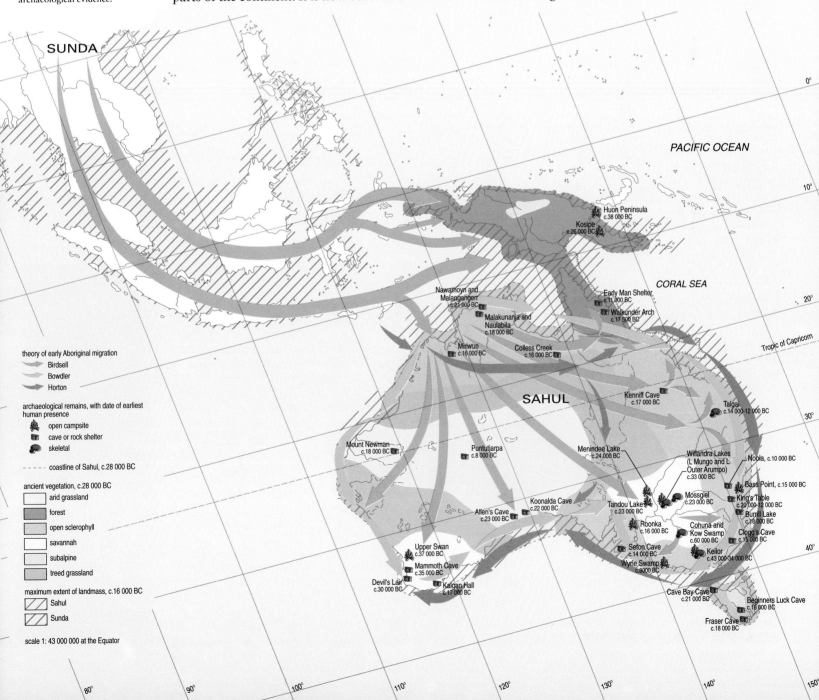

theory of early Aboriginal migration
- Birdsell
- Bowdler
- Horton

archaeological remains, with date of earliest human presence
- open campsite
- cave or rock shelter
- skeletal

– – – – coastline of Sahul, c.28 000 BC

ancient vegetation, c.28 000 BC
- arid grassland
- forest
- open sclerophyll
- savannah
- subalpine
- treed grassland

maximum extent of landmass, c.16 000 BC
- Sahul
- Sunda

scale 1: 43 000 000 at the Equator

SUNDA

PACIFIC OCEAN

CORAL SEA

Tropic of Capricorn

SAHUL

Huon Peninsula c.38 000 BC
Kosipe c.26 000 BC
Nawamoyn and Malangangerr c.21 000 BC
Early Man Shelter c.11 000 BC
Walkunder Arch c.17 500 BC
Malakunanja and Naulabila c.18 000 BC
Mirnwun c.16 000 BC
Colless Creek c.16 000 BC
Kenniff Cave c.17 000 BC
Talgai c.14 000-12 000 BC
Mount Newman c.18 000 BC
Puntutjarpa c.8 000 BC
Menindee Lake c.24 000 BC
Willandra Lakes (L Mungo and L. Outer Arumpo) c.33 000 BC
Noola, c.10 000 BC
Bass Point, c.15 000 BC
Mossgiel c.23 000 BC
King's Table c.20 000-12 000 BC
Koonalda Cave c.22 000 BC
Tandou Lake c.23 000 BC
Burrill Lake c.18 000 BC
Allen's Cave c.23 000 BC
Roonka c.16 000 BC
Cohuna and Kow Swamp c.60 000 BC
Clogg's Cave c.15 000 BC
Upper Swan c.37 000 BC
Seton Cave c.14 000 BC
Keilor c.43 000-34 000 BC
Mammoth Cave c.35 000 BC
Wyrie Swamp c.8000 BC
Devil's Lair c.30 000 BC
Kalgan Hall c.17 000 BC
Cave Bay Cave c.21 000 BC
Beginners Luck Cave c.18 000 BC
Fraser Cave c.18 000 BC

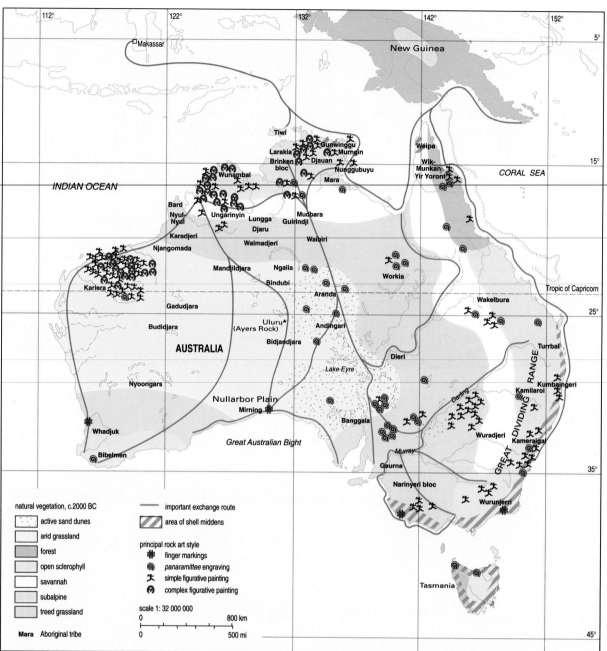

112°   122°   132°   142°   152°

Makassar

New Guinea

5°

INDIAN OCEAN

Tiwi
Larakia   Gunwinggu   Weipa
Brinken   Djauan   Murngin
bloc
Wunambal   Nunggubuyu   Wik-
Mara   Munkan
Yir Yoront   CORAL SEA   15°

Bard
Nyul-   Ungarinyin   Mudbara
Nyul   Lungga   Guirindji
Karadjeri   Djaru
Njangomara   Walmadjeri   Walbiri

Mandjildjara   Ngalia   Workia
Bindubi
Kariera   Aranda

Gadudjara   Tropic of Capricorn

Budidjara   Uluru   Wakelbura
(Ayers Rock)
Bidjandjara   Andingari

AUSTRALIA   Dieri   Turrbal
Lake Eyre   Kumbaingeri
Kamilaroi

Nyoongars   Banggala
Mirning   Wuradjeri   Kameraigal
Whadjuk   Nullarbor Plain
Gaurna
Bibelmen   Great Australian Bight
Narinyeri bloc   Wurunjeri
35°

Tasmania   45°

natural vegetation, c.2000 BC   important exchange route

active sand dunes   area of shell middens

arid grassland

forest   principal rock art style
finger markings
open sclerophyll   panaramittee engraving
savannah   simple figurative painting
subalpine   complex figurative painting

treed grassland   scale 1: 32 000 000
0   800 km
Mara   Aboriginal tribe   0   500 mi

In the late 19th and early 20th centuries anthropological scientists postulated that the Aborigines were the living remnants of Neanderthal man: they were not true *homo sapiens*, but a more primitive species that was styled archaic *homo sapiens*. This theory has since been discredited; the Aborigines are clearly modern man. The problem of classification, however, has remained. The Aborigines are often classed as belonging to a distinct Australoid race. But while some distinct racial characteristics can be found among the Aborigines, they share substantial similarities with other aboriginal groups in Asia, including the Mundas of central India, the Veddahs of Sri Lanka and, perhaps, the Ainu of Japan. It is now widely accepted that all these groups are descendants of a common ancestral race, but that the Aborigines developed their distinctive features in isolation and in response to changes in their environment that took place over a long period of time.

The event that led to the isolation of the Aborigines, setting them on a separate course of development, was the ending of the ice age. As the ice sheets retreated back to the poles, sea levels began to rise again, making the sea passages more treacherous. It was a process

that took thousands of years, during which it would have become increasingly dangerous for people to make the island-hopping trek from Southeast Asia. About 10,000 years ago the land bridges linking Australia with New Guinea and Tasmania disappeared beneath the waters of the Torres and Bass Straits, and the Aborigines were virtually cut off from outside influence. The Aborigines of northern Arnhem Land and Cape York Peninsula appear to have had some cultural links with Melanesia – the use of outrigger canoes by the eastern Cape York Aborigines probably came through contact with the Torres Strait Islanders – but they never developed the use of the bow and arrow, which was so much a part of life in New Guinea. There was pre-European contact, perhaps no more than 1,000 years old, with traders and fishermen from Makassar on the southernmost tip of Celebes (Sulawesi), and Chinese traders are also believed to have known this part of the world. But by and large, the ancient Australian civilization was left to develop undisturbed until the late 18th century.

As the climate warmed up, the environment of Australia altered. The land first occupied by the ancestral Aborigines had been a place of forests and grasslands, of lakes and rivers. For perhaps as many as 40,000 years the Aborigines shared the continent with a number of giant herbivorous marsupials, among them the lake-dwelling *diprodoton*, a hippotamus-like creature standing more than 2 meters high, and the giant kangaroo that reached a height of 3 meters. There was also a giant emu, which was only smaller than the now extinct *moa* of New Zealand. As the temperatures rose, the vegetation dried up, turning once lush grassland into arid desert, while the great lakes became featureless saltpans. With the disappearance of their habitats, the giant marsupials died out, perhaps helped on their way by the hunting activities of the Aborigines. Foraging would have reaped fewer rewards and the competition for sparse food resources would have intensified. Over time, the Aborigines adapted to their changed environment, exploiting new sources of food and learning to live in symbiotic relationship with the land.

The once popular view that the Aborigines were the last of the hunter–gatherers, the living fossils of humanity's common Stone Age past, is now completely discredited. While it is true that the Australian Aborigines survived into the modern world intact as

hunters and gatherers, their society and culture underwent various deep changes. A cultural pluralism grew up, developing out of their relationship with the land and the different uses to which it was put. This gave rise to different tribal characteristics, rituals and customs. There were an estimated 500 tribal groupings across Australia, and at least 260 language groups, with 600 dialects. Most tribal members were multilingual, with the ability to communicate in the languages or dialects of their immediate neighbors. This linguistic and tribal diversity was at the very least equal to, and probably greater than, the ancient tribal diversity of Europe. Unlike the Europeans, however, the Aborigines were virtually cut off from outside influences. Thus they retained more in common with one another than any other peoples on earth.

Aboriginal dreaming

Over tens of thousands of years, the Aborigines developed the close relationship with the earth that remains at the heart of all their beliefs and customs. Despite the considerable cultural diversity of the many Aboriginal groups in Australia, they share a belief in the "dreamtime" or "dreaming", as it is sometimes called, which

Below Uluru (Ayers Rock, as it was called by non-Aboriginal Australians until the late 1980s) is the world's largest monolith. It is of great spiritual significance to the Aranda peoples who are its custodians. Known simply as "the rock" to Australians, Uluru is the symbolic heart of the continent and has become one of the most potent images of reconciliation between the Aborigines and the more recent immigrants. Aboriginal proprietorial rights to the land were implicitly stated at a ceremony in 1988 that "handed back" Uluru to the Aranda. In 1992 native title to lands was officially recognized by the High Court of Australia's overturning of the rule of *terra nullius*, which held that Australia was unoccupied at the time of European colonization.

Left Aboriginal paintings of ancestral figures wearing elaborate costumes and headdresses that appear to resemble astronauts' helmets have led some writers of popular science to speculate that they are representations of aliens who visited the Earth in ancient times and were believed to be gods by the people living at the time. A much more reasonable interpretation of these figures is that they are part of ritualized tribal practice and have to do with the teaching of stories about the dreamtime and spirit worlds.

Below Weapons were mostly employed in hunting rather than fighting: though combats took place between individuals, intertribal warfare was uncommon in Australia before European contact. It is unlikely, however, that this woomera, or spear thrower, would have been used for hunting: highly decorated weapons of this kind, carrying clan stories, had totemic significance. Law-breakers were punished by ritual spearing, usually in the thigh.

is the time of creation. There is remarkable consistency in this belief across the continent. Regardless of where we look, dreaming (which is known as *altjiranga* by the Aranda peoples of central Australia, as *bugari* by the Karadjiri of the Kimberleys, as *wongar* by the Murgin peoples of Arnhem Land, and as *njidding* by the Nyungars) is the central tenet of Aboriginal society and culture.

The dreamtime refers to the origins of the Aboriginal peoples when the spiritual ancestors conspired to give order and form to the universe. The dreamtime laid down tribal and community laws. It was a constant spiritual presence manifested in the physical environment – in the rocks, the rivers, the billabongs, the sea, the desert, the animals and plants. All the moral laws and customs of the Aboriginal world take their reference from this coupling of the physical and spiritual universe. The living are guided from wrongdoing by the world of the spirits, who are contemporaneous with them. The dead are everywhere present, and the living and the dead are ultimately indivisible. When the time of creation is acted out in ritual, the participants enter the spirit of the dreamtime; that is, they enter into and become the actual spirit figures of the creation.

The Aranda term *altjiranga* refers to the making of the world by ancestral spirits. The phrase *altjiranga nganbakala* connotes individual eternity born of collective spirituality, while the derivative *altjira rama* refers to the active visualization, usually in ritual performance, of the eternal world of spirits. The dreaming, therefore, is not a fantastic or illusory state, as may be implied by the western meaning of the term, but one, though spiritual in origin, that is fully cognisant of the physical universe. All Aborigines read the landscape as a series of complex sign systems from which they derive meaning and spiritual truths. Spirituality is manifest in every physical feature, which means that the Aboriginal peoples have constructed intricate tribal histories and traditions out of their immediate environment.

The Wik people of the Gulf of Carpentaria, for instance, have developed dreamings out of the shark and the dingo, the Nyungars of southwestern Australia have developed associations out of the emu and the kangaroo, the Aranda have at the center of their dreaming the vast rock, Uluru (Ayers Rock). These totems provide the continuity between the ancestral past and the spiritual present. Totems signify the mystical links between tribal members, and form the foundations of laws governing the tribal estates, clans and, importantly, marriage – a highly selective process, based on the ancestral pasts, by which families construct their present identity.

Unlike many other belief systems, Aboriginal lore does not hold that there was a physical void before the moment of creation; the physical world existed, but it was without physical features or spiritual meaning. The spirits of the dreaming invested the mundane world with spiritual qualities, and embellished the physical universe with animals, plants and humans. Ancestry is located within these physical manifestations, and totems are self-evident truths of the creation. All Aboriginal tribes regard each member as connected, from conception to death and beyond, with the ancestral spirits who guide individual and group behavior. Babies are born of the spirits – conception is a spiritual not a physical act – and people live according to the requirements of their totem. When they die they are said to "go into the country".

cross-cousins (that is, a man would marry the daughter of his mother's brother or father's sister) was common to many groups. But there was a degree of flexibility, and men and women could sometimes marry outside their tribal group. Yet all marriages were seen to influence the social structure, so the determination of blood lines carried significant weight and tribal custom was strongly observed.

Aboriginal tribes were organized either through the patriarchal or the matriarchal line. By and large, the men were hunters while the women acted as food collectors. Gender segregation was observed in ritual; for example, at the communal song-dance performances, or corroborees, the men usually performed the mimetic dances with the women providing the rhythmic accompaniment. In addition, both men and women held gender-specific ceremonies in secret. Generally speaking, women were treated with a degree of brutality. Conception was believed to occur through the spirits, and no direct connection was made with sexual intercourse: thus the male was thought to have no role in procreation. Abortion was widely practiced, and infanticide was used to keep clan numbers down in times of scarcity: children who became a burden were abandoned and left to die. These brutal techniques were necessary for the tribe's survival, but are often ignored in discussion of Aboriginal society. Ritual mutilations such as scarring and circumcision were also commonplace. Male circumcision was widespread, though it was not practiced by the Nyungars.

The hunter–gatherer existence of the Aborigines was characterized by barter, reciprocity and the "payback". Barter was the simple exchange of goods of equal value. Reciprocity, practiced both by individuals and communities, involved the giving of gifts and incurring of debts. These debts were never canceled out, but were built upon to form a complex system of exchange. Pay-back was the system by which retaliation was made for wrong-doing, and much of it was performed by magic men. These practices formed the basis of tribal cohesiveness and the laws by which the people were governed. There were no formal institutions of worship or law; both were constituted organically within tribal communities, and were firmly prescribed by the estate to which the tribal adherents belonged. The spirits and tribal authority resided in the estate itself, and if the people were removed from it, they withered and died because they were removed from the very thing that certified their existence.

The tribe's custodians were every tribal member, but particularly the elders and wise men and women. In addition, there were the secret magic men and women (also held to be indivisible from the whole) who had various names and characteristics. They might be healers, such as the *margidjbu* of the Gunwinggu or the *gingin* of the Western Desert; these were not the same as the *mangorang* and the *mabanba*, clever men who possessed the powers of sorcery. The most best-known sorcerer figures are the *kurdaitcha* (meaning "feather foot", because they wore slippers made of emu feathers to remove all traces of their presence). Believed to possess spirit-like qualities, the *kurdaitcha* moved with stealth through the night and could change shape to ensure pay-back. They had the power to will individuals to death by the simple act of pointing a bone. The *kurdaitcha* secretly "sang" over the bone to put a curse on his victim; once someone learned he had been cursed in this way he very often began to fret, refused to eat and often died within a

Above Weaving was a technology known to the Aboriginal peoples. This woven basket would have been used for food-gathering. Fishing nets made of woven fiber were also common.

Social organization

The pre-contact Aborigines owned very few possessions. They had to walk wherever they went. Only objects such as spears and spear throwers were carried by the men; the women carried digging sticks and, in some areas, bark baskets or plaited pandanus leaf bags to hold foodstuffs. Such things as grinding stones, platters and wooden bowls were left at certain camps and were a means of defining their tribal territories. Though the term "tribe" is widely used in academic and popular discussions of Aborigines, and has even been assimilated into Aboriginal English, where it is used interchangeably with another word of English derivation, "mob", its meaning should not be confused with the hierarchical structures that are found among the peoples of Melanesia or Polynesia. Aboriginal "tribes", which can number from a few hundred to a couple of thousand, were made up of family groups, or clans, which were reasonably autonomous within the larger collective. Indeed the tribe may never actually have met in its entirety, even at ceremonial occasions, while family groups moved around within the same country, or estate.

It was commonly accepted in Aboriginal society that all the members would be married. Men habitually married in their twenties or early thirties, though this did not preclude earlier sexual relations. They generally took a pubertal wife. Since it was not uncommon for a man to take a second wife at the age of 50 or 60, the age range of his offspring could be substantial. In Aboriginal tradition, marriage took place between members of those groups that were deemed to be totemically compatible: though different laws governed marriage in different tribal circumstances, descent lines were always involved. The marriage of

short period. *Kurdaitchas* were very frequently deployed as avengers of wrong, and could remove what were called "sticks" (magical poisons) from an individual who had been "sung", or cursed. Most *kurdaitcha* were men, but could also be women.

The spirits and the law of the peoples were inclusive and were acted out in ceremonies such as corroborees. These were nonsacred occasions, intended for entertainment and relaxation. Other ceremonies were secret, and attended only by initiated men. Tribal dance was mimetic of the physical universe, not simply representational; when a kangaroo, for instance, was acted out in Nyungar ceremony the performers did not imitate the kangaroo, but invoked the kangaroo spirit. The correlation between the tribe and the kangaroo may have been even stronger and more practical. Aboriginal society may have learned survival techniques from observing the herd behavior of the kangaroo, which is not dissimilar to the social organization of many tribes, including habits of migration within clearly defined territorial boundaries. Kangaroos seek safety from external enemies by running in small groups, which are even known as "mobs". In everyday life, every tribal member was invested with a personal responsibility for the wellbeing of the tribe as a whole, and though tribal divisions existed – the most obvious being clan and gender divisions – everyone contributed directly to the whole. Laws and rules of behavior were not generally applicable across Aboriginal society, but were rooted in a particular estate and group – they were not transferable between peoples and lands. If members of one tribe were to stray into another's territory, they would immediately be dealt with by the law of that tribe,

which meant that individuals effectively remained within their own estate.

Within their tribal areas, the Aborigines held to firm rules of proprietorship. Given the spiritual significance of place, this is hardly surprising. Utilization of the environment involved a complex merger of belief and exploitation. The Aranda, for instance, set aside important ceremonial places, known as *pmara kutata*, within which hunting was prohibited. These areas were customarily marked out by landmarks such as a cave or a watering hole, in which the spirits were active. The setting aside of the land in this way meant that it effectively became a game-reserve, protecting an all-important source of tribal sustenance from over-hunting. Thus the *pmara kutata* served both a religious and an economic function.

Almost all Aboriginal societies were nomadic. It is a popular misconception – unfortunately one that is all too firmly enshrined in the misnomer "walkabout" – that their journeys took the form of random wanderings the length and breadth of the continent. Their migrations were confined within specifically delineated tribal areas. In arid parts of Australia, family groups moved from waterhole to waterhole along well defined tracks, and rarely established camp sites. In more fertile areas, tribal camp sites were recognized at particular places, nearly always close to water. The group would camp at these at certain times of the year, often when a particular food source became available. The Ngayawun of present-day New South Wales, for example, traveled every year to the Snowy Mountains following the annual migration of the bogong moth, considered by them a gastronomic delicacy. The Ngayawun would feast for several days, perhaps a few

Above This well-known 19th-century watercolor of an Aboriginal corroboree perpetuates a number of misconceptions about "primitive" Aboriginality. The dancing men are lined up as if for some kind of synchronized ritual suggestive of paganism, while their luminous body markings project an image of black magic. Aboriginal dance is much less uniform than the performance depicted here suggests. It consists of numerous complex movements as the dancers imitate particular animals and ritually reenact events – some early European observers were intrigued to see stories of European colonization being reenacted in dance.

Top right Because the Aborigines did not build permanent dwellings or appear to carry out any form of agriculture, Europeans were unable to conceive of them utilizing the land in a meaningful way, thus justifying the law of *terra nullius*. However, the Aborigines' huts, or *mia mia*, were well suited to their nomadic lifestyle. Usually made of bark, as here, they were easily erected and did not require specialized tools, which would have been cumbersome to carry.

Right This 1830s watercolor of an Aboriginal camp provides an insight into the way the clan or family group was organized as it moved around the tribal estate. The three larger structures may have housed extended families. The smaller huts probably provided shelter for young men and women, and the elderly.

weeks, and participate in important ceremonies before returning to the plains country that was their normal habitat. Some groups such as the Weipa in Cape York Peninsula and some of the Arnhem Land Aborigines, appear to have shifted less often. Their huts were built on the shore right up to the water's edge where they could harvest the abundant sealife that was their staple diet. In the wet season, they moved to higher ground, returning to the coast when the rains ceased. On the beach-front, over many thousands of years, they built up huge piles or middens of discarded crustacean shells. The significance of these is uncertain, but they appear to mark the regular pattern of their movements and may signify their permanent use and custodianship of the land.

Many of the Aboriginal tribes built themselves bark huts or shelters, often called *mia mia*, of simple construction for use during cold or rainy weather. In the north, where protection was needed against monsoonal rainfall, these were often raised on stilts. In arid parts of the country brush windbreaks were common. During fine weather most Aborigines preferred to sleep in the open. Clothes were minimal, though fur cloaks might be worn as protection against the cold.

Inter-tribal relations

Tribal areas, or estates, usually radiated out from sig-nificant landmarks, such as waterholes or billabongs. Alternatively, they could be prescribed by natural bar-riers such as rivers and waterways. The natural harbor on which Sydney stands today, for instance, formed the boundary between two tribal groups. They appear to have come rarely into contact with one another, and spoke very different languages, though they could see one another clearly across the water. Though the boundaries between estates were by no means always so well defined, their demarcation would have been well known to and understood by all tribal members. Sometimes the boundaries of neighboring estates overlapped. In these zones of interchange, the mem-bers of both tribes met as the occasion required to dis-cuss matters of mutual concern and settle important issues. Hunting and foraging across inter-tribal boundaries was permissible upon application, and requests were rarely refused – for the simple reason that reciprocity might be invoked in lean times. Illegal trespass into non-tribal areas brought immediate ret-ribution, including spearings, as customary law dic-tated. If the trespass were contrived by groups, war could result.

Periodic disputes broke out between neighboring tribes, and wars were not uncommon. However, dis-agreements were more often resolved in a ritualistic manner, either at a general corroboree or at an inter-tribal meeting of the elders, once payback had been satisfied; rarely, if ever, did they end in victory and capitulation. Aboriginal tribes had no interest what-ever in expanding their estates or in conquering oth-ers. The inter-tribal system broke down tragically with

the coming of the Europeans, who did not appreciate the totemic significance of tribal lands or the intricacy of tribal relations. When tribal groups were pushed off their estates and settled permanently on adjoining lands, the greatest and most violent disturbances in Aboriginal history broke out. The pay-back here could never be satisfied, and more Aborigines were probably killed in war in the 200 years after the arrival of the Europeans than in the previous 60,000.

Only recently have we begun to understand the intricacies of the Aborigines' trading systems – in the past, participation in a trading economy was con-sidered to have been well beyond the scope of their primitive subsistence lifestyle. However, recent archaeological and anthropological research have uncovered evidence of a complex interaction of exchange that linked tribes the length and breadth of the continent. Pearls from northwestern Australia, for instance, have been discovered in archaeological sites hundreds of kilometers away, while shells peculiar to the extreme north were used in barter the length of the continent, and have been found in southern Australia, over 3,000 kilometers from their source. Little is known of the actual routes that this ancient trade fol-lowed, but it seems clear that there was no traveling merchant class. Instead, tribes traded between one another, and precious objects were passed down the line. The existence of such a network of exchange would explain the speed at which news of the landing of the Europeans in 1788 passed between the tribes. When explorers began to journey into the interior, they discovered that the tribes they encountered there, with previous contact with white people, were already aware of the awesome potential of their guns.

Above This engraving was made in 1798. It shows Aborigines beside the river at Parramatta (an Aboriginal word meaning "head of the waters"), west of Sydney Cove. Rivers like this often formed the boundary between tribal estates. The figures are set in an Eden-like landscape and are depicted as innocents carrying out their way of life unencumbered by the trappings of civilized society. The gentle undulations of the hills and the soft outlines of the vegetation emphasize the innocence of the scene. Such romantic depictions of simple primitivism were fairly typical of the early European artistic response to Aboriginality but were quickly replaced by more hardened images that represented the Aborigines as debased savages. By the second half of the 19th century Aborigines had almost disappeared from the artistic record, except as costume-dressing in scenes of settler life, and they remained consistently absent from Australian art until the late 20th century when Aboriginal artists made Aboriginality once again the subject.

Right The dingo has totemic significance for many Aboriginal peoples. The evidence suggests that the Aborigines did not use dingoes in hunting, though in the wild they are formidable hunters, working in packs, but that they were camp dogs, following the clan groups as they traveled their ancient pathways. In the 19th century dingoes were hunted and killed by settlers as a threat to cattle and sheep, and dingo fences were erected in an attempt to confine the the dogs to non-pastoral areas. "Dingo" came to be used as a pejorative term for any cunning and untrustworthy character, and the legend grew up that dingoes killed small children. As recently as 1980 a dingo was blamed for the disappearance of a baby girl, Azaria Chamberlain, in a case that kept Australians spellbound for almost a decade.

Below The burning of grassland was an essential part of the Aboriginal peoples' custodianship of the land. Early colonists thought that the grass fires they observed were caused by campfires going out of control, and only recently have the land management techniques of the Aborigines been recognized for what they are. As the sweet new grass grew back after the burning, kangaroos and other game would be attracted back into the area; moreover, regular clearance kept down the accumulation of dry tinder over many seasons and so helped to prevent major bushfires of the kind that have devastated large areas of southeastern Australia in recent years.

Custodians of the land

While it is well known that the Aborigines had a deep spiritual attachment to the land, another widely held misconception is that they had no impact on the environment, simply hunting and gathering the food they needed and then moving on. This is far from being the case: their hunting activities over the thousands of years that they have inhabited the continent have had far-reaching effect on the shape of the landscape, and on its fauna. While the major factor in the extinction of the giant marsupials was undoubtedly the extensive climatic change brought about by the ending of the ice age, they may also have been prey to the weapons of the Aboriginal hunters.

But it was the advent of the dingo, or wild dog, that had the most devastating effect on wild life. The dingo, probably a native of Southeast Asia, has only been in Australia for between 5,000 and 3,000 years, and its presence may be explained by trading links between northern Aboriginal tribes and fishermen from Indonesia. Though never fully domesticated, it lived in close proximity to Aboriginal encampments. Before its arrival Australia was free of predatory mammals, though the thylacoko (the thylacine, or Tasmanian tiger or wolf), a scavenging carnivorous marsupial, would have been a threat to young marsupials and ground-nesting birds, and crocodiles and birds of prey such as the wedgetail eagle also take animals. In competition for the same food sources, the speedier dingo, which runs in packs, out-hunted the thylacoko, which disappeared from mainland Australia about 4,000 to 3,000 years ago. It survived in Tasmania – which was free of dingoes – until the present century.

We are only just beginning to understand the full

impact the Aborigines had on the land. While they treated it with respect as the center of their spiritual world, they also shaped it in accordance with their material and cultural needs. They did not till the land or plant and harvest crops, but they did clear substantial areas by burning. However, burning is integral to the survival of some of Australia's ecosystems. Fire caused by electrical storms rejuvenates grasslands, and forests such as the massive Karri in the southwest depend on heat to break open the seeds of trees. Only in very recent years have modern farmers and forestry workers come to recognize the positive function of burning. Through its controlled implementation they may yet reverse the greatest of Australia's ecological crises, that of soil degradation and aging forests. It seems that by burning the land, the Aborigines were acting as land managers and early conservationists, protecting from desertification the grasslands on which their survival depended.

Fire, tools and weapons

Fire for the Aborigines was not only an important land management technique; it was also an effective tool in hunting. Animals would be entrapped within a circle of flames. A small exit would be left, guarded by warrior hunters armed with spears, woomeras (spear throwers), waddis and occasionally boomerangs who would slaughter the animals as they tried to break through the gap. Fire was also used as a source of heat and for cooking. This was done over simple open fires, and involved the cooking of whole, unskinned carcasses, though crude ovens were also sometimes used. During the cold months in Tasmania, the Aborigines slept in small groups separated by small camp fires. Like the mainland Aborigines, they had mastered rudimentary skills of cooking, but unlike them, they do not seem to have learned the art of making fire. Instead, they seem to have been dependent upon on taking flames from the fires of electrical storms. These were kept alight by the use of fire sticks or torches, and each tribe attached great importance to having a burning torch always with it.

Though the Aborigines did not develop industrial techniques beyond the making of stone implements, fire was, for some, an important process in manufacturing. The head of the kodj ax, common to the peoples of southwestern Australia, was made by setting a fire against a granite outcrop. The rock would then be doused with water to cool it rapidly. The fractured pieces produced by the process of heating and cooling were then shaped and sharpened on both sides to form an ax-head. Two such pieces of sharpened stone were cemented end to end with gum from the blackboy plant and fixed to a length of wood about a third of a meter in length. The axhead and handle together weighed about half a kilogram.

The kodj manufacturing technique is a relatively recent one, which probably originated among the Aborigines of the southwest some 3,000 years ago. Much more ancient, and more widespread, was the percussive Kartan tool-making technique, which was in use at least 30,000 years ago and may have arrived in Australia with the Aborigines. The Kartan ax-heads were made from pebbles and small to medium-sized stones, only one face of which was worked, by being struck, scraped and flaked with another stone. The finished head was fixed to a haft with a resin made from ground spinifex seed, which was put to multiple use in weapon and tool-making, and secured with a fiber

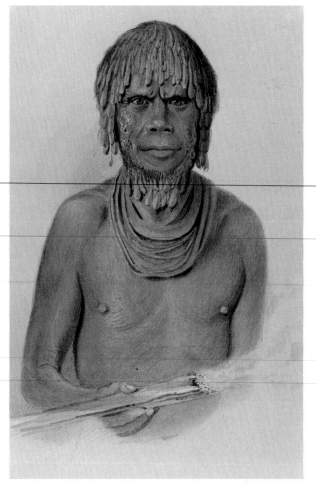

Left That the Tasmanians did not possess the ability to make fire was once put forward as evidence that they lacked the basics of civilization. Instead they were reported as carrying firesticks wherever they traveled. These sticks were lit from fires started by electrical storms or from the smoldering campfires that dotted the landscape – observers noted that the Tasmanian Aborigines often made several campfires and slept between them. This picture by Thomas Bock shows Mannalargenna, one of the "last of the Tasmanians" who were confined to Flinders Island in the 1830s, carrying a firestick. It was one of a series of pictures presented to the wife of Sir John Franklin (1786–1847), who as lieutenant-governor of Van Diemen's Land presided over the rounding up of the Tasmanian Aborigines.

string. Around 6,000 years ago, more finely worked stone implements known as microliths came into use. These were ground as well as being flaked, and even crude knives with serrated edges were manufactured.

Apart from the boomerang, which seems in any case to have had more of a ceremonial function than to have been used for hunting or warfare, the Aborigines' weapons and tools seem crude beside those of comparable hunter–gatherer cultures. Spears were used for hunting animals and fish, which formed an important part of their diet. Complex systems of traps and weirs were used to catch fish in the Berrima region of northern New South Wales and also in Arnhem Land, and fish-hooks were in use on the eastern coast, though there is no evidence of them earlier than 1,000 years ago. Nets were used throughout coastal and river regions. The relative scarcity of artifacts might lead to the assumption that the subsistence struggle for survival left little time in traditional Aboriginal life for cultural activity. Certainly no pottery or decorative use of metals have been found in Australia, though there is an array of shell and bone ornaments. Any such conclusion, however, is belied by the staggering variety of Aboriginal art.

Aboriginal art

Aboriginal art took many forms. Both men and women decorated their bodies with ocher and blood in ritual patterns for initiation ceremonies, and sometimes elaborate headdresses were worn. Unfortunately knowledge of many of the ceremonial styles of body-painting has been lost. Many of the tribes made sacred ritual objects such as decorated bark shields, ceremonial poles and carved figures, and others – especially the Arnhem Land Aborigines – made paintings

Right True boomerangs – carved, v-shaped throwing sticks, the aerodynamics of which allow them to return to the thrower – were rarely used in hunting, except to frighten animals into traps, but seem to have been used mostly for sport. Boomerang contests remain popular with Aboriginal groups and the sport is growing among non-Aboriginal Australians. Boomerangs, which are often elaborately decorated, were also used for cutting and digging, and as clapping sticks to accompany performance. There were many other types of throwing stick, not all of which were designed to return.

in ocher on sheets of bark. But by far the most abundant form of art, found in all parts of the continent are rock carvings and paintings. Many thousands of rock gallery sites have been listed, and as archaeologists catalog the vast collections they hold, more and more hidden masterpieces are discovered each year.

All dating of rock art must remain speculative and provisional, since estimates of the earliest appearances of particular forms are constantly having to be revised in the light of new discoveries. Among the oldest examples of Aboriginal art are simple finger markings scraped and chiseled across the soft limestone walls of caves. Such forms date back at least 20,000 years, but recent research suggests that some "secret" sites, used for the performance of exclusive rituals, in central Australia and the Northern Territory may go back more than 40,000 years. Around 15,000 years ago Panaramittee engravings began to appear. These marked significant sites; the carvings resemble the tracks of animals embellished with abstract shapes in particular circles and spirals.

Improved dating techniques of the ochers used in rock paintings suggest that these, too, were being made at a very early date, though fewer have survived. Rock paintings, from the Pilbra region of Western Australia and parts of central-northern Queensland, are between 12,000 and 13,000 years old. The first figurative representations began to appear around 10,000 years ago. These included drawings of humans and animals, some in the form of unique "X-ray"

paintings that depict the skeleton and internal organs. Abstract dot-paintings convey tribal and totemic knowledge.

All Aboriginal art – be it body-painting, carving or painting – was to be read in this way. Rock and tree paintings and markings contained coded messages for those trained to decipher them. They marked out the tribal group's physical environment and communicated important knowledge about it to the group as they made their way across the estate. The paintings delineated important ceremonial sites where secret rituals were enacted, and they carried information about tribal relations with the dreaming. They were a form of tribal history by which totemic lore and ancestral stories were passed down the generations.

The rock paintings were periodically retouched and added to. The tribal identity was passed on through the inherited designs, but contemporary circumstances could intervene to redefine relationships within the tribe and with neighboring groups, recasting aspects of history and belief. Today, many ancient rock galleries are under threat of disappearance because the custom of periodic retouching ceased with the removal of the Aboriginal peoples from their tribal land, and with the destruction of traditional ways of life. The location of many "secret" sites has been lost, and it seems likely that many hundreds of paintings have disappeared already. Those that remain communicate something to us of the world of the ancient peoples of Australia.

Right The Tiwi people of Bathurst and Melville Islands off the northern coast of Australia carve elaborate funeral poles called pukamini poles, which are placed round or near burial grounds; their intricate carved and painted designs tell clan stories and confirm totems. The makers of the funeral poles are chosen from within the totem. They carry the secrets of lineages and are highly regarded among their communities, where they form an artisan class. They were traditionally given ornaments, food and other goods in return for their services, but today are more likely to be paid in cash.

Aboriginal Art

The rock engravings and paintings of the Aboriginal peoples are located in galleries – areas of general exhibition – or sacred sites – marked areas of spiritual and ceremonial importance. The dispossession of tribes from their estates by European settlement meant that the significance of much rock art became lost. The disruption of tribal life similarly caused the disappearance of more ephemeral forms of art such as the decoration of weapons and body-painting. Archaeologists and anthropologists began keeping records of surviving sites and artworks in the 1930s but it is only since the 1960s that any systematic attempt has been made to catalog and preserve them. Since 1992, and the recognition of native title in Australia, rock art has become an important means of identifying the traditional custodians of the land. While the meaning of much art has been irredeemably lost, in more remote areas of the continent Aboriginal artists continued to retouch the ancient tribal rock paintings, and some record the arrival of European ships and of men on horseback carrying guns. Traditional ceremonial art is still practiced by some Aboriginal groups. There is also a thriving market for the paintings of modern Aboriginal artists, many of whom work in new media such as acrylics.

Above Art was central to traditional Aboriginal society. It carried coded information about the origins, lineages and beliefs of Aboriginal communities, and mapped the clan estates. Artists were selected on the basis of totem identities and rites of passage or initiation. Rock art is the most enduring form of Aboriginal art. Some rock engravings have been dated to more than 40,000 years old. This example of a maze-like design is from the oldest known site of Panaramittee engravings in South Australia.

Left Rock painting also has very ancient origins; it is most abundant in the center and north of the continent. In contrast to engravings, which are found mostly on open sites, rock paintings are generally in caves or on the walls or ceilings of rock-shelters, as in the case of this design of two human figures in the X-ray style (in which the internal organs and bone structure are shown), from Kakadu National Park in the Northern Territory.

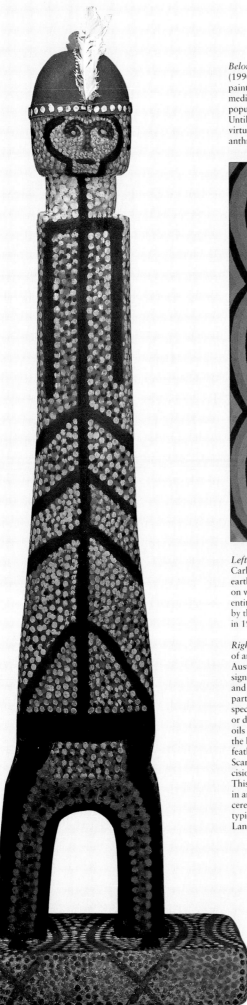

Below *Dream of Two Women* (1990) by Ronnie Tjampitjinpa is painted in acrylics on canvas, a medium that has became very popular with Aboriginal painters. Until recently Aboriginal art was virtually ignored outside anthropological museums, but in the early 1980s a remarkably vibrant art industry developed as galleries and private collectors outbid each other to purchase examples by living artists. In 1995 there were an estimated 5,000 Aboriginal artists working in Australia.

Left This sculpture by Paddy Carlton (Joolama, b. 1936), in earth pigments and natural binder on wood, 166 cm × 42 cm, is entitled *Bardadany*. It was acquired by the National Gallery of Victoria in 1992.

Right Body decoration was a form of art practiced throughout Australia. It carried deep religious significance. Motifs denoted clan and totemic identities, and particular designs were reserved for specific occasions such as initiation or death rituals. Ocher, clays and oils were commonly used to paint the body, and adornments included feathers, leaves, shells and rocks. Scarring was common, and circumcision was practiced by some tribes. This performer is about to take part in an open (ie. not secret) ceremony. His bold body design is typical of north-central Arnhem Land.

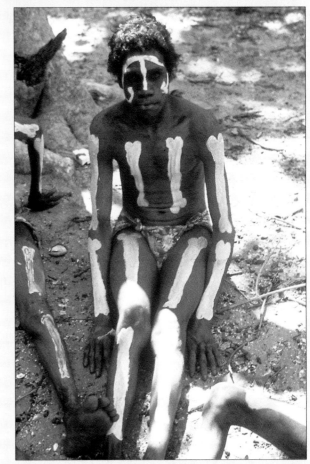

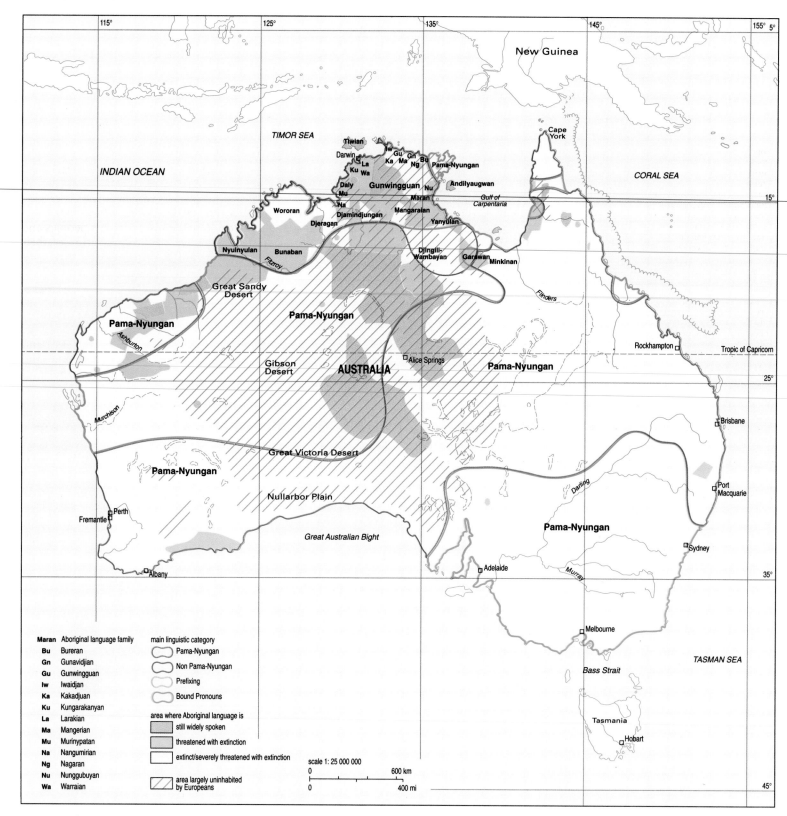

Maran	Aboriginal language family		main linguistic category
Bu	Bureran		Pama-Nyungan
Gn	Gunavidjian		Non Pama-Nyungan
Gu	Gunwingguan		Prefixing
Iw	Iwaidjan		Bound Pronouns
Ka	Kakadjuan		
Ku	Kungarakanyan		area where Aboriginal language is
La	Larakian		still widely spoken
Ma	Mangerian		threatened with extinction
Mu	Murinypatan		extinct/severely threatened with extinction
Na	Nangumirian		
Ng	Nagaran		scale 1: 25 000 000
Nu	Nunggubuyan		0 600 km
Wa	Warraian		area largely uninhabited by Europeans
			0 400 mi

Music and song

As with art, so Aboriginal music is intrinsic to belief in ancestry and the land. The mimetic ceremonial dances at corroborees were accompanied by songs chanted by a song-man to the rhythmic clapping of sticks and the drone of the didgeridoo - a long pipe of hollowed wood that was sounded by a combination of blowing and mouth movements. The songs and the dances reenacted the tribe's totemic identity, educating members in tribal law and reminding them of their shared responsibilities to the group. Some songs recounted myths and recited the tribe's history; others were employed to aid healing. More importantly, songs were a form of oral map-making. They described the tribal estate, naming significant places and landmarks, boundaries and points of contact with other tribes. These "songlines" were the means by which the tribe renewed its relationship with the land.

Open songs belonged to every member of the tribe, but some songs were the exclusive property of particular groups. Children, for example, had special songs to educate them in the lore of the tribe. Secret song-dance performances were part of the preparation for male and female initiation, and accompanied the initiation ceremonies themselves. The closed songs performed on such occasions carried secrets relating to specific spirits, to sexual knowledge and to sacred places. Other songs marked specific events in the phys-

Aboriginal languages
There were approximately 500 Aboriginal languages in Australia at the time of European colonization. It is tentatively suggested they shared a common linguistic root, proto-Australian. Only a fraction have survived into the present, though many hybrid forms have emerged. These can be classified as mixes of once differentiated languages, as mixes of Aboriginal and English, or as combinations of both. Around 51 language families have been identified, divided into two main subgroupings, Pama-Nyungan and non-Pama-Nyungan.

ical universe, such as changes in the season, or within the group, for example the birth of a child, a marriage or a special tribal occasion. Cult songs provided interpretations of the ancestors and of physical phenomena that would otherwise be difficult to explain, while clan songs were exclusive to particular family groupings.

The disappearance of a culture

Aboriginal society, customs and beliefs were fundamentally altered by European settlement. The first colonists believed they had an absolute right to the land: in legal terms Australia was *terra nullius*, an unoccupied land. As they moved into the interior, this appeared to give them a free hand to dispossess the Aborigines by any means they saw fit: the eradication of Aborigines from Tasmania was symptomatic of colonial attitudes. No attempt was made to understand or to accommodate Aboriginal value systems. It was only when the goal of ethnic cleansing seemed virtually to have been achieved that 19th-century anthropologists and scientists saw the need for systematic study of the "dying race". So opened a still more macabre chapter in the history of European–Aboriginal contact, as body-snatchers set out to fill the museums of Europe with specimens of the last of the hunters and gatherers.

Aboriginality was broken up by the invaders long before it could be explored and properly understood. Aborigines survived the genocide, but the world they now inhabited was substantially different. Even those who escaped the worst terror because they lived in remote areas could no longer narrate with full authority the culture and customs of their peoples – they could not tell their stories without recourse to the invaders. As a result, Aboriginality was studied as if it were a past that had vanished. The very qualities and nuances of Aboriginal existence are today refracted through the experience of contact, even when Aborigines tell their own stories, even where oral traditions such as songlines are still practiced. Where once songs were sung to celebrate the history of the peoples and their land, they now lament the desecration of their ways of life. Stories still recall tribal past times and beliefs; the religious significance of the land is still conveyed in song and performance and art; but the participants in these social memories inhabit conditions that are very different from those their forebears knew. The stories, the songs, the dance and the art may be authentic, but the references – the sites and landmarks, the intimate knowledge of the plant and animal life – and their deeper significance, have all now "gone into the country".

Below Aboriginal dance has become a major cultural industry in contemporary Australia. Here performers dance for tourists at Alice Springs in the center of the continent. Modern Aboriginal dance draws on ancient traditions and ceremonial, maintaining contact with the Aboriginal heritage, but blends contemporary themes. Aboriginal performers are finding an increasing audience for their art, both among the Aboriginal and non-Aboriginal communities. Many Aboriginal dance and song groups have made world tours. David Gulpilil from the Northern Territory, who made his debut as a young man with an international touring dance group, has since gone on to become an actor with many movies to his credit.

ACROSS THE GREAT OCEAN

First peoples

How and by whom were the islands scattered across the expanse of the world's greatest ocean settled? Different island societies offered their own accounts of their origins. Some spoke of descent from gods, or of ancestors emerging from underworlds, others told of great canoe voyages that brought their ancestors to their new lands. These accounts embodied important truths about the societies from which they came and helped to shape a common sense of identity. Later, when European mariners began to explore the islands of the Pacific, all sorts of theories were developed to explain the origins of the region's indigenous populations. Some were based on studies of the physical resemblances between the peoples of Polynesia and those of Southeast Asia; other explanations, emanating from the wilder shores of speculation, argued the existence of a lost continent or even suggested that a wandering tribe of ancient Egyptians had had a hand in shaping the culture of the Pacific islanders. The story of the peopling of the Pacific islands has become much clearer in recent years. Archaeology, the latest linguistic and genetic research, and a growing appreciation of the Pacific islanders' voyaging and navigational skills have all added to our knowledge. Just as modern study has pushed the earliest settlement of Australia back by several tens of thousands of years, so too the most recent research indicates that human migration into the Pacific islands began much earlier than was once supposed, at least 40,000 years ago. Yet the story is still incomplete, and there are many tantalizing questions that remain to be answered.

Given the existence of the land bridge between Australia and New Guinea during the Pleistocene glaciation, it is to be expected that the first peoples would have made their way into what is now New Guinea at about the same time, or not much later, than they arrived in Australia. Indeed, there is a case for arguing that they made their way by means of simple boats such as bark or dugout canoes or bamboo rafts across the short sea passages from Southeast Asia to New Guinea, and from there moved into Australia. For some years, the oldest known evidence of human activity came from the site of Kosipe in the highlands of eastern Papua New Guinea. Dating by Carbon 14 analysis suggested that some of the material from this site is up to 26,000 years old. As humans may have appeared in Australia as much as 60,000 years ago, and as the highlands of New Guinea would have been reached from earlier coastal sites, it seemed likely that evidence of earlier human presence would be found in the region. Recent excavations have provided it. The cave site of Matenkupkum on the island of New Ireland (part of the Bismarck Archipelago off the northeastern coast of Papua New Guinea) seems to have been inhabited about 33,000 years ago, while a date of around 40,000 years ago has been proposed for a site on the Huon Peninsula on the northern coast of the New Guinea mainland. The people of such coastal sites would have made use both of the rich marine

Below The peaks of the volcanic island of Bora Bora, one of the Society Islands of French Polynesia, are shrouded in mist. This 10-kilometer-long pimple of land lies in the vastness of the eastern Pacific Ocean. Yet more than 1,000 years ago, in the later phases of the process of exploration and migration that carried the Pacific peoples across a vast area of the globe's surface, highly skilled canoe voyagers found and settled it, together with many smaller, less conspicuous and more isolated islands.

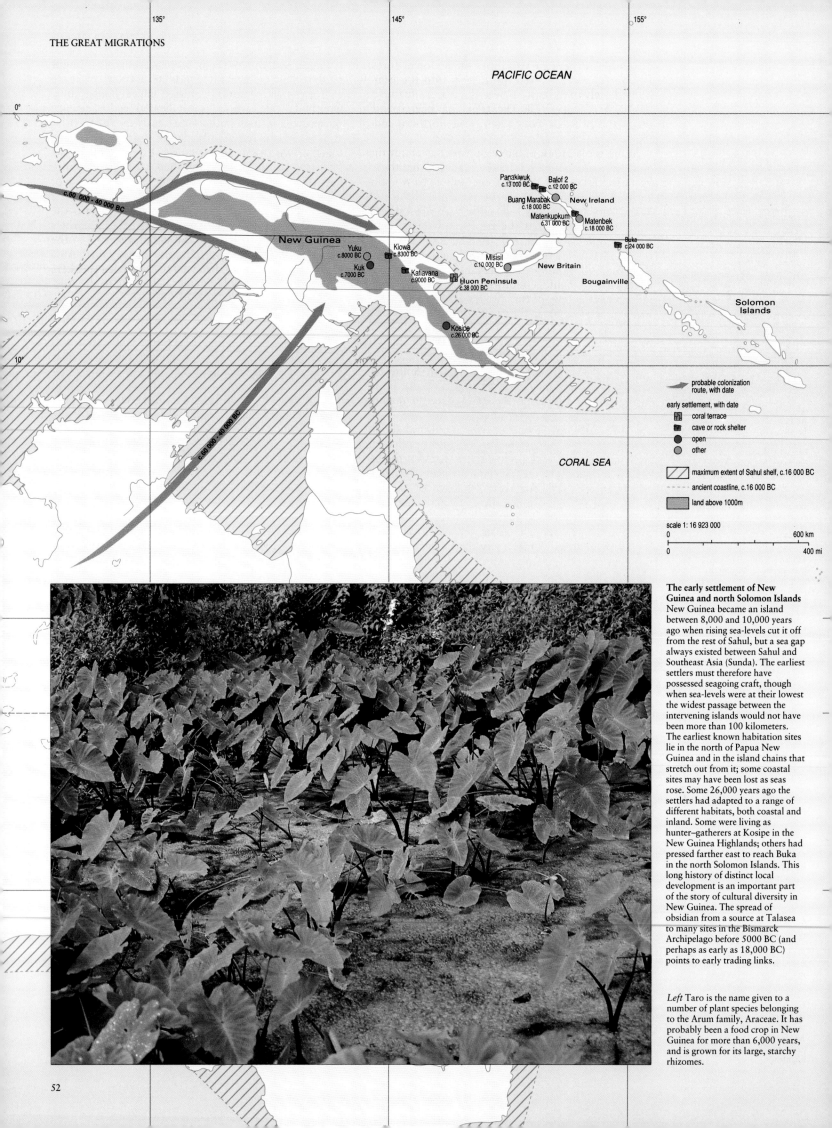

PACIFIC OCEAN

c.60 000 - 40 000 BC

New Guinea

Panakiwuk
c.13 000 BC

Balof 2
c.12 000 BC

Buang Marabak
c.18 000 BC

New Ireland

Matenkupkum
c.31 000 BC

Matenbek
c.18 000 BC

Buka
c.24 000 BC

Yuku
c.8000 BC

Kiowa
c.8300 BC

Kuk
c.7000 BC

Kafiavana
c.9000 BC

Misisil
c.10 000 BC

New Britain

Bougainville

Solomon
Islands

Huon Peninsula
c.38 000 BC

Kosipe
c.26 000 BC

c.60 000 - 40 000 BC

CORAL SEA

probable colonization
route, with date

early settlement, with date

coral terrace

cave or rock shelter

open

other

maximum extent of Sahul shelf, c.16 000 BC

ancient coastline, c.16 000 BC

land above 1000m

scale 1: 16 923 000

0   600 km

0   400 mi

The early settlement of New Guinea and north Solomon Islands
New Guinea became an island between 8,000 and 10,000 years ago when rising sea-levels cut it off from the rest of Sahul, but a sea gap always existed between Sahul and Southeast Asia (Sunda). The earliest settlers must therefore have possessed seagoing craft, though when sea-levels were at their lowest the widest passage between the intervening islands would not have been more than 100 kilometers. The earliest known habitation sites lie in the north of Papua New Guinea and in the island chains that stretch out from it; some coastal sites may have been lost as seas rose. Some 26,000 years ago the settlers had adapted to a range of different habitats, both coastal and inland. Some were living as hunter–gatherers at Kosipe in the New Guinea Highlands; others had pressed farther east to reach Buka in the north Solomon Islands. This long history of distinct local development is an important part of the story of cultural diversity in New Guinea. The spread of obsidian from a source at Talasea to many sites in the Bismarck Archipelago before 5000 BC (and perhaps as early as 18,000 BC) points to early trading links.

Left Taro is the name given to a number of plant species belonging to the Arum family, Araceae. It has probably been a food crop in New Guinea for more than 6,000 years, and is grown for its large, starchy rhizomes.

Above The Ambun stone, from the Ambun valley in the Western Highlands of Papua New Guinea, is a prehistoric carving of uncertain age, which may represent the embryo of the long-beaked spiny anteater that lives in the high mountain forests. It comes from the present-day territory of the Mae Enga people. The eastern Enga clans use stone objects, including ancient carvings, in rituals to propitiate ancestral ghosts, but they do not know where the carvings came from, nor what purpose their makers intended them for.

Far right The dark outline of a large ditch is visible on the wall of an excavation trench at Kuk plantation in the Mount Hagen region of New Guinea. Two such ditches, around 3 meters deep and each about 500 meters long, have been identified. They date from about 4000 BC and may have been used, with other smaller channels, to control levels of water in the soil in order to grow taro, most varieties of which require swampy or moist conditions. Evidence of such a drainage system suggests that agriculture was being intensified to support a growing and fairly densely settled population in the Western Highlands.

resources of the area and those of the lower forests. Some may have crossed quite early into the islands immediately to the east of New Guinea. A site that can be dated to about 26,000 years ago has been found in the island of Buka, which lies at the northern end of the Solomon Islands.

Stone tools are one source of evidence about these earliest Pacific peoples. It has been argued that the earliest assemblages of flaked stone tools of New Guinea show parallels with those of the Palaeolithic (Old Stone Age) in both Australia and Southeast Asia. This supports the idea that the peoples of these regions were originally connected. As the seas rose, they became separated from one another, and their cultures diverged as they adapted to very different climatic and other environmental conditions. The tools themselves indicate something of the way their makers used their local environments. In the earliest sites flaked ax-adzes appear alongside the waisted blades of hoe-like stone tools. Both were probably hafted. Tools of this kind suggest that the early New Guinea peoples were working away at the margins of the forest. Some have argued that they may even have practiced a limited form of horticulture, which would place them among the world's first crop gardeners. However, in the absence of any firm evidence of horticultural activity, such as drainage ditches or changes in the pollen analysis, most archaeologists have assumed that the people inhabiting these sites were hunters and gatherers.

The fullest archaeological sequence of the early occupation of New Guinea comes from the highlands. Some 15,000 years ago hunter–gatherers were present in the Kaironk valley. True settlement of the island's high central areas seems to have happened only when temperatures began to rise and the glaciers receded. Over 10,000 years ago, people were living in rock shelters at Kafiavana and Kiowa in Papua New Guinea's Eastern Highlands Province. The general settlement of the highlands may have been in progress by this time. Stone tools were becoming more sophisticated as edge-ground ax-adzes came into use. Changes in the pollens found in the archaeological record provide conclusive evidence that over the next few thousand years the forests were being cleared. By 3000 BC pigs and dogs were living with the highland peoples. They must have been brought across the water divide between New Guinea and Southeast Asia by humans, and their presence is a strong indication that agriculture by this stage had developed sufficiently to provide foodstuffs for their upkeep.

Crop cultivation in the Western Highlands may have begun well over 6,000 years ago. Traces of gutters, hollows and mounds at a site at Kuk in the Mount Hagen region of the New Guinea Highlands, which date from between 9,000 and 5,500 years ago, have been interpreted as evidence of a ditch and drainage system for the growing of the root crop taro, introduced from Southeast Asia. Complicated systems of water channels for swamp management, dating from 2,500 years ago, have also been found at a site at Manton in the Wahgi Valley area of the Western Highlands, together with wooden spades and polished stone ax-adzes very like those used in recent times. Agriculture may have developed more slowly in the Eastern Highlands, with a different root crop *Pueraria lobata* being cultivated, while hunting–gathering still remained important. The cultivation of other local plants, including sugar cane and bananas, may also have begun at an early date.

Pigs, new crops and tools were presumably brought to the New Guinea highlands as a result of trade exchanges with coastal peoples. Such exchanges must have had a long history, as is indicated by the presence of seashells in highland sites as early as 9,000 years ago. However, the appearance of domestic animals, together with signs of agricultural development, the presence of distinctive polished stone tools and, between 6,000 and 5,000 years ago, the production of pottery in some areas has suggested to scholars that a new influx of people had made their way into the northern coastal regions, from where aspects of their material culture spread to the peoples settled in the highlands. These new settlers are often called Austronesians, as they are believed to have been speakers of early forms of the languages belonging to the Austronesian family.

The Austronesians

The Austronesian language family is a large and ancient grouping of related languages, once known as Malayo-Polynesian. It includes all the languages of Polynesia, as well as some of those of Micronesia, Malaya, the Philippines, Indonesia, Taiwan, Vietnam, Cambodia and even Madagascar – over 800 in total. Austronesian languages are also widespread in the southwestern Pacific islands of Melanesia, where they are found alongside others that do not belong to that family (non-Austronesian – NAN – or Papuan languages). In mainland New Guinea, Austronesian languages are largely found in coastal areas. A widely accepted explanation of this distribution is that the ancestors of the Austronesians originated in southern China or Taiwan, but developed their culture after moving into the islands of Southeast Asia. From there,

they began to spread into the islands of the western Pacific some 5,000 to 6,000 years ago, coming into areas already inhabited by the descendants of earlier settlers.

The Austronesians introduced food plants of Asian origin, including taro and yams, and animals – pigs, dogs, and fowl. How many of these were really new to the region remains open to question. The earlier peoples had developed some horticulture, but the Austronesians had extensive agricultural and fishing skills to add to the early western Pacific cultural mix. They may have been the world's first really skilled seafarers. Reconstructed words of the Proto-Austronesian language (based on comparisons of words shared by the scattered members of the language family) not only include words for major Pacific food crops such as *tales* (taro), *qubi(s)* (yam), *nuir* (coconut), but also words connected with sailing and fishing technology, for example *kawil* (fishhook), *wangka* (canoe/boat), *katir* (outriggers – used to give greater stability to more sophisticated canoes). The Austronesians' sailing canoes were capable of longer and safer sea-crossings than the simpler craft used by the earlier settlers of Melanesia, and carried them along the coasts of New Guinea and to the island chains beyond.

The coming of the Austronesians may also explain some of the diversity in genetic make-up and physical appearance of modern Pacific peoples. The assumption is that the Austronesian-speakers were people of Southern Mongoloid stock, and their descendants are consequently related to the Mongoloid peoples of eastern Asia (as are the Native American peoples). They differed from the already established peoples of Australia, New Guinea and the nearby islands, who derived from a different genetic stock sometimes called Australoid – though the ancestors of the Australoids and Mongoloids may not have been completely unlinked. The peoples of Polynesia and Micronesia can be seen to owe most genetically to Austronesian, Mongoloid ancestors, while the peoples of Melanesia draw more upon Australoid ancestry, or on an admixture of Australoid and Mongoloid.

The picture of a new population – physically distinct, speaking distinct languages and bringing with them new skills and resources – beginning to spread through the Pacific islands around 6,000 years ago provides a clear framework for understanding further developments in the region. It is probably substantially correct, but the evidence is not yet conclusive. Though new archaeological features, new genetic-physical types and a new set of languages all appeared in the western Pacific around the same time, it is not easy to prove that they all derived from the same source: a specific new group of people. Present-day speakers of Austronesian languages vary considerably in physical appearance and genetic make-up, and there is no neat Australoid-Mongoloid split. Possibly this is a result of a mixing of peoples. For instance, contact between Austronesian-speakers and the existing NAN-speaking inhabitants of coastal New Guinea might have created a population who spoke an Austronesian language with some NAN features, but retained much of the genetic make-up of the earlier NAN-speakers.

The development of networks for trade and exchange in the islands of the western Pacific may also have helped to spread Austronesian languages. But our understanding of the processes by which the language spread and developed is still incomplete. Some scholars have proposed that Melanesia itself – possibly the islands north of New Guinea – was the original home of the Austronesian-speakers. Others have argued that the Austronesian-speakers may not have been a completely new set of people from Southeast Asia, but could have developed from a portion of the population already present in Melanesia. Recent genetic evidence seems to support the idea that the Austronesian-speaking ancestors of the Polynesians originated in Southeast Asia. But the study of skeletal remains found in association with the material evidence that archaeologists have linked to early Austronesian expansion remains very limited, and new findings could change the picture.

The story of Lapita ware

One particular type of archaeological evidence has been of great importance in tracing the spread of some of the Austronesian-speaking peoples through the islands of Melanesia and into the farther Pacific. This is a type of pottery known as Lapita ware. It is an earthenware, generally tempered with sand, and fired in open fires. There are a number of different forms including globular cooking pots, shouldered pots, open bowls and flat-bottomed dishes. Much of it is plain, but it is also found with a red slip, and some is patterned with a distinctive and attractive range of decorations stamped or incised into the surface. The stamping was often done with an instrument with a number of small teeth – something thought to be not unlike the tattooing chisels later used in Polynesia. This cutting and stamping was used to build up rows of decorative motifs or more complicated geometric designs, and even human faces. Because it is so distinctive, Lapita pottery is a valuable indicator of the spread of its makers – though in Melanesia at least, trade may have carried the pottery into areas not inhabited by Lapita people.

Lapita ware is named after an archaeological site on the west coast of New Caledonia excavated in the 1950s, but its actual place of origin is still disputed. Some archaeologists believe that Lapita ware originated in island Southeast Asia, though the earliest reliably dated pottery – from about 1600 BC – has been found in the Bismarck Archipelago. Some of the Lapita sites there are described as stable settlements – that is, they were occupied and developed over time – and some may cover an area of more than a hectare. Even if this indicates that Lapita producers in this area stayed put, the pottery itself spread quite rapidly to other areas. Early Lapita pottery (pre-800 BC) with similar decorative motifs has been found over a substantial part of the western Pacific, from the islands off northern New Guinea, through the Melanesian islands to Fiji and the islands of western Polynesia – Tonga, Samoa, Uvea and Futuna. The distant outposts of Fiji and Tonga could have been settled as early as 1300 BC. We have no firm evidence of human settlement in the Melanesian island groups south of the Solomon Islands before the arrival of Lapita-making Austronesians. Of course, this does not preclude the possibility that pre-Austronesian peoples, or other Austronesian-speakers, had moved into these areas before the Lapita makers, but nothing has yet been found to confirm it.

All the known Lapita sites have been found on coasts and on offshore islands, even when settling previously uninhabited islands. The presence of Lapita remains on fringing coral reefs suggests that the Lapita

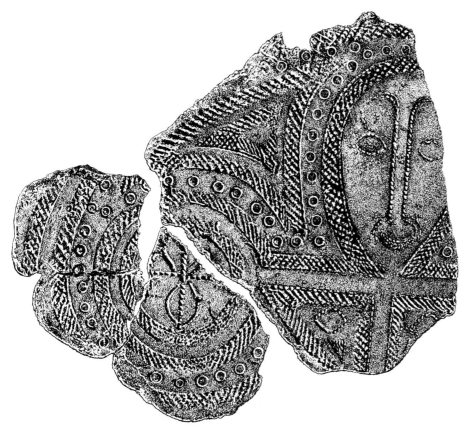

Even for the Lapita voyagers who first sailed between them, this was a significant distance and it was to have an influence on the subsequent history of the ancient Pacific peoples. Two distinct regions of Lapita culture developed, a western and an eastern. Lively contact continued within each region, but journeys between them were less frequent. The pottery found throughout the islands of Melanesia, from New Britain to Santa Cruz, Vanuatu and New Caledonia shares many decorative motifs; the similarities become weaker once Fiji and the islands of western Polynesia are reached. The language also seems to reflect this division, with the central Pacific languages of Fiji and Polynesia developing along separate lines from the Austronesian languages of the western Pacific.

The making of Melanesia

Some European writers have created the illusion that the societies of the Pacific islands were timeless and unchanging. This is far from the case; their histories are as much about change and innovation as those of any other part of the world. Internal evolution, adaptation to new environmental circumstances, new settler groups and contact between different societies all promoted change. Throughout the Pacific, identifying the first settlers and the likely nature of their society is only the beginning of the story.

As we have seen, New Guinea had already experienced some 34,000 years of human development by the time the Austronesians arrived. Their coming may have encouraged an intensification and elaboration of agriculture over a wide area beyond their own coastal settlements: there is evidence of extensive trading links with the interior. Yet the highland peoples were already in the process of developing into a number of horticultural and hunting–gathering societies, each

Above This combination of abstract patterns and a human face, found on pottery fragments from Nenumbo Gawa in the Santa Cruz Islands, is one of the most elaborate examples of known Lapita ware decoration. The most common decorative technique used by the Lapita potters was dentate stamping – the pattern being pressed into the soft clay with a short-toothed implement. Lapita sites may go back as far as 2000 BC, while in some areas Lapita-like pottery was still being made in the 2nd century AD. Generally, however, it began to give way to other ceramic traditions after 500 BC or was succeeded by plain "Lapitoid" pottery.

Left Flakes of obsidian (volcanic glass) provided razor-sharp cutting edges for a whole range of purposes. The spread of obsidian from Talasea in New Britain, which was being transported to neighboring New Ireland as early as 4500 BC, provides evidence of ancient trading links. Later it even found its way as far as Fiji.

Far right Yams (*Dioscorea*), here being planted in Fiji, are a widely distributed food plant of the Pacific. A vine with a tuberous root, yams favor drier soil conditions than most varieties of taro and are often grown on mounds, their vines trailed up a pole. The tubers normally weigh between 2.5 and 5 kilograms but they can reach lengths of 2 meters and weigh as much as 45 kilograms. They can be stored for several months.

people built some of their settlements on piles over the water. While they had pigs, dogs and fowl, as well as the major food crops of the Pacific, marine resources were clearly of great importance to them. Alongside stone tools, they used shell adzes, rubbing-stones or files of coral and sea-urchin spines, and shell scrapers, ornaments and fishhooks. The presence of oven pits on excavated sites shows that they cooked with hot stones in earth ovens, as is common throughout the Pacific region.

The seafaring skills of the Lapita people are shown not only by their ability to settle the more distant islands of the western Pacific but also by their apparent involvement in long-distance exchange. Obsidian (volcanic glass) was a valuable material for making sharp cutting tools. One important source was Talasea, on New Britain in the Bismarck Archipelago. Spectrographic analysis can identify obsidian as being from a particular source, and Talasea obsidian has been found in Lapita sites more than 2,500 kilometers from its place of origin. It spread as far as Vanuatu, New Caledonia and the Santa Cruz Islands. Two flakes have even been reported from Naigani in Fiji. Recent evidence shows that Talasea obsidian was "exported" long before the coming of the Lapita people, perhaps for more than 10,000 years. But the distances it was moved across water were probably under 30 kilometers. The Lapita voyagers made much longer journeys, crossing hundreds of kilometers of open ocean. Volcanic glass was not the only material they carried. Pottery and pottery-making materials, chert stone (a flint-like rock used for making flaked tools), stone adzes and oven stones all seem to have been transported over lesser distances. So there is considerable evidence to suggest that early Lapita history was not one of isolated settler communities but, rather, involved continuing contacts and exchanges based on two-way voyaging in sailing canoes.

The ocean gap between Vanuatu, the closest island group to the west, and Fiji is about 850 kilometers.

with its own linguistic and cultural distinctions. The discovery of what appear to be early agricultural drainage systems suggests that in some highland areas the population may have been larger than it was at one time believed to be.

Some of the early agriculturalists of New Guinea possessed items of material culture unknown to later inhabitants. Among the more striking of these are the distinctive stone mortars and pestles that are known to have been in existence before 1000 BC, but which may not be pre-Lapita. They have been found in the Bismarck Archipelago, northeastern New Guinea and the western highlands, with some in the northern Solomon Islands. Sometimes they have a strong decorative element that may incorporate bird-like forms. It has been suggested that the mortars and pestles were used to crush plant seeds and nut kernels.

The lowland peoples of New Guinea would have been growing taro, yam, sugar cane, banana, coconuts, and keeping pigs, dogs, and fowl, probably harvesting sago (from sago palms) and exploiting the natural resources of the coastal waters. Different communities may have had their own specialization, creating opportunities for trade: one village may have produced a particular highly valued item of food, another have been well placed to supply a particular type of stone. Among such specialized producers were the Lapita makers. We know that Lapita pottery was still being made in New Britain around 500 BC, but the Lapita culture gradually became absorbed into later societies that probably had their roots in several different traditions. However, the Lapita potting tradition lived on for a long time in places; at Yule Island on the Papuan Gulf, for example, red-slipped Lapita-like pottery was being produced as late as 1200 AD.

The Austronesian speakers of New Guinea had always lived alongside other peoples. The picture in the main island chain of Melanesia is rather different. The Solomon Islands, closest geographically to New Guinea, are most similar in terms of early settlement. At least some of the islands already had an established population by the time the Austronesians arrived. The cave site on the island of Buka, providing evidence of hunting, gathering and fishing activity around 26,000 years ago, has already been mentioned, and stone tools found on the island of Guadalcanal are similar to the ancient waisted ax-adzes of New Guinea. Excavations of the cave of Fotoruma on the same island show that it was inhabited for 3,000 years up to recent times. Certain items, types of tools, bead valuables and decorations such as arm rings made of shell run through many archaeological layers, suggesting a considerable continuity of culture down to some of the societies still living on the island. There is no evidence of the Lapita culture at this site, and yet Lapita coastal sites have been identified on the Santa Cruz Islands, some 390 kilometers east of the Solomons, that also date back 3,000 years.

Nor was Lapita the only pottery made in ancient Melanesia. On Buka, for example, pots were made using coiling techniques (Lapita is generally constructed from slabs of clay) and decorated with incisions and applied relief. These wares have been found from about 500 BC and continued in use for more than a thousand years. A similar type of pottery was being produced even earlier (perhaps 700 BC) in the central islands of Vanuatu, southeast of the Solomons along the Melanesian chain. There the pots are known as Mangaasi ware. It seems that the Mangaasi potters moved into an area in which there were already populations of Lapita people and perhaps even non-pottery-making Austronesians. The Mangaasi tradition in Vanuatu began to die out after about 1200 AD. Its end may have been caused by an increase in volcanic

Left Chickens descended from the jungle fowl of Southeast Asia are one of the major triad of domesticated animals found throughout the Pacific, the others being pigs and dogs. They were taken to the islands in the voyaging canoes of the Lapita-making peoples and their descendants, and even traveled as far as Easter Island on Polynesia's eastern edge. There, as elsewhere, they were a valued food – and one of the items offered in trade to the first European visitors.

Right In this photograph of the excavated "Roy Mata" site on Eretoka the main burial is seen towards the rear right of the picture. The skeleton of a man, possibly the 13th-century chief Roy Mata, lies on its back. A bundle of bones, perhaps those of a wife who died before him, is between his legs, and within his burial pit are the remains of four followers who accompanied him to the grave. Pairs of men and women, apparently also funeral sacrifices, have been uncovered in the foreground. Their bodies were carefully arranged, with the women seeming to hold the men.

Left This enigmatic bird-shaped stone pestle from the Papua New Guinea Highlands was excavated from a depth of about 3 meters. It is of unknown age. Stone pestle and mortars were no longer being made when Europeans first came into the area, and how far they stretch back into New Guinea prehistory remains an open question. There is uncertainty, too, about their original function.

activity, which culminated in a large eruption that broke up one island around 1400.

Another possibility is that the Mangaasi producers were driven away by a new group of settlers. This theory is supported by a remarkable meeting between local tradition and the findings of archaeologists. It is part of the oral history of the people of the island of Efate that a group of chiefs came to Efate and its neighboring islands, and established a new social order. An important name in this story is that of Roy Mata, who became a powerful leader in northern Efate. According to tradition he was buried on the small island of Eretoka, surrounded by a number of his followers, who were sacrificed – some of them voluntarily – to serve as his companions on his journey to the afterlife. Excavations on Eretoka in 1967 revealed a pit marked with stone slabs and large shells, which was found to contain the skeleton of a man with three other skeletons lying to his sides and a fourth across their feet. Around the main pit were 35 more burials, including 11 pairs of men and women buried together. A wide range of personal ornaments was also found, including necklaces of shell beads, whole shells, bone, stone and pieces of worked whale-teeth. There were pig-tusk bracelets and the remains of lower garments covered with shell beads. The wealth and complexity of the site and its Carbon 14 date, which places it in the 13th century, seem to fit the Roy Mata story – a testament to the power of oral tradition.

One point of disagreement between the oral and the archaeological account has to do with the direction from which Roy Mata and his people came. According to local history they originated in the south, but the archaeologists believe they came from the north. However this is eventually resolved, the islands of New Caledonia, lying to the south of Vanuatu, have their own complex prehistory. One of the mysteries of

New Caledonia's past concerns the hundreds of small conical mounds found on the mainland (Grande Terre) and the Isle des Pins. The mounds, which are about 2.5 meters high, have yielded Carbon 14 dates from 6000 BC and earlier. If they were made by humans, they show that people had reached the southern end of the main Melanesian chain far earlier than other evidence indicates. Since we now know that settlement of the northern end of the chain reaches back more than 20,000 years, this is not impossible. However, recent analysis of some of the tumuli suggests that they could be nesting mounds built by an extinct giant megapode bird. If that is the case, then New Caledonia falls more closely in line with the rest of southeastern Melanesia. The Austronesians, who arrived perhaps as early as 2000 BC, certainly by 1000 BC, probably played a part in the giant megapodes' extinction. In New Caledonia, Lapita ware was produced alongside another kind of pottery with designs pressed on by carved wooden paddles or dies, often combined with incisions and applied clay relief. It is probable that at least two or three different groups of Austronesian settlers came to New Caledonia, contributing to its later cultural complexity.

The fact that Melanesia as a whole has the longest history of human occupation in island Oceania means that there has been greater diversification of its populations into a host of different groups with enormous linguistic and cultural variation. The number of languages in Papua New Guinea alone exceeds 700, and the other island groups also show a high degree of linguistic diversity. The likelihood that initial settlement of the islands was by genetically and linguistically distinct peoples – the Papuans and the Austronesians – is important to the understanding of Melanesian prehistory. But the diversification of cultures today is the outcome of many processes working over time.

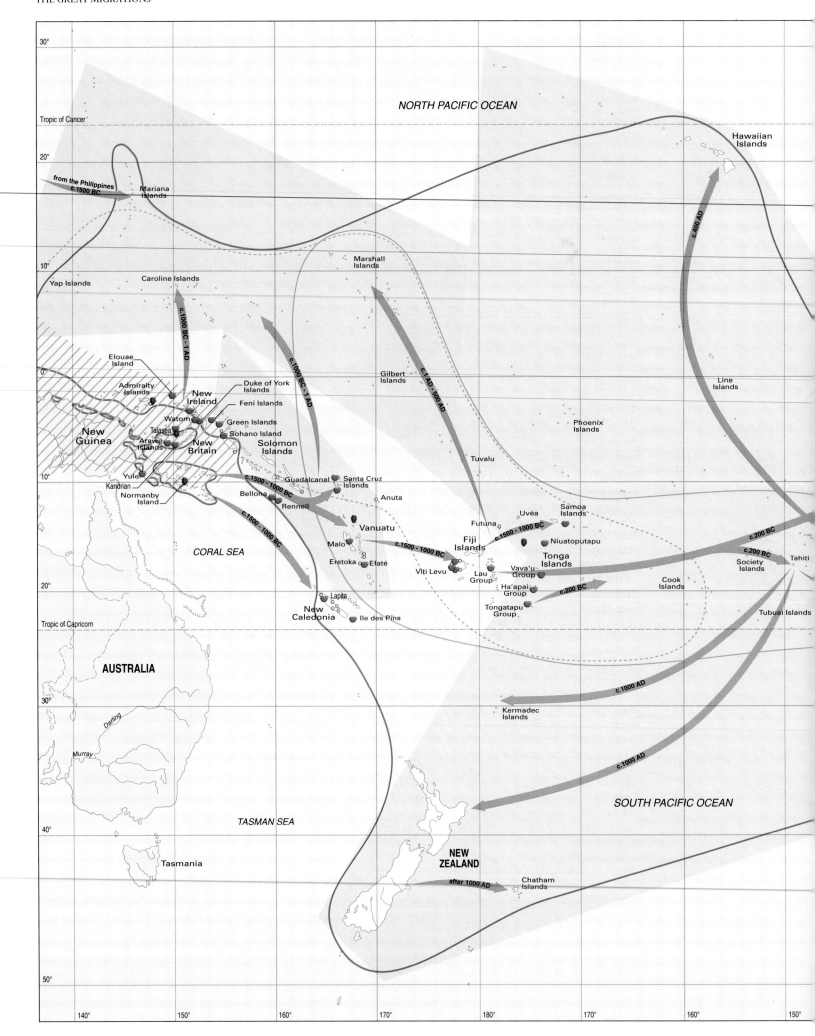

NORTH PACIFIC OCEAN

Tropic of Cancer

30°
20°
10°
0°
10°
20°
Tropic of Capricorn
30°
40°
50°

Hawaiian
Islands

from the Philippines
c.1500 BC.

Mariana
Islands

Yap Islands

Caroline Islands

c.1000 BC - 1 AD

Marshall
Islands

Line
Islands

c.400 AD

Elouae
Island

Admiralty
Islands

New
Ireland

Duke of York
Islands

Feni Islands

Watom

Green Islands

Talasea

Sohano Island

New
Guinea

Arawe
Islands

New
Britain

Solomon
Islands

c.1000 BC - 1 AD

Gilbert
Islands

c.1 AD - 500 AD

Phoenix
Islands

Tuvalu

Yule

Kandrian

Normanby
Island

c.1500 - 1000 BC

Guadalcanal

Santa Cruz
Islands

Anuta

Bellona

Rennell

Samoa
Islands

Futuna

Uvéa

c.1500 - 1000 BC

Niuatoputapu

c.1500 - 1000 BC

Vanuatu

Fiji
Islands

c.200 BC

c.1500 - 1000 BC

Malo

c.1500 - 1000 BC

Tonga
Islands

c.200 BC

CORAL SEA

Eretoka

Efaté

Viti Levu

Lau
Group

Vava'u
Group

Society
Islands

Tahiti

Ha'apai
Group

c.200 BC

Cook
Islands

AUSTRALIA

Lapita

New
Caledonia

Ile des Pins

Tongatapu
Group

Tubuai Islands

Darling

c.1000 AD

Murray

Kermadec
Islands

c.1000 AD

SOUTH PACIFIC OCEAN

TASMAN SEA

Tasmania

NEW
ZEALAND

Chatham
Islands

after 1000 AD

140°   150°   160°   170°   180°   170°   160°   150°

land settled by 8000 BC

probable colonization route, with date

archaeological site
- Lapita
- other

obsidian stone reserve

principal area

wild breadfruit and taro

cultivated breadfruit

cultivated taro

Austronesian language group

cultural zone

Melanesia

Micronesia

Polynesia

scale 1: 40 000 000

0   1000 km

0   700 mi

Marquesas
Islands

Tuamotu
Archipelago

to Easter Island c.300 AD

c.1000 AD

Iles
Gambier

140°   130°

Settlers of the further Pacific

In broad terms, the foundations of Polynesian society developed from an Austronesian language-speaking base in the Fiji-Tonga-Samoa triangle. Polynesian seafarers then carried their ways of life into central eastern Polynesia. From here, later voyages went to the corners of the great Polynesian triangle. Arrows on the map should not be read as implying precise points of origin. A Polynesian outlier region is shown within Melanesia, reaching into Micronesia: this indicates the presence of Polynesian island populations, whose closest language affinities are with Samoa and islands to the west, within the region of island groups that are predominantly Melanesian (so, for instance, Anuta is a Polynesian island while the Santa Cruz group is Melanesian). The settlement of Micronesia is less clear, with the the possibility of influxes of Austronesian-speakers from a number of areas. The movement of peoples is reflected in the distribution of the plants such as taro and breadfruit they carried into the further Pacific. The map shows their core areas of cultivation.

Right One breadfruit tree bears about 150 starchy fruit a year and they are an important foodsource, especially in eastern Polynesia.

Fiji and the making of Polynesia

Fiji is usually seen as belonging to present-day Melanesia, but the cultural boundary between Melanesia and Polynesia has little relevance in prehistory. Fiji is clearly part of a region in which the ancestral Polynesian culture developed out of the culture of the Lapita-making Austronesians. To talk, therefore, of the later Fijians as a "mixture" of Melanesian and Polynesian is misleading since to do so suggests the blending of ready-made groups. Rather, the main characteristics of the Fijians and their society emerged in the same historical development that led to the Melanesian/Polynesian distinction. This development left Fijians with features that seem to belong to both sides of the divide.

The Lapita-makers were establishing themselves throughout the island triangle of Fiji, Samoa and Tonga by about 1000 BC. (The first Fijian sites may be some 300 years or more earlier, but their radiocarbon datings are dubious.) The story of eastern Lapita ware is one of progressive simplification and eventual disappearance. Over the period down to 500 BC, the decoration was gradually reduced almost to nothing, while the number of different pot forms also decreased. In Samoa, Lapita ware was succeeded by simple bowls of what has been called Polynesian Plain ware. By the early 1st century AD, pottery-making seems to have ceased altogether in Tonga and Samoa, the Lapita trail, that has been so important in tracing the eastward movement of early Pacific cultures, almost runs out at this point. Though they were almost certainly the descendants of the Lapita-makers, later Polynesians did not possess pottery-making skills themselves. Why the tradition died out remains unanswered, though the exhaustion of clay sources, changes in food preparation techniques or in the role played by pottery in trade and exchange have all been put forward as possible explanations.

The appearance of other, later pottery types in Fiji suggests that there were further waves of migration from Melanesia. Paddle-impressed wares, similar to those of New Caledonia, were produced in Fiji from about 700 BC. From 1100 AD another pottery tradition, possibly related to the Mangaasi ware of Vanuatu, appears. It is difficult to know how large the later groups of settlers were, or how much they contributed to the distinctive Fijian genetic and cultural mix. But the later Melanesian arrivals may have helped to consolidate distinctions already developing between the Fijian peoples and the Polynesians of neighboring island groups. Archaeological evidence shows that after 1100 increasing numbers of earthwork fortifications were built on Fijian islands such as Viti Levu, Vanua Levu, and Taveuni. It is possible that the later arrivals may have added to the rivalries and competition for resources between Fiji's expanding populations of agricultural peoples. Traditional history tells of considerable intergroup conflict extending down into the last century.

Scholars have abandoned the attempt to identify one specific area – be it Tonga, Samoa, the eastern islands of Fiji, or any other island in western Polynesia – as the single place where Polynesian culture began. It now appears much more likely that the origins of Polynesian culture lie within the region as a whole – a view supported not only by the spread of Lapita ware but also by recent linguistic study, which has moved away from the idea that the shared language of the early settlers simply split in two to create the ancestral Fijian and ancestral Polynesian languages. There appear to have been greater interconnections between Fiji and the western Polynesian island groups in this early period than was once believed and it is more probable that a chain of related dialects extended from Fiji into the islands, one of which became the basis for Proto-Polynesian.

It is now argued that a distinct archaic Polynesian society had emerged by about 500 BC. Archaeology and the reconstruction of Proto-Polynesian words have both been used to try to show what that society was like. These ancestral Polynesians lived by a combination of agriculture and food-gathering. They grew taro and yam, used tree products such as breadfruit, coconut and chestnuts, kept animals such as pigs, dogs and chickens, and harvested fish and shellfish from the sea. Proto-Polynesian words have been reconstructed for a range of fishing techniques, including netting, fish traps and night fishing with torches. These people were probably already producing a barkcloth from the beaten inner bark of paper mulberry trees, and had developed at least one long-term food storage technique, the use of pits to keep fermented breadfruit paste, that could be used in times of shortage. They lived in small villages of several households, mainly near coasts. Language reconstructions and comparison with later Polynesian societies suggest that there were landholding groups based on descent from a common ancestor and that these were headed by hereditary chiefs. While there is no clear archaeological evidence of differences in rank, it seems probable that the foundations of the later hierarchical societies of Polynesia were already in place.

In the course of the next 1,500 years the Polynesians expanded their settlement eastward into the more distant islands of the Pacific. There was also some movement back to the west, with Polynesian populations being established on a number of small islands within Melanesia, such as Tikopia and Bellona, and Micronesia (Nukuoro and Kapingamarangi). The major voyages, however, would carry the Polynesians across great expanses of the eastern Pacific in the greatest seaborne expansion the world had seen.

The Great Triangle

By 1000 AD the Polynesians had settled a vast triangular region in the central and eastern Pacific, with its three corners at Aotearoa (New Zealand), Hawaii and Easter Island. In the center of this triangle were the high islands of the southern Cook Islands, the Society Islands, Austral Islands and the Marquesas, and the many atolls of the Tuamotu Archipelago and the Gambier Islands. The conventional view is that there was a considerable delay between the development of the archaic Polynesian culture in the Fiji/Tonga/Samoa area and the Polynesian spread into the eastern Pacific. Those who support this line argue that the earliest firm evidence of settlement in the east, found in the rugged high islands of the Marquesas, dates from around 300 AD. However, some scholars now believe that the delay was not as long as once thought. There is some unclear radiocarbon dating evidence from the Marquesas that suggests that the Polynesians may have reached them before 200 BC; and the archaeological record of island groups such as the Cook and Society Islands (closer to Tonga and Samoa than the Marquesas) is not complete enough to be sure that even earlier sites might not exist there. In the case of the Society Islands – which include Tahiti – early coastal sites may have sunk below sea-level as tectonic processes caused the volcanic islands to subside. Whatever the date of the earliest settlement of eastern Polynesia, it seems that it was from the more central island groups, particularly the Marquesas and Society Islands, that the Polynesians spread into the corners of the Great Triangle. Hawaii was first settled, probably

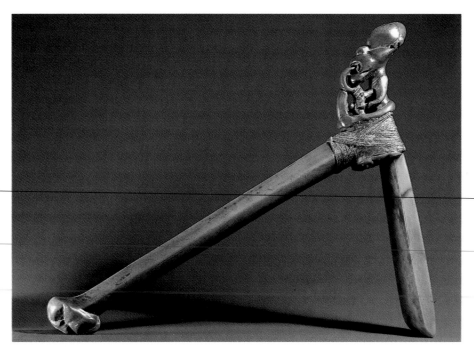

from the Marquesas, between 300 and 500 AD; Easter Island (known to the Polynesians as Rapa Nui) was also settled in the earlier part of that period.

The last frontiers of Polynesia lay in the islands to the south. Around 1000 AD people using the stone adzes and wearing the whale-tooth ornaments that were characteristic of central eastern Polynesia came to the rocky and relatively isolated Kermadec Islands. These settlements would eventually be abandoned. But about 1,000 kilometers to the southwest lay New Zealand. The ancestors of the Maori people established themselves there between 800 and 1000. They called it Aotearoa ("the long white cloud"), and one famous Maori legend of discovery tells of the coming of Kupe, a chief of Hawaiki (a name often applied to the legendary homelands of the Polynesians), who is said to have reached Aotearoa when he was out fishing and pursued an octopus that continually stole his bait. Kupe's is by no means the only discovery myth, however, and there are doubts about how widespread it was among the Maori.

Aotearoa constituted by far the greatest landmass to be colonized by the Polynesians – larger than the rest of Polynesia put together (over 250,000 square kilometers) – and there they encountered a world quite unlike that of the tropical islands in which their society had formed. Yet, despite many adaptations to their new setting with its different climate, animals and plants and its very varied topography, the Maori continued to draw on the traditions of their island Polynesian ancestors. The most extraordinary of the creatures they met were the large flightless birds they called *moa* – the name used in the tropical islands for chickens, which can be traced back to Austronesian roots. The *moa* inhabited the temperate forests that covered the North Island and the eastern side of the South Island. There were several different species; some were only about the size of a chicken, but the tallest was over 3.7 meters. These large flightless birds, which lacked any natural predators, proved an easy source of meat for the early settlers, and they were rapidly hunted to extinction.

Settlement spread quickly to both islands, confined mainly to coastal regions, particularly on the eastern, more sheltered, side; sea mammals – whales, seals and

Above Among the new materials discovered by the Polynesian settlers of Aotearoa was greenstone (nephrite). This form of jade was worked into personal ornaments, weapons and other objects of great beauty and value. Te Wahi Pounamu ("the place of greenstone") is one of the Maori names for the South Island, most of this precious resource coming from sites along its west coast. Illustrated here is a ceremonial adze with a finely-shaped greenstone blade. Such a *toki pou tangata* ("adze that establishes a man in authority") was a chiefly emblem of rank and a great heirloom.

Right According to one set of Maori legends about the discovery of Aotearoa, Kupe was instructed in a dream to sail his canoe southwest from Rarotonga in the Cook Islands. After a long voyage the first signs of the new land were seen. Kupe's wife called out "He ao!" – "A cloud!" The name Aotea ("white cloud") was given to Great Barrier Island at the northeastern end of the Hauraki Gulf, and the mainland became known as Aotearoa ("long white cloud").

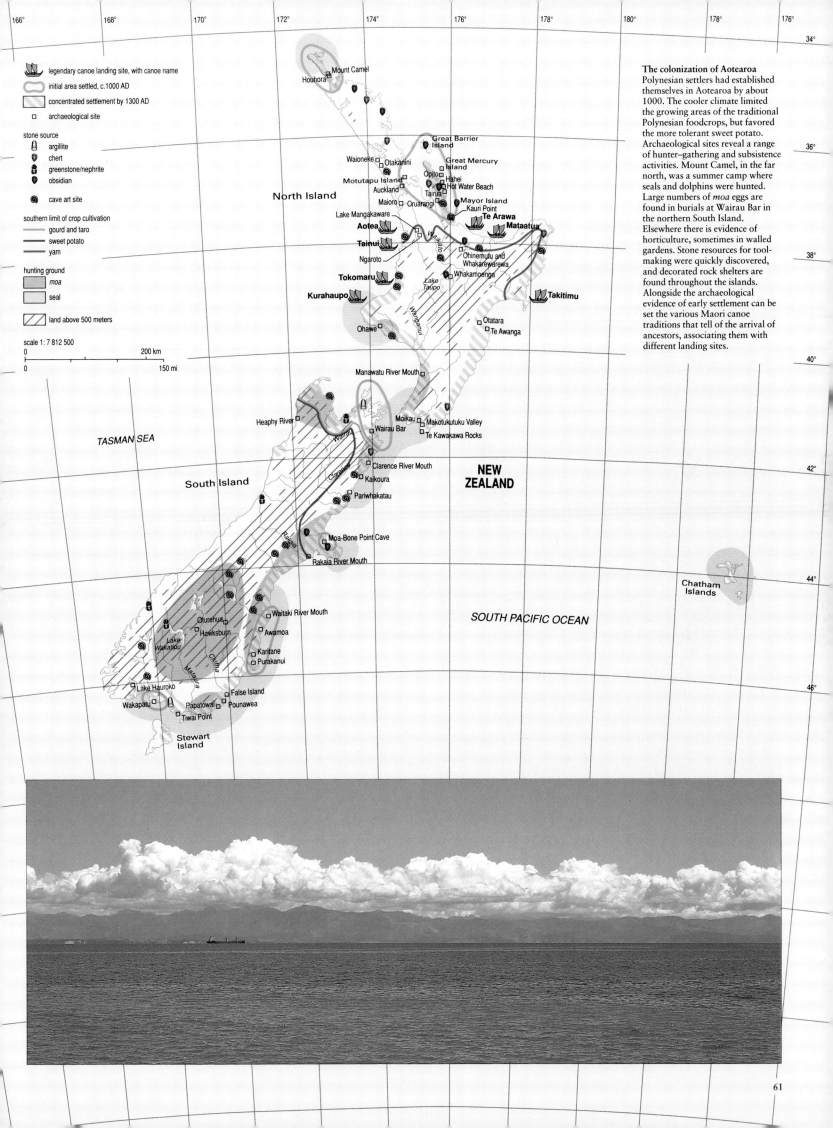

166° 168° 170° 172° 174° 176° 178° 180° 178° 176°

34°

legendary canoe landing site, with canoe name

initial area settled, c.1000 AD

concentrated settlement by 1300 AD

archaeological site

stone source

argillite

chert

greenstone/nephrite

obsidian

cave art site

southern limit of crop cultivation

gourd and taro

sweet potato

yam

hunting ground

moa

seal

land above 500 meters

scale 1: 7 812 500

0   200 km

0   150 mi

The colonization of Aotearoa
Polynesian settlers had established
themselves in Aotearoa by about
1000. The cooler climate limited
the growing areas of the traditional
Polynesian foodcrops, but favored
the more tolerant sweet potato.
Archaeological sites reveal a range
of hunter–gathering and subsistence
activities. Mount Camel, in the far
north, was a summer camp where
seals and dolphins were hunted.
Large numbers of *moa* eggs are
found in burials at Wairau Bar in
the northern South Island.
Elsewhere there is evidence of
horticulture, sometimes in walled
gardens. Stone resources for tool-
making were quickly discovered,
and decorated rock shelters are
found throughout the islands.
Alongside the archaeological
evidence of early settlement can be
set the various Maori canoe
traditions that tell of the arrival of
ancestors, associating them with
different landing sites.

36°

Mount Camel
Houhora

Great Barrier
Island
Waioneke   Otakanini   Great Mercury
Island
Motutapu Island   Opito   Hahei
Auckland   Tairua   Hot Water Beach
North Island   Maioro   Oruarangi   Mayor Island
Kauri Point
Lake Mangakaware   **Te Arawa**
Aotea   **Mataatua**

Tainui   Ohinemutu and
Whakarewarewa
Ngaroto   Whakamoenga

Tokomaru   Lake
Taupo

Kurahaupo   **Takitimu**

Ohawe   Otatara
Te Awanga

38°

Manawatu River Mouth

40°

TASMAN SEA   Heaphy River   Moikau   Makotukutuku Valley
Wairau Bar   Te Kawakawa Rocks

Clarence River Mouth

**NEW
ZEALAND**   42°

South Island   Kaikoura

Pariwhakatau

Moa-Bone Point Cave

Rakaia River Mouth   SOUTH PACIFIC OCEAN

Chatham
Islands   44°

Lake
Wakatipu   Oturehua   Waitaki River Mouth
Hawksburn
Awamoa
Karitane
Purakanui

Lake Hauroko   46°
False Island
Wakapatu   Papatowai   Pounawea
Tiwai Point
Stewart
Island

dolphins – seabirds and shellfish of all kinds were eaten in quantity. The cool climate restricted crop cultivation to the North Island and to the north of the South Island. The first settlers brought yams, taros and other tropical plants with them, but it was the sweet potato, or *kumara*, introduced into eastern Polynesia from South America, that proved the most successful food crop. The roots of the native fern (*Pteridium esculentum*) and of the New Zealand cabbage tree (*Cordyline australis*) were also eaten. Fiber from the native flax (*Phormium tenax*), belonging to the Agave family, was used to make clothing in place of the bark-cloth garments that were commonly worn elsewhere in Polynesia. Sources of stone were also exploited, par-

ticularly greenstone, found at several sites in the South Island, which was carved into ornaments and other fine objects such as ceremonial adzes.

The cultivation of the sweet potato – a native of the Andes – by the eastern Polynesians and the Maori raises the question of whether migration into Polynesia may have come from the Americas. The most powerful advocate of this theory was Thor Heyerdahl, the Norwegian ethnologist and explorer who caught the public imagination in the late 1940s by sailing his raft *Kon-Tiki* from Peru to an atoll of the Tuamotu Islands. In the decades since this impressive exploit, the overwhelming burden of evidence – linguistic links, the Lapita trail, genetic relationships – seems to

Above Hauraki Gulf in the northeast of the North Island is strongly connected in the oral tradition with the arrival of canoes from the north. Samuel Marsden, one of the earliest missionaries to visit New Zealand, was told by a Maori priest in 1819 that the first person to come to Aotearoa was the demigod hero Maui, guided to Hauraki by the god Tawhaki. Accounts of the landing places of the great canoes associated with the origins of the different Maori tribes vary, but the promontory of Whangaparaoa in the northwest of Hauraki Gulf is a legendary landfall of the Tainui, Arawa and Maataatua canoes.

confirm the western origins of the Polynesian peoples. But if the idea that the Polynesians originated in America is no longer tenable, this does not mean that there were no contacts at all. The presence of the sweet potato can only be explained by some limited contact early in the prehistory of eastern Polynesia. Whether this was provided by the drift voyage of a South American raft or by the exploratory voyaging of a Polynesian canoe it is impossible to say. But recent studies of Pacific voyaging have given greater insight into the capabilities of the early Polynesian navigators.

Pacific voyagers

The voyaging craft of the Pacific were canoes. Often these were craft of considerable size and sophisticated design. In historical times Micronesians favored outrigger canoes with built-up traveling platforms and sails that could be swung from one end of the boat to the other, allowing it to tack about as bow became stern. On some islands the hull was made deliberately asymmetrical to balance out the drag of the outrigger. The larger canoes of Fiji and western Polynesia had twin hulls, though in Fiji the hulls of the great *drua*, perhaps 24 meters long, were of unequal size, a feature also found in outrigger canoes from Tonga and Samoa. The eastern Polynesians had sailing canoes with equal-sized hulls. It seems likely that the canoes observed by the earliest European visitors to this part of the Pacific and illustrated in 18th-century watercolors resembled those used in its settlement. Wooden planking and a steering paddle found on the island of Huahine in the Society Islands are thought to have been part of a 24-meter-long double-canoe; they have been given a Carbon 14 date of between 850 and 1200. Such canoes had the capacity to hold substantial stores, including the livestock and food plants needed for colonization, as well as two dozen or more settlers. They would have been able to cover the vast distances necessary to reach the furthest corners of the Great Triangle.

Some Pacific scholars long argued that the scattered islands of Polynesia were settled as a result of accidental drift voyaging; once an island was reached, there could be no hope of return to the islands of origin. Others held that the navigational skills and canoes of the Polynesians were sufficient to have allowed them to make two-way exploratory journeys, followed by voyages of settlement. Recent studies support the second view. Of course, that does not rule out the possibility that some settlements came about through accidental voyages; return voyaging from the extremes of Polynesia, such as Aotearoa, to the islands at its center would have presented considerable difficulty. Yet computer simulations of canoe journeys using data on winds and currents, different seasonal starts and other information strongly suggest that the ancestors of the Polynesians would have been unlikely to have reached the Fiji/Tonga/Samoa area, let alone the far corners of the Polynesian triangle, without deliberately navigating a course.

We cannot tell exactly what navigational and sailing techniques these early settlers had. However, a number of studies into the skills practiced in the islands today – particularly those conducted by David Lewis in Micronesia and the Solomon Islands – have revealed a wide range and sophistication of seafaring knowledge. These island navigators align features on the shore to give the initial direction. Bearings are then taken from the rising point and trajectory of a large

number of familiar stars – steering by "star paths" enables the skilled navigator to make allowances for the effects of drift by winds and currents. Some navigators have complex ways of visualizing the spatial relationships between the canoe, the point of destination, known (and even imagined) locations, and the rising and setting points of particular stars. A knowledge and understanding of the pattern of ocean swells created by distant winds enables adjustments of direction to be made. The navigator will study all manner of phenomena – the path of bird flights, the movement of cloud formations and the reflections of lagoons on to cloud bases, the direction taken by driftwood and rafts of seaweed. He will be able to identify the swells deflected off different islands. All these things will help him "home in" on his targeted landfall.

A number of experiments have been made applying the islanders' traditional navigational techniques to long-distance voyaging. The most notable of these took place in 1976 when *Hokule'a*, a reconstruction of a Polynesian double-hulled canoe, successfully covered more than 2,000 nautical miles in a voyage from Maui in the Hawaiian Islands to Tahiti, sailing without instruments but using the skills of a Micronesian navigator. *Hokule'a* later sailed from central Polynesia to New Zealand. It would be wrong to assume that all the sailing and navigational skills possessed by today's Pacific islanders were present from the earliest period of expansion into the eastern Pacific, but it does seem reasonable to assume that such knowledge was steadily developed during the centuries-long process of discovery and settlement.

One question about the Polynesian exploration and settlement of the Pacific that can probably never be fully answered fully is "why?". What led the colonizers of the eastern Pacific to take the risks they did? Of course, we can guess at a number of particular reasons. Overpopulation on some islands, environmental problems such as recurring drought on others, may have reduced the ability of the land to sustain the whole community, bringing many to a point of starvation. In certain cases inter-group conflicts and rivalry over status may have encouraged migration. But these are only partial answers. There seems a wider, more general possibility: from the time of the first expansion of the Austronesian-speaking peoples into the Pacific, the islanders appear to have developed an intimate relationship with the sea. It may be, then, that the urge to voyage and explore became an integral part of their cultural tradition.

The "small islands" of the west

North of the Melanesian islands and west of Polynesia lie the chains of small islands that are conveniently referred to as Micronesia. Archaeological knowledge of much of this region is even younger and more incomplete than elsewhere in the Pacific, and there are still many gaps to be filled in its prehistory. In appearance most Micronesians are similar to the Mongoloid Polynesian peoples, and they speak Austronesian languages. Before the discovery of the spread of Lapita culture through Melanesia into Polynesia, it was frequently argued that the Polynesians' ancestors must have followed an eastward migration through the Micronesian islands.

Current evidence suggests that different groups of settlers entered Micronesia from both west and east. The languages of Palau and the Marianas have affinities with the western Austronesian languages of

Overleaf This reconstruction of a Polynesian double-hulled sailing canoe is of modest size compared to some of the canoes seen by early European visitors, said to be up to 30 meters long. The available evidence suggests that most voyaging canoes were between 15 and 22 meters long – the best known modern reconstruction, the two-sailed Hawaiian canoe *Hokule'a*, falls within this range and has shown itself to be capable of a 3,000 kilometer voyage. Such canoes, guided by their sails and a rear-mounted steering oar, could probably average between 100 and 150 nautical miles over 24 hours.

Left The *latte* pillars of the Marianas were probably still supporting important houses and canoe sheds when the Spanish took possession of the islands in 1565, but by the time the English navigator George Anson reached Tinian in 1742 they had fallen into disuse, as this engraving shows.

Left Two rows of *latte* stones have been reerected at Agana, the capital of Guam. Depending on the area, either coral limestone or volcanic rock were used in *latte* construction.

Below Some Marianas Red pottery is decorated with impressed lines and circles filled with white lime. Known from archaeological sites in the southern Marianas, this type is central to an unresolved debate that seeks to link Marianas Red to the pottery traditions of the Philippines.

Indonesia and the Philippines, while the languages of most of the other Micronesian islands are more closely related to those of eastern Melanesia (the Solomon Islands and Vanuatu). The earliest archaeological material yet found in Micronesia, dating back more than 3,000 years, comes from the high islands of the west, Saipan and Guam in the Marianas. Pottery was produced on these islands, the earliest being a mainly plain red-slipped ware known as Marianas Red. The closest relations of the rarer decorated Marianas Red seem to be in the ancient pottery traditions of the Philippines, and it therefore appears quite likely that settlement of the Marianas came from that area, though some archaeologists favor a less specific origin in Southeast Asia.

There appears to have been a good deal of continuity in the early culture of the Marianas. But around 1,100 years ago it entered into what has been called the Latte Phase. The *latte*, standing like two rows of gigantic stone toadstools with inverted caps, some over 5 meters high, were the supports for house floors, the larger ones possibly for communal men's houses. They are a remarkable use of stone in building that is unlike anything else in the Pacific. Rather than suggesting the arrival of a new group of settlers, however, the *latte* may just mark a shift from the use of wood to the use of stone, a local cultural development. They were probably in use until the disruption of the local population patterns by the Spanish in the 17th century. *Latte* sites have produced fishing gear, hooks and net weights, together with pounders similar to those used in many parts of the Pacific for mashing taro.

The cultures of the other main island groups of western Melanesia, Palau and Yap (the most westerly of the Caroline Islands) appear to have developed relatively independently of each other over a period of about 2,000 years from c.500 BC, each having their own set of possible external cultural and genetic inputs. In the case of Palau, early influences from both Indonesia and the Philippines seem probable. On Palau, large hill forts came into existence, with terraces that were probably used for taro cultivation as

Below Part of the massive outer wall, built of basalt blocks, of the burial enclosure of Nan Douwas, part of the settlement and ceremonial center of Nan Madol in eastern Pohnpei. Built on about 100 artificial islets within a shallow lagoon, Nan Madol has been called "the Venice of the Pacific". According to oral history, it was from here that the Saudeleur dynasty of chiefs, the Lords of Teleur, ruled Pohnpei for several hundred years. The site covers an area of about 0.65 square kilometers. Tradition says that the chiefly and administrative center, where the Lords of Teleur are said to have lived on the L-shaped islet of Pankatira, was in the south; the priestly and burial area in the north. Though some accounts suggest that Nan Madol may have been in use as late as the 18th century, there are arguments to support the view that it was abandoned prior to European contact.

well as defense. There were stone pavements, and platforms for houses. The later inhabitants of Yap are known to have sailed to Palau to obtain a particular kind of rock used in the production of the large stone disk valuables that are sometimes called the stone money of Yap. But there is little clear evidence as yet of any early links between the island groups.

In eastern Micronesia, the earliest known settlement sites, in the Marshall Islands, date from around 50 BC, though some radiocarbon dates a thousand years earlier have been recorded in Bikini Atoll. However, there are strong doubts about their validity – Bikini's recent history as an atomic test site does not invalidate the Carbon 14 data, but makes it much harder to assess. Linguistic analysis points toward eastern Melanesian origins for the earliest eastern Micronesian peoples, but the archaeological evidence remains inconclusive. Pottery found on the high island of Pohnpei in the Carolines could have developed from late Lapita ware, but no actual Lapita decoration has ever been found in Micronesia. Nevertheless, it seems likely that the initial settlers were Lapita people or similar Austronesians.

It is the high islands of the Caroline chain that offer the most spectacular evidence of later cultural development. Large structures of stone on Pohnpei and

Kosrae are, it seems, the products of quite densely settled and stratified societies. It has been suggested that the platforms and tombs lying within walled burial enclosures that began to be constructed on Pohnpei from the 9th century were linked to status. They became more elaborate in form, culminating in Micronesia's most famous archaeological site – the ruins of Nan Madol, seemingly no longer in use by the time Europeans first set foot here in the 16th century. In the past, these impressive buildings were explained as being the work of a new wave of settlers, but the current view is that Nan Madol, and similar smaller stone structures on Kosrae, were built by the established island peoples.

The picture we have of the early Micronesian past is highly fragmentary. It may change with the emergence of new discoveries. For example, even less is known about the archaeology of the low-lying atolls than of the high islands, and much investigation remains to be done here. But what has been established is consistent with the picture that has been pieced together elsewhere in the Pacific, a story of Austronesian peoples using their seafaring abilities to settle the many scattered islands of the region, adapting to local conditions, and developing distinctive local cultures over time.

CHANGING WORLDS OF THE ISLANDS

By the time that the first Europeans arrived in the Pacific, a vast range of societies had become established throughout the islands. To build up a picture of what their different social worlds were like, we are able to draw on oral traditions and the journals of the early European explorers as well as modern Pacific writers. This does not mean, however, that the island societies were unchanging, though continuity in custom and tradition was and is an important element in their social structures. Each of the islands has its own particular history: it is only recently, however, that these histories have been written down. What we are able to glimpse from the evidence available to us is a series of moments in a long process of change.

It will be clear from the story of settlement in the previous chapter that the cultural history and boundaries of the Pacific are not as clear-cut as the grouping of its islands into the subdivisions of Melanesia, Polynesia and Micronesia suggests. The terms are simplifications introduced by European commentators in the 19th century. Yet, in the absence of anything better, they still have currency, even in the political relations of the modern Pacific nations. They are used here simply as convenient starting points from which to trace some cultural connections and establish the different lines along which Pacific societies have developed.

Of the three, Polynesia – though much the largest in geographical area – is linguistically and culturally the most homogeneous. The peoples of its different island groups, including the Maori of Aotearoa, speak closely related languages, with the languages of eastern Polynesia forming a subgroup of their own. Melanesia, by contrast, has a huge number of languages (more than 1,000 according to some assessments) and distinct cultural groups. While its societies have some broad outlines in common, the region is far more diverse than Polynesia. Micronesia, too, includes a number of distinct cultures, and its Austronesian languages fall into a number of different subgroups. Three main cultural areas can be identified: western Micronesia, which includes the Chamorros of the Mariana Islands, the Yapese and the Palauans; central Micronesia, consisting of the scattered atolls and reefs of the Caroline Islands, with the Polynesian outlier islands of Nukuoro and Kapingamarangi in the south and the distinct cultures of Pohnpei and Kosrae at its eastern extreme; and eastern Micronesia, peopled by the Marshallese, the Nauruans and the Gilbertese (the people of the main island chain of Kiribati). Whatever their social and cultural distinctions, however, the traditional material bases for living in the Pacific's three major regions are very similar; the differences between them can be seen as variations within a broadly shared set of resources.

Living from the land and sea

From very early times the island economies were based on subsistence farming and marine resources, supplemented in some areas by hunting. In many islands, a form of shifting agriculture was practiced. A plot was

Left For the people of the Trobriand Islands of New Guinea, yams are not just a foodstuff but are a form of wealth, the possession of which represents status and power. Much of the crop is grown for presentation or ceremonial exchange. Women are the gardeners, and the yams from a household garden are seen as belonging to particular women. At harvest time, the yams are heaped in conical piles in front of the yam house of the owner's husband, and a few days later they are loaded into the yam house itself, as seen here. For a man, a full yam house is like a healthy bank account which, as long as the yams are not eaten and do not rot, can be drawn on to purchase other goods and services.

cleared of trees and vegetation, and crops were grown for two or three years before the plot was allowed to revert to scrub again for 15 to 20 years. Plows were unknown, and the tubers or sprouts of plants were set in individual holes prepared with digging sticks. In Aotearoa there is evidence of stone-walled field systems, and a long-term cycle of cropping and fallow was probably followed to maintain soil fertility.

Root crops – taro, yams and sweet potato – were chiefly cultivated; the only evidence of a cereal-growing tradition in the Pacific islands is found on the more fertile of the Mariana Islands, at the Asian edge of Micronesia, where the Chamorro people cultivated some rice. Taro was grown throughout the tropical Pacific. As well as the plant's starchy root, the green tops of some species of taro were eaten. It is a plant that requires moist conditions, and it was most productively cultivated in swamps or artificially created pond-fields. Some of the mountainous islands saw the development of elaborate terracing and pond-field systems, irrigated by a controlled water supply – Captain Cook observed such a system in New Caledonia, and they were also used in the Cook Islands and Hawaii. These systems grew larger with expanding populations, and their creation and maintenance required much labor and considerable organization beyond the level of the household or extended family. Taro horticulture was generally simpler and smaller in scale on the coral atolls of Micronesia, where a related species, the "atoll taro" (*Cyrtosperma chamissonis*), was able to tolerate the quick-draining, sandy soils: pits were sometimes dug to enable the roots to tap below the water table.

Right The great trilithon on the Tongan island of Tongatapu known as the Ha'amonga 'a Maui (the Burden of Maui) is the most impressive of Polynesian stone monuments and stands over 5 meters tall. A myth relates that the demigod hero Maui brought its three massive stones from the Wallis Islands, but it seems to have been built from local coral limestone and beachrock. Even so, the construction must have been an enormous task. Possibly a gateway, it forms part of a group of monuments that may represent a former chiefly capital at Heketa in the northeast of the island. Another local tradition suggests that the Ha'amonga was built around 1200 on the order of the high chief Tu'itatui, the eleventh holder of the title Tu'i Tonga, to symbolize the bond of brotherhood between his two sons.

The cultivation of yams, which prefer dry, well-drained conditions, was most important in parts of Melanesia and western Polynesia. In Tonga they were once the main item given in tribute to the sacred paramount chief, the Tu'i Tonga, in the annual first-fruits ceremony. In the Trobriand Islands of Papua New Guinea, possession of a full yam house is still an important symbol of wealth. As already noted, the sweet potato, which is tolerant of cool conditions, was the major crop of the Polynesian Maori in Aotearoa, where the tubers were stored over winter in roofed storage pits. It is well-suited to the highlands of New Guinea, and has become the main crop there since its introduction less than 400 years ago after Spanish and Portuguese colonizers had brought it to island Southeast Asia. Its cultivation may have made possible an expansion of population in parts of the highlands.

Other foodplants such as coconuts, breadfruit and bananas were grown in plantations often surrounding garden plots and fields. The coconut palm was the most important tree crop of the tropical lowlands. Its uses were numerous: the soft flesh and liquid of its inner kernel provided food and drink, the husk of the nut was a source of strong fibers, the shell could serve as a drinking vessel, and the leaf fronds were used for roofing or woven to provide baskets. The seedless fruit of the breadfruit tree was of major importance in parts of Micronesia and eastern Polynesia, particularly the Society Islands and the Marquesas, where it was fermented in pits and stored for future use. On many atolls, however, the pandanus – which was more tolerant of salt conditions – was more widely grown, while the sago palm was better suited to the swampy lowlands of New Guinea. The Tahitian chestnut,

Left Barkcloth, known to the Polynesians as *tapa*, is made from strips of inner bark, most commonly that of the paper mulberry (*Broussonetia papyrifera*). The strips are beaten out on wooden anvils with wooden mallets to form thin, papery sheets that can then be layered into thicker cloth. *Tapa* had many functions, both practical and symbolic. It was the stuff of everyday clothing, an important item in ritual presentation, and was used to wrap the sacred images of the gods. Patterning was applied in different ways across the island groups. The pattern on the *tapa* from Western Samoa shown here (known locally as *siapo*) was probably made by rubbing pigment onto cloth that had been laid over a wooden board onto which the design had been carved.

Right The seed or nut of the areca palm, taken with lime and the leaves of the betel plant (and therefore known rather misleadingly as the "betel-nut"), is chewed in many parts of Southeast Asia and the western Pacific. It is a mild stimulant that produces feelings of wellbeing and reduces hunger. Its effect probably come from the release of alkaloids that act on the body like nicotine. Chewing betel-nut stains the saliva red, and frequent use colors the teeth and lips, as seen in this man from the Sepik region of New Guinea.

Far right Kava is known as *yaqona* in Fiji where it has been used in religion ritual from very early times, but the more social form of the *kava* ceremony may have developed from the Tongan influences felt in Fiji in the 18th century. Here, *yaqona* is being mixed in a *tanoa*, the Tongan and Samoan form of *kava* bowl that is now also typical of Fiji. Formal *yaqona* drinking involves an elaborate etiquette of status and respect that is reflected in the position of the drinkers in relation to the bowl, in the order of drinking from the coconut-shell cup, and in specific actions such as clapping when the emptied cup is returned. Even on less formal occasions, some of the etiquette of ceremonial *yaqona* drinking remains.

Far left In the Sepik region of New Guinea a log is hollowed and shaped into a dugout canoe. Dugouts have been the basic river and coastal craft of many of the Pacific islands throughout their history. Where the available timber allowed, large dugout hulls were even used for long-distance voyaging canoes. In the past axes or adzes of stone would have been used to shape the canoes, in place of the metal tool seen here.

Left Decorative combs from the Solomon Islands are made from the mid-ribs of palm leaves, fastened together and ornamented with finely interwoven leaf-strips. On a miniature scale, they suggest the refinement of the weaver's art that can be found in many of the Pacific islands and are just one of the many uses to which the palm lends itself.

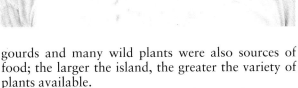

gourds and many wild plants were also sources of food; the larger the island, the greater the variety of plants available.

As the coconut palm suggests, plant products were put to all kinds of uses, and were a vital part of the economy and culture of the Pacific. Buildings varied in form, but were usually of wood, which was sometimes highly carved. Some canoes were made of dug-out logs, the long-distance outrigger canoes of planks lashed together with fibers. The timber shortage on some islands could lead to remarkable forms of construction, use being made of any piece of wood that was available; the assorted pieces were lashed together and sealed with breadfruit sap and coconut fiber to produce seaworthy and efficient craft. Sails were made of barkcloth, produced by pounding together the fibers of the inner bark of trees such as the paper mulberry and breadfruit tree. In Polynesia and Melanesia, barkcloth, sometimes highly decorated, was used for poncho-like garments, wraps and waistcloths; skirts were formed from strips of shredded leaf or inner bark, or fiber string. Pandanus and other leaves were woven into fine matting, while loomed wraps of hibiscus and banana fiber were produced in the Caroline Islands. The Maori made cloaks and skirts from the local flax plant.

Alcohol and tobacco were unknown to the Pacific islanders before the arrival of the Europeans (a possible exception is the coconut toddy made in parts of Micronesia, though its use may have arisen through early Spanish contact). However, two plant products – betel and *kava* – were valued for their stimulant effects: generally, where betel was used, *kava* was not. Betel – the nut of the areca palm, mixed with powdered lime and wrapped in the leaves of an astringent species of pepper – was chewed in a number of areas of Melanesia and in the western islands of Micronesia: its use is widespread in Southeast Asia and probably

spread from there. Items of betel-chewing equipment, particularly the carved spatulas used to add the lime, are among New Guinea's finest small artworks. *Kava*, a drink that in sufficient quantity produces mild euphoria and eventual drowsiness, was prepared by mixing the chewed or pounded roots of another species of pepper with water. *Kava* is a Polynesian word, and it was drunk throughout Polynesia except for Easter Island and Aotearoa. The ceremonial that surrounded the drinking of *kava* – in which the order of drinking reflected social status – was most fully developed in Fiji (where it is called *yaqona*) and the islands of western Polynesia. It was also drunk on Pohnpei and Kosrae in the Caroline Islands of Micronesia, where it was known as *sakau*, and was reasonably widespread in Melanesia.

It has already been noted that pigs, dogs and chicken were carried by the early migrants throughout the Pacific. Domesticated animals were seldom served as everyday food, but were reserved for feasting. This included dogs – the English botanist Sir Joseph Banks, visiting Tahiti with Captain Cook in 1769, reported that a dog prepared and cooked by the islanders made an excellent dish. A species of Polynesian rat, *Rattus exulans*, was also eaten on some of the islands, but is more likely to have arrived there as a stowaway on voyaging canoes than to have been deliberately introduced. From the evidence of archaeology, it seems that not all these animals were introduced to every one of the islands. No pig or chicken bones have been found in New Zealand, though dogs and rats were eaten, while in the Marquesas Islands the dogs brought by the early settlers later died out. Easter Island had only chickens, and many of the smaller islands supported no domesticated animals at all. In the highlands of New Guinea, the building up of large pig herds was a major form of wealth accumulation, the possession of which demonstrated individual and group status.

To all the coastal-dwelling peoples of the Pacific, the sea was naturally an important provider of protein and other resources. Fishing canoes allowed the islanders to go beyond the reefs in search of oceanic fish, which were caught with the use of sophisticated hooks and lures. The reefs themselves were generally rich in marine life; shellfish, sea urchins, sea cucumbers, sea slugs and seaweed all featured in the islanders' diet. Seabirds and turtles were also eaten. Shells, including turtle shell, were worked into articles of personal ornamentation, and "shell money" – often consisting of strings of small shell disks – was found in parts of Melanesia and Micronesia. Shells might also be used as scrapers or knives. On atoll islands, where the usual tool-making materials were hard to find, large shells ground into adzes and other tools took the place of the polished stone tools that were used elsewhere in the Pacific.

The subsistence tasks of food production and preparation were most commonly organized within the household or extended family. In some of the highly ranked societies, chiefs and nobles took no part in these activities but were provided with food by others. Elsewhere, there was no great difference between the work performed by the leaders and the other members of the community. What singled the leaders out was their ability to accumulate food surpluses, either through the work of their family and supporters or by way of offerings or tribute. The division of labor between women and men also varied, but it was not uncommon for men to be responsible for initial land clearance, while the continuous agricultural work fell to women. Fishing in the open sea was generally seen as a male activity, while women gathered shellfish and other marine life from the reefs and shoreline.

The Pacific peoples adapted successfully to their island habitats. However, it would be a mistake to infer from this that they lived in perfect harmony with the natural world. In the first place, the introduction of alien animal species had major environmental impact – rats and dogs preyed on ground-dwelling birds that had no natural animal predators. Humans also caused devastation – several indigenous bird species were brought to extinction in the hunt for food and feathers, and forests were cleared for farming and to provide fuel and building materials. Recent studies show that Easter Island had a rich vegetation before the arrival of the Polynesians, and it was their destruction of the natural tree cover that ultimately caused the environmental degradation that contributed to a population crash in the 18th century. Throughout the Pacific, the availability and distribution of natural resources influenced the way that human societies developed. The narrow resources of the smaller islands limited population size, restricting the growth of complex social organization: this is particularly true of the scattered atoll islands of Micronesia and Polynesia. On the larger islands, and in some of the larger island groups, the uneven distribution of resources encouraged the development of systems of exchange between different groups and became a focus for competition, and even warfare.

Descent and rank in Polynesia

Throughout the Pacific islands, kinship was fundamental to social organization. In Polynesia, island societies were divided into named groups, loosely described as clans or tribes, that claimed descent from common ancestors. Elders and acknowledged experts

Left Shell money is an important traditional form of wealth in Malaita, one of the Solomon Islands. Its value reflects the great amount of work involved in producing the individual beads that form the long strings, and it has remained an important part of the exchange ceremonies that help to uphold the relations between individuals and between groups. Here, shell money is displayed at a wedding, a presentation of bridewealth from the husband to the wife's family.

in tradition had an extensive knowledge of genealogy running back over dozens of generations, sometimes to the divine ancestors of mythical times. Though there was a bias toward patrilineal descent, this was not the exclusive basis for group membership: links through female lines could be (and commonly were) used to establish rights within a particular clan. Lands were divided between different segments of the clan and an individual could choose which descent group to belong to according to where he wanted to live. Rights in the group's land were maintained by living and working on them. This degree of choice and flexibility proved of value when some groups, having grown in numbers, were experiencing land shortage and pressure on resources, while others were not. On the high islands, the land was divided into wedge-like sections running from the center of the island down to the fringing reef, thereby offering the various clan-segments a range of resource zones to exploit. On the atolls, descent groups often controlled different islets.

Considerations of status might also influence an individual's choice of group affiliation – opting for matrilineal rather than patrilineal links could bring closer ties to those of higher rank. Social rank derived from closeness to the common ancestor, which was traced through seniority of birth. So in principle the highest rank, and title of chief, within a clan belonged to the eldest son of the senior male line, the line of eldest sons. Descendants of younger sons and daughters were of lower standing. As populations expanded, clans divided into local subgroups, each having its senior male head. These clan-segments were themselves ranked in relation to each other. The head of the highest group would be overall or paramount chief, the focus of ritual and political power.

The Fiji-Tonga-Samoa triangle
It is from the Lapita potters of the Fiji-Tonga-Samoa triangle that ancestral Polynesian society emerged. The potting tradition died out in Tonga and Samoa as they began to develop their own distinct Polynesian cultures. These are reflected in their later archaeological sites, which include the enigmatic star-shaped mounds of Samoa (possibly the platforms for godhouses) and the stone-clad, terraced chiefly tombs at Lapaha in Tonga. In Fiji, new pottery traditions emerged as it diverged from its Polynesian neighbors, their styles and techniques suggesting new influxes of people from Melanesia. But while each group maintained a cultural distinctiveness, there is also evidence of extensive later links between them. There seem to have been a number of Tongan incursions into Fiji. Tongan influence was particularly strongly felt in Fiji's Lau Islands. These include Karaba and Fulaga, noted in the 18th century for the wood-working skills of Tongan and Samoan craftsmen based there. The "direction of trade" arrows on the map show the broad pattern of the exchange of prestige goods, viewed from the perspective of Tonga. The ties between the groups also included those of chiefly marriage.

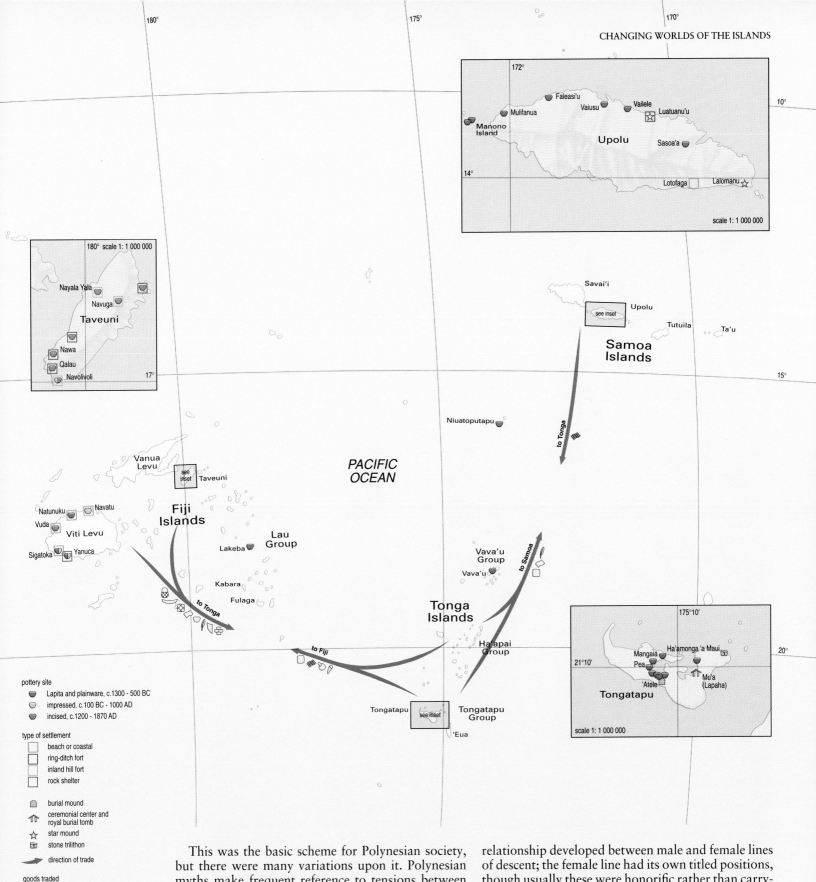

pottery site
- Lapita and plainware, c.1300 - 500 BC
- impressed, c.100 BC - 1000 AD
- incised, c.1200 - 1870 AD

type of settlement
- beach or coastal
- ring-ditch fort
- inland hill fort
- rock shelter

- burial mound
- ceremonial center and royal burial tomb
- star mound
- stone trilithon
- direction of trade

goods traded
- bark cloth
- baskets
- canoes
- decorated bark cloth
- fine mats (Samoan)
- ornaments
- other mats
- pottery
- red feathers
- sails
- sandalwood
- whales teeth

scale 1: 7 500 000
0   200 km
0   150 mi

This was the basic scheme for Polynesian society, but there were many variations upon it. Polynesian myths make frequent reference to tensions between elder and younger brothers. Many historical traditions tell of lower-ranked individuals and groups attempting to claim power and status. In the history of Hawaii for instance, the high chieftainship was repeatedly seized by members of junior lines. Though the formal political titles were usually held by men, women were often involved in important political processes such as creating and holding together group alliances, and in some instances they held high office.

In some Polynesian social systems, ritual authority and actual political power could be separated. In western Polynesia, for example, a complementary relationship developed between male and female lines of descent; the female line had its own titled positions, though usually these were honorific rather than carrying actual power. In Tonga, sisters outranked brothers in terms of formal honor and ritual authority. A father's sister was owed great respect, while sisters' children had a specific relationship of ritual power over their mother's brothers, including the right to take some of their possessions. This relation between gender and rank had its effects at the height of Tongan politics, since the paramount Tongan chief, the Tu'i Tonga, was formally outranked by his sister, and by her sons. To circumvent the threat this posed to the succession, the Tu'i Tonga's sister was by custom married to an outsider, usually a Fijian chief.

The nature of the Tu'i Tonga's power apparently changed over time. Oral traditions suggest that the earliest holders of the title combined sacred and secular authority. The great coral trilithon or archway known as Ha'amonga 'a Maui, the purpose of which is uncertain, and the 13th-century ceremonial center at Lapaha, which contains the large burial mounds of the high chiefs, give some indication of the resources at the disposal of these early leaders. But the chiefdom later became enthralled in power struggles. Sometime around the 15th century, tradition relates, the 23rd Tu'i Tonga was assassinated. His sons are said to have pursued the assassins, conquering other islands in the Tongan group. After this a new title was created, Tu'i Ha'atakalaua. Its holder was given control of day-to-day government while the Tu'i Tonga continued to fulfill his ritual functions as sacred head, receiving tribute and interceding with the gods for the fertility and wellbeing of the chiefdom. Some generations later a third title came into being, that of Tu'i Kanokupolu, its holder taking over as *hau*, or temporal ruler. The chiefly Ha'atakalaua line continued, but without the same civil powers. The last Tu'i Ha'atakalaua died in battle in 1799. The present king of Tonga is descended from the Kanokupolu and Ha'atakalaua lines.

Warfare appears to have been an integral part of Polynesian culture from earliest times: *toa* ("warrior") is a reconstructed Proto-Polynesian word, and oral traditions indicate that intergroup rivalry for lands and status was fierce. European sources from the 18th century also indicate that fighting was common in many of the island groups. In 1774 Cook observed a war fleet assemble on Tahiti to attack the neighboring island of Moorea. In some of the Polynesian islands the role of the warrior chief became more strongly emphasized than in others. On Mangaia in the Cook Islands, for example, there were two *ariki*, chiefs with ritual functions, but political control, particularly over the distribution of lands, lay with the leader who held *mangaia* (a word implying temporal power) by virtue of the military and political dominance wielded by the clan, or alliance of clans, he headed. Mangaian traditional history lists many battles in the course of which the *mangaia* passed from one group to another. Similarly, in the later phases of Easter Island's history before European contact, there seems to have been a

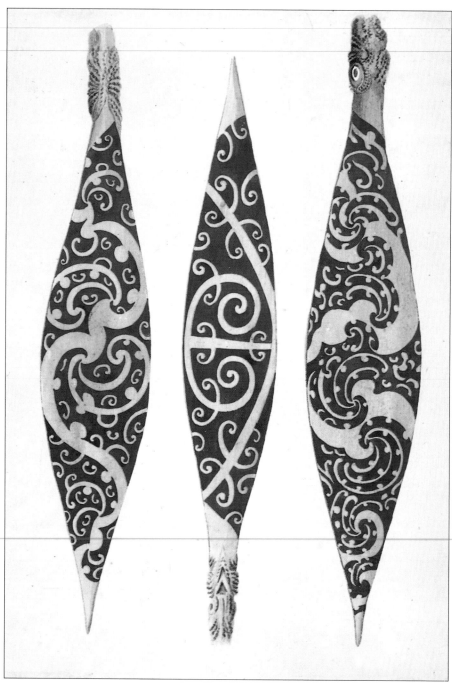

34°
36°
38°
40°
42°
44°
46°
48°

Legend

● important commercial center

Tuhoe principal Maori tribe around 1800

Maori routeway
— land
‑‑‑ sea

/// distribution of *pa*, or fortified settlements

percentage distribution of Maori population
by region, late 1700s
☐ Northern (Iwitini) – 82%
☐ Central (Waenganui) – 15%
☐ Southern (Te Wahi Pounamu) – 3%

scale 1 : 6 250 000
0 ——— 150 km
0 ——— 100 mi

Left Part of the impressive Tahitian warfleet assembled in April 1774 for an attack against Mahine, the paramount chief of Moorea, as observed by the artist William Hodges. The fleet was made up of some 160 war canoes and another 170 smaller double sailing canoes, and Cook estimated that it carried almost 8,000 men.

Below left In October 1769 Cook's ship *Endeavour* met six canoes, carrying about 50 men, off the east coast of Aotearoa. Though wary at first, the Maori eventually agreed to an exchange of goods. The items of trade included finely decorated canoe paddles, some of which may form the subject of the sketch by Sydney Parkinson shown here.

Later Maori society

By the 15th century, the easily hunted *moa*, a valuable food source, was virtually extinct in the North Island and scarce in the South Island, and there was greater use of marine resources and of foods such as fern root. The development after c.1500 of fortified settlements (*pa*) probably reflects tensions arising from increasing population pressure and competition for resources in the crop-growing areas. At the time of Cook's visit there were Maori communities from the extreme north to the far south, though the vast majority of population and tribes were located in the North Island, with coastal areas usually being the most densely settled. Trade networks, some running for long distances, had been built up from the times of earliest settlement. These allowed for the exchange of unevenly distributed resources such as greenstone, found only in the South Island.

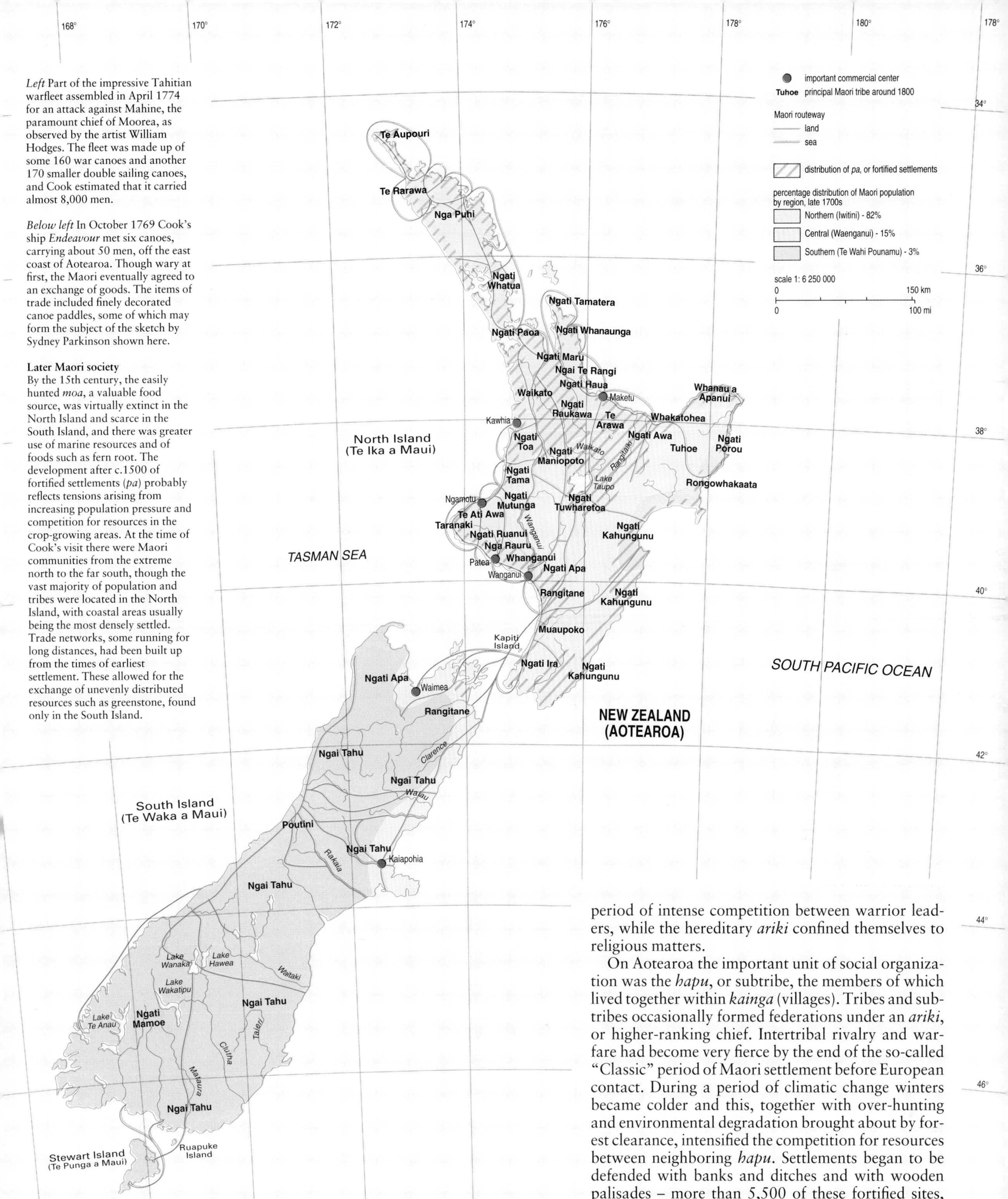

Map labels

Te Aupouri
Te Rarawa
Nga Puhi
Ngati Whatua
Ngati Tamatera
Ngati Paoa
Ngati Whanaunga
Ngati Maru
Ngai Te Rangi
Ngati Haua
Waikato
Maketu
Kawhia
Ngati Raukawa
Te Arawa
Whakatohea
Whanau a Apanui
Ngati Toa
Ngati Maniopoto
Ngati Awa
Tuhoe
Ngati Porou
Ngati Tama
Lake Taupo
Ngamotu
Ngati Mutunga
Te Ati Awa
Ngati Tuwharetoa
Rongowhakaata
Taranaki
Ngati Ruanui
Ngati Kahungunu
Nga Rauru
Patea
Whanganui
Wanganui
Ngati Apa
Rangitane
Ngati Kahungunu
Muaupoko
Kapiti Island
Ngati Ira
Ngati Kahungunu

North Island
(Te Ika a Maui)

TASMAN SEA

SOUTH PACIFIC OCEAN

NEW ZEALAND
(AOTEAROA)

Ngati Apa
Waimea
Rangitane
Ngai Tahu
Clarence
Ngai Tahu
Watau
Poutini
Ngai Tahu
Kaiapohia
Ngai Tahu
Rakaia

South Island
(Te Waka a Maui)

Lake Wanaka
Lake Hawea
Lake Wakatipu
Lake Te Anau
Ngati Mamoe
Ngai Tahu
Waitaki
Taieri
Clutha
Mataura
Ngai Tahu

Stewart Island
(Te Punga a Maui)
Ruapuke Island

period of intense competition between warrior leaders, while the hereditary *ariki* confined themselves to religious matters.

On Aotearoa the important unit of social organization was the *hapu*, or subtribe, the members of which lived together within *kainga* (villages). Tribes and subtribes occasionally formed federations under an *ariki*, or higher-ranking chief. Intertribal rivalry and warfare had become very fierce by the end of the so-called "Classic" period of Maori settlement before European contact. During a period of climatic change winters became colder and this, together with over-hunting and environmental degradation brought about by forest clearance, intensified the competition for resources between neighboring *hapu*. Settlements began to be defended with banks and ditches and with wooden palisades – more than 5,500 of these fortified sites, known as *pa*, have been identified in the North Island. Raids were often made by one *hapu* upon another to exert *utu* – the repayment of former injuries – and captured enemies were sometimes eaten, though the incidence of cannibalism should not be overplayed.

Power, sanctity and taboos

There was considerable variation in the degree to which rank operated within Polynesian societies. On the atolls of Pukapuka and Tokelau, the only distinction of rank was between a small number of chiefs and priests and the rest of the population. Land was controlled by kin groups and production supervised by family heads. Village meetings or councils were held to discuss matters concerning the whole community, such as the use of land, and decisions were taken, as far as possible, by consensus. Chiefs had a personal sacredness, but few symbols of rank marked them off from the rest of the community. Nor was Maori society strongly stratified, but was divided between those belonging to the chiefly families, the *rangatira,* and the *tuatua,* or commoners. Many people, however, would have had a kinship link to the chiefly groups. A kind of slavery existed, consisting of those captured in war.

The most elaborate social hierarchies were those of Tonga, Tahiti and Hawaii. In Hawaii, the ruling aristocratic group was virtually closed off from those of lower rank. Paramount chiefs headed political units of up to 30,000 people. At the level of paramount, brother-sister and brother-half-sister marriages took place, keeping rank and privilege within a single descent line. New paramounts would redistribute lands to their supporters. These chiefs installed stewards to oversee the use of the land, the organization of

work such as the maintenance of irrigation systems, and the provision of tribute. The commoners carried out the productive labor, and could be removed from the land they worked by those of higher rank.

As landowners, the Hawaiian chiefs exercised a high degree of economic control. Production was organized to generate food surpluses, which were given in tribute to the chiefs, whose mediation between the human and supernatural worlds had made them possible. Tribute flowed up through the levels of chiefs and a good part of the food offerings and other goods were redistributed, particularly in feasting. It was said that a wise paramount should feed all those who brought him gifts, but much of the tribute received at the highest level, including prestige items such as fine feathers, was probably distributed within the chieftain group, thereby helping to secure their ties to the paramount chief. Polynesian chiefs generally were the focus for tribute offerings and were also responsible for their redistribution. How far that redistribution reached down through all levels of society seems to have depended on the numbers of ranks of chiefs there were.

The chief and those of high rank had a greater degree of *mana,* or effective power, than others. The ultimate source of *mana* was the gods, but though its origins were supernatural, it could be revealed in the successful outcome of practical action. So evidence of

Above The Maori fortified settlement, or *pa,* at One Tree Hill in the southern suburbs of Auckland occupies the slopes of a volcanic cone. The outlines of massive earthworks, terraces, houses and storage pits can be clearly seen. To reach the final strongpoint on the volcano's summit an attacking force would first have to cross the terraces on the lower slopes and then fight its way through a sequence of ditches and palisades, engaging in hand to hand combat with the defenders. Clubs and stabbing spears were the main weapons and surprise would have been the first requirement for a successful assault. The Maori appear to have begun to develop their formidable military defense works in about the 14th or 15th centuries. The *pa* at One Tree Hill may have accommodated as many as 5,000 people. Today the summit is crowned by an obelisk erected as a memorial to the Maori people in the early 20th century.

Above In the highly-ranked society of Hawaii possession of feather-covered crested helmets and feather cloaks known as *'ahu'ula* was a mark of high chieftainship. To make a cloak like the one shown here thousands of feathers were needed from Hawaii's unique species of native birds such as the red *'i'iwi* and the golden *o'o*. Cloaks of the same kind were once used to dress images of gods and, worn by a chief, symbolized his sacredness and power.

important chief's shadow were to fall on a food store, the food within it would become inedible to anyone else. The degree of personal sanctity accorded to a chief varied from society to society; the more stratified the society, the more elaborate the *tapu*. In the stratified chiefdoms of Hawaii the paramount chiefs shared with the gods the *kapu moe*, a taboo requiring prostration on the ground in their presence. Infringement of their sanctity might be punished by immediate death at the hands of their retainers, rather than by supernatural intervention.

Myths and arts of Polynesia

The close affinities between the cultures of the Polynesian islands are reflected in their common mythologies. Stories of the trickster-hero Maui are widely distributed: he gave fire to humankind and, seated in his canoe, is said to have pulled up several of the Polynesian islands, including those of Aotearoa, from the sea with his fishhook. Many eastern Polynesians traced the origins of the known world, including human beings, back to a sky father and earth mother: Avatea and Papa, as they are known in the Cook Islands. They were often presented as the parents of a number of prominent gods, such as Rongo, as he was known to the Maori and eastern Polynesians (Lono to the Hawaiians), Tangaroa (Kanaloa), Tu (Ku), and Tane (Kane): only the first two, however, were known in Tonga and Samoa.

mana could be seen in the power to sway followers, in a plentiful crop harvest, or in victory in war. The chief was a channel through which *mana* could be brought to bear on the wellbeing of his people. But divine power should not be compromised by contact with impure things, and those with little *mana* could be threatened by contact with the more powerful. So chiefs, and their possessions, became hedged about with ritual restrictions – they became *tapu* (from which the English word "taboo" derives). To break such restrictions was dangerous: it could invite illness or death. *Tapu* might be deliberately extended over land or other items that chiefs wished to conserve and protect. But it might be passed on accidentally: an account from the Maori refers to the fear that if an

The gods were generally linked to specific areas of human interest and activity. For the Maori, Rongo was associated with crops and harvest, Tangaroa with the sea and fishing, Tu with warfare, and Tane with the forest and the use of its products. Before an individual or a group went fishing, or prepared the land to grow sweet potatoes, or made an expedition of war, or cut trees for building, offerings would be made to the appropriate god. There were also a number of local gods and goddesses, such as the goddess Pele,

Right The *marae* of Tahiti and the other islands of central eastern Polynesia were places of worship, sacred open spaces used for meetings and ritual. The reconstructed Arahurahu *marae* in the west of Tahiti is an impressive reminder of the larger type of ritual site found in coastal areas. At one end stands the stepped *ahu* platform on which images of gods would have been displayed and from which priests might have spoken as the possessed mouth-pieces of the gods. The larger *marae* were probably used for tribal ritual, though the many smaller ones may simply have been sites where individual families could call upon their ancestors. All sorts of occasions would have been marked by *marae* ceremonial, including seasonal festivals, funerals, chiefly investitures and war ceremonies. In the latter case, human sacrifices would have been added to the animal sacrifices made in the *marae*.

Religion in Polynesian Art

Throughout Polynesia the arts, especially the art of the carver, were used both to represent gods and ancestors and to produce material vehicles for their *mana*, or power. They communicated ideas about the world of myth and furnished the objects that were central to ritual practice. While Polynesia has a greater unity than the other cultural regions of the Pacific, religious beliefs did vary from island group to island group, and there were distinct local cults. Yet certain mythical figures were found very widely, among them the hero Maui, who fished up land, stole fire, and wished to overcome death. Similarly, Tangaroa (also known as Tagaloa, Ta'aroa and Kanaloa) was a major god of both western and eastern Polynesia. In the east he was particularly identified with the things of the ocean, as part of a family of gods with different functions, who were often treated as ultimate ancestors. Gods were sometimes represented by figures of human or near-human form, but in other cases the representation was more abstract, with certain materials, techniques or colors playing a part in symbolizing the god.

Below Easter Island's "birdman" cult is reflected in this small wooden carving. An annual competition to obtain a seabird egg was important in establishing ritual and political leadership. The warrior leader of the successful group became *tangata manu* (birdman) for the year. He lived in a secluded hut, probably as a representative of the creator god Makemake.

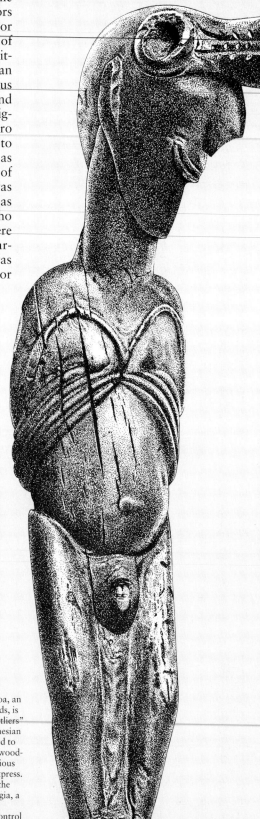

Below Most famous of the *ti-i*, images of ancestors or gods, from the island of Rurutu (Austral Islands, French Polynesia) is this carving of the god A'a. It was taken from Rurutu by missionaries in 1821. A removable back panel gives access to a hollow interior, in which other smaller figures were once stored.

Left The island of Nukuroa, an atoll of the Caroline Islands, is one of the Polynesian "outliers" of Micronesia. Non-Polynesian influences may have helped to shape both its distinctive wood-carving style and the religious tradition it was used to express. The figure seen here is of the goddess Kave de Hine Aligia, a powerful and potentially dangerous being said to control Nukuoro in the absence of a more benign god. The carving probably stood in a godhouse, a focus for offerings.

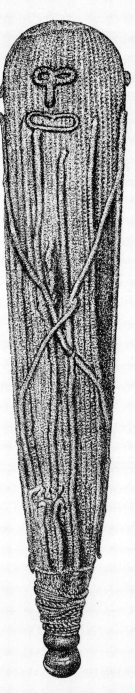

Left A temple figure from Kona on the island of Hawaii represents Ku, one of four major gods. He was especially linked with warfare, fishing, canoe-building and sorcery. Ku had many aspects and many names – Ku-olono-wao (Ku of the deep forest), Ku-mauna (Ku of the mountains), Ku-waha-ilo (Ku maggot-mouth, god of sorcery) among them. Most celebrated of the battle-god images of Ku was Ku-ka'ili-moku (Ku the snatcher of land), owned by Kamehameha, the chief whose conquests created the Hawaiian kingdom.

Right In Tahiti and its neighboring islands the worship of the four great eastern Polynesian gods, known there as Tane, Ta'aroa, Ro'o and Tu, had by the mid 18th century become secondary to the worship of 'Oro, son of Ta'aroa, whose cult spread from the island of Raiatea. Tahitian images of 'Oro were produced by plaiting sennit (coconut fiber) about a wooden core. These were originally decorated with red feathers, marks of the sacredness of 'Oro.

Left Maori tradition makes Hine-nui-te-po (Great woman of the night/underworld) both ancestress of humankind and death goddess. Myth tells how the trickster-hero Maui sought eternal life for all by trying to reverse the process of birth. This bone-chest, a container for the bones of a high-ranking person, shows Maui between the goddess's legs, about to enter her. He would be crushed as she awoke, roused by the laughter of one of his bird companions.

Right Identification of the staff god figures of Rarotonga, Cook Islands are uncertain, but this upper portion of a staff god may represent Tangaroa, the creator-god, with generations of lineage ancestors below. The full staff would have been more than 3 meters long, its center wrapped in a bundle of barkcloth within which were red feathers and pieces of pearlshell symbolizing the spirit of the god.

79

Easter Island – Rapa Nui

Easter Island, or Rapa Nui, was settled by 400 AD, possibly from the Marquesas group. Lying at the isolated eastern corner of the Polynesian triangle, it evolved its own distinctive culture. A limited range of foodstuffs – sweet potato, taro, yam, sugar cane, gourds, fish and chicken – supported the island's population, which expanded into two confederations of clans. By 1000 AD a great phase of building and artistic production had begun, and in the following 500 years – a period of relative peace – the different kin groups vied in the making of the island's famous stone statues. By the time the first Europeans arrived in 1722 this phase had long passed, giving way to a period of interclan warfare when the island's older structures, including statues, were overthrown. Spearheads of volcanic glass were produced in great numbers and the Poike Ditch in the east of the island may be a defensive work from this period. Recent studies suggest that these later changes in society were linked with environmental degradation, which increased the competition for limited resources and led to a fall in population. The Polynesian settlers themselves seem to have contributed to the environmental crisis through progressive deforestation. European-introduced diseases dealt a final critical blow to dwindling numbers, and a slave raid in 1862 carried away much of the remaining population to Peru. Only a small number returned later. The island was annexed by Chile in 1888.

Right One of Rapa Nui's great stone figures (*moai maea*), with its red topknot replaced and inlaid eyes restored. Many of the toppled statues have been put back on their ceremonial platforms (*ahu*). These were a key element of the ceremonial complexes that on Easter Island were a development of the *marae* found elsewhere in eastern Polynesia and which served the ritual needs of local kin groups. The largest erected statue weighed over 80 tonnes. Like the others, it would have been carved out of the rock with stone mauls, or wedging tools, then transported from the quarry on a wooden sled or rollers and erected with ramps and levers – a massive investment of effort.

Left From the rocks of Orongo carved birdman figures look out toward the island of Motu Nui. The *manutara* or birdman cult was part of the later history of Easter Island. The village of Orongo, established around 1500, became the ceremonial center where each September a competition took place between groups headed by the most powerful *matatoa*, the warriors who controlled secular power in the island's warring society. Their representatives swam out to Motu Nui to see who would be the first to return with the egg of a Sooty tern. The leader of the successful group became birdman, a cult leader and, perhaps, the island's nominal ruler for a year.

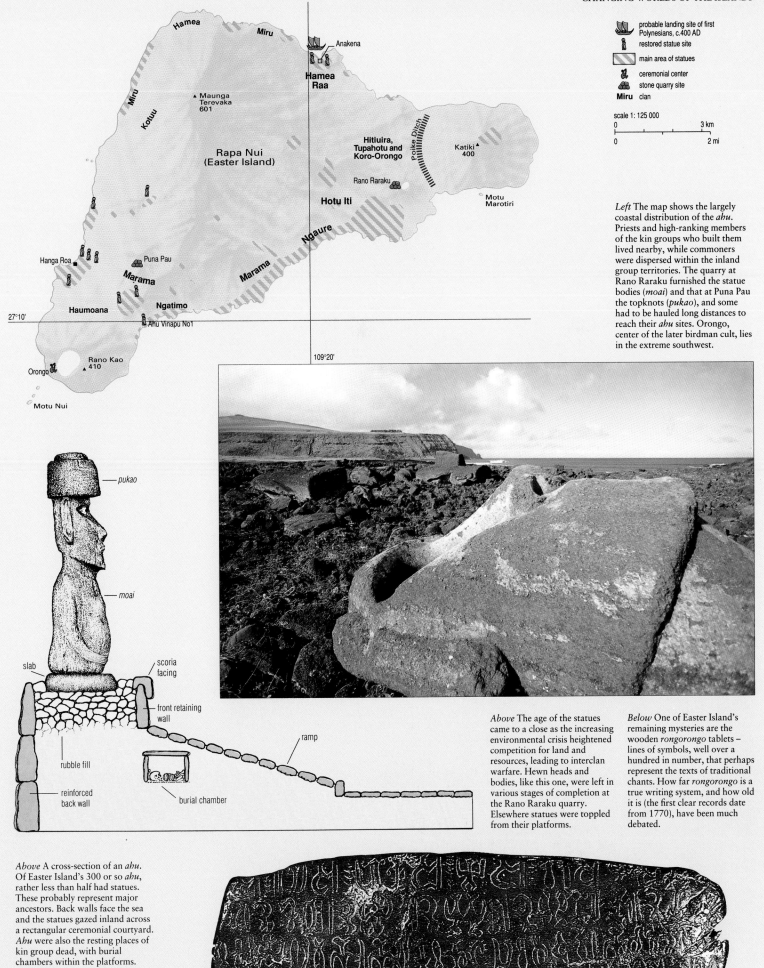

probable landing site of first Polynesians, c.400 AD

restored statue site

main area of statues

ceremonial center

stone quarry site

Miru clan

scale 1: 125 000

0   3 km

0   2 mi

Left The map shows the largely coastal distribution of the *ahu*. Priests and high-ranking members of the kin groups who built them lived nearby, while commoners were dispersed within the inland group territories. The quarry at Rano Raraku furnished the statue bodies (*moai*) and that at Puna Pau the topknots (*pukao*), and some had to be hauled long distances to reach their *ahu* sites. Orongo, center of the later birdman cult, lies in the extreme southwest.

pukao

moai

slab

scoria facing

front retaining wall

rubble fill

reinforced back wall

burial chamber

ramp

Above The age of the statues came to a close as the increasing environmental crisis heightened competition for land and resources, leading to interclan warfare. Hewn heads and bodies, like this one, were left in various stages of completion at the Rano Raraku quarry. Elsewhere statues were toppled from their platforms.

Below One of Easter Island's remaining mysteries are the wooden *rongorongo* tablets – lines of symbols, well over a hundred in number, that perhaps represent the texts of traditional chants. How far *rongorongo* is a true writing system, and how old it is (the first clear records date from 1770), have been much debated.

Above A cross-section of an *ahu*. Of Easter Island's 300 or so *ahu*, rather less than half had statues. These probably represent major ancestors. Back walls face the sea and the statues gazed inland across a rectangular ceremonial courtyard. *Ahu* were also the resting places of kin group dead, with burial chambers within the platforms. Cremation pits are sometimes found nearby.

Tattoo

The term "tattoo" first became known in late 18th-century Europe through the writings of Captain Cook, who observed the Polynesian art of skin decoration, *tatau*, on his voyages across the Pacific. Tattooing was very widely distributed among the islands of Polynesia, suggesting that its origins lay deep in the past, probably among the Lapita-making Austronesian ancestors. Tattooing was also practiced in the the Caroline and Marshall Islands of Micronesia, while within Melanesia tattoo traditions were scattered from Papua through to Fiji.

The typical Polynesian tattooing tools were fine bone chisels with teeth, mounted like small adzes. Dipped in pigment, these were tapped into the skin with a light mallet, leaving the color in the puncture holes. It was a very painful process, and extensive tattoos needed many sessions spread out over months or even years. The work was done by master craftsmen and their assistants, and was often surrounded by ritual. Both men and women had tattoos, those on men covering more areas of the body. In the Marquesas Islands, which had one of the most sophisticated tattoo traditions, women might have patterns on their hands and arms, stomach and lower back, while full tattoo for men involved almost every part of the body, including the face. Having a tattoo was not necessarily a mark of rank, but status could be reflected in its quality. Tattooing was discouraged by European missionaries and died away in many areas. But there were exceptions, and in recent years there has been a revival of the art in some places, for instance among urban Maori communities. Old as well as more modern tattooing techniques are used, with aspects of traditional design giving expression to present-day identities.

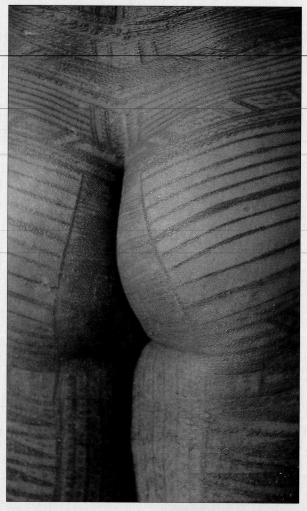

Right This drawing by Sydney Parkinson shows a style of Maori male facial tattoo seen in the north of Aotearoa (New Zealand) by those aboard Captain Cook's ship *Endeavour* in 1769. Maori myth tells that the art of tattooing (*moko*) was originally brought back by a visitor to the spirit underworld. The tattooing tools found on archaeological sites of early date suggest that tattooing skills were introduced by the first settlers from island Polynesia. But Maori *moko* developed characteristics of its own. The teeth of tattooing chisels became shorter or vanished, to produce a tool that cut much deeper into the skin so that grooved scars formed the main lines of a pattern. The curvilinear designs that became the most widespread can be related both to woodcarving styles and to the painted patterns on house rafters. Areas of the body covered by tattoo varied between regions. Women's *moko* was often confined to the lips and chin, but men might be tattooed over the whole face, and on the lower body, buttocks and thighs. *Moko* designs were individual variations on common decorative themes, a particular pattern being closely identified with its wearer, a source of identity. It was said that while other things that you valued could be lost through misfortune, only death could deprive you of your *moko*.

Above Despite a decline in the colonial period, there is a strong continued tradition of tattoo in Samoa, where it was traditionally a sign of adulthood for both sexes. The fuller male tattoo involves elaborate patterns that may extend over much of the body from the middle of the back to a little below the knee. Here a tattoo is being applied to the buttocks and thighs in a strong rectilinear design, using toothed chisels or "tattooing combs".

Left A youth's body is washed off after a tattooing session. Being able to show that they can bear the pain of such work is one important reason why young men choose to have tattoo done. The intense pain of extensive male tattoo is compared to women's pain in childbirth. Pride in Samoan culture, family pride in being able to mount the ceremony and appeal to the opposite sex also play their part.

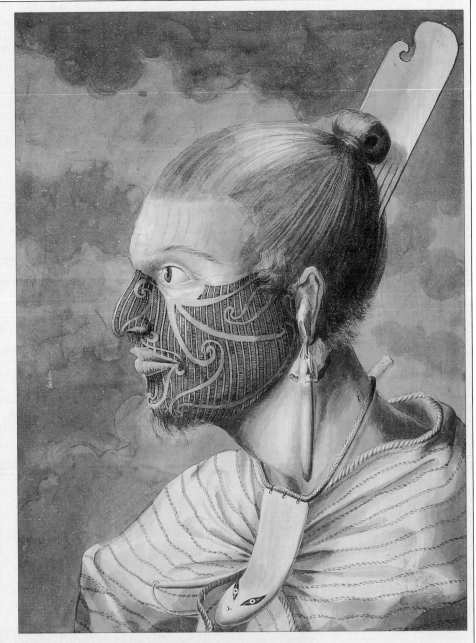

Left In some areas of Melanesia, thorns, shell and stone flakes replace the bone tattooing chisel. Here, in eastern Papua, a grandmother works a design on her granddaughter using a tattooing tool consisting of a twig with a thorn from a lime bush. A mixture of oil and charcoal is used as the pigment. The tools used in Fiji were very similar to those of their Polynesian neighbors. There were important differences, though, in who was tattooed. In Fiji, tattoo was restricted to women, and carried out by female tattooists. It appears to have been an aspect of initiation to adulthood, with the tattoo being applied to the pubic area, in some instances extending from the midriff to the upper thighs. Such tattoo was covered by the *liku* skirt of womanhood, but more readily visible marks were placed around the mouth and sometimes on the hands.

who were associated with the volcanic activity of the island of Hawaii. Kin groups would generally have their own particular objects of worship, often powerful ancestors who had become part of the spirit world. The Tongans and Samoans probably had wooden god-houses for their cults, but in central and eastern Polynesia ritual activities (including human sacrifices) took place in the open, and sacred sites were in the form of walled open spaces or courtyards called *marae*. At one end there would be a stone platform (*ahu*) where the spirits or gods resided. In the Society Islands these stone temples became very elaborate, with complex multi-layered platforms; in Aotearoa, by contrast, the *marae* was simply a flat open space within a settlement.

Polynesian arts frequently reflected the relations between the living, the ancestors and the gods, and the relations within society. Many of Polynesia's finest carvings are images of gods and goddesses, or of ancestors. The great stone figures (dating from about 1100–1680) that look out from the slopes of Easter Island or stand on stone platforms represent ancestors. The Cook Islanders kept intricately carved wooden figures to represent the gods in ritual. The images carved on a Maori meeting house might encompass the entire history of the group that owned it. Possession of a particularly fine object could enhance *mana*, and particular items came to be regarded as symbols of rank. These varied from island to island. Objects of finely worked feathers were especially valued among the Hawaiians, and cloaks covered with thousands of red and yellow feathers were worn by the chiefs as a mark of status. Beautifully shaped and polished personal ornaments, ceremonial adzes and clubs of greenstone (nephrite jade) were among the heirlooms of the Maori chiefs.

Facial and body tattooing was widespread throughout Polynesia ("tattoo" is another word of Polynesian origin). The tattoos were worked in complex designs, and the size and quality of an individual's tattoo was often an indication of rank. The possession of special artistic and technological skills was generally highly regarded by the Polynesians. Crafts such as woodcarving and canoe-building were practiced in combination with religious rituals, and the Maori applied the term *tohunga* – meaning a specialist or expert – both to those skilled in particular arts such as tattooing and carving and to those concerned with religion. There were special schools where priestly *tohunga* were taught sacred knowledge, while others became adept in ritual and chant in order to preside at all kinds of ceremony, or were trained in history and genealogy. Ceremony played an important part in Polynesian life, and the performance of ritual dance, song and oratory were all highly valued.

Social organization and leadership in Melanesia

Commentators frequently draw a contrast between the large, hierarchical chiefdoms of Polynesia and the small communities of Melanesia where little value was given to social rank – individuals obtained status and leadership through their own abilities, particularly their skill in acquiring and manipulating wealth. Though this summarization does capture some important differences between Polynesian and Melanesian societies, it nevertheless oversimplifies matters. Melanesia historically was a region of enormous cultural diversity. Political groupings could range from a few dozen people to several thousand in the highlands

of New Guinea or in Fiji, and settlements vary from scattered homesteads to highly-organized villages.

Nor was political leadership restricted to a single form, though the type most often discussed is that of the "big man" who actively attracts supporters through his abilities, especially in feast-giving and ceremonial exchange, and emerges through competition with others. But the power of big men varied greatly with the scale of the society and the resources at their disposal. Sometimes they were no more than influential figures in the communal decision-making of a men's house or body of elders. In other cases they exercised a stronger leadership role. Among the Kwaio of the Solomon Islands today, for example, big men achieve their position of leadership by successfully manipulating wealth in the form of pigs and shell bead

strings. Descent groups (largely but not exclusively patrilineal) gain prestige by staging impressive mortuary feasts. Substantial presentations of valuables are made to the relatives of the deceased by the rival descent groups attending the burial. When they in turn stage their own mortuary feasts, the recipients of past gifts are expected to make presentations at least as large in return. These exchanges form part of the competition for prestige. A big man will be at the fore in assembling the wealth his group needs for such occasions, contributing to feasts and providing the resources needed for marriages. So he builds up a network of obligations toward himself, which is realized as political support. His leadership rests not on any formal title but on the decision of group members to follow him and accept his guidance.

Above A group of Hewa men from the Highland region of New Guinea are decorated for a festivity. In Melanesian societies men usually take on the major public roles and play the most prominent part in key ceremonials. At the same time, women often have their own ideas of worth or status and their own techniques of achieving these, distinct from those of the men.

Right Frigate birds appear frequently in the art of the Solomon Islands, often symbolizing ancestral spirits. The carvings on this wooden paddle from Isabel Island are said to show the spirits of the drowned returning to advise living fishermen. A part-human part-bird figure can be seen at the top right.

Body adornment in Papua New Guinea

More than one and a quarter million people live in the Highlands of Papua New Guinea. They are divided into different language groups, some of which may contain only a few hundred people, others more than one hundred thousand. Both similarities and cultural differences can be traced in the rich traditions of body adornment found in the region. The most elaborate forms of self-decoration have been associated with festivals of ceremonial gift exchange and with religious cult performances. Self adornment is an important part of dance performances and nowadays is displayed when dancers travel to compete in regional cultural shows, or Sing Sings.

Many elements help to make up the decorations. Particularly striking is the use of feathers, mainly in headdresses, from Papua New Guinea's dazzling array of bird life. Some of the most highly prized plumes come from the country's unique Bird of Paradise species. But, besides these, feathers from parrots, eagles, cassowaries and many other birds are used. Shells of various kinds and sizes, some shaped into crescents or disks, are another important element. To these can be added ornaments made from pigs' tusks or the fur of marsupials such as the cuscus and the tree kangaroo. Human hair is used for the sculpted wigs that are often worn by Highland men. Flowers, strings of seed pods, plaited fibers, colored and scented leaves are interwoven into the decorations, and today are supplemented with beads, plastics and other imported materials. A range of face-painting and, less commonly, body-painting styles add to the overall effect. Though different cultural groups may be distinguished by particular decorative styles, there may be more subtle variations within a local set of decorative elements that convey messages about the social roles of those wearing them. Women and men have different decorative styles, with male decoration generally the more elaborate. At ceremonial exchanges in the Mount Hagen area the different categories of people taking part – donors, helpers and recipients – may adorn themselves in a particular way to distinguish themselves from the others.

Left Two men from the Mount Hagen area of the Western Highlands wear long wig-headdresses topped with further decorations. Both sport headbands made of marsupial fur; the man on the right has incorporated the graceful crown plumes of the King of Saxony Bird of Paradise and the long, dark tail feathers of the Princess Stephanie Bird of Paradise. The bamboo sticks on his chest form a tally representing the number of pearl shells given away in ceremonial exchanges.

Above A Huli man from the Tari area of the Southern Highlands wears the *manda tene*, or downturned wig. The wigs are formed from human hair and decorated with a variety of plumes and dried flowers.

Far left A Hewa woman has a pearlshell crescent at her neck, an ornament widely worn in the Highlands. Cowrie shells form a necklace and decorate her head covering. The trade of decorative shells from the coast into the Highlands dates back into the distant past.

Center Yellow and red are the principal colors used in Huli self-decoration. Here a young man makes use of a car mirror to help him apply his face paint. Paints are now often bought rather than manufactured locally.

Left Self adornment is considered to be more truly a male activity, but when women do decorate for particular occasions, as here, their use of feathers can be more profuse than that of men.

Many Melanesian societies shared versions of this form of leadership. The qualities associated with big men were wide-ranging. They included ambition and organizational skills, as well as generosity in the distribution of wealth. It was important that a big man should have the backing of close kin to place their resources at his disposal and be able to call on the production skills of several wives to grow crops and raise pigs for distribution at exchange ceremonies. In some cases proven ability in warfare was necessary to back up his claim to leadership, and the power to sway decision by his oratory might also be required. Among the Kwaio, highest success as big men falls to those who are eldest sons, but though it may be some advantage to be the eldest son of an existing big man, there is no guarantee that the big man status will stay in the family. However, it appears that big men sometimes groomed a close kinsman or other chosen candidate to succeed them. For a time at least, the big men of New Guinea highland societies such as the Melpa were drawn from a closed dominant group that monopolized the major exchanges of valuables, and in this respect at least, some of their status was ascribed to them rather than achieved.

True inherited chieftainship could also be found in Melanesia. In the Trobriand Islands leadership of high-ranking subclans was based on descent from a common female ancestor; in New Caledonia patrilineal succession through the eldest male line was more frequent, with clans coming together in alliances under paramount chiefs. Fiji, closest to Polynesia, developed a complex, hierarchical chiefdom with similarities to the systems of western Polynesia. On Papua New Guinea, the Purari of the south coast had hereditary chiefs and a system of social ranking. But this was accompanied by competitive exchange, and the chief's influence in the community was related to his ability to establish a substantial holding of shell ornaments and to maintain a network of obligations through the giving of food.

One of the most interesting forms of inherited chieftainship existed among the Mekeo, living farther east along the same coast. The titles of chief passed mainly from father to eldest son, but they evolved a system of dual chieftainship, each subclan having civilian and military leaders. The senior and junior civilian chiefs were "chiefs of the village", men of peace whose job was to ensure harmony within the community. In addition there was the "chief of the spear", a war chief, seen as potentially dangerous, but whose aggression might be called upon if it became necessary to fight an external enemy. It is possible that at some time, as in some Polynesian societies, junior subclan members had taken over the military powers that had belonged to their seniors. Here wealth seems to have had a limited part in leadership; the chiefs' powers were inherited by descent, and lying behind them were the supernatural forces of sorcery.

Trade, exchange and warfare

Integral to the role of leadership in Melanesia was the ability to gain control of the prestige items that entered the region through trade and exchange. This trade took a variety of forms, from straightforward barter to elaborate ceremonial exchange, and networks were established that linked peoples of different language and culture. In the Solomon Islands and a number of other large islands, the people of the interior would exchange vegetables for the fish caught by the coastal

peoples. In New Guinea items such as shells would pass through several sequences of exchange as they made their way up into the highlands, while bird of paradise feathers, prized as items of personal adornment, traveled down to the coast. In this way the people of the Mount Hagen area of the Highlands received the shells that became central to their highly developed local ceremonial exchange system, giving in return goods that had themselves been traded into their area, such as bamboo tubes containing oil for decoration and packs of salt. Such trade was organized through a network of trading relationships between pairs of individuals or "trade-friends".

Most Melanesian societies were self-sufficient in food, but some manufactured specialist products that they exchanged for particular foodstuffs. The Motu

Above Pigs are staked out for presentation in a major ceremonial exchange in the New Guinea Highlands. Pigs have long been an important form of wealth in Melanesia, and are the most valuable items in the *tee* exchange system of the Tombema-Enga people of the Western Highlands. Men with the longest lines of pigs are acclaimed big men.

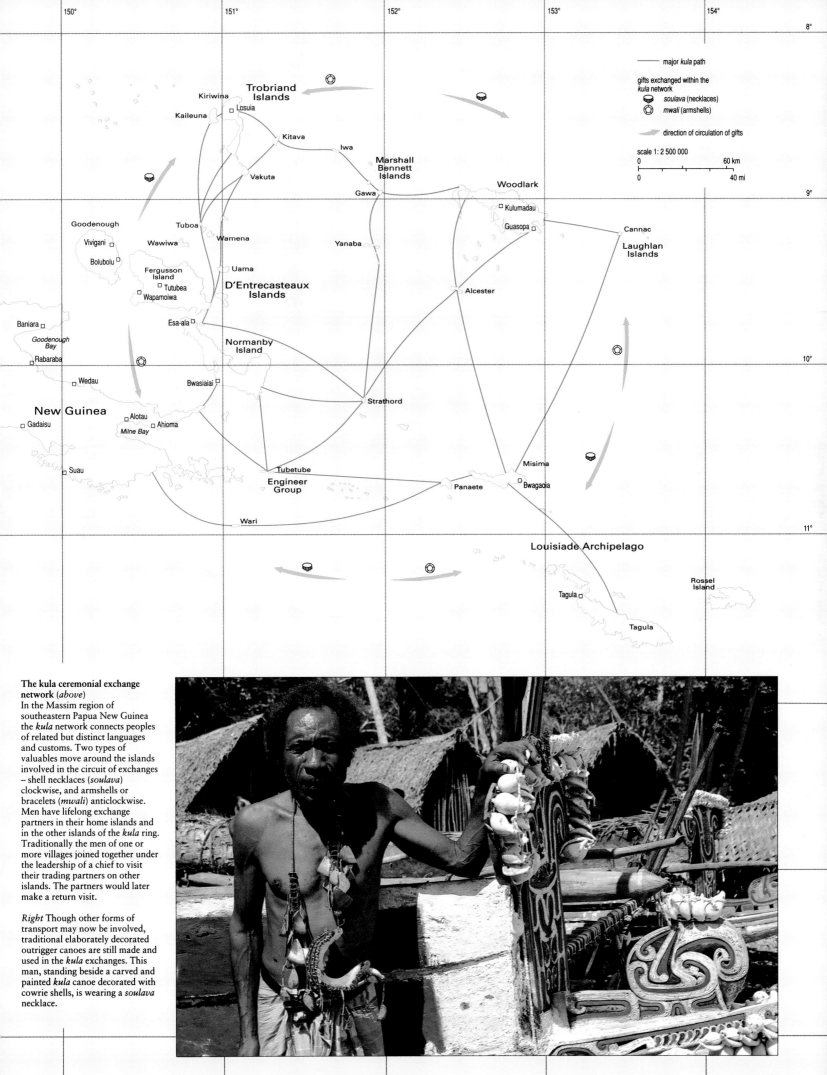

The kula ceremonial exchange network (*above*)
In the Massim region of southeastern Papua New Guinea the *kula* network connects peoples of related but distinct languages and customs. Two types of valuables move around the islands involved in the circuit of exchanges – shell necklaces (*soulava*) clockwise, and armshells or bracelets (*mwali*) anticlockwise. Men have lifelong exchange partners in their home islands and in the other islands of the *kula* ring. Traditionally the men of one or more villages joined together under the leadership of a chief to visit their trading partners on other islands. The partners would later make a return visit.

Right Though other forms of transport may now be involved, traditional elaborately decorated outrigger canoes are still made and used in the *kula* exchanges. This man, standing beside a carved and painted *kula* canoe decorated with cowrie shells, is wearing a *soulava* necklace.

Map labels:

major *kula* path
gifts exchanged within the *kula* network
soulava (necklaces)
mwali (armshells)
direction of circulation of gifts

scale 1: 2 500 000
0   60 km
0   40 mi

Trobriand Islands
Kiriwina
Kaileuna
Losuia
Kitava
Iwa
Marshall Bennett Islands
Woodlark
Gawa
Kulumadau
Guasopa
Cannac
Laughlan Islands
Goodenough
Vivigani
Tuboa
Wamena
Yanaba
Bolubolu
Wawiwa
Fergusson Island
Tutubea
Uama
Wapamoiwa
D'Entrecasteaux Islands
Alcester
Baniara
Goodenough Bay
Esa-ala
Normanby Island
Rabaraba
Wedau
Bwasiaiai
Strathord
New Guinea
Gadaisu
Alotau
Ahioma
Milne Bay
Misima
Bwagaoia
Suau
Tubetube
Engineer Group
Panaete
Wari
Louisiade Archipelago
Rossel Island
Tagula
Tagula

150°   151°   152°   153°   154°
8°
9°
10°
11°

people, for example, living in the area of present-day Port Moresby, were producers of pottery that they carried in multi-hulled trading vessels along the coast to be traded for sago. On the northeast coast, the sailing skills of the Siassi enabled them to become ocean-going middlemen, establishing a substantial network of trade in various goods, including pottery, dogs and pigs, between mainland New Guinea and the islands of New Britain. The best-known of all the Melanesian ceremonial exchange networks is the *kula* ring, which linked many of the islands of the Solomon Sea off Papua New Guinea's southeastern promontory. It may be about 500 years old. Two categories of valuables passed around the *kula* ring: necklaces of red shell disks in a clockwise direction, and white armshells the other way. On being presented with one of these valuables, an individual was obliged at a future date to give one of the other type, of equal value, in return. Men had *kula* partners, in relationships that lasted for life. Some would be local but others lived overseas, and *kula* voyages, rich in ceremony and magic, were organized to allow men to visit their partners for exchange ceremonies. Prestige was acquired by the number and quality of the *kula* shells that passed through an individual's hands, especial worth being attributed to the finest and most celebrated shells. Trading in other goods went on alongside the formal exchanges of the *kula*.

Ceremonial exchange reflects the positive side of Melanesian intergroup relations. To judge by the evidence of the recent past, feuding and warfare were widespread. Sometimes formal links with trading partners or special exchange arrangements allowed goods to pass between groups that were otherwise in a state of hostility. Exchanges could also help to cement alliances and re-establish good relations between groups that had been in conflict. Warfare usually took the form of small-scale skirmishing, or surprise attacks by raiding parties; in some cases, formalized confrontations took place on recognized fighting grounds, with only limited casualties being incurred. But hostilities could be more extensive than this, as in the political-military competition for supremacy between the Fijian chiefdoms, in which contending chiefs sought to win the support and co-operation of widely ranged groups through a combination of arms and diplomacy. In New Guinea, particularly the west and parts of the Sepik River region, and in some of the Solomon Islands, the taking of heads was an integral part of warfare, and sometimes a motivation for it. Among the Asmat people of western New Guinea, group and individual masculinity resided in success in head-hunting. Though the immediate motive for a head-taking raid might be revenge for some previous killing, raid or slight, heads brought spiritual force to the community and were needed for the rituals of male initiation.

Rituals and difference

Though men frequently relied on women's labor and occupied most public positions, it is difficult to generalize about the status of Melanesian women. In the Trobriand Islands, in the north of the *kula* area, items such as skirts and banana leaf bundles are considered part of women's wealth and were given away in mortuary ceremonies in which women compete with each other for prestige. Husbands are expected to assist in assembling the wealth needed for these presentations. But in many Melanesian societies the relations

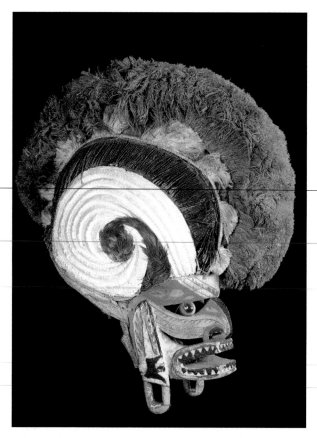

Left This *tanua* or *tatanua* mask, representing an ancestor, is one of the elaborate painted woodcarvings used in the *malanggan* ceremonies of New Ireland, in the Bismarck Archipelago of Papua New Guinea. *Malanggan* feasts honored the ancestors who would lead away the spirits of the more recent dead. The initiation of boys would sometimes take place at the same time. The design of each *malanggan* mask was the property of the carver who made it, and the particular combination of elements could not be reproduced by members of other families.

Above This carved stopper would have been placed in one end of a transverse flute from the eastern Sepik region of Papua New Guinea. Sacred flutes were commonly played in pairs by initiated men and were kept from the sight of women.

Left A New Guinea house-door is decorated with the "x-ray" drawing of a pregnant woman. While children are valued in their own right and as new members of kin groups, some Melanesian societies regard the process of childbirth as potentially polluting. Women only attend and there may be a separate birthing hut.

Above Large upright slit-drums or *tam tam* are characteristic of central and southern Vanuatu, particularly the islands of Ambrym and Malekula. They were used for signalling as well as to accompany ceremonial songs and dances. Drums of the kind seen here might be grouped on a dancing ground connected with the ceremonial of a graded society. Each time a man progressed to a new grade a tree-fern sculpture was placed beside the dancing area, its form reflecting that grade. The carving on the drums sometimes echoed those of the sculptures.

between men and women were ritually regulated in the belief that women polluted masculine power and should not be allowed to come into contact with things that were sacred. Amongst the Kwara'ae of the Solomon Islands, women were regarded as being especially polluting during menstruation and childbirth, and at these times were expected to stay in a special house outside and downhill from the main settlement. Because they were not supposed, at any time, to pass above men or sacred things, they had to remain downhill from the houses where men met or ancestral relics were stored, and they could not step over a man or bathe upstream from one.

Separate men's houses where sacred objects such as spirit masks were kept and where initiated men talked, worked and slept were common in Melanesia. Initiation often involved becoming familiar with ritual secrets and objects like the sacred flutes of northeastern New Guinea – long bamboo flutes arranged in pairs with a longer male and shorter female; women and children are told that their sounds are the voices of spirits. In some groups there were graded men's clubs or societies: individuals progressed through the different grades by undergoing a series of initiations and gathering further secret knowledge at each stage. On South Pentecost in Vanuatu, for example, men moved up through the successive grades of the *warsangul* by making payments and sacrifices, and by taking part in ever more complex rituals; there were ten such grades in recent times, and each was harder to enter than the previous one. This male society was paralleled by a women's society of three basic grades.

Ritual was the focus for much artistic creation. Cult houses were often elaborately decorated. Among the Abelam of New Guinea's Sepik region, the high fronts of the houses connected to their *tambaran* cult were covered with paintings of the spirits linked to their clans. Masks, costumes, slit gongs and other instruments all had their ritual roles in music and dance performances. The destruction and recreation of ritual objects was not unusual during such performances – for example, the complex carvings of the *malanggan* ceremonies of New Ireland were created again for each new celebration, and the designs were owned by individuals. While it is possible to trace affinities in artistic styles across language groups to characterize a whole island or subregion such as the middle Sepik, which is distinguished by its dynamic inventiveness and its vigorous use of different materials such as wood, plaited rattan and decorated barkcloth, many styles were highly localized – yet another reflection of the cultural diversity of Melanesia.

Kinship groups of Micronesia

In Micronesia, social organization differed yet again from either Polynesia or Melanesia. Here local land-holding groups were often based on kinship traced through the female line, which in turn were part of a wider grouping, the matriclan. Marriage would take place between members of different matriclans. The early society of the Yap Islands may have been like this, but it evolved into a system in which men remained in possession of a landed estate, passing it on to their sons, but clan membership was determined by descent in the female line. Since marriage took place outside the matriclan, a man's sons did not belong to his own clan but to that of his wife; as a result, landed estates regularly passed between matriclans.

Traditional Pacific Building Styles

The cultural diversity of the Pacific is reflected in the architectural variety to be found in the region. It is to be expected that different forms of social organization and different aspects of social life lead to different types of building. These range from meeting houses for whole communities to houses built for individual chiefs, small family dwellings or larger houses shared by unmarried men, or even by all the families of a village, as among the Kiwai of Papua. In one social setting the importance of the cult house may be reflected in its distinctive architecture, in another a yam store may become an elaborate structure. There are also more basic differences of building style. Even within one cultural group there can be variations. A study of the Mountain Arapesh of Papua New Guinea in the 1930s suggested that at that time they had seven distinct house styles.

Yet there are widespread parallels in the kinds of materials used in traditional building, in techniques, and in the ways the builders responded to their island environments. Substantial construction with stone is rare, more likely to be used in a ceremonial context rather than domestically – as in the ceremonial center of Nan Madol in Pohnpei or in the dancing grounds of the Marquesas Islands. The large standing *latte* stones of the Marianas were the supports for houses of importance. More modest stone-faced house platforms are to be found in some parts of Polynesia such as the Cook Islands and the Marquesas. Nonetheless, timber and thatch, lashed with plant materials, are the basic components of almost all traditional Pacific building. One common form is a rectangular house with a ridgepole carried by two or more posts, with

rafters running down from it to horizontal members supported by the wall posts. Horizontal laths bound to the rafters provide points of attachment for the thatch, often made of palm or pandanus leaves. The building of houses on piles is not uncommon in parts of Melanesia. This provides protection in areas that are prone to flooding and allows houses to be built over shallow water. For building on dry land it has other advantages, including the creation of a sheltered area below, and better ventilation. The two or three level pile-built houses of the Mekeo (Papua New Guinea) provide an upper closed sleeping area and an airy lower level for use in the daytime. On many of the tropical islands ventilation is provided by building open-sided structures, either direct onto the ground or raised on platforms.

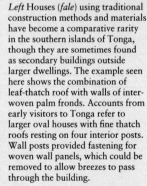

Below Members of a Gilbertese community sit in a modern version of the *maneaba*, the large open-sided thatched meeting house that has for centuries provided a focus for the social lives of villages in Kiribati. While still a building in which various conventions of respect are applied, the ceremonial rules that once guided all activity in the *maneaba* have faded, in part with changes in religious belief. Traditionally the *maneaba* was a structure charged with symbolism and itself due respect. The completion of such houses by the covering of the ridgepole was surrounded by ritual. In some areas the breaking of the thatching awl was taken as a sign of approaching misfortune. For anyone to strike any of the stone studs on which the edges of the roof rested was seen as a grave offense. Different kin groups had their own specific sitting area within the *maneaba*.

Some estates carried higher status than others. From the point of view of the clan, therefore, it was desirable that female members should marry into higher-status estates; a Yapese saying held that women were like canoe navigators seeking out lands for their clans, while men were like the stone moorings to which the canoes were secured. Young women were considered ritually impure but with childbirth and age they became gradually purer and more powerful, so that older women had a substantial say in the affairs of the estate. But even in Micronesia's more strictly matrilineal systems, which gave women considerable influence in group affairs, lineage and clan leaders were customarily male.

At the opposite end of Micronesia, in Kiribati, the kin groupings of the Gilbertese were rather more like those of Polynesia. Descent was traced through both male and female lines, and rights to the lands of a particular hamlet could come through either; however, people generally preferred to live on the lands of their father's family. Land rights were linked with rights to occupy particular traditional seating places in the *maneaba* – the Gilbertese' distinctive large, open-sided rectangular meeting houses with high thatched roofs. The southern Gilbert Islands (southern Tungaru) was divided into different *maneaba* districts, and the *maneaba* system was the basis of political authority. The different landholding kin groups were represented within the meeting houses by elders who discussed community affairs and tried to resolve internal conflicts by consensus between themselves. The *maneaba* was also the center of other community activity including feasting and ceremonial.

In contrast to the relative equality of the south, northern Kiribati had a system of social ranking in which chiefs and nobles exercised authority over those of lower status. In some areas paramount chiefs arose out of competitions for power. An invasion of the more northerly islands from the south, probably during the 17th century, introduced the *maneaba* system into most of the northern Gilbert Islands, but the chiefly traditions of the north continued, and struggles for power and land carried on there into the 19th century. Inter-island warfare seems to have been common in the central islands of the group, and it appears that the *maneaba* system was more successful at settling differences within districts than at resolving conflicts between them. Many examples still exist of the remarkable suits of armor, made of coconut fiber, that the warring Gilbertese wore to protect themselves against fearsome weapons edged with shark's teeth.

Inherited chieftaincy was the most common pattern of leadership in Micronesia, with complex systems of ranking developing on the larger islands such as Palau, Yap and Pohnpei. Pohnpei saw the rise of the Saudeleur dynasty of chiefs, who attempted to control the island from their stone-built complex of Nan Madol until it was conquered by an invasion from Kosrae. At a later date Pohnpei was divided into five distinct districts, each of which had two parallel lines of ranked titles descending through matriclans. At the head of one of these was the paramount chief, the *Nanmariki*. His person was sacred, and all behavior toward him had to reflect this. At the head of the other line was the *Naniken*, the adviser and spokesman for the paramount chief, who had charge of daily affairs. This development parallels to some extent the separation of ritual and practical power to be found in parts of Polynesia.

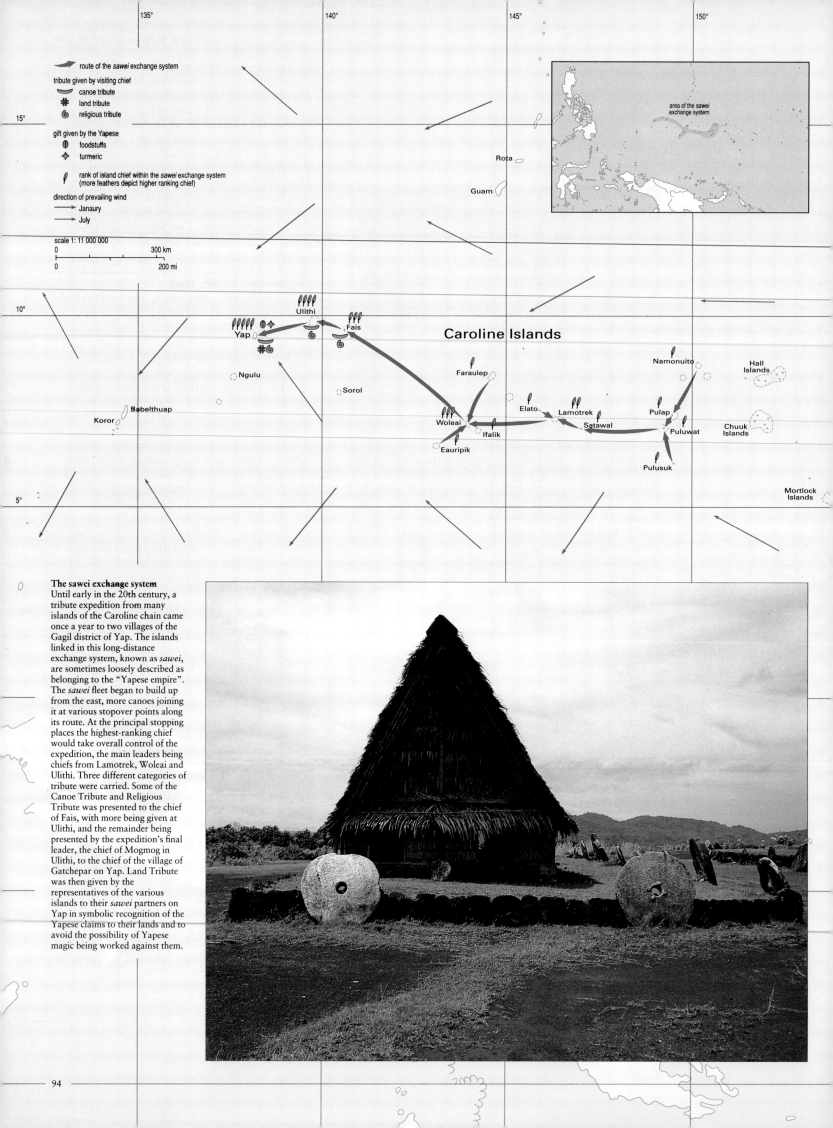

Map labels

- route of the *sawei* exchange system
- tribute given by visiting chief
  - canoe tribute
  - land tribute
  - religious tribute
- gift given by the Yapese
  - foodstuffs
  - turmeric
- rank of island chief within the *sawei* exchange system (more feathers depict higher ranking chief)
- direction of prevailing wind
  - January
  - July

scale 1: 11 000 000

0   300 km
0   200 mi

area of the *sawei* exchange system

Rota

Guam

Caroline Islands

Ulithi

Yap   Fais

Namonuito   Hall Islands

Ngulu   Faraulep

Sorol

Elato   Lamotrek   Pulap

Babelthuap   Woleai   Satawal   Puluwat   Chuuk Islands

Koror   Ifalik

Eauripik   Pulusuk

Mortlock Islands

The sawei exchange system

Until early in the 20th century, a tribute expedition from many islands of the Caroline chain came once a year to two villages of the Gagil district of Yap. The islands linked in this long-distance exchange system, known as *sawei*, are sometimes loosely described as belonging to the "Yapese empire". The *sawei* fleet began to build up from the east, more canoes joining it at various stopover points along its route. At the principal stopping places the highest-ranking chief would take overall control of the expedition, the main leaders being chiefs from Lamotrek, Woleai and Ulithi. Three different categories of tribute were carried. Some of the Canoe Tribute and Religious Tribute was presented to the chief of Fais, with more being given at Ulithi, and the remainder being presented by the expedition's final leader, the chief of Mogmog in Ulithi, to the chief of the village of Gatchepar on Yap. Land Tribute was then given by the representatives of the various islands to their *sawei* partners on Yap in symbolic recognition of the Yapese claims to their lands and to avoid the possibility of Yapese magic being worked against them.

Above The bead money of Palau contains pieces of glass and ceramic beads. The original provenance of these fragments remains open to question, but they hint at links into Micronesia from Asia and may even have been passed along the traderoutes that crisscrossed the ancient world from Rome to China.

Below left Pieces of Yapese stone money, or *fae*, rest against the platform of a house. All but the very largest disks could be carried by putting a pole through the central hole. But the *fae* usually remained on clan estates, perhaps standing round or lining the paths to men's houses – symbols of wealth and prestige. While the argonite stone for the *fae* was transported by canoe from Palau over the course of several centuries, some of the largest disks may have been brought to Yap in the late 19th century by an adventurer called O'Keefe who used them to trade coconuts.

Overleaf A dancer from the Asaro valley in the Eastern Highlands of Papua New Guinea removes his mud mask. The pale gray color of the clay from which these masks are made, and which coats the bodies of the so-called mudmen, is associated with death and with the world of spirits. The role of the mudmen traditionally was to protect other dancers, to raise the morale of local warriors and to frighten enemies.

Exchange and tribute

While Micronesia resembled Polynesia in its emphasis on inherited rank, it was nearer to Melanesia in the opportunities it provided for status competition. For an individual to take possession of a chiefdom in Pohnpei, he had not only to be a member of the correct clan, but also had to demonstrate his wealth and resources. Usually this was done at feasts, when the individual, or his kin-group, had to produce large quantities of high-quality foods and other goods for ceremonial exchange. In more extreme cases status and power were gained through warfare. Sometimes competition involved the manipulation of particular valuables. This seems to have been the case in the islands of Palau, where wealth included a form of bead "money", which incorporated glass and ceramic fragments such as glass beads and segments of bracelets. These were not of local manufacture – it has been suggested that the glass pieces came from the Philippines, but their ultimate origin may lie as far away as China or the Roman empire. The most spectacular of such exchange valuables were the large stone disks, some as much as four meters in diameter, known as *fae*, which were used on Yap as money in exchanges connected with marriage. They were given by the woman's side to the man's side, who presented shell money in return. The stone from which these disks were made came from quarries in the islands of the Palau group, from where it had to be brought by canoe, a journey of 250 kilometers.

As in Melanesia, networks of exchange linked particular groups of islands. At the most local level, different islets of the same atoll might arrange to share out temporary surpluses of food, but the Micronesians – every bit as skilled in canoe-building and navigation as the Polynesians – also operated exchange systems across wide expanses of ocean. In the central Caroline Islands, for example, a local network of exchange linked the islands of Lamotrek, Elato and Satawal: the chief of Lamotrek received tribute of coconuts, breadfruit and sea turtles from the others, granting them in return the right to use the resources of certain smaller islands and reefs claimed by Lamotrek, as well as the promise of assistance during periods of food shortage. But a much wider exchange system known as the

sawei also linked many of the atolls, some as many as 1,100 kilometers away, to particular villages on Yap, on the western edge of the network. Once a year each of the outer islands would assemble a fleet of canoes to carry tribute offerings of woven mats and skirts, shell valuables, coconut oil and sennit twine (coconut fiber twine valued in the construction of buildings and canoes) to Yap. The tribute-bringers would stay with their *sawei* partners and, on their departure, would receive from them exchange gifts of goods in short supply on the atolls, such as turmeric, flint, wood for canoes and items of food. The high-ranking Yapese involved in this system saw their relation with the outer islanders as being symbolic of the relation between fathers and children, with the children enjoying the use of their fathers' land.

Beyond the idea of tribute, both the local and the more wide-ranging networks of exchange in the Caroline Islands brought large numbers of small, scattered islands voluntarily together within a single economic system, facilitating the movement of materials and foodstuffs between them and making their perilous subsistence economies less vulnerable to climatic disasters such as typhoons. In the western (Ralik) chain of the Marshall Islands, greater political force seems to have been involved in establishing a system of wealth and food-surplus accumulation. There, the paramount chief and his retainers made regular tribute-gathering voyages to subject islands. It has been suggested that the redistribution of these resources may have helped to offset food shortages caused by periods of drought or storm damage.

These patterns of tribute and exchange hint at the development of local craft specializations in some of the islands, and certainly there was considerable diversity in craft skills within Micronesia. In a number of areas canoe technology was sophisticated: some 12 different canoe types are recorded from Woleai in the Caroline Islands, each of them adapted to a specific purpose: one for ceremonial, two for travel on open ocean, two for ocean fishing, two for lagoon fishing; the rest types of paddling canoe. Distinctive styles of decoration – sometimes, for example, the prows were elaborately carved with intricate designs – made it possible to identify the place of origin of particular canoes. Palau was noted for producing wooden objects such as bowls and boxes decorated with shell-inlay work. On Pohnpei and Kosrae fabrics were woven from the fibers of banana and hibiscus plants. Body decoration in the form of sophisticated tattooing was found in the Caroline and Marshall Islands.

Micronesia thus adds its own distinctive dimensions to the cultural wealth of the Pacific region. Scattered throughout the vast ocean were island societies rich in traditions stretching back to founding ancestors or mythical origins. The sense of continuity derived from these connections with the ancestral past was greatly valued, but this was never a world of static cultural development. All the island societies were subject to processes of change as they colonized and adapted to new lands and environments, evolved new systems of food production, established economic and political contacts with neighboring groups, experienced population growth and internal social development. These diverse island cultures were soon to be subjected to the cumulative impact of European contact as, from the beginning of the 16th century, sailors from the other side of the world showed increasing interest in the peoples and places of the Pacific.

PART THREE
POST-EUROPEAN CONTACT

THE PACIFIC AND THE
EUROPEAN IMAGINATION

Beyond the gaze of God

Even before their first frail ships ventured beyond the realms of the "known world" into the Pacific, Europeans had long speculated about a mythical southern continent. When eventually they did reach the Pacific, their perceptions were colored by these accounts. Because Europeans came to predominate over the indigenous inhabitants of Australia, New Zealand and the Pacific, their myths have created arguably the most enduring images of the region and its peoples. And in the settler societies of Australia and New Zealand, where people of European origin came to dominate numerically as well as politically, their stories of exploration, conquest and pioneering form the standards of literature, history and art.

These imaginative reconstructions of the Pacific have their roots deep in European culture and history. For the ancient peoples of the Mediterranean, the world consisted of three landmasses: Europe, Asia and Africa. Greek and Roman geographers reasoned that

the world was round, and that the landmasses of the north must be balanced by equally massive lands in the south. As early as the 5th century BC, the Greek historian Herodotus recorded in his *Histories* a story that had been told him by a sailor. "The Egyptian king Necho . . . sent out a fleet manned by a Phoenician crew with orders to sail westabouts and return to Egypt and the Mediterranean by way of the Straits of Gibraltar . . . The Phoenicians sailed from the Arabian Gulf into the southern ocean, and every autumn put in at some convenient spot of the . . . coast, sowed a patch of ground, and waited for the next year's harvest." Restocking with provisions for the journey in this manner, the Phoenicians sailed on for two years. In the third year they reentered the Mediterranean, passing through the Pillars of Hercules (the Strait of Gibraltar). Herodotus recorded that as the Phoenicians sailed west, "they had the sun on their right to northward of them". This strongly hints at the story's authenticity, for it is a detail sailors are unlikely to

Spanish exploration of the Pacific
The Spanish were the first European sailors to explore the Pacific. Magellan, sailing under the Spanish flag, entered the Pacific from the Atlantic through the Strait of Magellan in 1520 with the intention of finding a westward route to the Spice Islands (Indonesia). He managed to bypass all the main island groups except Guam before reaching the Philippines, but his pioneering voyage established the ocean's extent. Later expeditions went in search of the fabled land of Ophir, site of King Solomon's mines (which gave their name to the Solomon Islands), and the other supposed riches of the south. Torres was the first to confirm that New Guinea was an island by passing through the strait that separates it from Australia in 1606.

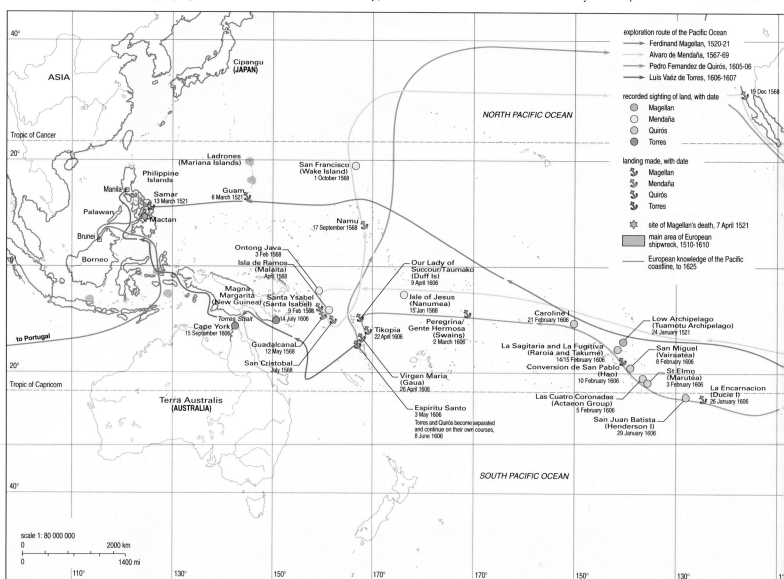

have invented and shows that the Phoenicians must have crossed the Equator and circumnavigated Africa.

The Phoenicians' epic voyage thus raised the possibility that the world was round, and that unknown land lay in its southern hemisphere. Herodotus did not believe the story himself. Others were not so skeptical. Plato and Aristotle entertained the possibility of a southern land, but it was the astronomer, mathematician and geographer Ptolemy, working in Alexandria in the mid 2nd century AD, who became the best-known classical proponent of the theory. He argued that it stood to reason that a great south land existed, so that the world was balanced both sides of the Equator. Ptolemy's maps show the *Indicus Oceanus* (Indian Ocean) surrounded by a great land that stretched fully east to west from approximately 10 degrees south of the Equator.

The Arabs, Chinese and Indians also calculated that the world was round, and that unknown lands lay to the south. The Venetian traveler Marco Polo (1254–1324) brought back from his journey into China fabulous stories of a vast southern continent of extraordinary wealth. But the notion that people resided in an unknown hemisphere, away from the gaze of God, was too much for medieval churchmen. Christianity proved implacably hostile to geographical and astronomical investigation, and the European mind resorted to believing that the earth was flat. Nothing of any consequence could exist beyond what God had already revealed about his creation – and if it did, it could only be a terrestrial purgatory inhabited by ungodly creatures beyond the great fires that were believed to burn on the Equator.

Ways into the Pacific

The expansion of Europe into the Pacific is often seen as part of the process of the enlightenment by which reason overcame superstition. For men to sail beyond the limits of the certain world required not only individual strength of character, but scientific and technological knowledge. The development of the compass and other navigational aids, together with improvements in shipbuilding, especially sail-rigging, gave European sailors the confidence to venture into unknown waters. They began to navigate their way through a maze of intellectual and theological doubts into those regions that had previously existed only in the imagination of eccentric and heretical men, madmen and blasphemers, voyaging out from Europe in the name of God, monarchs and commerce, with a new sense of destiny and fired by missionary zeal. Whole new worlds awaited to be discovered, to be "civilized" and exploited.

In 1492 Christopher Columbus crossed the Atlantic to "discover" the Americas in the belief that he had sailed to India and Japan. In correcting the error, he made a second mistake by thinking that the Indian Ocean lapped the southwestern seaboard of the Americas and that Asia was connected to the Americas in the north. Before their own riches were known, the Americas were seen as a barrier to the wealth of the Far East and the imagined riches of the great south land. In 1513 the Spaniard Vasco Nuñez de Balboa crossed the Isthmus of Panama to become the first European to sight the Pacific, though he had no notion that what he was observing was the world's greatest ocean. Convinced that a western passage could be found to the Pacific, and thus to the riches of Asia, the Portuguese navigator Ferdinand Magellan (c.

1480–1521) persuaded the Spanish king, the emperor Charles V, to fit out an expedition. In September 1519 Magellan sailed westward across the Atlantic with five ships under his command and entered the Pacific through the strait that separates the southern tip of South America from the island of Tierra del Fuego, which now bears his name. As Magellan entered the ocean, its deceptive calm led him to name it the Pacific.

Like Columbus, Magellan believed that the world was very much smaller than it actually is; had he even an inkling of the extent of the Pacific, he would probably not have attempted the crossing. European ships of the 16th century, although a significant advance on those that preceded them, were not designed to cross the world's largest ocean, and could carry only a minimum of provisions. Most of Magellan's crew starved: the survivors lived off sawdust and rats. In the course of this terrible journey they landed at Guam in the Marianas, and the Philippines, where Magellan was killed by islanders. The expedition's one surviving ship limped back to Spain in September 1522, having circumnavigated the globe.

Terra australis incognita

The possibility of an unknown land of vast riches in the south – *terra australis incognita* – burned deep in the European imagination. In 1567 the Spanish viceroy of Peru fitted out Alvaro de Mendaña de Neira with two ships to search for this mythical place. The first Spaniard to venture into the South Pacific, he eventually stumbled upon the Solomon Islands. Believing he had found the great south land, he stayed there for six months, visiting the islands of Guadalcanal, San Cristobal and Malaita, before returning home. It took nearly 30 years of petitioning the Spanish court before he was able to mount a second expedition in 1595, but his charts from the first were so inaccurate that he landed this time in the Marquesas. Despite the vast distance between the two island chains, he believed he had reached his original landfall. Mendaña was killed by islanders, and the survivors made their way back to Peru via the Philippines.

Undaunted by this failure, the pilot on Mendaña's second voyage, Pedro Fernández de Quirós (1560–1614) returned to the South Pacific in 1605. After passing through the Tuamotu Archipelago and continuing westward he reached an island that, thinking he had struck the eastern shore of the great south land, he called Austrialia de Espiritu Santo (today shortened to Espiritu Santo, the main island of Vanuatu). Mutiny among his crew and conflict with the islanders soon forced him to retreat, but even as late as the early 20th century some Roman Catholic histories credited de Quirós with the discovery of Australia. De Quirós's ship became separated from the rest of his fleet and returned to Acapulco. Luis Vaéz de Torres took command of the of the other two ships, which went on to sail through the strait that is named after him, between New Guinea and the northern tip of Cape York Peninsula on the Australian mainland, thereby proving that New Guinea is an island. However, the Spanish kept the news of the discovery a secret, and no one was to follow Vaéz de Torres through the strait until Captain Cook did so in 1770.

Earlier in 1606, the Dutchman Willem Jansz (c.1570–c.1629) sailed the *Duyfken* from the Dutch trading settlement at Batavia (present-day Jakarta) in the Spice Islands (Indonesia) to explore the southern coastline of New Guinea. He reached the Torres Strait

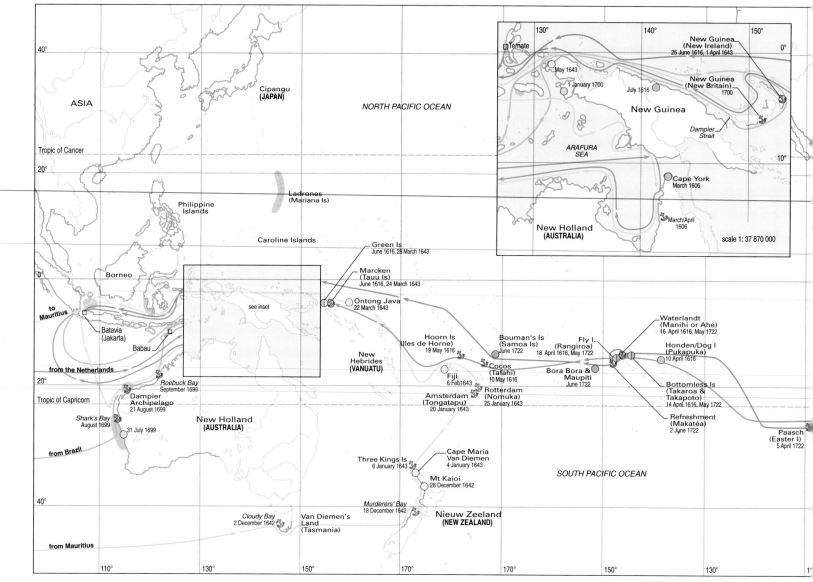

but did not enter it, instead turning south to reach the northern coast of Cape York Peninsula on the Australian mainland, which he followed south, penetrating far into the Gulf of Carpentaria. His charts, however, show that he thought the peninsula was attached to New Guinea. Ten years later his compatriot Dirk Hartog arrived by accident on the west coast of Australia, having sailed too far south of the Cape of Good Hope on his way from the Netherlands to Batavia. He and his men came ashore at what is now Dirk Hartog Island, and left a pewter plate inscribed with the name of their ship and its officers.

The Dutch were now taking the lead in exploring the South Pacific in search of the fabled southern land. In 1615 Willem Cornelisz Schouten and Isaac Le Maire had rounded Cape Horn for the first time and crossed the Pacific, discovering the northern outliers of the Tonga Islands, Futuna and Alofi (which they called the Hoorn Islands) and some of the New Guinea islands. In 1626–27 Pieter Nuyts explored almost 1,600 kilometers of the southern coast of the landmass discovered by Jansz (which the Dutch were now calling New Holland), and other Dutch mariners added to knowledge of its north and west coasts. Most important was the voyage of Abel Tasman (?1603–?59) who in 1642 was dispatched by the Dutch governor-general at Batavia, Anthony van Diemen, to find the southern continent. Sailing from the west, Tasman passed to the south of Australia until he came to the

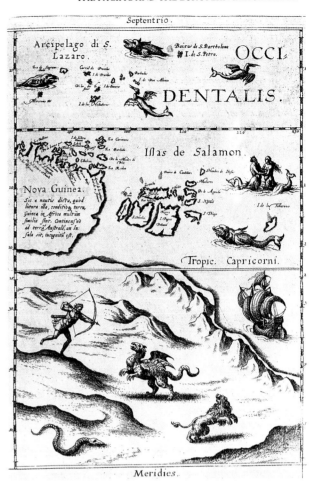

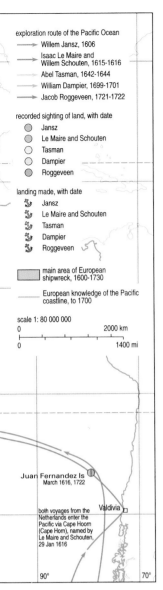

island that now bears his name, Tasmania, but which he called after van Diemen. Tasman continued east, becoming the first European to sight New Zealand – named after a province in the Netherlands – and gave his name to the sea that separates it from Australia. He sailed on to Tonga and Fiji before returning via New Guinea to Batavia.

The coastal wastes of New Holland described by the Dutch mariners were so unpromising that people refused to believe that they could belong to the fabled southern continent. Indeed, by the mid 17th century some doubters were beginning to question its very existence. "The country being so large, so free from the incumbrances of frosts and ice, and endless winters," wrote one English skeptic in 1670, "I have oft marvelled with myself that no further progress has been made in discovery of it." Yet explorers, scholars and artists simply refused to give up the idea of a great wealthy land in the south. "It is clearly known, that the two continents, the land which lies on the north-side [of the Equator]" reported Peter Heylyn's *Cosmography* (1657) "is four times at least as large as that which lies south thereof; and therefore since the earth is equally poised on both sides of the center, it must needs be that the earth is in answerable measure and proportion must advance itself some places above the sea, on the southside of the line, as it does in others of the north." However, the reports of the English explorer and former buccaneer William Dampier (1651–1715), who visited New Holland's northern coast in 1688 and returned again in 1699 to explore its western coast, were so unfavorable that no other

The Dutch in the Pacific
Exploration of the Pacific in the 17th century belonged to the Dutch. It was from Batavia, the main trading post of the powerful Dutch East India Company, that Tasman sailed on his great voyage of 1642–44. The English explorer William Dampier surveyed the western coast of Australia in 1699.

Top right Cartographers in the 16th century were able to map the Solomon Islands and the north coast of New Guinea with some degree of accuracy. But though de Jode's atlas of 1593 shows New Guinea as an island, its south coast and the great southern continent below it are figments of the map-maker's imagination.

Right Hessel Gerritsz was the official cartographer to the Dutch East Indies Company. His 1622 chart of the Pacific, of which this is a detail, added to earlier Spanish discoveries new information gleaned from the recent voyages of Jansz, Hartog, Schouten and Le Maire, described in the document's extended captions.

Left In 1697 Willem de Vlamingh replaced the original pewter plate that Dirk Hartog left in 1616 to mark his landing on an island off the west coast of Australia with this one, now in the National Library of Australia.

Mapping the Great South Land

Centuries before Europeans investigated the southern hemisphere they had constructed elaborate images of worlds beyond their own. Maps dating back to the geographer Ptolemy around 150 AD depicted a vast southern continent to balance the landmass of Europe and Asia in the northern hemisphere. On medieval maps, which were drawn to show Jerusalem at the center of the world, the lands beyond its known boundaries were peopled with demons and other fantastic beings.

After Christopher Columbus, searching for a western passage to China, opened up the Americas to European exploration, rumors of a fabled city or country of gold, El Dorado, began to take hold on the European imagination. The idea of an unknown southern continent, *terra australis incognita*, persisted in European minds, and when El Dorado was found not to lie in South America, it was popularly believed that its riches were contained within the great south land instead. In 1520 Ferdinand Magellan rounded the southern tip of South America to enter the vast

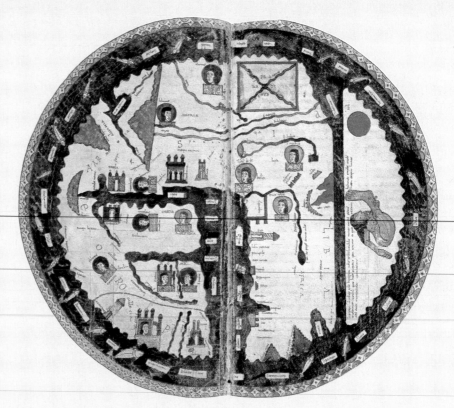

Above This world map of the early 13th century shows Asia, Europe and Africa joined to each other around the Mediterranean Sea. Asia occupies the upper half, Europe the lower left quarter and Africa the lower right quarter. Africa ends at Libya and beyond it, separated by a narrow tract of water, lies a fourth continent. The legend on it reads: "The fourth continent is unknown to us and uninhabitable on account of the blaze of the sun. There sciapodes are alleged to live, one-legged beings of incredible speed, who…lie on their backs in the shade of their enormous foot."

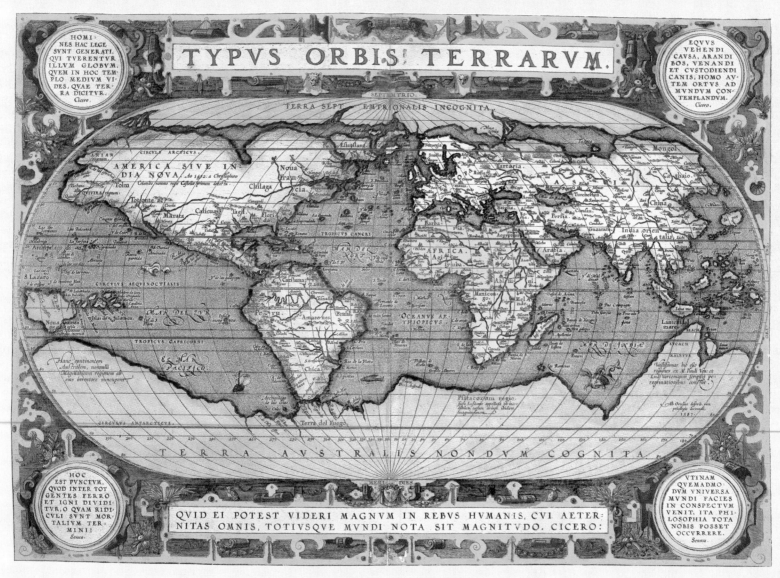

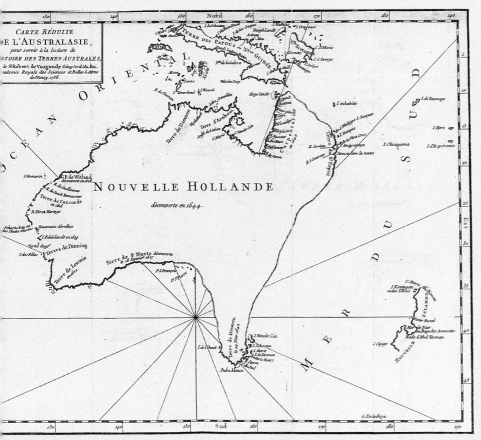

expanse of the Pacific Ocean. But he and subsequent voyagers failed to discover any sign of the southern continent. It was only when Dutch traders to the East Indies, hoping to complete their voyages from Europe faster, sailed southward from the Cape of Good Hope to pick up the prevailing westerlies of the lower latitudes that a coastline of any extent was discovered in the southern seas.

The Dutch gave the barren and monotonous land their mariners visited the name of New Holland. In this guise Australia now found its way on to European maps, but few believed that it was part of the fabulous southern continent of popular imagination. Tasmania (Van Diemen's Land) was charted by Tasman, but the final piece in the jigsaw did not fall into place until James Cook sailed along the entire length of Australia's eastern seaboard in 1770. His subsequent expeditions in the Pacific confirmed that no other southern continent, with the exception of Antarctica, existed. The myth of the great south land of untold riches was finally laid to rest.

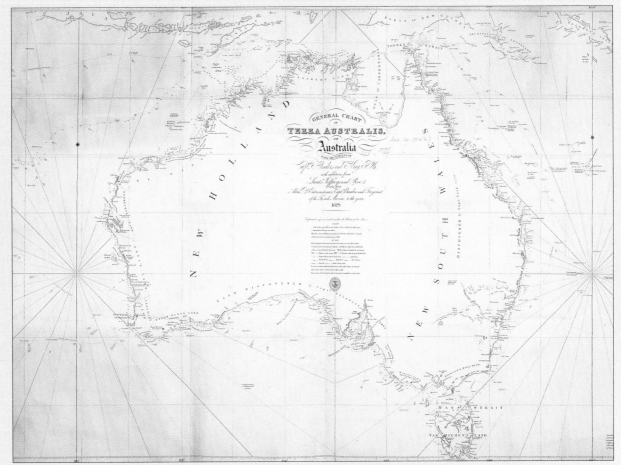

Left In 1570 Abraham Ortelius, a Dutch cartographer, produced what some have called the first modern atlas. In the lower part of his world map, illustrated here, he has depicted a vast landmass with the legend: TERRA AVSTRALIS NONDVM COGNITA (the southern land not yet discovered). Tierra del Fuego, south of the Straits of Magellan, is shown as part of this landmass, but New Guinea (on the extreme left edge of the map) is an island, though the cartographer notes "Whether [it] is an island or part of the southern continent remains uncertain". Though Luís Vaéz de Torres was to sail through the dangerous waters of the straits that separate Australia and New Guinea, and which now bear his name, in 1606, his exploit remained unpublicized and European map-makers would remain in doubt as to whether or not New Guinea was an island until Captain Cook sailed through the strait in *Endeavour* more than 150 years later.

Above By the mid 17th century Dutch mariners had charted large sections of the northern and western seaboards of Australia (which they called New Holland), and Tasman's voyage of 1642 had added Tasmania and part of New Zealand to European maps (Tasman himself believed that the stretch of New Zealand coast he discovered was part of the southern continent). Robert de Vaugondy's map of New Holland, published in Paris in 1756, was one of those carried by Cook on his first Pacific voyage. It incorporates all the known information about Australia at that time, but draws a hypothetical coastline between Nuyt's Land in the west and

Tasmania, and all along the eastern seaboard. De Quirós's discoveries in Vanuatu (Terre du St Esprit) have been tacked on to the northeast corner of the continent, but New Guinea is shown separated by a broad strait.

Above Australia was not circumnavigated for more than 30 years after Cook charted its eastern coast. In 1798 Matthew Flinders (1774–1814) and George Bass passed through the Bass Strait to prove that Tasmania was a separate island, and Flinders completed the

first circumnavigation of the continent between 1801 and 1803, charting large sections of the coast. The General Chart of Terra Australis or Australia (as the continent now became known), based on his surveys, was the first map to reveal its true shape.

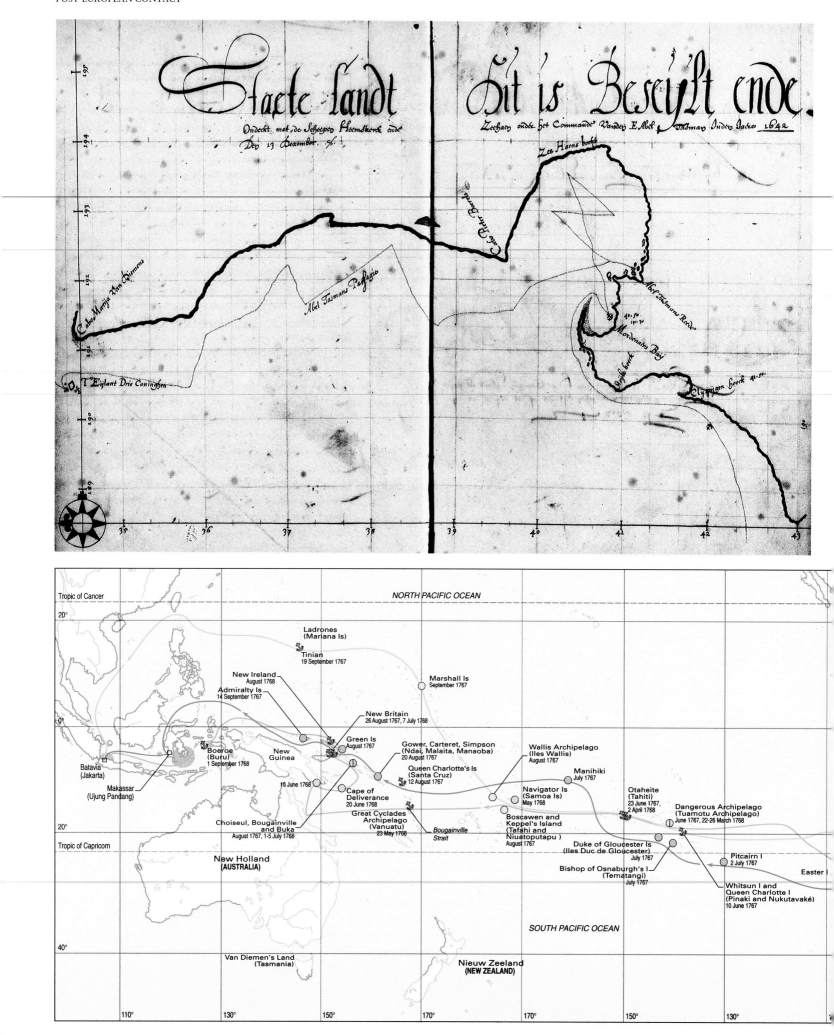

Far right William Dampier, the first Englishman to make landfall in Australia in 1688, wrote unfavorably about Australia and its inhabitants, whom he described as mere "brutes".

Left Tasman charted a considerable stretch of the coast of New Zealand (which he originally called Staten Landt). Shown here is the northern part of the South Island and the west coast of the North Island, with the track of his ship, the *Heemskerck* (north is on the right). The Dutch did not attempt to follow up Tasman's discoveries, and New Zealand remained unvisited until Cook's first voyage in 1769.

Below right This portrait by Jacob Gerritsz Cuyp of Abel Tasman with his second wife, Joanna Tiercz, and their daughter was painted c. 1640, shortly before the Dutch East India Company commissioned him to search for the southern continent.

18th-century explorers before Cook
Naval competition between the French and the British in the 18th century reached its height in the Seven Years' War (1756–63). It gave both access to better and faster ships and to improved methods of navigation. In the uneasy peace that followed, British and French became involved in a race for influence in the South Pacific, the last part of the globe to remain unexplored. Wallis and Carteret's expedition was undertaken by the British with the specific aim of finding the southern continent. Hard on their heels was the French navigator Bougainville, the most famous of Cook's precursors.

expeditions were sent there. Voyagers simply bypassed it altogether, traveling farther to the south and east.

By the middle of the 18th century the British and the French had become engaged in a race to outdo each other in further discoveries in the southern oceans. In 1767 a British expedition was sent to the South Pacific under the command of Captain Philip Carteret in HMS *Swallow* and Captain Samuel Wallis in HMS *Dolphin*. They separated near the Strait of Magellan, and Carteret went on to discover Pitcairn Island before crossing the Pacific to make landfall in New Britain, while Wallis became the first European to visit Tahiti in the Society Islands. Within months he had been followed there by the French navigator Louis de Bougainville (1729–1811), who spent some time on the island before sailing north along the Great Barrier Reef and concluding that land must lie not far beyond it. Almost immediately after him Captain James Cook (1728–79) came to Tahiti, sent there by the Royal Navy, ostensibly to observe the transit of the planet Venus as it made an eclipse of the sun. But he carried with him secret dispatches ordering him to confirm the existence of the southern continent and to report on its suitability for settlement.

After leaving Tahiti in June 1769, Cook sailed around New Zealand, charting the coast, before journeying on to make a detailed survey of the east coast of Australia. After 250 years of European exploration in the Pacific, Cook finally confirmed that New Holland was indeed the great south land. With the confirmation, the European dream of finding "flourishing kingdoms" in the south came to an end. Cook, however, helped ease disappointment by reporting that the southeast corner of the continent, which he called New South Wales, was at least capable of supporting a transported civilization: "The coast of this country

. . . abounds with a great number of bays and harbors," he recorded in his log in 1770. "The country itself so far as we know does not produce any one thing that can become an article of trade to invite Europeans to fix a settlement upon it. However, this eastern side is not that barren and miserable country that Dampier and others have described the western side to be."

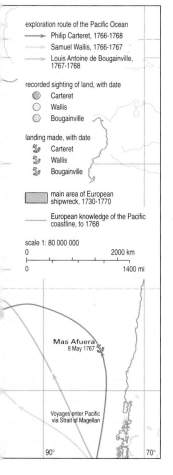

Captain James Cook

James Cook, a Yorkshireman by birth, was apprenticed into the Whitby shipping trade at the age of 18. Life on the stout coal-carrying barks of the North Sea gave him a tough training in the practical skills of seamanship and he was offered the command of a ship at the relatively young age of 27. Cook, who had begun the study of mathematics in his spare time, turned it down, preferring instead to join the Royal Navy as an able seaman. Within two years he had been made master of HMS *Pembroke*, which took him to Canada where he saw action against the French during the Seven Years' War (1756–63).

Already marked out as a man of promise, with the ending of the war Cook was engaged to make a survey of the coast of Newfoundland. In 1766 he sent details of his observations of an eclipse of the sun to the Royal Society, the premier scientific organization in Britain. When, two years later, the Society, in conjunction with the Admiralty, began arrangements for the first British scientific exploration of the Pacific, Cook, though an obscure noncommissioned officer, was appointed to head the expedition. He was created lieu-

tenant and given command of HMS *Endeavour*, a sturdy collier-bark of the kind he had been used to sailing on the North Sea. Though the ostensible purpose of the expedition was to observe the transit of Venus across the sun, Cook carried with him instructions to search for the "great south land" and to "take possession of convenient situations in the country in the name of the King of Great Britain".

The expedition reached Tahiti on 13 April 1769, nearly a full two months before the predicted eclipse on 3 June. Cook made use of the intervening time to map the islands and collect specimens of plants and animals. Once the eclipse was past he was free to turn his attention to the search for the southern continent. From Tahiti previous navigators had struck west, following the trade winds across the Pacific. Cook set a different course, sailing south and southwest. The east coast of New Zealand was sighted on 7 October, and Cook spent the next six months meticulously mapping its entire 3,860 kilometers of coastline. The expedition left New Zealand on 31 March 1770, continuing due west, and two and a half weeks later came upon the

Below Cook's skills as a maritime surveyor helped recommend him to the Lords of the Admiralty to lead the *Endeavour* expedition and it is testimony to his unrivalled surveying skills that his accurate maps of nearly 4,000 kilometers of New Zealand coastline and 5,000 kilometers of eastern Australia were made without the aid of a chronometer, without which he was unable to fix longitude accurately. The chronometer pictured here is the one that he carried on his later voyages.

Capt.ᵗ James Cook
of the Endeavour.

Left William Hodges (1744–97) was the best trained of all the artists who accompanied Cook on his voyages. In this portrait, made about 1775, the painter has captured the intensity of Cook's personality more successfully than the efforts of more fashionable portrait painters. The searching yet kindly eyes and earnest expression show him to be a man of the Enlightenment and of science, for all that he is also depicted as a brusque and practical sea captain.

Right Cook made his second and third voyages in HMS *Resolution,* Like the smaller *Endeavour,* it was a former Whitby collier-bark. These vessels, built for the often treacherous waters of the North Sea, were slow and rolled heavily, but their sturdiness made them supremely reliable at sea, and being straight-sided and flat-bottomed, they had capacious holds. Cook's second expedition was perhaps the greatest voyage ever made under sail. For three years the ship was pushed to its limits as it encountered every type of weather from the icy waters of Antarctica to the doldrums of the Equator.

Below Icebergs were met again on Cook's final voyage, this time in the Arctic. The expedition ended in tragedy when, having failed to find a north passage into the Atlantic, Cook returned to the Hawaiian islands. On Kealakekua, a violent argument broke out over the theft of a cutter. After firing on the angry islanders, Cook was clubbed and stabbed to death on the beach.

southeast coast of Australia. Turning north, and surveying as he went, Cook sailed the 5,000-kilometer length of its eastern coastline, stopping briefly to make landfall at Botany Bay. On 11 June the *Endeavour* struck a spur of the Great Barrier Reef and was forced to beach at Endeavour Bay to make repairs. Continuing around the coast, Cook sailed through the Torres Strait to reach Batavia, where 31 men – a third of the total complement – fell victim to shore fever. The remainder arrived back in England on 13 July 1771, after an absence of almost three years.

Cook made two further expeditions to the Pacific in 1772–75, and in 1776–79. On his second voyage he sailed farther south than any one before him to enter Antarctic waters and complete the first circumnavigation of Antarctica. Cook was charged on his third trip with the task of discovering whether an Arctic passage existed between the Atlantic and Pacific Oceans. Sailing north from Tahiti, he discovered the Hawaiian group, which he named the Sandwich Islands, in early 1778 and then continued northward to explore the coasts of North America and Alaska. But his search proved fruitless and he returned to Hawaii in early 1779, where he was killed in a sudden violent dispute with a group of islanders.

Left This illustration showing Vasco da Gama's men in lusty pursuit of naked nymphs on the "island of love", while cupids playfully scatter flowers over the scene, comes from an 1805 edition of Luís de Camoes' epic poem, *The Lusiads* (1570). This rich work, which celebrates the achievements of the Portuguese navigator and is enlivened by many classical allusions, set the fashion for placing paradise islands in the southern oceans. The abode of love presided over by Venus, where the pleasures of the flesh are freely available to all men, has a very long history in European literature, but came to be applied with particular fervor to the Pacific islands.

Right Pacific fantasy islands have taken many different forms in literature. *The Swiss Family Robinson*, first published in two parts in 1812–3, was described by an early critic, Charles Nodier, as "Robinson Crusoe in the bosom of his family". Recounting the story of a shipwrecked family who make their lives on their island with only a few possessions that have been washed ashore, it demonstrates the strengths of European civilization in paradise. The marooned family triumphs over adversity through honest toil, pious faith and cooperative effort.

Islands of the imagination

Alongside the myth of the great south land, the idea of the paradisiacal island had long exercised a powerful hold on the European imagination dating back at least as far as the classical Greek myths of Atlantis and Hesperides and the various island communities described in Homer's *Iliad*. In a different tradition, Celtic legends had long told of the island of Avalon. The tourist brochures of today that extol the virtues of exotic island lifestyles are their modern equivalent. One of the first literary evocations of a "dream island" in the Pacific was written by the Portuguese traveler and poet Luís de Camões (1524–80). In Camões's epic poem *The Lusiads* (1572) recounting the voyages of the great Portuguese navigator Vasco daGama, he and his crew are rewarded by Venus for their discovery of a sea route to India by being transported to a "love island" in the southern seas. In the lush forests, the men frolic with the nymphs and "all was forgotten in the ecstasy of love": in a vision, da Gama is told of a time when Europeans will cast their influence all over the vast southern ocean. Thus Camões paved the way for the European imagination to colonize the Pacific. The force of this imagination was at times quite overpowering, leaving little room for the region's indigenous populations – whether Pacific islanders or Australian Aborigines – to articulate their sense of place and belonging. For Europeans, the Pacific would represent, alternatively, paradise lost and paradise regained.

In 1719 the English author Daniel Defoe (1660–1731) published *The Life and strange surprising Adventures of Robinson Crusoe*, based on the actual experiences of Alexander Selkirk, a sailor on

one of Dampier's expeditions around the world, who was put ashore at his own request on the island of Juan Fernandez in 1704 and was rescued five years later. In Defoe's story the shipwrecked Crusoe is able to live independently of European civilization for 27 years on his "desert" island, but he does this by producing in miniature the social and economic order he has left behind. The book relates in meticulous detail how Crusoe, with the aid of a few tools and stores salvaged from the wreck of his ship, sets about building a house, growing crops and domesticating a goat. The more that Crusoe practices the virtues of perseverance, thrift and self-control, the more God rewards him. In many ways, the book is an object-lesson in how to be a successful colonizer. Indeed, after the arrival of the savage Friday and the Spaniard, Crusoe says "My island was now peopled, and I thought myself very rich in subjects, and it was a merry reflection which I frequently made, how like a king I looked. First of all, the whole country was my own mere property, so that I had an undoubted right of dominion. Secondly, my people were perfectly subjected: I was absolute lord and law-giver. . . ."

Defoe achieved enormous popularity with his story, which became a stereotype of the "desert island" adventure. Within a few years it had been translated into many European languages, and it has had many imitators over the years. Among the most popular and successful was *Swiss Family Robinson* (1812–13), by Johann Rudolf Wyss (1781–1830). This tells the story of a Swiss family marooned on an uninhabited Pacific island where they build a happy community and utilize the resources they have at their disposal, showing great fortitude in all their reversals of fortune.

The antipodes

Since classical times, the term commonly used for the people dwelling on the opposite side of the globe was the antipodes, literally meaning "having the feet opposite". In the popular imagination things there were the wrong way round and men walked upside down. The early Christian theologian and author of *The City of God*, St Augustine (354–430), debunked the idea, ridiculing "that fabulous hypothesis" that maintained that men "walk a part of the earth opposite to our own, whose feet are in a position contrary to ours, and where the sun rises when it sets with us." Nevertheless such speculations opened up immense imaginative possibilities of "topsy turvy" lands, and on medieval maps the *terra australis incognita* was peopled with exotic creatures walking on their heads, or with grotesque man-devils and other monsters. It was such notions of the antipodes that the 17th-century English poet Andrew Marvell lampooned when he wrote:

> But now the *Salmon-Fishers* moist
> Their *Leathern Boats* begin to hoist
> And like *Antipodes* in Shoes,
> Have Shod their *Heads* in their *Canoos*.

From here, it was a short step for writers who were out of sympathy with their own times to seize upon the idea of the antipodes being the antithesis of things as they were in Europe in order to criticize the existing social order. The most enduring, and the most devastating, of such critiques is *Gulliver's Travels* (1726), by the satirist Jonathan Swift (1667–1745). In Part I of the four-part book, Gulliver is marooned on Lilliput, a land of small people who are at war with their neighbors on the island of Blefuscu. The pretensions of the diminutive Lilliputians, and their arguments over whether eggs should be broken at the big or small end, are used to satirize the English political parties and religious dissensions of the day. Swift places Lilliput "to the North-West of Van Diemen's Land" at a "latitude of 30 degrees two minutes South" – in other words in present-day South Australia, almost due north of Adelaide. The setting for Part IV, the land of the Houyhnynms – horses endowed with reason who are contrasted with the Yahoos, beasts in the shape of men – is located in the Great Australian Bight south of Nuyt's Archipelago.

In the 19th century it became a popular pastime among the European middle classes to plot their particular antipodean fantasies on maps of the world, and the myth of the antipodes still lingers in the joke told to children in Europe that if they dig a tunnel through the earth they will find Australians standing on their heads. It is ironical that today the term antipodes, in the sense of being on the opposite side of the world, is used exclusively to describe Australia and New Zealand, the two Pacific societies that are closest in social and cultural formation to European society. However, the Australian poet James McAuley (1917–76) harked back to the earlier meaning of the word when, in "Terra Australis" (1946) he wrote:

> Voyage within you, on the fabled ocean,
> And you will find that Southern Continent,
> Quiros' vision – his hidalgo heart
> And mythical Australia, where reside
> All things in their imagined counterpart.

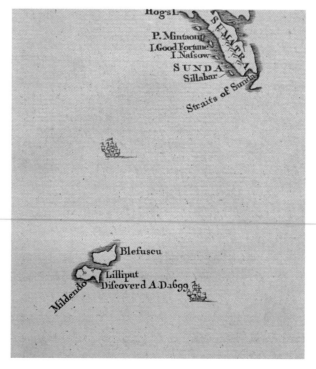

Left Like Defoe, who based *Robinson Crusoe* on the experiences of Alexander Selkirk, a shipwrecked sailor on one of Dampier's expeditions, Jonathan Swift used the published account of Dampier's voyages as the inspiration for his sustained satire *Gulliver's Travels*. Gulliver, in the first of many shipwrecks, is washed ashore on the island of Lilliput, populated by earnest but overly concerned small people who are in conflict with the inhabitants of the neighboring island of Blefescu. Precise compass references are provided for the location of the islands, which Swift places in the empty ocean between Sumatra and Van Diemen's Land. In reality, they would be situated on the Australian landmass just north of Adelaide.

Left Gulliver among the Yahoos in the land of Houyhnhnms, from an 18th-century edition of Swift's works. This episode in Gulliver's voyages opens up a dialog between reason and savagery. The Houyhnhnms (who are horses) are idealized rational creatures while the human Yahoos lack any form of civilized values. They were once civilized, but have become degraded and returned to a more rudimentary condition. Today Yahoo is a term of derision used by Australians and others for those who do not conform to polite manners and style.

Below This drawing by a Scottish convict artist, Thomas Watling (1762–??), entitled "A Groupe on the North shore of Port Jackson New South Wales", was completed in 1794, just six years after the arrival of the First Fleet in Australia. The Aboriginal family conforms to Dampier's description of rude barbarianism, being devoid of clothes and having virtually no possessions, but the delineation of the figures suggests that the artist was influenced by the romantic ideas of the 18th-century philosophers who held savagery to be the state of nature, free from the constraints and conflicts of degraded civilized society.

Brute savages

The peoples of the Pacific presented a conundrum for Christian theology. Though they were not the grotesque upside-down creatures of medieval imaginings, they did challenge European beliefs concerning the nature of God's creation and man's place within it. Classical thinkers from Aristotle onward had perceived of life as a "great chain of being", reaching upward from inanimate plants at the bottom through the various kinds of animated life-forms to man at the top. The teaching of the church, which ranked man as lesser than the angels but higher than the beasts, endorsed and elaborated this hierarchical arrangement. Yet it was difficult to accept that the primitive peoples of the Pacific, living in a state little better than the animals, unlettered, without social comforts and lacking the arts and skills of civilization, were on the same rung of the ladder as European man. The 17th-century rationalist Thomas Hobbes (1588–1679) argued that such primitiveness meant that "every man is enemy to every man". In the condition of slavery "there is no place for industry...and consequently no culture of the earth;...no knowledge of the face of the Earth; no account of time, no arts, no letters; no society." Thus, Europeans began to see the mission of colonizing as being essential to the spread of civilization, which must extinguish savagery.

Willem Jansz, the first known European to make landfall on the Australian mainland, described the Cape York Aborigines he encountered near Weipa in 1606 as the "most wretched and poorest creatures". One of his crew members was killed in a violent scuffle with some of their number, thereby foreshadowing the course that contact between Europeans and the peoples of the Pacific would all too often take in the future: mutual curiosity leading to suspicion, then to misunderstanding and finally to open hostility. William Dampier's opinion of the Australian Aborigine was no better: "The inhabitants of this country are the miserablest people in the world...[they] have no houses and skin garments, sheep, poultry and fruits of the earth...setting aside their human shape, they differ little from brutes....They have no sort of clothes, but a piece of rind of a tree tied like a girdle about their waists, and a handful of long grass, or three or four small green boughs, full of leaves, thrust under their girdle...Whether they cohabit one man to one woman, or promiscuously, I know not: but they did live in companies, 20 or 30 men, women and children together...I did not perceive that they did worship any thing. . . ."

Nearly one hundred years later Cook, too, placed the Aborigines he encountered on the east coast of Australia at the bottom of the chain of being; yet, infused with the romantic views of 18th-century Europe, he was rather more positive about their "savage conditions". "In reality", he wrote, "they are far more happier than we Europeans, being wholly unacquainted not only with the superfluous but the necessary conveniences so much sought after in Europe. . . . They live in a tranquillity which is not disturbed by the inequality of condition: the earth and the sea of their own accord furnishes them with all the things necessary for life, they covet not magnificent houses, household stuff etc....In short they seemed to set no value upon anything we gave them, nor would they ever part with anything of their own for any one article we could offer them; this in my opinion argues that they think themselves provided with all the necessaries of life and that they have not superfluities."

Scientific Exploration

The European ships that explored the Pacific in the late 18th century were little less than floating laboratories, equipped with the most up to date scientific and navigational instruments to observe the planetary movements in the southern skies, study the currents of the Pacific, take soundings of its depths, chart its islands and collect specimens of its flora and fauna. When the *Endeavour* left England in 1768 it carried on board not only Sir Joseph Banks, then aged 23 and newly elected to the Royal Society, but also the botanist Daniel Carl Solander. Born in Sweden in 1733, Solander was a pupil and colleague of Carl Linnaeus (1707–78), the preeminent natural scientist of his day, responsible for the first systematic classification of plant and animal species. Solander had been settled in England since 1760 and had formed a close association with Banks. It was the latter who proposed they should both accompany the expedition the Royal Society was sponsoring to the Pacific, and contributed £10,000 of his own money to finance it. A contemporary observed: "No people ever went to sea better fitted for the purpose of Natural History. They have got a fine library of Natural History; they have got all sorts of machines for catching and preserving insects; all kinds of nets, trawls, drags and hooks for coral fishing, they even have a curious contrivance of a telescope, by which, put into the water, you can see the bottom at a great depth." "Experimental gentlemen", as the ships' crews termed the scientists on board, were present on Cook's two subsequent voyages, and French expeditions to the Pacific were similarly well equipped for serious scientific investigation.

Right William Dampier's account of his voyage to New Holland, published in 1703, contained some of the earliest drawings of the animals of Australia seen in Europe, thereby laying the foundation for natural observation of the unique antipodean wildlife. His crude drawings and rudimentary notes ("The head and greatest part of the neck of this bird is red and therein differs from the Avosetta [Avocet] of Italy") may be compared to the detailed comments that Sydney Parkinson, one of the professional artists on the *Endeavour*, made on the back of a

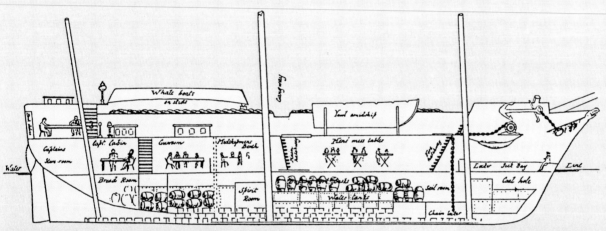

Above In 1831, when still only 22 years of age, Charles Darwin (1809–82) was chosen as the official naturalist on HMS *Beagle* as it surveyed the coastline of South America and the South Pacific; his observations on the 5-year voyage would later lead him to formulate the theory of evolution. The cramped conditions in which shipboard scientists had to work and store their specimens can be gauged from this cross-section of *Beagle* – considerably larger than either of Cook's ships.

Left An amateur who used his private wealth to support his enthusiasm for scientific investigation, Joseph Banks, painted here by Sir Joshua Reynolds, became the leading botanist of his day. He retained a lifelong interest in the Pacific and Australia, though he never revisited them after 1770.

Right Accompanying Cook as naturalists on his second voyage were the German-born Johann Reinhold Forster (1729–98) and his son George (1754–94). They lacked the flair of Banks and the credentials of Solander but nevertheless made a number of important contributions to knowledge of the Pacific.

Place this P. 123.

F.3.

A Noddy of N. Holland. P.123 & 143

F.5.

The head & greatest part of ẙ neck of this bird is red, & therein differs from the Avosetta of Italy.

A Comon Noddy. P.143

F.6.

F.4.

The Bill & Leggs of this Bird are of a Bright Red.

drawing of a tree fuchsia collected in New Zealand: "The calyx deep crimson on the inside as are also the filaments and stile, the top of which is yellow. The petals dark purple, the outside of the calyx paler and tinged with green, anthera yellow tinged with red, the upper part of the leaves dark grass green, the under part white with a cast of green and veined with green, the capsula green, the stalk gray green." Parkinson died at Batavia on the way back to England, but James Miller made this painting (*far right*) from his sketch and written description.

Above George Forster was only 18 when he made this drawing of a New Zealand tui, revealing a good eye for detail. He later went on to establish a reputation as an ornithologist. His *Voyage round the World* is one of the liveliest accounts of Cook's journeys.

Right Louis XVI personally commissioned and financed La Pérouse's voyage of 1785–88, which explored more of the Pacific, particularly its northern Asian coastline, than any previous expedition. The king is seen in this painting by Nicolas-André Monsiau issuing his instructions to La Pérouse. The last known sighting of La Pérouse's two ships was at Botany Bay in March 1788, when they were seen by members of the recently arrived First Fleet. They subsequently disappeared without trace. In 1791 D'Entrecasteaux was sent to search for La Pérouse; accompanying him was the naturalist Labillardière, a friend and correspondent of Banks. When Labillardiere's botanical collections, amounting to some 10,000 specimens, were captured by the Royal Navy, Banks arranged for their return to France – a reminder that the bonds of scientific knowledge were sometimes stronger than the enmities of war.

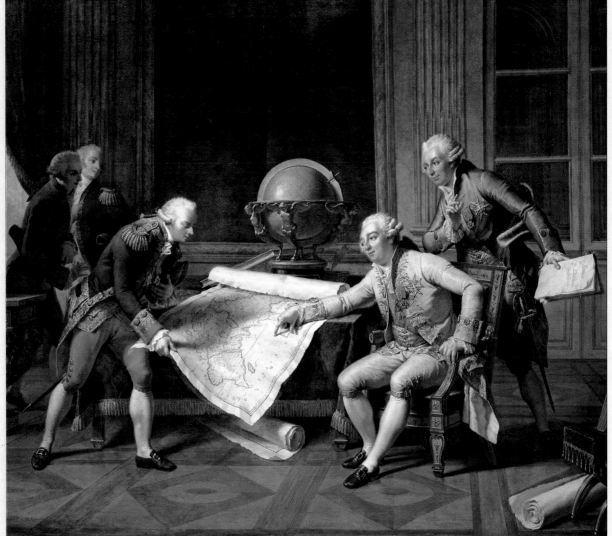

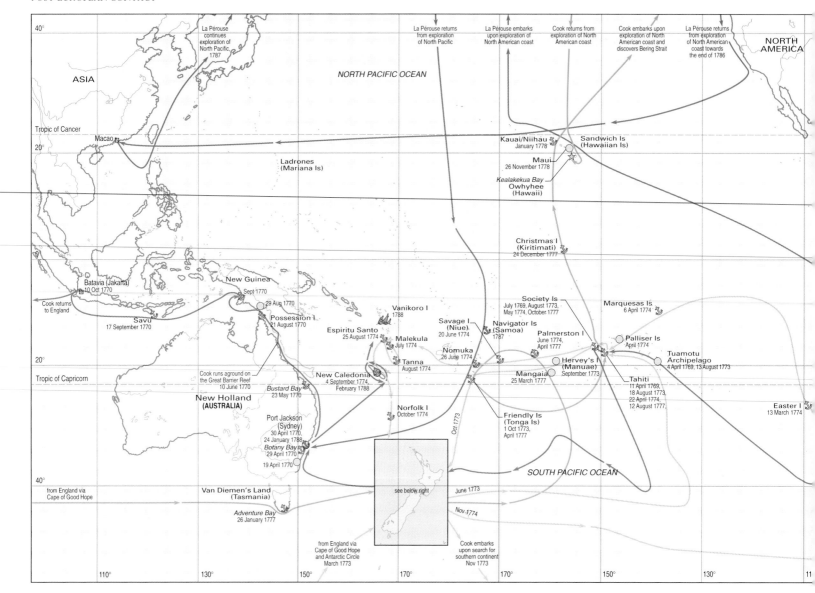

The voyages of Cook and La Pérouse

Missing links

Dampier's published accounts of his four voyages around the world which achieved enormous popularity and helped – with other travelers' tales – to fix the image of the Pacific "savage" in the European imagination. And if man lived in the Pacific in a savage and brutish state, then it was not impossible that a creature providing the "missing link" between man and the animals dwelt there also. Such ideas were inspired in the literary imagination by the writings of James Burnett, Lord Monboddo (1714–99), a Scottish lawyer and amateur anthropologist who (though he never actually visited the Pacific) studied the lore and customs of primitive peoples and explored the origins of language and society in his monumental work *Of the Origin and Progress of Language* (1773–92). Monboddo's theories brought him popular fame and notoriety. In some of his conclusions he anticipated the principles of Darwinian evolution and he was widely ridiculed for several of his notions, especially his belief that man is related to the orangutan and that children are born with tails.

Monboddo's ideas were clearly lampooned in the imaginary account of a journey to the Pacific written by the pseudonymous Hildebrand Bowman and published in the same year as the first volume of Monboddo's work. Bowman describes how, while traveling in the southern seas, he discovers a creature, which he names the Taupinieran, that proves the link

between humans and apes, having an animal face resembling a pig, the body of a human and – a tail. "I examined it over and over", wrote Bowman, and "both sexes were furnished with these small appendages." The publication, a century later, of the English naturalist Charles Darwin's famous work, *The Descent of Man and Selection in Relation to Sex* (1871), inspired the same kind of burlesque. Darwin wrote that the early progenitors of man were "no doubt once covered with hair, both sexes having beards; their eyes were pointed, and capable of movement, and their bodies were provided with a tail having proper muscles." Soon after appeared a satirical fantasy by E. W. Cole (1832–1918) in which he claimed that a traveler by the name of Jones had discovered in New Guinea the missing link in human evolution. The Elocwe (an anagram on the author's name) could be found "within a few hundred miles of important English, Spanish and Dutch settlements in the Eastern Archipelago". The form, attitude and motions of the Elocwe were discernibly those of "a species of gorilla, remarkably approaching human form", and Jones was greatly astonished to hear these creatures utter distinct human speech.

Journeys of scientific inquiry

Up until the late 18th century Europeans knew more about the celestial bodies than they did about the other side of the world; at least they could observe the skies.

The voyages of Cook and La Pérouse
Cook was without doubt the greatest European navigator of the Pacific. His three voyages of exploration revealed his talent for navigation and accurate charting. Jean-François de Galaup, comte de La Pérouse (1741–88) crossed even greater expanses of the ocean in his attempt to find the Northwest Passage, the object of Cook's final voyage. He visited the coasts of Chile, Alaska, California, China, Sakhalin Island and the Kamchatka peninsula (from where his journal and charts were dispatched overland to France) and then went on to explore the South Pacific. Several expeditions were sent in search of his ships, last sighted at Botany Bay in March 1788. It was not until 1828 that the French explorer Dumont d'Urville finally established that they had gone down off Vanikoro, one of the Santa Cruz Islands.

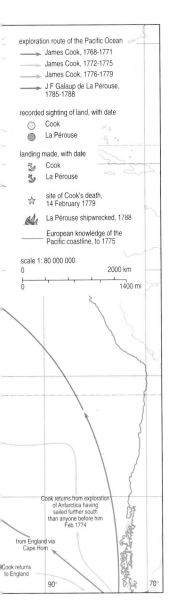

exploration route of the Pacific Ocean

⟶ James Cook, 1768-1771
⟶ James Cook, 1772-1775
⟶ James Cook, 1776-1779
⟶ J F Galaup de La Pérouse, 1785-1788

recorded sighting of land, with date
○ Cook
● La Pérouse

landing made, with date
🏞 Cook
🏞 La Pérouse

☆ site of Cook's death, 14 February 1779

⛵ La Pérouse shipwrecked, 1788

—— European knowledge of the Pacific coastline, to 1775

scale 1: 80 000 000
0   2000 km
0   1400 mi

Cook returns from exploration of Antarctica having sailed further south than anyone before him Feb 1774

from England via Cape Horn

Cook returns to England

90°   70°

Cook in New Zealand (*right*)
Cook visited New Zealand on all three of his Pacific voyages. On the first occasion, in 1769–70, he spent six months there, meticulously charting the coastline. Many features were named for his ships' officers or for members of the Admiralty board, which sponsored the expedition.

In the course of the century, French and British expeditions to the Pacific came to take the form of scientific journeys of inquiry, and within a very short period of time the Pacific had become one of the most researched places in the world. It was a region of great interest to science for it helped to complete the picture of life and culture on the planet. The Pacific's geographical location on the "other side of the world" from Europe helped make sense of the known world because the vast ocean and its peoples filled out knowledge of the world and its peoples – the "other" world defined the "self". It is not without significance that Charles Darwin's voyages in the Pacific provided the material from which he derived his influential ideas. In 1831–36 he sailed as a naturalist on HMS *Beagle,* which was making a scientific survey of South American waters, later visiting the Galapagos Islands, Tahiti, New Zealand and Tasmania. The mass of notes and information Darwin collected on this voyage were to form the basis of *The Origin of Species by Means of Natural Selection* (1859) in which he formulated the theory of evolution through the survival of the fittest.

The mariners dispatched by the French and the British to investigate and chart the Pacific were required to keep shipboard logs in which they made accurate and exhaustive daily entries. Bougainville, who was himself a noted mathematician, had an astronomer and a botanist on board; Cook's expeditions were sponsored by the Royal Society, Britain's foremost scientific body of research, founded in 1660. His meticulous charting of the Pacific was greatly aided by the use of the sextant, which had come to replace the much more inaccurate astrolabe as an instrument of navigation earlier in the century, and later by the chronometer. He was accompanied by the botanist Joseph Banks (1743–1827) who collected plants at every opportunity: Botany Bay, the site of Cook's first landing on the east coast of Australia, was so named by Cook in commemoration of the great number of specimens that Banks gathered there. From 1733 artists were specially trained at the Portsmouth Naval Academy for the purpose of making a visual record of the plants and animals encountered, as well as the islands and their human inhabitants. In the words of Johann Forster, who accompanied Cook on his second voyage: "My object was nature in its greatest extent; the earth, the sea, the air, the organic and animated creation, and more particularly that class of beings to which we ourselves belong."

The Arcadia of the south

There was always an ambivalence in European imagining about the savage inhabitants of the Pacific. Against the view that they were mere brutes incapable of reason was counterposed the idea that they were primitives unencumbered and uncorrupted by the weight of civilization, living in a state close to nature and in tune with the essential goodness of the human spirit. The concept of the noble savage had its origins in the "golden age" of classical antiquity, but had been given new force and popularity through the writings of the 16th-century French philosopher Montaigne. The English poet John Dryden (1631–1700) gave voice to the idea in his play *The Conquest of Granada* (1672):

> I am free as Nature first made man,
> Ere the base laws of servitude began,
> When wild in the woods the noble savage ran.

Daniel Defoe took up the theme in *A New Voyage Round the World* (1724), in which he reworked Dampier's "brutes" into beings of savage innocence who – though they walked the earth stark naked, both men and women – "had something singularly honest, and sincere in their faces, nor did we find any thing of falsehood or treachery among them." As Europe moved into the age of the Enlightenment, the Swiss philosopher Jean-Jacques Rousseau (1712–78) reworked the theme of the noble savage yet again, and made it the fashionable talk of the literary and political *salons* of mid 18th-century Europe. In his *Discourse on Inequality* (1754), for example, he argued that "man is naturally good and only by institutions is he made bad". Men such as Banks and Bougainville, educated and privileged, were embued with these ideas. They were not slow to identify the inhabitants of Polynesia with the noble savage, and to compare them to classical beings. "These gentlemen, like Homer of old," wrote Banks of the Tahitian islanders, "must be poets as well as musicians." Bougainville described them in even more effusive terms. "I never saw men better made," he exclaimed, "and whose limbs were more proportionate." And if the men were easily likened to Mars and Hercules, then the women were the living incarnations of Venus, possessing the "celestial form of that goddess". Echoing Camões's love island, Bougainville named Tahiti the "New Cythera", after the island of Greece dedicated in classical times to the goddess of love. For him, Tahiti was paradise before the fall. "Often," he wrote in *Voyage autour du monde* (*A Voyage round the World*, 1771) "I thought I was walking in the Garden of Eden," and he compared Tahiti with the Elysian island of Greek mythology where only the souls of the pure reside.

Thus the first reports of the Tahitian islanders showed them to be both amiable and intelligent.

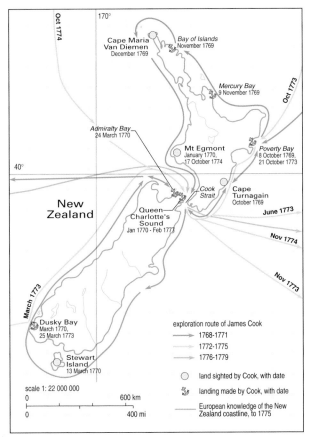

Oct 1774

170°

Cape Maria Van Diemen
December 1769

Bay of Islands
November 1769

Mercury Bay
9 November 1769

Oct 1773

Admiralty Bay
24 March 1770

40°

Mt Egmont
January 1770,
17 October 1774

Poverty Bay
8 October 1769,
21 October 1773

Cook Strait

Cape Turnagain
October 1769

June 1773

New Zealand

Queen Charlotte's Sound
Jan 1770 - Feb 1777

Nov 1774

Nov 1773

March 1773

Dusky Bay
March 1770,
25 March 1773

Stewart Island
13 March 1770

exploration route of James Cook
⟶ 1768-1771
⟶ 1772-1775
⟶ 1776-1779

○ land sighted by Cook, with date
🏞 landing made by Cook, with date
—— European knowledge of the New Zealand coastline, to 1775

scale 1: 22 000 000
0   600 km
0   400 mi

The Noble Savage

European exploration of the Pacific coincided with a period of intense philosophical debate concerning the "state of man". Under the stimulus of the scientific Enlightenment and of romanticism, its literary and artistic counterpart, ideas about the perfectibility of man and the civilizing effects of society came increasingly into question. The romantics were critical of the forces that were shaping industrializing Europe and sought instead to elevate and praise the "state of nature" in which innocent, prelapsarian man lived a virtuous and happy life uncorrupted and degraded by artificial society. The concept of the "noble savage" can be traced back to classical writers such as Homer, Pliny and Xenophon who idealized the Arcadians and other primitive groups, both real and imagined. In the 18th century its greatest popularizer was Jean-Jacques Rousseau (1712–88) who argued in *Emile* (1762) and in the autobiographical *Confessions* (1765–70) in favor of the innate goodness of man. The romantic attitude toward primitivism had a great influence on European conceptualizing of the Pacific. Both Cook and Banks, for example, extolled the "primitive" virtues of the Polynesians. The artists who accompanied them depicted the men in heroic, classical mode and the women as the nymphs of classical mythology. Such images had long-lasting place in popular imaginings of the Pacific, and their influence has never been entirely removed.

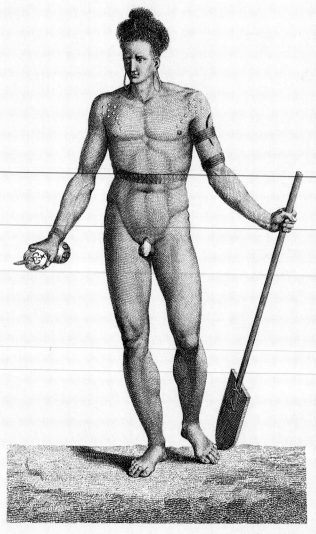

Below William Hodges accompanied Cook's second voyage to the Pacific. On his return he was employed by the Admiralty, on a retainer of £250 per annum, to record his impressions of the Pacific and was particularly regarded for his accurate depiction of atmospheric conditions at sea, from the storms of Antarctica to the becalmed waters of the doldrums. His paintings of Tahiti, however, while topographically precise, owe more than a little to the romantic imagination. In *Oaitepeha Bay, Tahiti* (1776), innocent nymphs are to be seen frolicking near and in the water. Such paintings, harking back to the tradition of Venus's island of love, contributed significantly to neoclassical images of the Pacific. The same influence is seen still more strongly in John Webber's painting of *Poedooa (below right)*. His portrait of the daughter of a chief of Raiatea in the Society Islands typifies the sensual Polynesian woman of the romantic imagination.

Left This engraving of a native of the Admiralty Islands (part of the Bismarck Archipelago of Papua New Guinea) appeared in Labillardière's *Account of the voyage in search of La Pérouse* (1797). In contrast to the soft, sensuous images of Polynesian women, the noble savage here (whose posture is closely modeled on classical Greek statuary) is presented in unsentimental terms. His attitude of heroic stoicism reflects the values of republican France as seen in the paintings of Jacques Louis David – an example of the way that European artists imposed their own preoccupations on their depictions of the inhabitants of the Pacific.

Right European engravers transcribed the images of the Pacific painted by the artists who traveled there and popularized them for the reading public. This engraving by T. Chambers, entitled *Two of the natives of New Holland advancing to combat* (1773), is based on Sydney Parkinson's visual record of the Aborigines who opposed Cook's landing at Botany Bay. In facial features and body shape, these warriors, with their inaccurately depicted sword, spear and shield, remind us of statues of Greek and Roman soldiers. Their body markings, too, are quite false. The figures draw attention to the European desire to make classical virtue out of the savage condition.

Above In 1774 Tobias Furneaux, captain of the ship that accompanied *Resolution* on Cook's second Pacific voyage, brought back to England a young Polynesian called Omai. He was presented to George III, who gave him a sword, and was courted and feted by polite society. This painting by William Parry (1776) shows Omai with Joseph Banks and Dr Daniel Carl Solander, Banks' fellow botanist on board the *Endeavour*, seated here on the right. Though Omai dressed in European costume for his royal audience, he is portrayed here as the noble savage in a toga-like robe. Omai was not the only such Pacific visitor to Europe – Bougainville introduced the Tahitian Aotourou to Paris and was criticised by some for having removed him from his happy island to the corrupting influences of French society. Cook, too, was doubtful about the wisdom of having brought Omai to England.

According to Cook's journals, he often elicited navigational advice from the Polynesian islanders: he records that Maori map-makers drew the two main islands of New Zealand for him in charcoal on the deck of his ship, the *Endeavour*. The image of the noble savage was further advanced by the reception in Paris of the Tahitian Aotourou, brought back by Bougainville to be introduced to the society of the *philosophes*, while a few years later fashionable London was enlivened by the visit of Omai, another Polynesian. But not everyone held a high opinion of primitive nobility. One of those who were critical of the European philosophers who exalted the noble savage was the French navigator La Pérouse. When, during his wide-ranging explorations of the Pacific, his ships reached the Navigators' Islands (now Samoa) in 1787, a group of islanders set upon and murdered the commander of the *Astrolabe*, together with a number of his men. This brutal event caused La Pérouse to remark with some bitterness that "despite the academies which award the crown to the paradoxes of philosophers, the almost savage man, living in anarchy, is a being more malicious than the wolves and tigers of the forest."

Watkin Tench (c. 1758–1833), in charge of the contingent of British marines who accompanied the First Fleet – the 11 ships that carried the first group of white settlers to Australia in 1788 – similarly admonished the romantic disposition that had invented the noble savage: "I wish those European philosophers, whose closest speculations exalt a state of nature above a state of civilization could survey the phantom, which their heated imaginations have raised," he wrote. Then they might learn that the savage "roaming for prey amidst his native deserts is a creature deformed by all those passions which affect and degrade our nature, unsoftened by the influence of religion, philosophy and legal restriction." Tench was in no doubt that the Aborigines were the most primitive, and

therefore the most brutish and debased, of all people on earth.

The attitudes of other visitors to the Pacific were more ambivalent. William Lockerby, who was in Fiji in 1809, said of the islanders that "in war they are fearless and savage to the utmost degree, but in peace their disposition is mild and generous to their friends, and the affection they bear towards their relations is very seldom found among Europeans." Thus, the inhabitants of the Pacific were both cannibals and an intimate community of loving people: the two concepts of brutish savagery or primitive nobility coexisted in the European mind, shaping and prejudicing attitudes towards them. At the bottom of the scale were the Aborigines, regarded as mere brutes, and the Melanesian head-hunting tribes of New Guinea, often described as the last Stone Age peoples to enter the civilized world. By and large, Polynesians tended to embody primitive nobility, though the warlike Maori of New Zealand, for example, were described alternately as noble savages and brutish cannibals.

Paradise found and lost

Polynesia and its people, especially the island of Tahiti, long continued to exercise their innocent charms over European visitors. A French sailor wrote of the island: "If happiness consists in the abundance of all things necessary to live, in living in a superb land with the finest climate, in enjoying the best of health, in breathing the purest and most salubrious air, in leading a simple, soft, quiet life, free from all passions, even from jealousy, although surrounded by women, if these women can themselves even disperse happiness, then I say that there is not in the world a happier nation than the Tahiti one." It became a commonplace that Polynesian women would avail themselves without any notable inhibitions to sailors, many of whom had been months at sea without female company. (More recently, however, revisionist scholarship has

Above The concept of the Pacific islands as paradise seized the European imagination and was seen as a contrast to the crowded and smoky cities of industrializing Europe. Here the Arcadia of the south seas has been reproduced on a French painted wallpaper of the early 19th century entitled *Peoples of the Pacific Ocean*. It shows highly romanticized Polynesians enjoying the fruits of nature. The death of Captain Cook, depicted in the left background, hints at coming conflict.

suggested that "lower caste" women were sent by the island leaders to greet the sailors and offer themselves for sex in order to defuse potential conflict.)

Tahiti became famed as a rest station where men could recover from scurvy and the other privations of shipboard life as they luxuriated in the abundance of fresh tropical fruits and the delights of the flesh. In the mid 19th century the American novelist Herman Melville (1819–91) wrote "it seems a fairy land, all fresh and blooming from the hand of the creator", and some time later the pseudonymous French writer Pierre Loti (Julien Marie Viaud, 1850–1923), also evoked the seductions of the island "where misery is unknown and work useless, where each has his place in the sun and in the shade, his place in the water and his food in the woods". But it is in the paintings of Paul Gauguin (1848–1903), who abandoned the artistic life of Paris "to live like a savage" in the "primitive paradise" of Tahiti, and later the Marquesas, that the sensuous beauty of Polynesia, especially its women, found its most explicit and haunting images.

Herman Melville, the New York-born son of a failed businessman, was one of those who contributed most powerfully to the imaginative view of the Pacific as paradise before the Fall. He went to sea as a cabin-boy at the age of 16 and spent several years sailing on whalers in the South Seas. His experiences formed the basis for three of his most memorable writings: *Typee* (1846), *Omoo* (1847), and *Moby Dick* (1851). The first of these – subtitled *A Peep at Polynesian Life* – is a record of his adventures in the Typee valley of the Marquesas, where he spent a month as the captive of a cannibal tribe. He reckoned to have found true innocence among the Typee people, maintaining that they lived in a prelapsarian state of nature. Criticizing the so-called civilization of the western world for its materialism, Melville celebrated the pure simplicity, as he saw it, of the savage way of life: "There are none of those thousand sources of irritation that the ingenuity of civilized man has created to mar his own felicity." In keeping with the classical imagery of the noble savage, Melville's islanders dance in the waters as nymphs, "springing buoyantly into the air and revealing their naked forms to the waist." The character of Fayaway – who became the literary type in western imaginings of Polynesian women – is both beautiful and amoral: "The easy unstudied graces of a child of nature like this, breathing from infancy an atmosphere of perpetual summer, and nurtured by the simple fruits of the earth, and removed effectually from all injurious tendencies. . . ."

In 1907 the American novelist Jack London (1876–1916) – who, like Melville, had been a sailor in early life – arrived at the Marquesas in search of Typee. Failing to find Melville's paradise, he recorded his disillusion. The valley of the Typee had degenerated into an "abode of some dozen wretched creatures, afflicted by leprosy, elephantiasis, tuberculosis"; life in paradise had rotted away, forcing London to conclude, like Melville, "that the white race flourishes on impurities and corruption". The Pacific clearly held few charms for London. Of the Solomons he wrote: "Fever and dysentery are perpetually on the walk about...loathsome skin diseases abound...the air is saturated with a poison that bites into every pore, cut or abrasion and plants malignant ulcers, and many strong men who escape dying there return as wrecks to their own countries....The worst punishment I could inflict on my enemies would be to banish them

Below The American novelist Herman Melville belongs to a long line of writers who contributed to the popular romantic image of the Pacific islands, and particularly to the characterization of Polynesian women as love objects. This illustration from an early 20th-century edition of *Typee* is typical of its kind. Fayaway, Melville's Polynesian nymph figure, inspired many adventurers and writers such as Jack London to voyage to the south seas in search of paradise.

to the Solomons." And while the white man may have corrupted the southern paradise of the noble Polynesians, among the Melanesians, according to London, the highest instinct was to "catch a man with his back turned and to smite him a cunning blow with a tomahawk that severs the spinal column at the base of the brain". On some islands, he continued, "social intercourse is calculated in homicides. Heads are the medium of exchange, and white heads are extremely valuable."

One writer who attempted to dispel European myths about the Pacific, and introduce instead a degree of measured realism, was Robert Louis Stevenson (1850–94), the author of *Treasure Island* (1883) and other adventure stories. After contracting tuberculosis he made a journey in 1888 to the South Pacific in an attempt to restore his health. Chartering a yacht, he visited the Marquesas, Fakarava Atoll, Honolulu and the Gilbert Islands before settling in Samoa where he built a house, Vailima, for himself and his family and lived out the last years of his life in patriarchal style. During his travels in the Pacific he made a careful study of the islands and their inhabitants, writing perceptively about them in *A Footnote to History* (1892) and *In the South Seas* (1896). On his tombstone he had inscribed a dedication that reads in part: "Here he lies where he want to be;/Home is the sailor, home from the sea."

Yet, despite the best intentions of many to destroy it, the myth of the Pacific as a paradise has proved remarkably tenacious. The American writer James Michener (b.1907) began writing *Isles of the South Pacific* (published in 1947) while he was serving with the United States forces in the Pacific during World War II. As he has explained in an interview: "I was in the Navy on Espiritu Santo in the South Seas. The mosquitoes drove me batty and the humidity was terrible," but he was sure that the people who were grumbling about conditions would not remember the islands that way. So he planned the stories as a record of the way things really were. His narrative was to become the basis of the alluring Rodgers and Hammerstein musical *South Pacific*, first shown on Broadway in 1949 and then turned into a movie box office hit. Michener later protested that he had had nothing to do with the musical, and did not attend any of the rehearsals. It seems that Rodgers and Hammerstein did to Michener's interpretation of life on a Pacific island what Defoe had done to Dampier's brutes more than two centuries earlier.

A continent apart

Eighteen years after Cook had reported the existence of the southern continent, Captain Arthur Phillip (1738–1814), charged with establishing the first colony in New South Wales in 1788, claimed it as British territory in the name of George III, drawing an imaginary line down the center of Australia to exclude the despised land in the west. The objective now was to carve a civilization out of disappointed expectation. Cook himself had set the tone: "We are to consider that we see this country in a pure state of nature", he wrote. "The industry of man has had nothing to do with any part of it, and yet we find all such things as Nature has bestowed upon it in a flourishing state."

Initially the early settlers of Australia were too busy fulfilling the truth of Cook's observation that "it can never be doubted but that most sorts of grain, fruits, roots etc of a kind would flourish here... planted and

Gauguin in Paradise

At the end of the 19th century a number of European artists, in reaction against what they perceived as the decadence and decay of civilized society, looked to the primitive for inspiration, venturing to Africa, the Middle East and the Pacific in search of new forms and modes of artistic expression. Among those who did so was the French painter Paul Gauguin (1848–1903). He had made his early career as a banker but the French financial collapse of 1883 provided the excuse to abandon the bourgeois way of life, which he more and more detested, and take up painting, which was his passion. He moved first to Brittany and then, separating from his wife and family, announced his decision to leave Europe for good.

Arriving in Tahiti in 1891, he developed his aesthetic theory of *synthèsisme*, which he had first evolved with Emile Bernard in Brittany. This attempted to link naturalistic and symbolic forms through the use of simple techniques and bold colors and is his major contribution to European art. After two years he returned to Paris but by 1895 had been lured back to the Pacific, where he spent the last eight years of his life. For all his detestation of metropolitan life, Gauguin remained an expatriated Frenchman. He transported his theory of primitive art with him to the Pacific, and his works tend to essentialize Polynesian life. He continued to reproduce in his paintings the myth of the love islands, even when his own fortunes had deteriorated and he had grown despondent about his failing physical condition. He died in the Marquesas Islands in 1903.

Gauguin's *Self-portrait with Idol* (*below left*), painted in c. 1893, shows the artist in contemplative mood, drawn towards the primitive that lurks within each man, sublimated beneath the veneer of shallow civilized values. He was to remain poised between the two worlds of his imagination. In Tahiti he lived mainly in the capital, Papeete, then a rough shanty town and port, and did not venture too far into the primitive. (*Right*) In *Merahi Metua No Tehamana* (*Tehamana has many ancestors*), Gauguin has set his portrait of Tehamana, the young Polynesian girl who was his mistress and is here wearing European clothes, against the background of her ancestors. Back in France, his paintings received little acclaim and he became increasingly vitriolic against European manners and society. He determined to return to the Pacific, and this time would go deeper into the heart of his chosen imaginative world.

Right Hina Tefatou (Moon and Earth) shows a young woman standing by a pool. The composition is characteristically uncomplicated and the painting is technically unsophisticated, in reaction to the complex and sophisticated forms of Europe. Gauguin's Polynesians remain in harmony with nature and the natural order of things.

Below Te Raau Rahi (The Big Tree) is one of two paintings by Gauguin that carry this name. The scene is a simple idyll of primitive life. Here, as elsewhere, Gauguin depicts the Polynesians not as noble savages, neoclassical figures that recall the mythologized past of Europe's imagined golden age, as in early European representations of the Pacific, but as childlike innocents. This was in keeping with the new mood of paternalism that was coming to characterize Europe's relations with its Pacific colonies, and Gauguin's paintings grew steadily in appeal. He died not knowing that the critics and collectors who had previously rejected his work were now coming to applaud his endeavors, and his final painting was of a Brittany landscape.

cultivated by the hand of industry," to be concerned with cultural considerations. The settlement of Australia was first and foremost a practical affair, a matter of little or no interest to artists. Unlike Cook's scientific expeditions, the First Fleet was not accompanied by an official artist. The first European painters in Australia were not stylists, but amateurs employed as draftsmen simply to provide a visual record, for practical purposes, of the landforms and topography of the new continent. Though there was a printing press on board the First Fleet, no one in the colony knew how to operate it. Any hopes of a flourishing colonial literature would have to wait seven years for the printers to arrive.

The earliest artistic responses to Australia capture something of the confusion of the colonists in finding themselves in so strange an environment, with unfamiliar trees and plants and animals that hopped on two legs. The settlers made what they could of this exotic place, and their first response was to bend everything into existing patterns of European thought and, as a consequence, very little art and literature of significance was produced until the 1890s. The colonial response to make familiar the unfamiliar was reflected in early colonial architectural designs, which – whether of small peasant cottages, official barracks and standard government buildings – were all transplanted from the old world. Only gradually did art and literature make use of the new environment.

Even the names the settlers gave their settlements clung to the familiar: Adelaide was named in honor of one British queen, Victoria and Queensland after another, Sydney and Hobart after colonial secretaries, Melbourne after a British prime minister. Other names, such as Perth, were chosen simply as reminders of places left behind in the abandoned old world. Relatively few places were accorded Aboriginal names. It was a means of taming the "melancholy weirdness" of the Australian environment, of coming to terms with alienation in exile. Some names were ridiculously optimistic (or ironic), such as Utopia, Eden, and a plethora of Hopes and Hopetowns up and down the coastline. Names such as Mount Misery, Broken Hill, Mount Mistake, Lake Disappointment, Useless Loop, Cape Tribulation, Anxious Bay capture the settlers' feelings toward the unrelenting landscape in which they struggled to make a living. These names may be contrasted with those of the forested and fertile islands of New Zealand, where the few that sound a note of warning or regret, such as Doubtful Sound in the South Island and Poverty Bay in the North, are more than adequately compensated for by Doubtless Bay, Bay of Plenty, Golden Harbour, and Preservation Inlet.

Australia was to prove ultimately a disappointment for those who had hoped for more – there was no great south land of untold riches; no El Dorado. Disillusionment took some time to become fully articulated, but its beginnings are unmistakable. The first disappointment for those who hoped to build a neo-classical paradise in the antipodes were the Aborigines. Governor Phillip quickly found that they were not interested in meeting European myths of the noble savage – as Cook had noticed, they placed no value upon anything Europeans had to give them. So enthusiasm passed instead to the land itself and to the newly arrived contingent of convicts, marines, officials and their wives who had sailed with the First Fleet under his command. "There are few things more pleasing than the contemplation of order and useful arrangement, arising gradually out of tumult and confusion," he wrote, "and perhaps this satisfaction cannot anywhere be more fully enjoyed than where settlement of civilized people is fixing itself upon a newly discovered savage coast."

Australia was to become a new-world society of prosperous, happily transplanted Europeans, a civilization built upon the labor of slaves, the convicts. Aboriginality descended in the European mind from nobility to mere nuisance, leaving the Australian-born poet Henry Kendall (1839–82), in a poem significantly entitled "The Last of his Tribe", to lament the passing of the race that had given way to progress:

He crouches, and buries his face on his knees,
And hides in the dark of his hair;
For he cannot look up to the storm-smitten trees,
Or think of the loneliness there –
Of the loss and the loneliness there. . . .

Will he go in his sleep from these desolate lands,
Like a chief, to the rest of his race,
With the honey-voiced woman who beckons and
   stands,
And gleams like a dream in his face –
Like a marvellous dream in his face?

Literature and art left the Aborigines to die out, and they went unrecorded – except as a problem in the frontier lands. The silence of the imagination was an indication of just how little society cared. The Aborigines did not fit into the new narratives of public works and nation-building. They did not equate with the new heroes of the outback – the noble frontiersman, the itinerant white worker – and so they were ignored. In contrast, the imagination positively blossomed when it came to celebrating the accomplishments of the settlers.

Seen through the eyes of others

When the American writer Mark Twain (Samuel Clemens, 1835–1910) visited Australia in the 1890s, he wrote "Australian history is almost always picturesque; indeed, it is curious and strange, that it is itself the chiefest novelty the country has to offer, and so it pushes the other novelties into second and third place. It does not read like history, but like the most beautiful lies. And all of a fresh and new sort, not mouldy old stale ones. It is full of surprises, and adventures, and incongruities, and contradictions, and incredibilities; but they are all true, they all happened." Many other visitors, remarking on the contrariness of Australia, helped to reinforce the myth of the antipodes. Still others did so without ever leaving Europe. One of the most extraordinary of those who visited Australia only in the imagination was the English visionary poet, painter and engraver William Blake (1757–1827), who at one time eked a living by painting commissioned watercolors of Aborigines for the delectation of London's salon society.

The novelist Charles Dickens (1812–70) toyed from time to time with the idea of emigrating to Australia, but never did so. Two of his sons, however, became successful colonists and – seemingly possessing some of their father's oratorical skills – entered Australian politics. In a number of Dickens' novels – for example, *Pickwick Papers* (1837), *Nicholas Nickleby* (1839), *David Copperfield* (1850) and *Great Expectations* (1860) – characters are transported to Australia, where they survive and prosper, unlike those that remain behind: his optimistic portrayal of Australia as a place of hope for both free settler and convict was in marked contrast to his gloomy descriptions of the conditions endured by Britain's industrial poor. Dickens did not paint immigrant America in the same hopeful colors – his portrayal of American manners and behavior in *Martin Chuzzlewit* (1844), for example, caused much offense in the United States at the time of its publication – and he seems to have been influenced in his view of Australia by Caroline Chisholm (1818–77) who had lived there from 1838 to 1846. On returning to England, she established the Family Colonization Society, which chartered ships to take

Below Travel brochures continue to promote the sensual image of the Pacific islands. In this advertisement for the Cook Islands – "A Special Place, A Special People, A Special Magic" – a beckoning Polynesian girl replaces the seductive nymph figure of the 19th-century imagination. The man on the beach luxuriates in the sun as he awaits the spell of the Pacific to do its unfailing magic.

THE Cook ISLANDS

A SPECIAL PLACE. A SPECIAL PEOPLE. A SPECIAL MAGIC.

An Unforgettable South Pacific Experience

settlers to Australia and encouraged the emigration of women in particular. Another writer to visit Australia in the imagination was Charles Reade (1814–84), whose *It is Never too Late to Mend* (1856), a novel about prison and convict life, was a powerful influence on Marcus Clarke (1846–81). The latter's *For the Term of his Natural Life* (1874), which tells the story of a convict transported for a crime he did not commit, was one of the most important literary works of 19th-century Australia.

Among the European authors who did visit Australia was Henry Kingsley (1830–76), younger brother of the better-known Charles Kingsley, who migrated to Australia during the goldrushes of the 1850s and remained there for several years before returning to Britain. He wrote several novels about Australian life, the best-known of which is *The Recollections of Geoffrey Hamlyn* (1859). The novelist Samuel Butler (1835–1902) spent five years as a sheep-breeder in New Zealand from 1859 to 1864. In *Erewhon* (1872) and *Erewhon Revisited* (1901) he sited the mythical land of Erewhon (Nowhere backwards) in a remote valley of that country, and used it to satirize the hypocrisy of Victorian society – a new twist on the antipodean theme. In the 1870s, Anthony Trollope (1815–82), then at the height of his popularity as the chronicler of English ecclesiastical and political life, visited his emigrant son in Australia, continuing on to New Zealand. His impressions were published in a series of travelogs as *Australia and New Zealand* (1873) – a form of writing then very popular with the British reading public. The diaries of women travelers were particularly sought after, the foremost Australian exponent of this genre being May Vivienne (d.1917), the "poetess of the pastoral".

When the English historian James Anthony Froude (1818–94) visited Australia and New Zealand in the mid 1880s he recorded his impressions on his return in *Oceania*. It contained many errors of fact about their settler societies and provoked a sharp response. Among the most vocal of Froude's critics was Edward Jermingham Wakefield, son of the chief architect of the systematic colonization of Britain's overseas territories, Edward Gibbon Wakefield (1796–1862). In reply to Froude's derogatory remarks, Wakefield acclaimed Australia and New Zealand as "these wonderful young countries, where the process of civilization which occupied twelve centuries in England has been completely achieved in fifty years." The white settler society of Australia and New Zealand was by now confident enough to refute the misconceptions and misinterpretations of those seeking to describe them from outside. By contrast, the indigenous peoples of the Pacific, without the same access to education and to the newspaper and book trade, were not in a position to correct the false impressions created by the literatures of the colonizers and to challenge the European-centered visions of their place and societies. This deficit of the imagination to a considerable extent continues today, for the island communities are still essentialized and given stereotypical treatment in travel and popular literature, in tourist brochures, in the visual arts, and in their portrayal in television and film. Distinctive literatures and arts are now developing to resist the process of colonization and to present an authentic indigenous view but they face a monumental task in proposing alternative visions to the European gaze that has for so long defined the Pacific and its peoples.

FRONTIERS AND RESISTANCE

The history of the European "discovery" and later colonization of the Pacific falls neatly into separate periods: the 16th century belonged to the Portuguese and the Spanish; the 17th century and first half of the 18th century to the Dutch; the second half of the 18th century and the 19th century to the British and the French. The 19th century carried Europe to the zenith of its colonial ascendancy as protectorates were established and territories annexed by France (French Polynesia, New Caledonia, Wallis and Futuna) and Britain (Fiji, the Solomon Islands, Papua New Guinea, the Gilbert and Ellice Islands, Tonga). Germany was the last European nation to join in the hunt for spoils in the South Pacific, acquiring interests in Samoa and Micronesia and in 1884 annexing northeast New Guinea, while the white settler colonies of Australia and New Zealand participated in (and later took control of) the administration of Britain's island possessions. In 1888 Easter Island was annexed by Chile, and in 1898 the United States annexed Hawaii and seized Guam in the Spanish-American War. The next year it purchased by treaty all Spain's former territories in Micronesia and acquired American Samoa by agreement with Germany and Britain.

European intervention in the Pacific was often ill conceived and crudely executed. Yet it represented a profound opening up of the world for all concerned. In the process of making maps and writing down their often exaggerated stories of discovery, and in bringing back live and dead specimens of the region's exotic plant and animal life, including its human inhabitants, Europeans acquainted themselves with worlds that were previously unknown to them. The voyages of exploration thus brought the Pacific and its peoples

European colonialism in the Pacific
The history of European intervention in the South Pacific falls into three phases. In the 16th and 17th centuries the Spanish and Dutch, operating from their profitable trading bases in the Spice Islands, drove the search for profit and gain. By the end of the 18th century the British and French were leading the exploration of the scattered islands of the eastern Pacific and filling in the final spaces on the map; the beginnings of white settler societies had been established in Australia and New Zealand. The second half of the 19th century was the apogee of colonial influence in the region as one European power after another annexed territories for their own commercial and political gain.

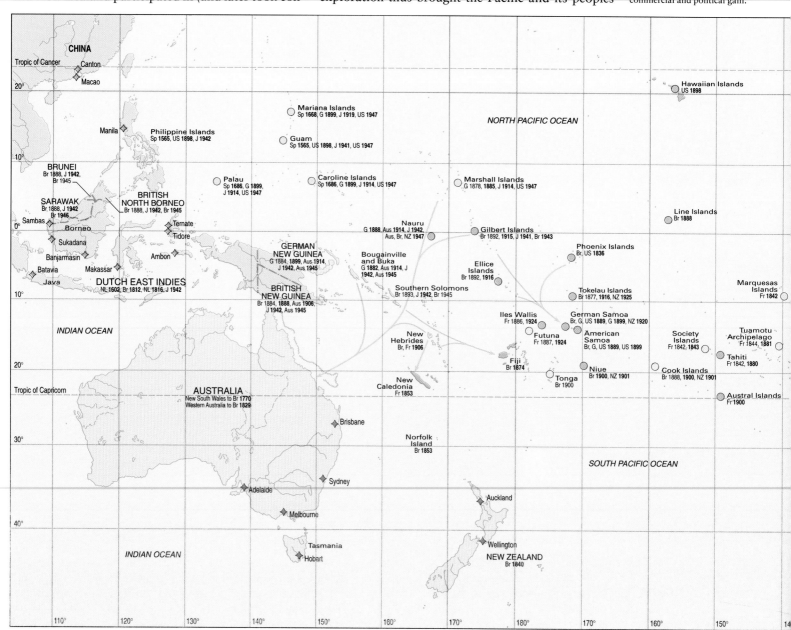

FERDINAN:MAGAGLIANES

Right Though Ferdinand Magellan (c.1480–1521) was born in Portugal he was sailing under the Spanish flag when he made his momentous voyage across the Pacific Ocean in 1520–1. His early years as a navigator had been spent in Portuguese service in the Indian Ocean but in 1517, after a disagreement with the Portuguese king over terms of pay, he offered his services to the Spanish crown. His purpose in making his Pacific voyage was to show that the spice-yielding Moluccas Islands (known to him from his earlier voyages though he probably had not visited them himself), lay west of the line of demarcation established by the Treaty of Tordesillas, and therefore fell within the half of the globe assigned by papal decree to Spain.

period of first European contact
- 16th century
- 17th century
- 18th century

major colonial power

Aus	Australia
Br	Britain
Ch	Chile
Fr	France
G	Germany
J	Japan
NL	Netherlands
NZ	New Zealand
Sp	Spain
US	United States

1844   date protectorate was established
1844   date of annexation or cession
    international boundary, late 1800s
    flow of slaves/indentured workers, c.1860-1910

important trading post
- ◆ by 1670
- ◆ by 1850

scale 1: 61 000 000
0   1000 km
0   900 mi

◉ Pitcairn Island
Br **1839**

Easter Island ◉
Ch **1888**

130°   120°   110°

into European view and into European systems of knowledge. The indigenous peoples, whose cosmologies had not previously entertained the possibilities of peoples arriving from "other worlds", interpreted the pale-skinned mariners as returning spirits from the ancestral dead – an almost universal response among both the Pacific islanders and the Australian Aborigines. Ironic as it may be, European discovery and colonization of the Pacific ultimately enabled the indigenous peoples to begin to visualize the extent of their own civilizations.

There were, of course, many more less positive by-products, including diseases that wiped out whole populations and a conceit that led the Europeans to value their own achievements ahead of those of the indigenous cultures and to impose their own systems of belief and economic structures on them, or else ignore and marginalize them altogether. With musket in one hand and the Bible in the other, the 19th-century colonizers set about peopling the Pacific with their own kind, in an attempt to make the new world they found into a mirror image of the one they had left behind. Where it was expedient they indentured the indigenous peoples as a species of slave labor, where it was not they simply shoved them aside.

European ethnocentricity is revealed in the very claim that Europeans "discovered" the Pacific. The focus on Europe's great navigational journeys obscures the achievements of the Polynesians, the original discoverers, explorers and settlers of the Pacific. Magellan's voyage in 1520–1 was remarkable in that he was the first European to cross the Pacific, but it is significant that he bypassed without ever seeing the many islands that had already been explored and settled by the Polynesians. Later, as the great 18th-century voyages established the number and extent of the Pacific's scattered island societies, Europeans were so in awe of their own achievements and the magnitude of the Pacific itself that they were prevented from seeing the Pacific civilizations in proper perspective. All kinds of theories were invented to explain how the islands had come to be settled rather than admit that the Polynesian canoe voyagers were capable of matching the navigational skills of men such as Wallis, Bougainville, Cook and La Pérouse.

Pacific conquistadores

The first recorded contact between Europeans and Pacific Islanders occurred when Magellan's fleet reached the island of Guam in Micronesia in March 1521. It set an unfortunate standard by which further contact would take place. Both sides were initially curious, but when the islanders tried to claim a skiff from the Europeans, the reprisal meted out to them was bloody and disproportionate, even by the standards of the day. Magellan landed a force of 40 men who then proceeded to attack and kill the offending islanders. Between 40 and 50 of their houses were burned to the ground and a number of their canoes destroyed.

As Europe's foremost maritime nations, Spain and Portugal quickly become rivals during the "Age of Discovery" for trade and possessions in the expanding global economy. In 1494, in the Treaty of Tordesillas, Pope Alexander VI divided the known and unknown worlds into equal halves. The imaginary longitudinal line of demarcation ran 2,000 kilometers west of the Cape Verde Islands in the mid Atlantic; everything east of it belonged to Portugal, everything west to Spain. The Treaty of Zaragoza (1529) extended this principle to the Pacific so that the eastern portion belonged to the Spanish and the western portion to the Portuguese. But because the Pacific had not yet been explored and no one knew how big the globe was, it was unclear where the line actually fell. Magellan's voyage was in a large measure intended to prove that the prosperous Spice Islands (present-day Indonesia), which lay on the sea-route between the Indian Ocean and China and were claimed by Portugal, fell within the Spanish sphere. Though experience later showed this theory to be incorrect, subsequent treaties gave Spain control of the Philippines, settled in 1565, which were nominally in the Portuguese hemisphere. Trade links were forged between Spain and the islands by way of its possessions in Mexico.

Subsequent Spanish exploration of the Pacific was motivated by the desire to find the supposed vast riches of the southern continent and by missionary zeal to spread the Catholic faith. Mendaña's failure to establish settlements on his expeditions of 1567 and 1595 was a powerful lesson that colonization of the Pacific islands would not be an easy enterprise. De Quirós, however, who mounted the next expedition into the Pacific, burned with the ambition of the *conquistador* to convert the continent's presumed millions of inhabitants to Christianity while seizing its treasures for the greater glory of Spain and the Catholic faith. Following his retreat at the hands of hostile islanders from Espiritu Santo in 1606 he was unable to enlist further support for a colony in the south seas. His death in 1614 ended the Spanish dream of establishing a Catholic empire in the south, and Spain subsequently concentrated all its colonizing efforts in the Americas.

Nevertheless the Spanish retained some influence in the Pacific. The galleons that sailed the trade route between Mexico and the Philippines would habitually call in at Guam in the Marianas to take on water and supplies. By 1600 it had become a regular staging post, and in 1668 Jesuit missionaries arrived there to establish a permanent settlement. In their estimation, there

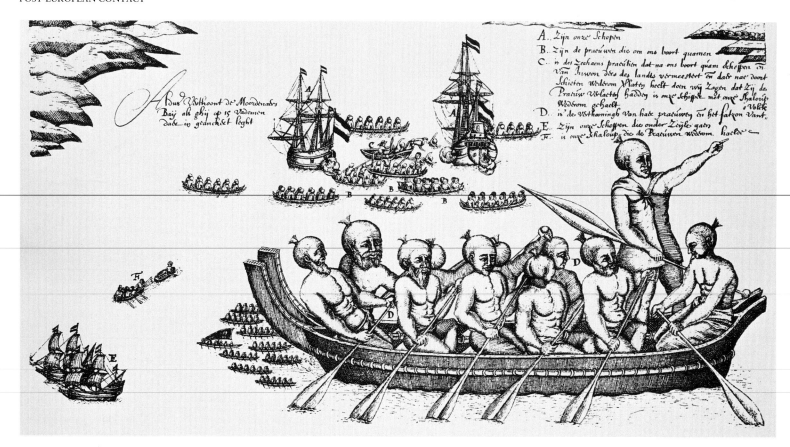

A. Zijn onze Schepen
B. Zijn de pracütten die om ons boort quamen
C. in des Zeehaens pracütten dat na ons boort quam schepen in
Van Inwon des des landes vermeestert en dat nae doort
Schieten Wedrom Platty heeft doen wij Zagen dat Zij de
Pracüw Vrlaeten hadden is onze schepen met onze Shalouip
Wedrom gehaelt
D. in de Vrthoonigh Von hate pracüwen en het falten Vant
E. Zijn onze Scheppen die onder Zeijle gaen
F. is onze Shaloup die de Pracüwen Wedrom haeld

were probably about 70,000 indigenous Chamorro throughout the islands, almost half of them living on Guam. In just over a century after first coming into contact with Europeans this number had fallen to 1,318 – one of the most dramatic reductions of populations the world has ever known. The Chamorro were either killed in massacres, died of introduced diseases, or were shipped off as slaves and indentured laborers to the Philippines. Though Chamorro numbers in the late 20th century have recovered to around 10,000, virtually all vestiges of their indigenous culture have been replaced by a strict adherence to Roman Catholicism. The population of the Marianas today is predominantly of mixed European, Asian and Polynesian descent.

Dutch explorers
In 1609, the Dutch won control of the Spice Islands from the Portuguese, renaming them the Dutch East Indies. The Dutch East India Company was formed to protect Dutch trading interests by granting monopoly licenses. It was illegal for Dutch merchants to trade privately within the area of the Dutch East India Company's monopoly, which included the whole Pacific region, and contact between Dutch traders and Pacific islanders was forbidden unless it was carried out under the auspices of the Company. Le Maire and Schouten – despatched from the Netherlands to search the Pacific for commercial opportunities – were viewed with suspicion by the Company's officials when they arrived in Batavia in 1616 to report their successful rounding of Cape Horn and their discovery of Tonga. In 1622 Jacob Roggeveen was seriously disciplined and had his ships confiscated after making an east–west crossing of the Pacific via Easter Island, Samoa, Bora Bora and Maupiti, back into the seaways controlled by the Company. It was as an employee of the Company that Abel Tasman made his expedition in 1642. Having explored the southern coast of

Australia and become the first European to sight Tasmania and New Zealand before returning to Batavia, he was chastised for bringing back "no riches or things of profit but only the said lands and apparently good passage were discovered".

The Dutch showed little enthusiasm for establishing trading colonies anywhere in the South Pacific, least of all along the barren and miserable coast of northern and western Australia: they were much more concerned with defending and extending their prosperous trading empire in the Dutch East Indies. Contact with the indigenous peoples of the Pacific was mainly in the form of occasional skirmishes between landing parties of mariners and defending groups of warriors. Typical of such meetings were the experiences of Schouten and Le Maire in the Tongan Islands. While still at sea, they came upon a rigged double canoe, or *tongiaki*, carrying a group of Tongans, seemingly on a trading mission to Samoa. The Dutch at first mistook the *tongiaki* for a barque, a European vessel of similar size, and fired two warning shots across the bow before despatching an armed boat to apprehend whoever it was in these waters. Panic seized the Tongans as the armed Dutch came alongside. Several blackened their faces with charcoal and leapt into the water, while the remainder fell to their knees and began kissing the feet and arms of the Dutch sailors. Those who had not drowned were retrieved from the water and a form of order returned as the Dutch offered the islanders trinkets and knives. The pale skin of the Europeans, and their odd clothing, must have appeared bewildering to the Tongans, who may have believed they were sea monsters, or perhaps returning dead ancestors, the spirits of the great Polynesian navigators. (The name that was later given to Europeans by the Tongans, *palangi*, which means men from the sky, seems to point to an early belief that they were returning spirits from the ancestral dead, or at least, spirits.) Whatever the case, those on board the *tongiaki* seemed

Above As in many parts of the Pacific, violence marked the first encounter between Europeans and Maori. This drawing by a Dutch artist shows a group of hostile Maori canoes encircling Tasman's two ships, the *Heemskerck* and the *Zeehaen*, after they had anchored in a bay on 17 December 1642. It may be that the European ships had strayed within a *tapu*, or protected, tribal fishing ground; the Maori seem to have interpreted an exchange of trumpet calls as a challenge to fight. The crew of one of the ship's boats was attacked and in the ensuing struggle four Dutch seamen were killed.

disorientated; when released by the Dutch they headed in a southeasterly direction, away from their original route, towards an empty expanse of the Pacific.

The next day Schouten and Le Maire came upon the island of Tafahi in the Tongan archipelago, where they were approached by many more *tongiaki*. The Tongans did not appear to exhibit any warlike intentions, and a brisk exchange of goods ensued. However, when the Dutch despatched a boat to look for better anchorage, it was almost immediately set upon by 14 or more canoes. These dispersed when the Dutch fired their muskets, hitting at least one man in the chest. Trading resumed the next day, and soon the chief arrived with 35 canoes from the neighboring island of Niuatoputapu. He presented Le Maire with a pig, but when a gift of *kava* was refused, for fear that it might be poisonous, it appeared that a grave offense had been committed. The following morning an army of a thousand or so warriors attacked the Dutch force and a bloody battle ensued. Again the deployment of firearms repelled the Tongans, but the Dutch decided that the islanders could not be trusted. As they departed, the name Traitors' Island was entered onto the map.

A similar confrontation occurred in New Zealand when, in late December 1642, Tasman sailed his two ships, the *Heemskerck* and *Zeehaen*, into Golden Bay on the north coast of the South Island. Warriors of the local Hgati Timata-kokiri tribe went to meet them, sounding a "Moorish-like trumpet". A crew member on board the *Heemskerck* was ordered to respond in like kind. The Hgati Timata-kokiri seem to have interpreted the exchange of trumpet calls as a challenge to fight, and the canoes attacked, killing four crew members. Tasman retreated without putting ashore, and subsequently called the place Murderers' Bay. The Dutch did not publicize their discovery of New

Zealand. It seems that Tasman's descriptions of the islands' potential for trade so impressed his Company superiors that they determined to keep them a secret from the rest of the world. However, they did nothing to exploit their find, and no further contact with the Maori took place for well over a century, until Cook's first voyage in 1769–70.

British and French in Polynesia

By the second half of the 18th century rivalry between the maritime empires of the French and the British, spreading around the globe, had spilled over into the South Pacific, where it started up a scramble for trade and influence. Competition was keen in Tahiti and the Society Islands. The first recorded contact between Europeans and Tahitians took place when Samuel Wallis sailed HMS *Dolphin* into Matavai Bay in June 1767. The *Dolphin* was dangerously short of food and water, so boats were dispatched to make landfall. These were immediately challenged by a number of canoes carrying warriors who seemed intent on gaining whatever was valuable from the strangers. They also seemed less curious about the appearance of the pale-skinned creatures than were many other Pacific islanders, and they were unperturbed by the spectacle of the ship and its smaller boats. It is possible that in the course of their sea voyages around the neighboring groups of islands the Tahitians had heard stories about the Dutch ship *Afrikaanishe Galei*, which had been wrecked off Takapoto in the Tuamotu Archipelago in 1722. The islanders of Takapoto had salvaged goods from the ship which they had either kept or traded with the surrounding islands. The Pacific islanders quickly discovered that the iron and steel nails, knives and axes of the Europeans were much more efficient tools than their own stone or shell implements, and goods of these kind may already have made their way into the possession of the Tahitians, who were keen traders as well as being skilled sailors and navigators.

In all events, Wallis's report states that the canoes that came alongside the *Dolphin* and its boats "behaved very insolently". The Tahitians demanded nails and trinkets before they would hand over any articles for trade. They crowded round the boats and scuffles broke out in which several British sailors were struck. It is possible that the Tahitian canoes were intent on sinking the boats in order to profit from the salvage. A group on shore appeared especially threatening and Wallis ordered his crew to fire their muskets into them; one islander was killed and another wounded. Thus, as was to be the case so often in the Pacific, trade was sanctioned out of the barrel of the gun. The *Dolphin* then attempted to find anchorage farther into the bay but became stranded on a sandbar. Its plight encouraged the islanders to renew their attacks, and once again Wallis was drawn to give a demonstration of his superior firepower. The ship's cannons were loaded with grapeshot and bags of musket balls. When the men in the canoes began to attack, throwing "stones like hail", the grapeshot was fired with an effect like a scatter-gun, killing several of the assailants. Trading then began again, but the British sailors were unable to prevent the islanders removing by stealth many of the valuable items they coveted.

Both Bougainville and Cook, visiting the island not longer after Wallis's departure, were equally plagued by incessant stealing – the first time that Bougainville came ashore and dined with a chief, one of his officers

Below Cook clashed with the Pacific islanders and with the Maori on a number of occasions, but peaceful relations were most rapidly established through setting up a system of barter. In return for water and food, his crew would distribute goods such as nails and other small goods. This picture, popularly attributed to Joseph Banks who is known not to have been an accomplished artist, shows an English officer exchanging a small piece of cloth for a crayfish.

had his pocket picked. Theft was not common among the Tahitians themselves. Their houses were open, and they had few personal possessions to steal. They were, however, unable to resist the treasury of, to them, exotic and useful articles that the European ships carried: needles and pins, nails, metal buttons, beads, pieces of paper, glass vessels, not to speak of more valuable items such as tools. From this arose the European legend that the Polynesians were skilled and inveterate thieves. The power of the gun, however, proved to be an effective means of enforcing discipline and facilitating trade. One of Cook's men on his second visit to Tahiti in 1773, six years after the *Dolphin*'s sojourn, recorded: "None of us ever received the least insult of incivility from any of them, nor did they come within our lines without leave: so terrible did Captain Wallis make the sight of a gun to the inhabitants of Otahitee [the name by which Tahiti was originally known in Europe]."

Before his departure from Tahiti in June 1767, Wallis had annexed the island to the British crown by the simple ritual of hoisting a Union Jack and firing a volley of shots. The following year Bougainville claimed Tahiti for France in the name of Louis XV. The British and the French were forever suspicious of each other's activities in the Pacific, but neither was powerful enough to establish an uncontested hegemony. In any case, the French Revolution and the wars that engulfed Europe in its aftermath forestalled the French from following up their claim to Tahiti. At this period, trade and influence were more important than outright possession. It was not until 1842 that Tahiti formally became a French protectorate. In 1880 it became a French colony, the largest island in what is today the overseas territory of French Polynesia.

The Friendly Islands
On his second Pacific voyage, Cook continued westward from Tahiti to make landfall in the Tonga Islands in September 1773, returning the following June to Nomuka in the same group. Cook found the

Above Nearly all the early European visitors to the Pacific commented on the incessant stealing of goods from their ships and persons by the Polynesian islanders. This engraving, from the English edition of *The Voyage of La Pérouse* (1798), is entitled "A Devilish Propensity to Theiving" and shows Polynesian beauties engaged in distracting French officers from their scientific observations of Easter Island while others pick their pockets.

Left The London Missionary Society was one of the first religious organizations actively to proselytize in Polynesia. After a number of setbacks, its missionaries succeeded in converting Pomare II, chief of the Matavai Bay area of Tahiti, whose high priest is seen here kneeling in front of a British officer, backed by a group of LMS missionaries and their wives. Missionary support was a powerful instrument for local chiefly rulers, who were able to gain access to European arms and influence.

Above Boxing and wrestling were favorite pastimes of the islanders, and competitions were specially staged for early European visitors. John Webber, an artist on Cook's later Pacific voyages, depicted such a bout.

apparently abused for refusing to take a girl who seemed to be offered by her parents. The French navigator Bruni d'Entrecasteaux, who visited Tonga in 1793 while trying to discover the fate of La Pérouse's expedition (which had disappeared after leaving Botany Bay in 1788 and was later assumed to been wrecked off Vanikoro Island in the Santa Cruz islands), reported that "men of the most obliging disposition took pleasure in informing strangers that they might be favorably received by the softer sex."

Traders and missionaries

The Polynesian islanders readily supplied the first European ships that visited them with much-needed food supplies – fruit, vegetables and meat. Cook reported that in Tahiti a pig could be had for the price of a hatchet. It was his custom to release some of the livestock carried on board his ships onto the islands he visited, and to plant a few seeds. Tahiti soon supported considerable numbers of the larger European pig as well as goats, and cattle and sheep also became established in the islands of Polynesia within a short period of time. Citrus trees, vines, papaya, pineapples, root vegetables and cereals were among the plants that early European visitors introduced, helping to create a constant source of goods for trade with European ships. In the course of the 19th century Tahiti's importance as a commercial station grew as the trading ships that visited the Pacific in increasing numbers stopped off to take on supplies, and whalers came ashore to refit their vessels. In their dealings with the Europeans, the islanders were quick to identify the relationship between supply, demand and price. From the beginning, women were part of this trade. Wallis reported that his men were offered several handsome young girls at a rate fixed at a "thirty penny nail each time", and Cook noted that "they set great value upon spike nails, but as this was an article many in the ship were provided with, the women soon found a much easier way of coming at them than by bringing provisions."

The Tahitians particularly valued red feathers, which were imported from Samoa and Tonga, and they were soon used as a primitive form of currency; by the 1790s alcohol was also in use as a medium of trade. At this time Tahiti started to supply the then starving settlement at Port Jackson in New South Wales with pigs, and a thriving export trade developed; more than three million pounds of pork were traded into New South Wales between 1801 and 1826. As a result of this trade, the Tahitians were able to acquire firearms but – unlike in New Zealand – this did not result in an arms race between rival tribal groups: the Tahitians were more interested in acquiring hardware and other commodities, which they kept for personal use or else traded among themselves or in their traditional areas of commerce among the other Society Islands. By the middle of the century dried coconut flesh, or copra, from which oil for soap and candles was produced, had become the mainstay of trade in the islands.

Missionaries soon followed the first European voyagers and traders in Polynesia. In 1797 the London Missionary Society (LMS) sent a group to Tahiti. They met with little success initially, and this first mission was abandoned in 1809. Eventually, however, the Tahitian chief Pomare II, who controlled the area of Matavai Bay, was converted to Christianity. Backed by his missionary advisers, Pomare was able to assert his authority over the other island chieftains and

Tongans very welcoming – it was he who named the islands the "Friendly Islands" – but his journals noted the nuisance created by constant "thieving". This was also commented upon by a Spaniard, Francisco Antonio Mourelle, who came upon the previously uncharted island of Vava'u in 1781. During their two-week stay on the island his crew were entertained by displays of boxing and wrestling, including contests between women. According to Mourelle's journal, the islanders "never gave us grounds for complaint, unless by their propensity to thieving, which is impossible for Indians to suppress."

When Tasman had visited Nomuka more than a century earlier, he too had been struck by the friendliness of the islanders, especially the women, who had seemed intent on feeling in the genital region of the Dutch sailors, apparently desiring "fleshly intercourse". This is an early example of Polynesian women being credited by Europeans with extreme sexual licentiousness, but it is probable that they were only interested in discovering whether or not these strange beings, clothed in loose breeches and shirts, were in fact men – Tongan women, after all, were lighter-skinned than the men because they did not go into the sun so much, while Tongan men went almost naked except for a penis sheath. Cook described the Tongans as "very submissive and obliging", and was establish himself as "king", promulgating a code of law for the island in 1819. A British trader, John Russell, noted an earlier philosophical discussion with Pomare in which he showed himself to be considerably skeptical of Christian beliefs. "He demanded of me where Jehovah lived," Russell recorded. "I pointed to the heavens. He said he did not believe it. His brother, if possible was still worse...with a haughty and disdainful indifference...and observed, we could bring down the sun and the moon by means of our quadrant, why could we not bring down our Savior by a similar operation?" European visitors, who made little attempt to understand indigenous religious beliefs and rituals, which they regarded as mere sorcery, formed the impression that the Polynesians were more interested in trade than in the soul, and with material rather than spiritual wellbeing. Christianity received many setbacks. The chiefs who accepted it cut themselves off from their traditional *mana*, and in 1830 there was an uprising against the Christian missions by those who supported a return to the old ways.

Early proselytizing in the Tongan archipelago – which between 1790 and 1852 was embroiled in civil war between the islands' chiefly lines – also met with rebuffs. The first missionaries arrived in 1797, but it was not until 1831 that Methodist missionaries succeeded in converting the chief Taufa'ahau. With their help, he was able eventually to bring to an end the long period of feuding, and in 1845 he took the title King George Tupou: his long reign was to last until 1893, by which time the majority of the islanders had become Christian and Tonga had developed many of the institutions of European government, with a legal code, constitution and administrative structure. A similar partnership developed in Samoa in the 1830s between John Williams, a member of the LMS, and the holder of the Malietoa (district chief) title, whom he converted. As a result, Christianity spread rapidly through Samoa, but a number of heretical movements sprang up, reflecting the resilience of traditional beliefs. When, in the late 19th century, Germany,

Britain and the United States began to contest political control of the islands between them, rival chiefs headed Samoan resistance to foreign interference.

Throughout the Pacific, European proselytizing of the islanders had more devastating effect than even the most ardent Christian intended. Because they had no natural immunity, the diseases transmitted by Europeans to the islanders proved fatal to them, mowing down whole populations. Measles and influenza, both transmitted in droplets of saliva sprayed during coughing, were the biggest killers. The discrete family groupings of island societies might have prevented the spread of these diseases, but missionaries of all denominations encouraged people to congregate for divine worship. As measles and influenza gained their foothold, ironically and tragically, the islanders intensified their communal prayers. Venereal diseases also spread through Pacific societies as a result of European contact, causing sterility, derangement, premature death, and the birth of countless deformed babies who were promptly abandoned or killed.

Settlement and resistance: New Zealand

On his first visit to New Zealand, Cook spent six months charting the coastline while Joseph Banks and the other scientists and the artists accompanying the expedition made detailed records of the land and its flora and fauna. Cook's first encounter with the indigenous peoples was no more friendly than Tasman's had been, but with the help of Tupaia, the Polynesian who joined Cook's expedition in Raiatea and acted as interpreter, the English crew began to barter goods in return for food and water, and better relations were established. There were misunderstandings and hostile confrontations from time to time, when Cook did not hesitate to demonstrate the superior power of the musket, but in the course of this and two subsequent visits he came to form a high opinion of the intelligence and abilities of the Maori – the name, deriving from the term *tangata maori* ("local people"), by which they came to describe themselves.

Left Overfishing of the Atlantic whaling grounds and the growing demand for sperm whale oil, which until the discovery of petroleum in the 1850s was the most valuable source of oil for lighting and for industrial lubricants, attracted whaling fleets from Western Europe and the eastern seaboard of the United States to the rich waters of the South Pacific at the beginning of the 19th century. Four-year cruises were not uncommon, and the whalers established stations along the coast of New Zealand where they repaired their ships and processed the blubber, rendering it down for oil. As shown in this engraving, the whales were caught from small rowboats crewed by six men armed with hand harpoons and a coiled line to play the whale, which was killed with a hand lance once it had become exhausted. Vast numbers were slaughtered in this way. Herman Melville's *Moby Dick* (1851) is the best-known fictional narrative of whaling life. In it Captain Ahab's pursuit of the great white whale becomes a metaphor of the human drive for conquest and revenge.

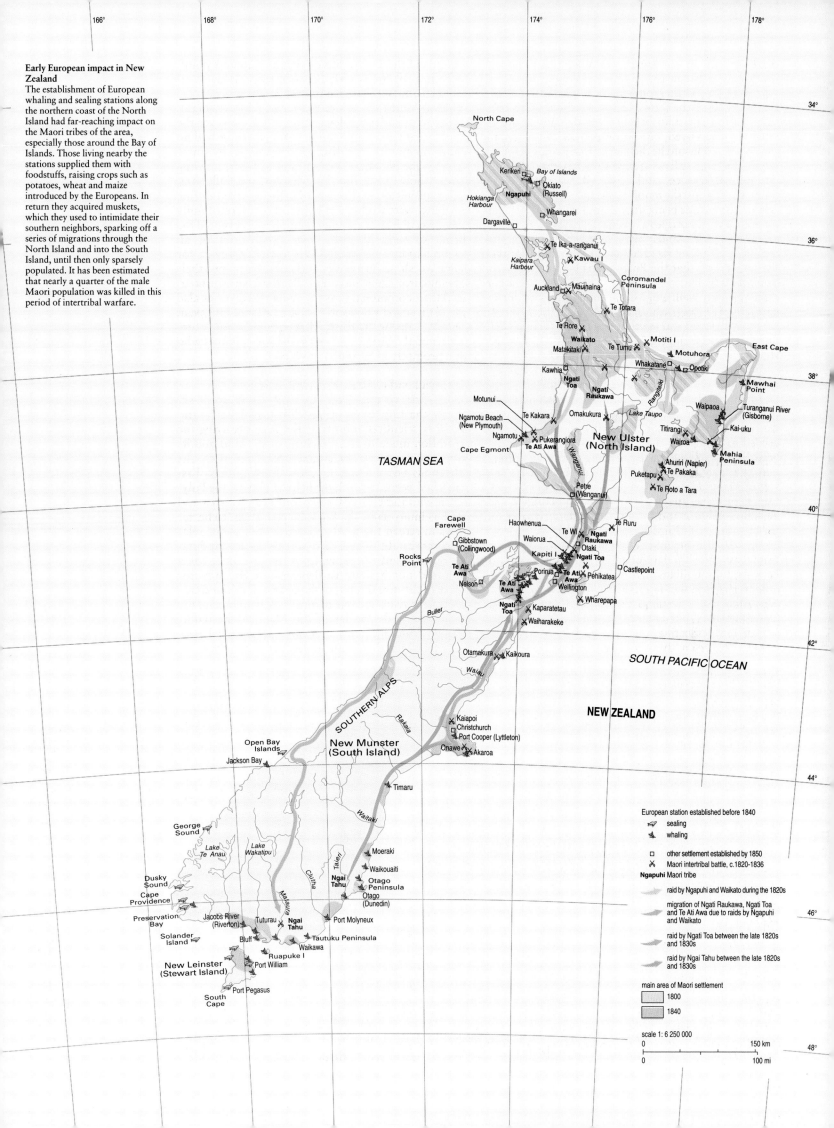

Early European impact in New Zealand

The establishment of European whaling and sealing stations along the northern coast of the North Island had far-reaching impact on the Maori tribes of the area, especially those around the Bay of Islands. Those living nearby the stations supplied them with foodstuffs, raising crops such as potatoes, wheat and maize introduced by the Europeans. In return they acquired muskets, which they used to intimidate their southern neighbors, sparking off a series of migrations through the North Island and into the South Island, until then only sparsely populated. It has been estimated that nearly a quarter of the male Maori population was killed in this period of intertribal warfare.

166°   168°   170°   172°   174°   176°   178°

34°   36°   38°   40°   42°   44°   46°   48°

North Cape

Kerikeri
Bay of Islands
Okiato (Russell)
Ngapuhi
Hokianga Harbour
Whangarei
Dargaville

Te Ika-a-ranganui
Kaipara Harbour
Kawau I
Coromandel Peninsula
Auckland   Mauihaina
Te Totara
Te Rore
Waikato   Motiti I   East Cape
Matakitaki   Te Tumu   Motuhora
Kawhia   Whakatane   Opotiki
Ngati Toa   Te Roto a Tara   Mawhai Point
Ngati Raukawa   Rangitaiki
Motunui
Ngamotu Beach (New Plymouth)   Te Kakara   Omakukura   Lake Taupo   Waipaoa   Turanganui River (Gisborne)
Ngamotu   **New Ulster (North Island)**   Titirangi   Kai-uku
Te Ati Awa   Pukerangiora   Wairoa
Cape Egmont   Wanganui   Ahuriri (Napier)   Te Pakaka   Mahia Peninsula
Puketapu
Petre (Wanganui)   Te Roto a Tara

TASMAN SEA

Cape Farewell
Haowhenua   Te Ruru
Gibbstown (Collingwood)   Waiorua   Te Wi   **Ngati Raukawa**
Rocks Point   Kapiti I   Otaki   **Ngati Toa**
Te Ati Awa   Porirua   **Te Ati Awa**   Pehikatea   Castlepoint
Nelson   **Te Ati Awa**   Wellington
Ngati Toa   Kaparatetau   Wharepapa
Buller   Waiharakeke

Otamakura   Kaikoura
Waiau

SOUTH PACIFIC OCEAN

NEW ZEALAND

SOUTHERN ALPS
Rakaia
Kaiapoi
Christchurch
Port Cooper (Lyttleton)
Open Bay Islands   **New Munster (South Island)**   Onawe   Akaroa
Jackson Bay

Timaru
Waitaki

George Sound
Lake Te Anau   Lake Wakatipu   Moeraki
Waikouaiti
Dusky Sound   **Ngai Tahu**   Otago Peninsula
Cape Providence   Clutha   Otago (Dunedin)
Taieri
Mataura   Port Molyneux
Preservation Bay   Jacobs River (Riverton)   Tuturau   **Ngai Tahu**
Solander Island   Bluff   Tautuku Peninsula
Ruapuke I   Waikawa
New Leinster (Stewart Island)   Port William
Port Pegasus
South Cape

European station established before 1840
🛶 sealing
⚓ whaling

□ other settlement established by 1850
✕ Maori intertribal battle, c.1820-1836
Ngapuhi Maori tribe

raid by Ngapuhi and Waikato during the 1820s

migration of Ngati Raukawa, Ngati Toa and Te Ati Awa due to raids by Ngapuhi and Waikato

raid by Ngati Toa between the late 1820s and 1830s

raid by Ngai Tahu between the late 1820s and 1830s

main area of Maori settlement
1800
1840

scale 1: 6 250 000
0   150 km
0   100 mi

The Maori Meeting House

The meeting house, or carved house (*whare whakairo*), was – and continues to be – an important feature of the *marae*, the ceremonial open space that is the center of a Maori community, used for life-crisis events such as weddings and funerals and for religious and secular gatherings. Both the *marae* and the meeting house underwent changes after the coming of Europeans to New Zealand. But they continued to draw on the traditional symbolism, art and ritual that was central to the identity of tribe, subtribe or community. The houses give shelter and provide accommodation for visitors. Though some are relatively small and simple, in some areas size and the quality of the decoration came to be seen as the reflection of group pride and prestige. The finest meeting houses demonstrate Maori construction and artistic skills at their highest. They represent the owner group and its history in a very direct way. The house is often named after a specific, usually male, ancestor, whose body it symbolizes. The ridgepole of the roof is the ancestral spine, the rafters are ribs. At the same time, they are lines of descent. The ridgepole is the senior line, while from it other lineages, the rafters, lead down to the figures of more recent ancestors around the walls. So within the house generations of descendants, living and dead, are brought together within the "belly" of their shared ancestor. The earliest carved meeting house to survive almost complete is the splendid Te Hau ki Turanga (The Spirit of Turanga), now in the National Museum in Wellington. Carved with iron tools, it was built at Manutuke in Poverty Bay, eastern North Island, in six months in 1842–3.

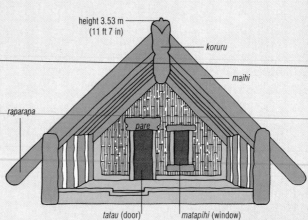

height 3.53 m (11 ft 7 in)

koruru

maihi

raparapa

pare

tatau (door)

matapihi (window)

Right and above The main parts of a meeting house are identified in the ground plan of Te Hau ki Turanga. Looking out from the interior, the left side of the house is relatively "sacred", or *tapu*; it is linked with men and is the correct side to place visitors. The right is relatively "common" (*noa*) and is associated with women and local people. The facade reflects the ancestor symbolism of the meeting house. The *koruru* at its apex is the head of the ancestor, the bargeboards (*maihi*) his arms and the carved *raparapa* his fingers. The window (on the left looking out) is *tapu* while the door is *noa*.

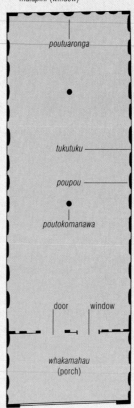

poutuaronga

tukutuku

poupou

poutokomanawa

door   window

whakamahau (porch)

Right Te Hau ki Turanga shows the development of a vibrant and influential regional style. The team of 18 carvers was headed by the chief craftsman Raharui Rukupo whose self-portrait stands to the right of the house door.

Left The ridgepole and rafters of Te Hau ki Turanga are richly painted in the traditional colors of black, white and red. The ridgepole is supported at the far end on a finely carved half-treetrunk, the *poutuaronga*. In the foreground stands a *poutokomanawa*, a more slender ridge support. The ancestral image it rests on is more naturalistic in style than the relief carvings on the *poupou* panels around the walls. Between them are patterned lattice-work panels (*tukutuku*) of bleached or dyed flax.

Cook's journals, published in 1773 and 1777, stressed the natural advantages of the land, and other European explorers, particularly the French, followed close behind him to New Zealand. In 1772, an expedition led by Marion du Fresne clashed violently with a Maori tribe in the Bay of Islands. Du Fresne and 15 of his crew were killed, and in reprisal the French destroyed three villages, inflicting heavy casualties. The first Europeans to set up permanent settlements in New Zealand, from about 1802, were sealers and whalers working in the southern waters of the Pacific, who established land stations on safe harborages along the coast. Here they repaired their ships and processed their hauls of sealskins and whale oil for onward shipping to the growing commercial port of Sydney in New South Wales, from where the burgeoning New Zealand trade operated. Abundant supplies of timber and New Zealand flax formed the basis for a developing shipbuilding industry on the North Island, particularly around the Bay of Islands, and were also exported in quantity. In time Kororareka (later known as Russell) became a thriving port; on one day in the 1830s, more than 30 ships carrying crews of more than 1,000 were counted in dock.

The Maori called the white men *pakeha* (the derivation of which is uncertain, but may refer to the indigenous white turnip). There were a number of disputes and revenge killings on both sides, but in the main relations between the whalers and sealers and the Maori were stable. The Maori tolerated the presence of the Europeans because they had valuable goods – fish hooks, axes, other iron implements and muskets – to trade in return for food, other essentials and women. Those Maori who lived closest to the centers of European settlement on the northern coast were the most affected by the European presence. They learned new farming skills with the use of iron tools and – more significantly – gained *mana* from the possession of European goods. Very soon individual leaders began to acquire muskets, which they used to intimidate their southern neighbors, displacing them from their lands and sparking off a series of migrations that was to lead to a widespread redistribution of population. Soon the possession of arms was widespread, and a period of endemic intertribal warfare followed – the so-called "Musket Wars", which lasted from 1818 into the 1830s. It has been estimated that between 20 and 25 percent of the male fighting population were killed in the wars, but the sharp decline in Maori numbers that took place in these years owed even more to the spread of European diseases.

As in other parts of the Pacific, missionaries arrived in New Zealand hard on the heels of European traders. In 1814 Samuel Marsden (1764–1838), chaplain to the penal colony of New South Wales and quick to acclaim the high level of civilization achieved by the Maori (by comparison with the Aborigines, as he saw it), helped to establish a mission run by the Church Missionary Society in the Bay of Islands. Conversions were at first slow, but Anglican, Methodist and Roman Catholic missionaries continued to arrive, and during the late 1820s set themselves up as mediators in the Maori Wars. At the same time, they offered skills as doctors and teachers. A written form of the Maori language was produced and literacy became a skill that gave its Maori possessors *mana*. Missionary success among the Maori in the 1830s and 1840s seemed to challenge traditional values and authority through its attacks on cannibalism, tribal warfare and the power of *tapu*, and to signal the supremacy of European culture. Items of European dress began to be worn and other aspects of European culture, including the use of money, tobacco and alcohol, were adopted, particularly by those tribes that had had longest contact with Europeans. However, Maoris living in more remote areas were unaffected by such changes, and for very large numbers of Maori "converts", Christian belief was merely an accretion on their traditional culture and religion. Prophetic cults, mingling Old Testament figures with tribal history, were not uncommon.

During the 1830s the nature of European settlement in New Zealand began to alter. At the beginning of the decade there were about 200 Europeans living there permanently, mostly in the North Island; by 1840 the number had risen to 2,000, all of whom were British with the exception of 50 Americans and 20 French. Many more settlers arrived after 1840 under the auspices of the New Zealand Company, founded in 1837 to create a British colony under the scheme of land grant purchases thought up by Edward Gibbon Wakefield (1796–1862). Under his plan, devised in 1827 whilst he was a prisoner in London's Newgate jail, "systemic migration" to the colonies would be encouraged by selling land at a price above its value and placing the surplus in a fund to subsidize the fares of those wishing to make new lives for themselves in the colonies. The higher value of the land meant that those who came out on assisted passages would have to work for a few years as hired labor before they could accumulate enough funds to become landowners themselves. By these means the colonies would never go short of workers, and the money to fund further assisted passages was assured so long as there was

land to sell The scheme was tried first at Adelaide in South Australia in 1836, but its greatest success was to be in New Zealand, where settlements based on Wakefield's ideas were established on land purchased around Cook Strait at Wellington, Wanganui and New Plymouth in the North Island and Nelson in the South Island.

The activities of the New Zealand Company were undoubtedly a factor in the British government's decision to acquire sovereignty over the whole of New Zealand through its formal annexation – a move that would make all land sales a crown monopoly. The increasing interest being shown in the islands by the French also acted as a spur to annexation. At this period the New South Wales government exerted *de facto* authority over the European settlers in New Zealand. There was no official British representative there until the appointment of James Busby as British Resident in 1833. Busby was a vocal supporter of annexation and was the unofficial spokesman for the settlers. In January 1840 William Hobson, dispatched to New Zealand by the Colonial Office in London, began the process of negotiation with the Maori chiefs that would cede sovereignty of the North Island to Britain. The fact that the British were so concerned to find legal sanction for their act of annexation shows the very great contrast between the nature of settlement in New Zealand and Australia, where the doctrine of *terra nullius* allowed the Aborigines no rights at all.

On 5 February 1840 a treaty was presented to a large gathering of Maori at Waitangi. By its terms, the Maori ceded sovereignty in return for guaranteed proprietorship and full use over their lands. Sale of land would extinguish the original title and any further

Above The *heitiki*, usually carved from greenstone but also sometimes from other stone or wood, is one of the most prized of Maori ornaments, and is worn as a pendant. Its origins are disputed, but it possibly represents a human embryo, perhaps a stillborn child. The *heitiki* gave its wearer *mana* associated with fertility and creation. This 19th-century *heitiki* is supposed to have been presented to a missionary.

Left This reconstruction of the signing of the Treaty of Waitangi, painted in 1949, was used as the front cover for a New Zealand farming journal. It perpetuates colonial attitudes toward the treaty, showing the savagery of the Maori tribes being tamed by the civilizing virtues of European rule. The impression given is one of order and honorable exchange, but even before all the signing ceremonies at different treaty sites had been completed, many Maori were beginning to doubt the wisdom of having accepted British authority. The unequal terms of the treaty left lasting resentment and formed a focus for Maori resistance that continues to this day.

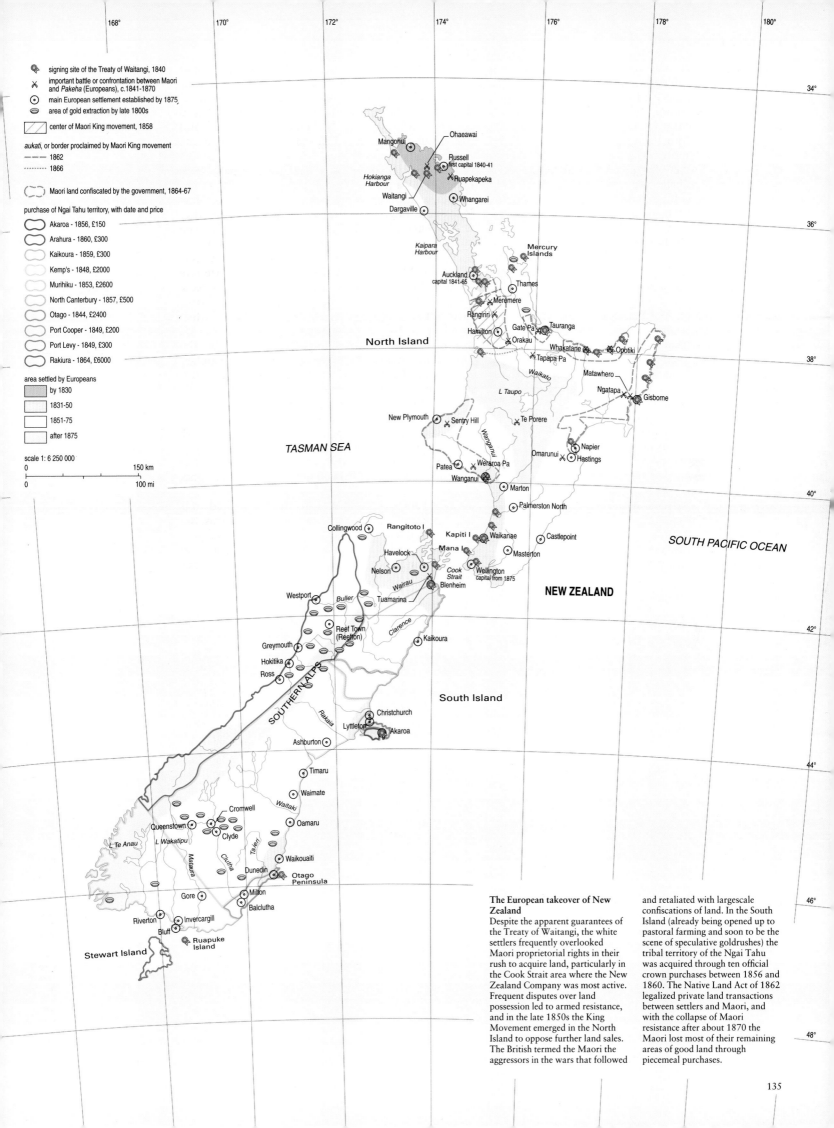

signing site of the Treaty of Waitangi, 1840

important battle or confrontation between Maori and *Pakeha* (Europeans), c.1841-1870

main European settlement established by 1875

area of gold extraction by late 1800s

center of Maori King movement, 1858

aukati, or border proclaimed by Maori King movement
— — — 1862
· · · · · · · · 1866

Maori land confiscated by the government, 1864-67

purchase of Ngai Tahu territory, with date and price

Akaroa - 1856, £150

Arahura - 1860, £300

Kaikoura - 1859, £300

Kemp's - 1848, £2000

Murihiku - 1853, £2600

North Canterbury - 1857, £500

Otago - 1844, £2400

Port Cooper - 1849, £200

Port Levy - 1849, £300

Rakiura - 1864, £6000

area settled by Europeans

by 1830

1831-50

1851-75

after 1875

scale 1: 6 250 000

0 — 150 km

0 — 100 mi

TASMAN SEA

North Island

Mangonui

Ohaeawai

Russell
first capital 1840-41

Hokianga Harbour

Ruapekapeka

Waitangi

Whangarei

Dargaville

Kaipara Harbour

Mercury Islands

Auckland
capital 1841-65

Thames

Meremere

Rangiriri

Gate Pa

Tauranga

Hamilton

Orakau

Whakatane

Opotiki

Tapapa Pa

Matawhero

Waikato

Ngatapa

Gisborne

L Taupo

New Plymouth

Sentry Hill

Te Porere

Wanganui

Omarunui

Napier

Hastings

Patea

Weraroa Pa

Wanganui

Marton

Palmerston North

Castlepoint

Collingwood

Rangitoto I

Kapiti I

Waikanae

Havelock

Mana I.

Masterton

Nelson

Cook Strait

Wellington
capital from 1875

Wairau

Blenheim

NEW ZEALAND

Westport

Buller

Tuamarina

SOUTH PACIFIC OCEAN

Reef Town
(Reefton)

Clarence

Greymouth

Kaikoura

Hokitika

Ross

SOUTHERN ALPS

South Island

Rakaia

Christchurch

Lyttleton

Akaroa

Ashburton

Timaru

Waitaki

Waimate

Cromwell

Oamaru

Queenstown

Clyde

L Te Anau

L Wakatipu

Taieri

Waikouaiti

Mataura

Clutha

Dunedin

Otago Peninsula

Gore

Milton

Balclutha

Riverton

Invercargill

Bluff

Ruapuke Island

Stewart Island

The European takeover of New Zealand

Despite the apparent guarantees of the Treaty of Waitangi, the white settlers frequently overlooked Maori proprietorial rights in their rush to acquire land, particularly in the Cook Strait area where the New Zealand Company was most active. Frequent disputes over land possession led to armed resistance, and in the late 1850s the King Movement emerged in the North Island to oppose further land sales. The British termed the Maori the aggressors in the wars that followed and retaliated with largescale confiscations of land. In the South Island (already being opened up to pastoral farming and soon to be the scene of speculative goldrushes) the tribal territory of the Ngai Tahu was acquired through ten official crown purchases between 1856 and 1860. The Native Land Act of 1862 legalized private land transactions between settlers and Maori, and with the collapse of Maori resistance after about 1870 the Maori lost most of their remaining areas of good land through piecemeal purchases.

135

claims, and the chiefs agreed to sell their lands only to crown representatives. In return the Maori were promised protection and the same rights and privileges as British subjects. Two versions of the treaty were prepared – one in English and the other in Maori. But there were significant differences. In the Maori version, the chiefs were guaranteed *"te tino rangatiratanga"*, or full chiefly authority over their lands. They believed that they were not giving up their right to customary law over their people. According to the English version the Maori ceded all rights to law and government. The discussions at Waitangi failed to make this distinction clear, and 45 chiefs signed the agreement without fully realizing the implications of what they were doing. Subsequent meetings were held for other chiefs to append their names, bringing the total number of Maori signatories to the agreement to more than 500: even so, not all the Maori subtribes (*hapu*) were party to the treaty. In May 1840 Hobson moved quickly to proclaim British sovereignty over the North Island by virtue of cession and over the South Island by right of discovery so as to forestall French plans to do so. At first New Zealand was legally part of New South Wales, but in 1841 it became a separate crown colony, with Hobson as its first governor.

The Maori Wars

The Treaty of Waitangi was vaunted by the British as New Zealand's Magna Carta, but from the beginning there were disagreements over its interpretation. All too frequently the treaty was abused by the settlers; in the Cook Strait area, for instance, the New Zealand Company often failed to check who actually held the proprietorial rights of the lands it bought, or if those rights were subject to dispute. A local chief, Te Rauparaha, led the Maori resistance to *pakeha* settlement, and conflicts with the settlers were frequent. But not all wars related to dispossession. Maori objectives in the Northern War of 1845–6 – in effect, a rebellion by chiefs Hone Heke and Kawiti of the Ngapuhi – had less to do with disputed land than with the decline in trade in the Bay of Islands area after the British shifted their administrative capital south from Russell to Auckland: the Maori had supplied foodstuffs and flax to the *pakeha* in return for clothing, guns, sugar and rum, and had had some share in the whaling and timber industries.

As an act of rebellion Hone Heke cut down the symbol of British authority, the flag-pole at Russell. It is possible that he believed he would be empowered by such an act, that the symbolism would translate into actuality; but the act was also consistent with *utu* (revenge) and the gaining of *mana* through an insult. The British dutifully restored their symbol of power and Hone Heke twice more cut it down. On the fourth occasion Heke's warriors sacked and plundered Russell, killing 19 *pakeha*. The British responded by attacking Heke's and Kawiti's *pa* – fortified stockades – at Puketu and Ohaeawai. The *pa*, however, proved very effective against musket fire, and the British were repelled. Though the British later claimed a military success against Hone Heke, he was defeated in 1846 by a factional alliance of Ngapuhi chiefs. Throughout the Maori Wars, intertribal conflict remained endemic, and the British – pursuing a military strategy they had already used to great effect in India – were to prove adept at exploiting differences and disagreements between rival *hapu*.

Though there were periods of comparative tranquillity and stability – for example, under the governorship of George Grey from 1845 to 1853 – relations between the Maori and the *pakeha* were frequently uneasy, and conflict was never far away. In the 1850s the settler demand for land increased. Among the Maori of Taranaki province, where the land shortage was most acute, a movement sprang up opposed to further land sales. After 1858 this merged into the King Movement, led first by the the Waikato chief "king" Te Wherowhero, and then by his son Tawhiao – which sought to protect Maori independence. The King Movement gained widespread support throughout New Zealand, and by 1860 government ineptitude in dealing with Maori grievances made a renewal of war inevitable.

Despite their technological disadvantage in weaponry, the Maori were remarkably skillful in adapting their *pa* to withstand artillery bombardment, replacing wooden barricades with earthen ones and building defensive bunkers. Defeat, however, was inevitable. During the 1850s the *pakeha* population quadrupled to around 100,000 and was larger than the Maori, whose numbers continued to decline. But the nature of Maori social organization itself worked against them. The warrior spirit was central to tribal life, but there was no separate army or warrior class in Maori society: everyone trained as a fighter and both men and women were ready to do battle when called upon. Ultimately, this counted strategically against them. The Maori were able to sustain battle for only a few days before a break was needed to gather food and water. No tribal structure existed to establish supply lines from the villages to the warriors remaining at the front and this allowed the British ample opportunity to mount a damaging counter offensive. Maori resis-

Right William Bradley's watercolor of 1788 shows ships of the First Fleet entering Botany Bay, where a group of vessels is already at anchor. To the Aborigines observing from the shore, the flotilla of European sailing ships seemed like "winged islands".

Below This 19th-century lithograph shows a Maori village within the stockade of a *pa*; the picture gives an impression of demoralization. The Maori faced overwhelming odds in their resistance to the *pakeha*. By the mid 1860s the British army in New Zealand numbered about 14,000 men, equipped with armored steamships, heavy artillery and telegraph communications – a modern fighting force. At best, the Maori could muster no more than 2,000 warriors at any one time. However, their resourcefulness in constructing sophisticated defensive fieldworks to protect their *pa* from artillery fire made it almost impossible for the British to inflict a single decisive defeat, and the war dwindled into sporadic skirmishing.

tance was effectively ended by the mid 1860s, though sporadic localized conflicts continued until the end of the decade. The last formal peace agreement, with Te Kooti, a guerrilla leader and founder of a religious cult on the east coast of the North Island, was not concluded until 1881.

By 1890 some 22 million hectares of a total land area of 26 million hectares were owned by the *pakeha*, acquired through crown and private purchase; most of the land remaining in Maori possession lay in remote parts of the North Island. The landless Maori subsisted by cropping, food gathering and by hiring themselves to the *pakeha* as laborers; forced to live in makeshift quarters, health conditions were poor and numbers continued to decline, to reach a low of about 45,000 at the end of the century. Maori society and culture, however, proved resilient to assimilating pressures. Passive resistance made itself felt in two ways: through political activity (an unofficial Maori parliament met from 1892 to 1907) and through the growth of popular millenarian religious cults, which predicted the downfall and expulsion of the British. By the turn of the century the initiative had passed into the hands of a new generation of leaders, the Young Maori Party, a Western-educated elite led by Apirana Ngata, the first Maori graduate. Able to work the *pakeha* machine to their own advantage, the Young Maori leaders helped to bring about a measure of economic and social improvement, and the population figures started slowly to climb again. At the same time, they succeeded in winning the support of the tribal leaders. In the 20th century, pressure for Maori rights would increasingly take the form of intervention in the political process and the intensification of cultural identity.

Settlement and resistance: Australia

Despite Cook's favorable report on the suitability of New South Wales for settlement, the British did not immediately take advantage of the opportunities it presented: Lord North's government – engaged in a colonial war in North America from 1775 – had other things to think about. The loss of the American War of Independence in 1783 made it impossible to resume the arrangement whereby Britain deported to America about 1,000 convicts a year, mainly to Maryland and Virginia, and the scheme to establish a penal colony in the southern continent began to take shape. On 13 May 1787 the "First Fleet", consisting of 11 ships, left Portsmouth for New South Wales with more than 750 convicts – 568 men, 191 women and 19 children – on board. Many were petty criminals, others hardened repeat offenders. They were to be the labor force that would establish Australia as a British colony. Accompanying them were 250 sailors, soldiers and marines, including 27 wives and 13 children.

The Fleet arrived in Australia in January 1788. The traditional custodians of the lands in the area of Botany Bay, the first landfall, and Port Jackson, the site of the earliest settlement, were the Eora and Dharuk. As the flotilla of small ships detached themselves from the pale horizon and drew into the bay proper, they seemed to the people watching from the shore like "winged islands", and the tribal elders no doubt recalled the stories of Cook's visit a generation

and in some case actively assume – aspects of indigenous culture: in North America, for example, traders such as the French *coureurs du bois* (forest runners) became a conduit through which some elements of the indigenous lifestyle entered colonial society. Similarly in many of the Pacific islands, as we have seen in Tahiti and in New Zealand, frontier traders arrived ahead of governments. In New South Wales, however, the government arrived first, and as "civilization" moved its borders from the first coastal settlements into the Aboriginal lands, the accommodation of Aboriginal value systems was actively suppressed. No attempt was made to write down the Aboriginal languages, or to interpret their civilization and pre-contact histories. Nevertheless, it is tempting to see in the lifestyles of the 19th-century itinerant workers of the outback some assimilation of Aboriginal nomadism. These heroes of Australian legend found employment as the seasons determined, picking up here and there whatever they needed for survival, and rarely possessing anything more than what they could carry in their swag. Like the explorers of the interior, they relied heavily upon Aboriginal bushcraft, and in the course of the 19th century they became organized into primitive unions, linked by the ties of "mateship", or group solidarity, in a way that possibly parallels the family groupings of Aboriginal tribal organization.

The actual number of Aborigines inhabiting Australia at the time of the European settlement is unknown: estimates range from between 500,000 to 3 million. It was obvious to the First Fleeters that the continent would have to be won in war, not simply settled. The jailed, the jailers and the free combined forces – willingly or otherwise – to dispossess the Aborigines from their lands in the name of empire. The settlers plundered, pillaged and raped for the greater good of civilization, and far greater atrocities were

Far left Massacres of Aborigines were commonplace, and the authorities moved slowly to curtail the violence inflicted by settlers. In 1816 the lieutenant governor of Van Diemen's Land, Thomas Davey, published a proclamation reiterating that the perpetrators of racial violence on both sides would be punished by law. The caption to a pictogrammic version of the proclamation points out with heavy-handed irony that since the "blackfellow" could not read, pictures would have to serve to deliver the message: the Aborigines, it was implied, were unfit for any of the gifts of civilization. The land seizures and attacks against the Aborigines continued, to be met with retaliatory raids. By the 1820s it seemed clear to the government that the conflict would only be ended with the total eradication of the Aborigines from the settled areas of Van Diemen's Land.

Right The last recorded punitive mission against and massacre of Aborigines occurred as recently as the late 1920s. A common feature of policing was to place Aboriginal men in neck chains, a practice (never inflicted on white convicts) that died out only slowly.

earlier, which had become part of the oral history of both tribes. On that occasion some of the men had threatened the newcomers with their spears but were repelled by musket-fire, after which they retreated to a safe distance and declined all further attempts to make closer contact. Now, though some stayed to watch as men and supplies were disembarked from the "winged islands", the rest had the good sense to flee when a musket was discharged. Later the Eora around Port Jackson came to accept presents such as beads and ribbons from the British officers, showing great interest in their clothes. But they were right to fear this incursion of pale-skinned intruders. For the Eora and Dharuk, as for all the Aboriginal peoples, the consequences of European contact would be catastrophic. First they would be devastated by European diseases. Then, as the European settlement extended its tentacles, they would be dispossessed of their lands, their languages and much of their cultural heritage.

Within the next three years, two more transport fleets arrived, bringing more convicts in chains, and more men to guard them. Social organization among the early colonists – forced into migration either in the service of the crown, or as prisoners – was strict, founded on the principle of the jailer and the jailed. The rigid application of British law allowed these immigrants little scope to experiment with alternative forms of social organization in the way the American colonists had done. Frontier traders have always had a disreputable image in settler societies. In order to carry out commerce, they needed to accommodate –

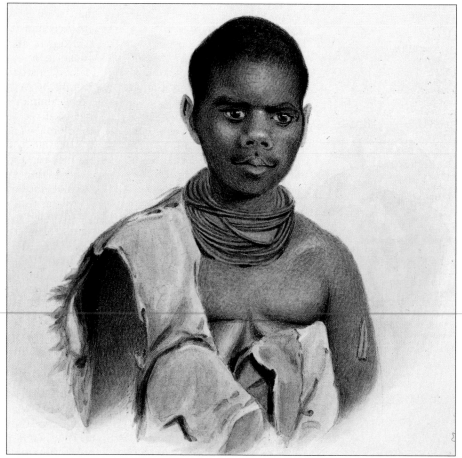

Left Truganini (1803–76) is popularly believed to have been the last full-blooded Tasmanian Aborigine. Thomas Bock painted this portrait of her in about 1831 for George Augustus Robinson, the "protector of the Aborigines", whose mistress she is alleged to have been. Truganini is variously cast as a patriot and a traitor. At the end of her life, as the only surviving "specimen" of the Tasmanian Aborigines, she became a scientific curiosity: she was examined in detail and all her physical proportions methodically noted. After her burial in 1876 her skeleton was exhumed and stored in the museum of the Royal Society of Tasmania. It was exhibited at Melbourne in 1888 as part of the commemorations of 100 years of European settlement, and formed part of the museum's public display between 1904 and 1947. In 1976 her remains were returned to descendants of the original Tasmanians and cremated in a private ceremony, her ashes being scattered on the waters of the D'Entrecasteaux Channel.

committed against the Aborigines than were ever inflicted in the transportation of convicts. Accounts of these wars, however, were never written down, and they did not enter the mythology of colonialism in the way that the Maori Wars did in New Zealand. History books purveyed the lie that the acquisition of Australia was a peaceful affair. It is true that comparatively few insurrections of the kind that occurred in Melanesia took place, and there were no colonial wars like those in New Zealand. Yet it seems probable that more people were killed in the fighting between the Aborigines and the settlers than in all other 19th-century Pacific wars of resistance. The pattern of Aboriginal resistance to the Gubbers and Miglews (as those living on the east and north of the continent termed the Europeans) and to the Wadjellas (the name for white settlers used by the Aborigines of Western Australia) took the form of organized hit and run raids. These amounted to a form of guerrilla warfare, which might last for a period of six months or even extend over a number of years, with extensive casualties being inflicted on both sides.

One of the fears held by early governors and colonial officials was that convicts and Aborigines would form a common front against the authorities. This, however, proved to be false – few escaped convicts managed to integrate with the Aborigines, though an exception was William Buckley (1780–1856) who after escaping from Port Jackson in 1803 survived among the local Aborigines until 1835. Another was the former convict, or emancipist, John Wilson, who

was accorded tribal initiation by the Eora of the Hawksbury area north of Sydney. This region of good farming land was the site of prolonged conflict between the colonialists and the Eora led by Pemulwuy, who managed to avoid capture from the time of his first attack in 1795 until he was shot dead by a settler in 1802. Pemulwuy's raids against the farmers gave considerable concern to the governor, who was reluctant to allow ex-convict settlers to take matters into their own hands for fear they might themselves revolt. Nonetheless, a reward of 5 gallons of rum (later increased to 20) was offered for the capture of Pemulwuy, whether taken dead or alive, and after his capture and death his head was presented to the governor who had it pickled and sent to Joseph Banks in London. Yagan, a member of the Wajuk tribe, led a similar war in Western Australia between 1829 and 1833 before he too was killed. Like Pemulwuy, he was decapitated. His head was "smoke cured" for several months before being shipped off to London to be studied by phrenologists.

These are only two examples of a familiar pattern of resistance and response throughout Australia. Attacks by white settlers led to the death of many thousands of Aborigines (some estimates put the number at around 20,000). The ethnic cleansing of Aborigines from Van Diemen's Land (as Tasmania was known until 1855) was symptomatic of colonial attitudes. So determined was the lieutenant governor Sir George Arthur (1784–1854) to rid the island of Aborigines that he formed a cordon of about 2,000 men

The Mutiny on the Bounty

A year after the arrival of the First Fleet in Australia, a second British settlement was made in the Pacific – this time at Pitcairn Island and without the sanction of the British government – by members of the mutinous crew of HMS *Bounty*. This celebrated historical episode has been endlessly written about and mythologized. In popular legend (and in at least three Hollywood portrayals) Captain William Bligh (1754–1817) has been demonized as a cruel tyrant who drove his crew beyond the point of endurance.

The voyage of HMS *Bounty* in 1787 was one of the first commercial ventures undertaken by the British in the South Pacific: the intention was to collect breadfruit tree seedlings from Tahiti and to take them to the West Indies, where it was hoped they might prove a staple food for slaves. While Bligh was noted for his acerbic temper and foul-mouthed abuse, he was a capable commander. At the age of 22, he had been master of the *Resolution* on Cook's third and final voyage, and he took especial pains to keep his ship in good repair and his crew healthy and scurvy-free. The *Bounty*'s complement of 46 spent five months in Tahiti while Bligh waited to make sure his seedlings were sufficiently advanced for transportation. During this time some of the crew formed amorous attachments with Tahitian women. The *Bounty* had been 24 days out at sea on the next leg of its journey, sailing on a westward course, when on 28 April 1789 it was suddenly seized by Fletcher Christian, the master's mate. After some confusion, Bligh and 18 others were set adrift in the *Bounty*'s longboat.

The mutineers returned to Tahiti and settled for a short time on Tubuai before splitting into two groups. Christian and 8 others, together with 19 Tahitian women and 6 men, sailed on in the *Bounty* to Pitcairn Island. Here they established a small community that remained undiscovered by the British authorities until 1808. The rest stayed in Tahiti, where they were arrested by a British frigate in 1791 and returned to England: three were later hanged. Popular history insists that it was Bligh's tyrannical behavior that caused the mutiny, but he appears to have been lighter with the lash than many other ship's captains of the day, including Cook. Bligh himself blamed the crew's discontents on the enchantments of Tahiti. To this can be added a number of other causes. The *Bounty* was a small ship, of only 215 tonnes. It had been fitted with tiers to hold the potted seedlings, making conditions even more cramped. There were no commissioned officers and no marines on board to help keep control, and Bligh's personal relations with his warrant officers, especially Christian, had fatally broken down.

Above The luckless William Bligh, portrayed here in 1803, faced two mutinies in his career, on board the *Bounty* in 1789 and twenty years later when, as as governor of New South Wales, he stood up to the colony's early land and rum profiteers. The ringleaders were found guilty of conspiracy, and Bligh was subsequently promoted to rear admiral (1811) and vice admiral (1814).

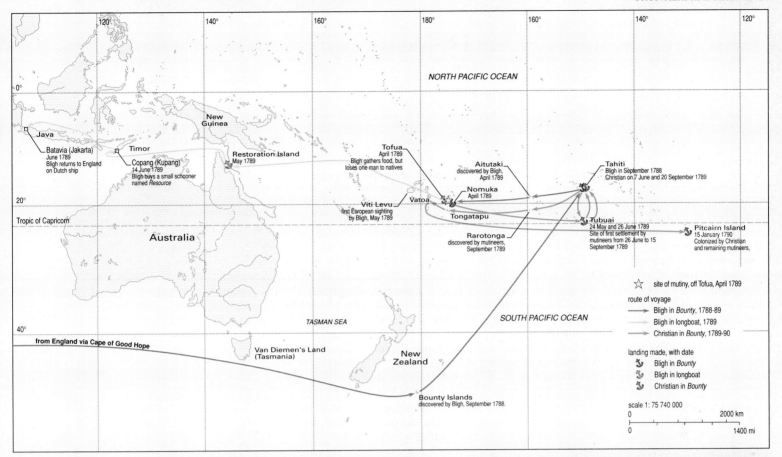

North Pacific Ocean

New Guinea

Java
Batavia (Jakarta)
June 1789
Bligh returns to England
on Dutch ship

Timor
Copang (Kupang)
14 June 1789
Bligh buys a small schooner
named *Resource*

Restoration Island
May 1789

Tofua
April 1789
Bligh gathers food, but
loses one man to natives

Aitutaki
discovered by Bligh,
April 1789

Tahiti
Bligh in September 1788
Christian on 7 June and 20 September 1789

Nomuka
April 1789

Viti Levu
first European sighting
by Bligh, May 1789

Vatoa

Tongatapu

Tubuai
24 May and 26 June 1789
Site of first settlement by
mutineers from 26 June to 15
September 1789

Pitcairn Island
15 January 1790
Colonized by Christian
and remaining mutineers,

Rarotonga
discovered by mutineers,
September 1789

Australia

Tropic of Capricorn

Tasman Sea

South Pacific Ocean

from England via Cape of Good Hope

Van Diemen's Land
(Tasmania)

New Zealand

Bounty Islands
discovered by Bligh, September 1788.

☆ site of mutiny, off Tofua, April 1789

route of voyage
→ Bligh in *Bounty*, 1788-89
→ Bligh in longboat, 1789
→ Christian in *Bounty*, 1789-90

landing made, with date
⚓ Bligh in *Bounty*
⚓ Bligh in longboat
⚓ Christian in *Bounty*

scale 1: 75 740 000
0 ____ 2000 km
0 ____ 1400 mi

Left Robert Dodd's painting of 1790 shows Bligh being set adrift in the *Bounty*'s longboat. He had a sextant and compass and some nautical tables but no charts. It is testimony to Bligh's skills of seamanship that seven weeks later, after a voyage of 5,800 kilometers, he succeeded in reaching Timor in the Dutch East Indies. Only one man out of the 18 in the boat with him had died, killed by the hostile inhabitants of an island where they landed to take on food and water.

The voyage of the *Bounty* (*above*) Bligh's orders were to enter the South Pacific round Cape Horn, but because departure from England was delayed until December, storms forced him to make for the Cape of Good Hope instead. Sailing south of New Zealand, he made the first European discovery of the Bounty Islands. After the *Bounty* left Tahiti in April, Bligh was cast adrift off Tofua in the Tonga Islands. The mutineers returned to Tahiti before proceeding to Pitcairn Island.

Below The south side of Pitcairn Island. Christian's choice of this tiny island as a safe haven proved sound. The soil was fertile, and the tiny settlement was able to flourish. No news was heard of it until 1808 when the island was visited by an American sealer, the *Topaz*. Because of the Napoleonic wars the British authorities neglected to investigate, and the next report of the colony came in 1814, when the captain of a passing British frigate found one mutineer, John Adams, still alive.

Above Knowing that they would never be able to return to England, save to face hanging, the mutineers scuttled the *Bounty* soon after arriving on Pitcairn. They dragged ashore everything they could use, including the ship's bell, which today is preserved as a pot for plants.

Below Thursday October Christian, Fletcher's son, was the first child born on the island. His house, partly made of *Bounty*'s timbers, is still standing. By the 1830s the population had outgrown the island's resources. The community was resettled on Tahiti and then, in 1855, on Norfolk Island where descendants of the original mutineers are still living today.

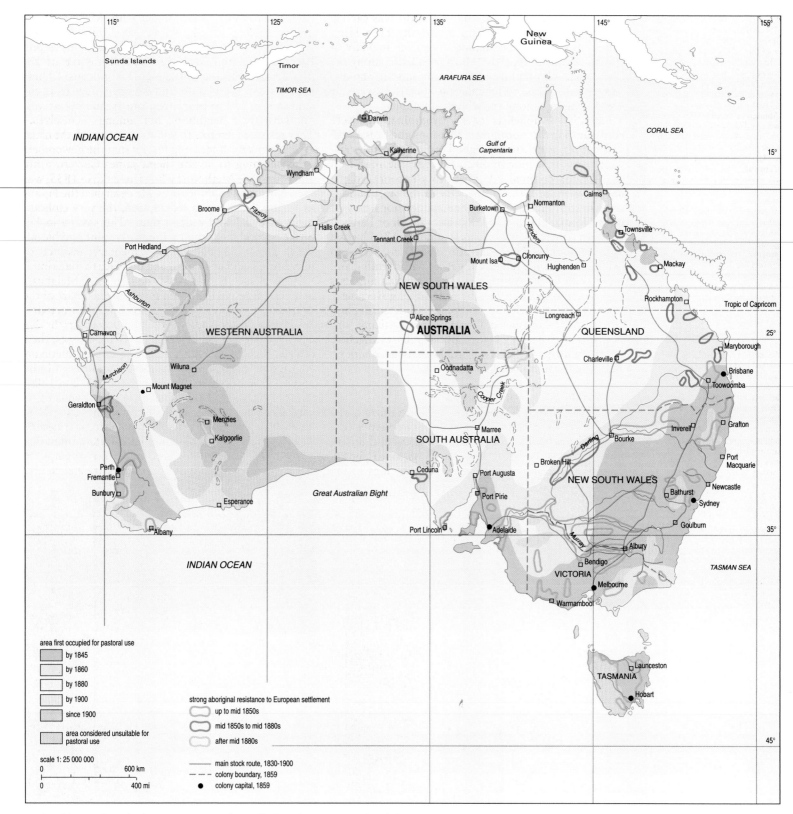

area first occupied for pastoral use
- by 1845
- by 1860
- by 1880
- by 1900
- since 1900

area considered unsuitable for pastoral use

scale 1: 25 000 000

0 — 600 km
0 — 400 mi

strong aboriginal resistance to European settlement
- up to mid 1850s
- mid 1850s to mid 1880s
- after mid 1880s

— main stock route, 1830-1900
--- colony boundary, 1859
● colony capital, 1859

and soldiers (the Black Line) to round up all the Aborigines in the eastern half of the island and to drive them into their last remaining outpost on Tasman's Peninsula. The mission cost more than £35,000, but only two Aborigines – one woman and one boy – were captured. In 1835 George Augustus Robinson was appointed the "protector of the Aborigines". His job consisted of relocating all remaining Tasmanian Aborigines to Flinders Island, where they were confined in primitive conditions.

Yet the guerrilla wars against the white settlers probably caused fewer deaths among the Aboriginal population than did intertribal fighting. The expansion of European settlement, and particularly the growth of the Australian wool industry which led to the seizure of large tracts of land for grazing, displaced tribal groups, forcing them on to lands not their own, at the expense of other tribes. Violence and wars resulted but, with the breakup of the traditional tribal patterns, the means no longer existed to settle disputes ceremonially, as in the past. Payback killings lasted for years, and even today deep hostilities can be found between dispossessed groups based on their original tribal affiliations. Other Aborigines died as a result of disease. There is considerable debate about how smallpox was introduced to Australia – some believe that it may have been present in the north before European contact, introduced by Indonesian traders. Other

European impact on the Aborigines
The settlement of Australia by the British brought immediate conflict with the indigenous inhabitants. The colonizers declared the land unoccupied, *terra nullius*, but more than 3,000 settlers died attempting to prove their claim over it. Casualty rates among the Aborigines were far higher but were unrecorded. In the first half century of settlement the fiercest resistance took place around the areas of close settlement in southeast Australia, in Tasmania, where the Aborigines were systematically eradicated, and around Perth and Fremantle in Western Australia. As the pastoralists extended their range into the interior, the forcible dispossession and removal of tribal groups into adjacent areas provoked intertribal conflict. In this century the activities of mining companies encroaching on traditional sites have aroused fierce opposition in the Northern Territory.

Below The Reverend John Williams of the London Missionary Society was killed by islanders in the New Hebrides in 1839. His death aroused great public excitement in Britain, where it was rumored that his body had been cooked and eaten, and he is shown here suffering a martyr's death. He had already had considerable missionary success in the Cook Islands and Samoa.

accounts suggest that the smallpox virus was carried for inoculation purposes on board the First Fleet. When an outbreak of smallpox occurred in 1789, it spread rapidly among the Aborigines living along the east coast, who had no natural immunity to the disease and no access to inoculation. Its effects were far less damaging among the white community.

Christian evangelists of all denominations were active among the Aborigines. Missions and "reserves" – places set aside for Aboriginal groups to reside on – were virtually synonymous, and until the mid 19th century the colonial administrators encouraged the development of the missions. One of the most famous (which still exists) is the Benedictine monastery at New Norcia, about 130 kilometers north of Perth in Western Australia, which was founded in 1846 by two Spanish monks, Dom Salvado and Dom Serra, to teach the Catholic religion together with farming and other skills to the Aborigines. The Christian missions declined in importance as the number of government reserves – all too often brutal places of detention and confinement – increased. Christian proselytizing continues to the present day, especially by evangelical groups who proclaim a spiritual renaissance among Aboriginal communities in the north.

Fiji and the islands of Melanesia
After de Quirós's ill-fated attempt to establish a settlement on Espiritu Santo in 1606, more than a century and a half was to elapse before French and British navigators, in the late 18th century, began to put the islands of Melanesia back on European maps of the

Pacific. Early European contact with Melanesia was not promising. Cook, who visited Fiji, the New Hebrides (Vanuatu) and New Caledonia on his second Pacific expedition in 1774, was dismissive of the islanders, remarking of the New Hebrideans: "These people are in a rude state, and if we can judge from circumstances and appearances, are frequently at war not with their neighbors, but among themselves." They resisted attempts to win them over with the usual gifts of trinkets, appearing fearful that the newcomers were planning to invade them. James Calvert, a fire and brimstone Methodist who visited Fiji in 1835, was even more uncomplimentary. He described the Fijians as "Cannibals beyond redemption, the very embodiment of evil," and judged that "The savage in Fiji broke beyond the common limits of rapine and bloodshed, and violating every elementary instinct of humanity, stood unrivalled as a disgrace to mankind."

Reports such as these cast the islands of Melanesia in a very negative light, and it was the last part of the Pacific region to be opened up to European activity. What first attracted visitors in any number was the discovery of sandalwood trees in the island forests; their timber, used in ornamental carving and cabinetmaking, had high value as a trading commodity in India and Asia. Within ten years of arriving in Fiji in 1804, cutters from Australia had stripped the islands of its sandalwood reserves, and had moved on to the New Hebrides by the 1830s and New Caledonia a decade later. These early traders were hard-bitten, often disreputable individuals. They made no attempt to extend control outside their coastal settlements, and

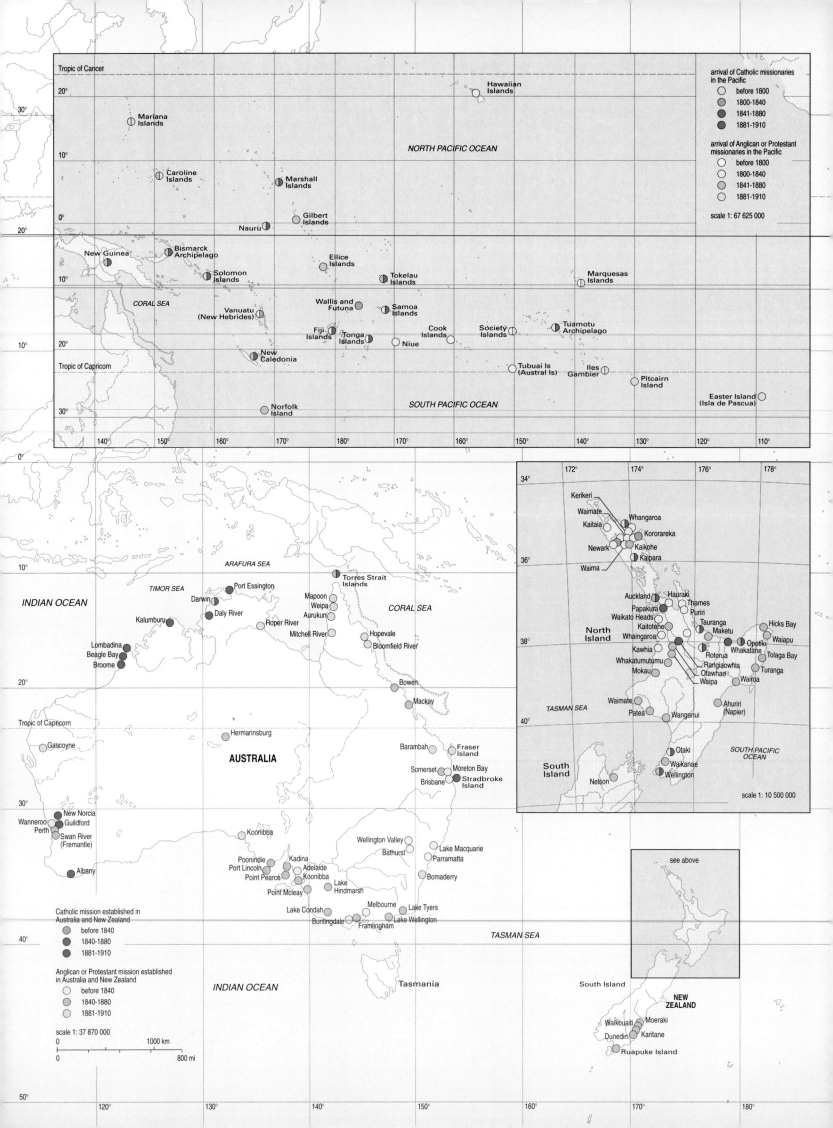

Arrival of Catholic missionaries in the Pacific
- ○ before 1800
- ◑ 1800-1840
- ◕ 1841-1880
- ● 1881-1910

Arrival of Anglican or Protestant missionaries in the Pacific
- ○ before 1800
- ◔ 1800-1840
- ◑ 1841-1880
- ◕ 1881-1910

scale 1: 67 625 000

Tropic of Cancer

20°

30°

Mariana
Islands

Caroline
Islands

Marshall
Islands

Nauru

Gilbert
Islands

NORTH PACIFIC OCEAN

Hawaiian
Islands

New Guinea

Bismarck
Archipelago

Solomon
Islands

Ellice
Islands

Tokelau
Islands

Marquesas
Islands

CORAL SEA

Vanuatu
(New Hebrides)

Wallis and
Futuna

Samoa
Islands

Fiji
Islands

Tonga
Islands

Cook
Islands

Niue

Society
Islands

Tuamotu
Archipelago

New
Caledonia

Tropic of Capricorn

Tubuai Is
(Austral Is)

Iles
Gambier

Pitcairn
Island

Easter Island
(Isla de Pascua)

Norfolk
Island

SOUTH PACIFIC OCEAN

Catholic mission established in Australia and New Zealand
- ◑ before 1840
- ◕ 1840-1880
- ● 1881-1910

Anglican or Protestant mission established in Australia and New Zealand
- ○ before 1840
- ◔ 1840-1880
- ◑ 1881-1910

scale 1: 37 870 000

0   1000 km

0   800 mi

INDIAN OCEAN

ARAFURA SEA

TIMOR SEA

Port Essington

Darwin

Daly River

Kalumburu

Roper River

Torres Strait
Islands

Mapoon

Weipa

Aurukun

Mitchell River

CORAL SEA

Hopevale

Bloomfield River

Lombadina

Beagle Bay

Broome

Hermannsburg

Bowen

Mackay

AUSTRALIA

Tropic of Capricorn

Gascoyne

Barambah

Fraser
Island

Somerset

Moreton Bay

Brisbane

Stradbroke
Island

New Norcia

Wanneroo

Guildford

Perth

Swan River
(Fremantle)

Koonibba

Wellington Valley

Bathurst

Lake Macquarie

Parramatta

Albany

Poonindie

Port Lincoln

Point Pearce

Kadina

Adelaide

Koonibba

Lake
Hindmarsh

Bomaderry

Point Mcleay

Lake Condah

Buntingdale

Framlingham

Melbourne

Lake Tyers

Lake Wellington

TASMAN SEA

INDIAN OCEAN

Tasmania

South Island

NEW
ZEALAND

Waikouaiti

Dunedin

Moeraki

Karitane

Ruapuke Island

New Zealand inset (scale 1: 10 500 000)

Kerikeri

Waimate

Kaitaia

Whangaroa

Kororareka

Newark

Kaikohe

Kaipara

Waima

Auckland

Hauraki

Papakura

Thames

Waikato Heads

Puriri

Kaitotehe

Tauranga

Maketu

Hicks Bay

North
Island

Whaingaroa

Kawhia

Rotorua

Whakatane

Opotiki

Waiapu

Tolaga Bay

Whakatumutumu

Rangiaowhia

Turanga

Mokau

Otawhao

Wairoa

Waipa

Waimate

Patea

Wanganui

Ahuriri
(Napier)

South
Island

Nelson

Otaki

Waikanae

Wellington

TASMAN SEA

SOUTH PACIFIC
OCEAN

see above

Above The illegal trade of blackbirding was responsible for transporting thousands of Melanesians to the sugarcane plantations of Queensland in the late 19th century. This drawing from the *Illustrated Melbourne Post* of 1872 shows kidnapped men being forced below deck. The trade was strongly criticized by the southern Australian colonies.

Christianity in the South Pacific
(left)
Christianity has had a profound effect on the cultures of the Pacific. The first missions were established by the Spanish in Micronesia in the 17th century, and from the end of the 18th century both Roman Catholic (mainly French) and Protestant missionaries were active in spreading Christianity throughout Polynesia. Missionaries translated the Bible into the different Polynesian languages, thereby giving them written forms, and missionary support for the chiefly rulers helped the spread of European cultural influences. Christianity became central to island life: in Fiji, for example, Wesleyan Methodism is almost a state religion. Throughout the Pacific – particularly in New Zealand and Melanesia – Christianity absorbed aspects of traditional religion and culture, leading to the emergence of new prophetic cults. In Australia, the diversity of indigenous languages prompted missionaries to teach the scriptures in English. At the same time they disdained Aboriginal cultural forms. They proved to be one of the main agents of cultural loss among the Aborigines.

were tolerated by the Melanesians, who could easily have expelled them, because they were able to offer them iron axes and other useful items.

Missionaries were often brutally received by the Melanesians. The Reverend John Williams of the London Missionary Society, continuing on to the New Hebrides from his successes in Samoa, was killed shortly after arriving on the island of Tanna in 1839. James Calvert did not flinch from the immensity of the task of civilizing the warlike Fijians. So ingrained were they in their wicked ways, however, there seemed to him little hope of their redemption. The Fijians' understanding of earthly wealth and power meant that they were quicker to grasp the benefits of trade than of salvation, and though the missionaries preached hellfire and damnation, the islanders' acceptance of Christianity was often no more than a pragmatic move of self-advantage. One tribal chief, Ratu Tui Levuka, was reported as saying "My right hand is Wesleyan and assists Mr Calvert; my left hand is the Pope's religion and assists the Priests; but the rest of my body is *vakatevoro* – heathen."

The first missionary inroads into Fiji had little longterm success, and it was not until the middle of the century that conversion became widespread. As the activities of European traders increased, together with the prevalence of muskets, new opportunities for wealth and power were opened up among the chiefly lines, sparking off a period of intense political rivalry. Cakobau, the chief who emerged as dominant from this process, was converted by Methodist missionaries in 1854, after which most Fijians were quick to follow his example. European missionaries elsewhere in Melanesia met with numerous setbacks. The Roman Catholic Marist Order, which attempted to set up missions in the New Hebrides and the Solomon Islands in the 1840s, was repulsed from both, and did not return until much later in the century. Presbyterian and Anglican missionaries made greater headway in the 1850s and 1860s, and both Protestants and Roman

Catholics were present in New Caledonia from the middle of the century.

The development that brought greatest change and upheaval to Melanesia was plantation agriculture, particularly in Fiji, where coconuts, cotton and, later, sugar cane were all established as commercial crops. The concept of land ownership was alien to the Fijians, and land sales to the mainly American and Australian-owned companies were a frequent cause of friction, while the recruitment of labor from elsewhere in the Pacific led to confrontations with the local population and helped to break up traditional Fijian society. When Fiji became a British crown colony in 1874 migrant sugar cane workers were introduced from India and at the end of their contracts of indenture were encouraged to become permanent settlers – a development that was to have longterm political consequences for the islands.

From the mid 19th century, large numbers of New Hebrideans and Solomon Islanders were also recruited, often through forcible indenture, to work on the plantations of northern Australia after the idea of using Aboriginal labor for this purpose had been abandoned. Within a few years there were approximately 2,000 Melanesians (or Kanakas, as they were then commonly called) working in the cane fields. Some were brought there on contracts of indenture that promised them payment of ten shillings a month. But a very great many were kidnapped and imported as slaves – a nefarious trade known as blackbirding. By 1895 more than 50,000 Kanakas had been introduced to the cane fields of Queensland and northern New South Wales. Morbidity rates were very high as the workers were kept in appalling conditions. Various acts were passed by the Queensland government to try to control the trade, but it was not until legislation was passed banning the trade by the Australian federal government in 1904 that the importation of Pacific islanders was brought to an end. After 1906 those already in Australia were required to be deported. Most were simply shipped off to the nearest islands and dumped; a great many died along the way.

Between 1864 and 1897 more than 22,000 French convicts (*bagnards*) were sent to New Caledonia, which had been annexed by the French in 1854 as a penal colony. Like the convict labor in Australia, the *bagnards* were largely employed in public works, constructing roads, harbor facilities and government buildings. They were also employed in forest clearance, mining and farming. As New Caledonia's plantation economy grew and mining developed, the French colonial administration drew upon large numbers of indentured workers from elsewhere in the Pacific, particularly the New Hebrides and the Solomon Islands, to supplement convict labor. At the same time it set out to encourage free white settlers to the islands, mainly from France, Australia and New Zealand. After 1872 a new group of *bagnards* began to arrive – political prisoners, including 4,000 *communards* from the 1871 Paris uprising. Political prisoners were not required to work though they could hire out their labor. Among the *communards* were many intellectuals and professionals whose skills were eagerly sought by the colony's administrators. Many worked as teachers and the socialist message they helped to put across has been cited as a factor in the social unrest that resulted in 1878 in an uprising, the first of several, among the Melanesian population. Land confiscations and the destruction of the islanders' garden plots to extend the area of settler agriculture were a major source of grievance. The colonial government dealt harshly with indigenous protest and by the end of the century the majority of Melanesians had been relegated to reserves.

The British established plantations on the islands of Efate, Epi and Ambrym in the New Hebrides in the 1870s, but French planters and traders, particularly those of the New Caledonian Company, came to play an increasingly important role in the developing economy of the area. In 1887 the islands were placed under the joint control of the British and French navies, and in 1906 this was succeeded by an Anglo-French condominium. The Solomon Islands were made a British protectorate in 1893, partly to prevent them being annexed by the French.

New Guinea

New Guinea is the second largest island in the world (excluding Australia). For centuries before it came to be drawn on European maps it had been visited by Malay traders, who valued it as a source of slaves and feathers. The first European to sight the island was the Portuguese navigator Antonío de Abrea, as early as 1511. But New Guinea was the last region of the Pacific to be opened up to European trade and colonization, and some of its most inaccessible highland areas were not penetrated by the outside world until the middle years of this century. In the 1930s, when light aircraft made exploration of the rugged terrain much easier, as many as one million people, previously unknown to Europeans, were found to be living in remote areas of the Eastern Highlands. Even today there are large numbers of Highland New Guineans who have never seen a European.

Though the Dutch claimed the western part of the island (present-day Irian Jaya) as part of the territory of the Dutch East Indies in 1828, they did not attempt to exercise any administrative control there until the end of the 19th century. Even after eastern Australia's rising agricultural and trading importance had made the Torres Strait an important waterway for European shipping, little interest was shown in colonizing southeastern New Guinea. The famed ferocity of the Torres Strait Islanders and the coastal-dwelling New Guineans no doubt served to dampen the bravest spirits; nor were the swampy lowlands on the south of the island and the rugged mountains on its northern side conducive to exploration and settlement. In the words of a report that appeared in the *Illustrated London News* in 1848, two years after a British landing party had been repulsed by a hostile group of islanders, the New Guinean coast had "hitherto only been seen from a distance, and not visited by navigators, on account of the dangers with which it is beset."

British interest in the island began to deepen in the last quarter of the 19th century. Captain John Moresby undertook a survey of the southeastern coast in the 1870s, and British planters began to move into the islands of New Britain and New Ireland. It was, however, only when the German-owned New Guinea Company moved into the northeastern part of the island in 1884 that Britain, at the prompting of the Queensland government, annexed Papua (the southeast part of the island). The costs of administration were shared between Britain and the governments of Victoria, New South Wales and Queensland. After 1906 Australia had sole administrative charge of Papua, and in 1921 it was officially mandated control

of German New Guinea (which it had annexed in 1914 on the outbreak of World War I) by the League of Nations.

One reaction of the New Guineans to the coming of Europeans was the growth of what later came to be known as cargo cults. The belief arose that European power resided in the wooden crates in which colonial officials received their supplies of goods. Tribesmen imagined that by carrying these crates, and by mimicking the marching of European soldiers or undertaking domestic duties such as setting tables, they would be able to tap the source of European power. The cargo cults – which were not confined to New Guinea, but also sprang up in the Solomon Islands and other parts of Melanesia – took on a millenarian, anti-European character, mingling aspects of Christian and indigenous belief. The end of the world was widely predicted, and a new age of blessing would be inaugurated by the arrival of a special cargo of goods sent by tribal gods or ancestors, who were expected to return with the cargo. Or the goods were expected to come through the Europeans, who were sometimes accused of having prevented them from reaching those for whom they were intended. Cargo cults proliferated during the 1930s. Airplanes as well as ships were expected to bring the cargoes, and symbolic airstrips were built in preparation for their coming.

Dramatic as the cargo cults were, it was the replacement of stone implements by highly prized iron axes that had the greatest impact on indigenous cultures and society. The new tools spread rapidly among the different tribes, and even penetrated the highlands in advance of European contact. By speeding up the clearance of forest plots for cultivation they became the means by which the subsistence economies of the hunters and gatherers were transformed into cash economies. Thus the iron ax played a major role in the renegotiation of tribal authority and law that followed as a consequence of European contact, and contributed directly to the breakdown of the old ways.

Above Cargo cults developed large followings throughout the Pacific, but particularly in New Guinea where the confusion of Christian teachings and materialist Melanesian cultures was a potent combination. The cults identified the cargo carried by Europeans as the source of their power; the means of their transportation, ships and later airplanes, were also the focus of attention. Pictured here is the effigy of a white "messiah" with a cross and a carving of an airplane.

Left The British flag is raised in Port Moresby on 6 November 1884 as Papua becomes a British protectorate. Australian interests, especially in Queensland, anxious about the threat of further German penetration into New Guinea, urged that Papua should be fully annexed. Britain was not keen to add to its imperial burdens and when annexation took place four years later, it shared the costs of the territory's administration with the eastern colonies of Australia. In 1914, on the outbreak of World War I, Australia took over the running of Germany's holdings in New Guinea, and in 1921 Papua New Guinea became an Australian protectorate. Independence was achieved in 1975.

Right Kaipel, a Wahgi man from the New Guinea Highlands, with his shield, painted with a design that is based on an advertisement for South Pacific lager. But this is not simply the corruption of Wahgi tradition that it might seem; elements of the advertisement have been subtly altered so that it refers to traditional clan rivalries.

A COMMUNITY OF THIEVES

An unlikely beginning

Few societies have had less inspired beginnings than Australia. Its first colonists were convicted felons – a mixed bag of murderers, rapists, prostitutes and pimps, petty criminals, political prisoners and hard cases. By all contemporary estimations, and by any social categorization we might choose to apply today, the First Fleeters were drawn from the low life of British and Irish society. The transportation of convicts to far-off places of incarceration was not a new phenomenon in 1788 (the British already sent convicts to North America, Bermuda and Gibraltar), but Australia was destined to become the only modern nation in the world to be founded on the basis of this particular form of human commerce.

By the late 18th century the "houses of correction" set up in the reign of Queen Elizabeth two centuries earlier were proving quite inadequate to contain the growing numbers of convicted felons who fell foul of England's increasingly draconian property laws or political prisoners detained by a government that was becoming fearful of the spread of sedition. After 1776, when transportation ceased to the American colonies, more and more criminals were crammed into prison hulks – permanently moored, rotting ships that listed low in the gray-brown waters of the Thames or at naval ports along the coast. Many sank in the slightest rough weather; they all stank with excrement and the corpses of expired inmates. These hulks caused alarm among townspeople, worried that they would bring the contagion of rebellion or disease – "jail fever" as it was called – to their doorsteps.

There was general agreement that an alternative to the hulks should be found. The problem of where to house Britain's criminal excess opened up a debate that ranged widely over questions about the political, practical and philosophical nature of crime and punishment. The building of penitentiaries, a system favored by the philosopher Jeremy Bentham (1748–1832) among others, was ruled out as being too expensive: Bentham's elaborate plan for a "panopticon" maintained by a sophisticated surveillance system had to await the electronic monitoring of the 20th century before it would become a practical proposition. His ideas for a central prison administration brought him into direct conflict with the local authorities who were responsible for the houses of correction. So transportation remained the best solution. The possibility of sending felons to established colonies was discussed, but the American revolution had left the government nervous of the risk of arousing colonial discontent, so it was dropped. Various locations on the west coast of Africa were considered – one plan put forward in all seriousness was to abandon the convicts on the beaches of the Ivory Coast, where they would presumably have perished. Another eccentric suggestion was to exchange convicts for Christian slaves in Algeria and Tunisia. A report on South Africa was commissioned, and for a time this looked a promising option. But the findings were unfavorable: the location lacked water. Had the report been more positive (and had Cook not happened to have made landfall at a well-watered spot on the east coast), Australia, the world's driest continent, might have waited longer to be colonized. One of the first to argue the case publicly for New South Wales to be

Above Captain Arthur Phillip (1738–1814) was a naval officer who had seen active service in the Seven Years' War before being appointed first governor of New South Wales in 1786. He commanded the First Fleet and chose Port Jackson as the site of the new colony on its arrival in Australia in January 1788. His letters of commission gave Phillip almost unlimited power, but he had difficulty in establishing his personal authority: his enlightened views on punishment brought him into conflict with the officers of the marines responsible for policing the colony, and he won few friends among the convicts either. Phillip returned to England for medical reasons in 1792 and resigned a year later. He resumed his naval career and was promoted to admiral just before his death in 1814, having retired from active service several years earlier.

made a penal colony was Joseph Banks, by now President of the Royal Society, who told a parliamentary committee in 1779 that it might serve as a place for the transportation of criminals, stressing its good climate, variety of soil, potential for agriculture, freedom from hostile inhabitants and beasts of prey, and abundance of timber and water.

The government of William Pitt, which came to office in 1784, was determined to resolve the prison problem once and for all. Accordingly, the prime minister announced to the House of Commons that "no cheaper mode of disposing of the convicts could be found" than to dispatch them to Australia, and in August 1786 the Admiralty was instructed to arrange for a fleet of convict ships, under the command of Captain Arthur Phillip, to be sent to Botany Bay. Given that the Pacific was an arena of intense and growing colonial rivalry between the European powers, more should be read into the government's decision than Pitt's simple statement suggests. Cook and Banks had indicated that New South Wales and Norfolk Island would be likely sources of essential naval supplies, and those urging their colonization were attracted by the possibilities of establishing a base to protect and enlarge Britain's trading interests in the South Pacific. What really seems to have prompted the British government to action were the rumors then circulating in London that the French were exploring the east coast of Australia. (The Colonial Office was also concerned by Dutch activity in the region.) That this was no idle threat was confirmed within days of the First Fleet's arrival in Australia, when two European ships were sighted in the vicinity of Botany Bay. These belonged to La Pérouse's Pacific expedition, which had left France two and a half years earlier. The French commander remained in Botany Bay for several weeks carrying out experiments and studying the fauna and flora, before making sail for the Pacific on 19 March 1788 – the last that was ever seen of his ships. As a parting gesture, La Pérouse gave his name to an area on the northern foreshore of Botany Bay.

The Starving Time

Far from containing the "fine meadow" promised by Cook, Botany Bay turned out to be a flat expanse of scrub that afforded poor, unprotected anchorage. Within days of his arrival Phillip had rejected it as the site of the proposed settlement, choosing instead Port Jackson inlet (Sydney Harbor), about 8 kilometers to the north, which he described as the best natural harbor in the world. It was well served by a freshwater spring, which today lies beneath the central business district of Sydney, Australia's oldest and premier city. Here, on 26 January 1788 (celebrated each year as Australia Day), Phillip hoisted the British flag and proclaimed the settlement of the colony of New South Wales in the name of King George III. In the words of an eyewitness to the event, a "flag staff had been purposely erected and an union jack displayed, when the marines fired several volleys; between which the governor and the officers who accompanied him drank the healths of his Majesty and the Royal Family, and success to the new colony."

Even before the departure of the First Fleet for Australia, Botany Bay had become synonymous in popular usage with New South Wales: in 1779 *The Times* newspaper reported that "Men of profligate principles empowered with the empanelling of juries, may give away the lives of every honest Englishman, and send people to the New Drop, or Botany Bay, who ought to go to some better place." The name stuck fast, despite the removal of the penal colony to Port Jackson, and in time it became the shorthand term for the whole system of transportation. In 1828 Botany Bay was described as an "immense hulk, as it were, a common sewer, into which the refuse of the jails of England periodically drains." The name passed into convict literature and become lodged in British, Irish and Australian folk memory: "Botany Bay" is the title of one of the best-known folksongs from the transportation period, still commonly sung today. It is somewhat ironic that Cook had initially considered calling the place Stingray Bay, after two large fish that his crew caught there, preferring instead to commemorate the quantity of botanic specimens gathered by Banks. The former name might have been the more appropriate, considering the sting that the convicts would feel in the tail of the lash.

By the time the Second Fleet reached Port Jackson in 1790 the tiny colony was on the verge of starvation. The land had proved far less fertile than had been hoped and the colonists lacked farming skills. Their first attempts to grow crops were unsuccessful: the meager cereal harvest had to be saved for seed for the next season's sowing, and vegetables failed to flourish. Though the colonists had brought livestock with them, many animals died or strayed, and game was scarce. At the end of 1788 Phillip was forced to send a ship to Cape Town to buy supplies, which returned in May 1789 with wheat, barley and flour, but even so strict rationing had to be introduced. Far from bringing hoped-for relief, the Second Fleet exacerbated the colony's problems. Heading south off the Cape of Good Hope to pick up the Roaring Forties, the fleet's storeship hit an iceberg, the food supply was jettisoned to save the boat from sinking, and the Second Fleeters arrived without the means to feed themselves, let alone supplement the settlement's meager resources. Not for nothing did this period become known in folk memory as "the starving time".

The condition of the Second Fleet was an ominous

portent of the full horrors of the transportation system. More than one thousand convicts had boarded the ships at Portsmouth, but 11 died while the ships were still preparing to leave England, a further 267 perished at sea, several were found to be dead on arrival, and one hundred more died on or soon after docking – in all, more than a third of the transportation's original rollcall. As the ships tied up to disembark their cargo, rotting corpses were simply tossed into the harbor and it became abundantly clear to all who had gathered to welcome the fleet that these were "hell ships", every bit as bad as the prison hulks they were intended to relieve. In the opinion of some, conditions were even worse than those of the African slavers, where financial incentives meant that ships' captains at least provided their human cargo with the minimum to survive. "The slave trade is merciful to what I have seen", one of the officers on board the Second Fleet recorded.

The Reverend Richard Johnson, who buried 86 of those who died in the period immediately after the fleet's arrival, described the scene below decks as "truly shocking to the feelings of humanity, a great number of them laying, some half naked and others quite nearly quite naked, without either bed or bedding, unable to turn or help themselves ... the smell was so offensive that I could scarcely bear it." His journal describes the wretched state of the survivors, many of whom were too weak to walk unaided, or able only to crawl on hands and knees into the fresh air. The overwhelming majority of those who pulled through were unfit to undertake any kind of work for a very long time. Others were permanently invalided, or went mad from their ordeal.

The mortality rate on board the Third Fleet, which arrived in 1791, was not as high as the Second (approximately one in ten), but once again many of those who disembarked were too sick or enfeebled to

contribute to the colony. By 1801 43 transport ships had arrived in Australia carrying 7,486 convicts, of whom 756 were dead on arrival. Corrupt officials, sadistic masters and crews, and drunken or incompetent surgeons contributed to this appalling record. Men perished at the rate of one in every eight; women fared better, but the death rate of one in 28 was still lamentable. In 1802 the colonial administration took a leaf out of the page of the slave trade and began paying surgeons a financial incentive for every prisoner landed fit for work, while captains received a bonus of £50 for a ship arriving in good order. For a time, conditions on board the transports improved markedly, and the mortality rate declined.

Moral discipline was imposed among those who survived the voyage through the dual tyranny of hard labor and the lash. In the early days of the settlement, the authorities were so little concerned for the spiritual welfare of the felons (as indeed they were for that of the Aborigines) that Governor Phillip refused to give any help toward building a place of worship. His first priorities were law, order and public works. It has often been suggested that this decision sowed the seeds of the secularism for which Australian society has come to be noted. Despite the growing numbers of Irish prisoners, the observance of Catholic mass was banned absolutely until 1821. Skepticism of religious and secular authority grew to be a tenacious characteristic among following generations of Australians, enshrined in the attitude that holds that Jack is always as good as his master. In the late 19th century agnostic Australians developed the name "Hughie" to signify the deity, who might, for example, be entreated to bring the rains with the disrespectful incantation, "Send it down Hughie."

On the other side of the world from home and off the commonly used shipping routes, Port Jackson was a natural prison – the "gulag of the south seas", as

Left This picture of convicts aboard a transport ship shows a relatively ordered scene: though the prisoners are confined in cages, conditions below deck appear sanitary and well-lit. This was far from being the case during the early years of transportation. The surgeons aboard the overcrowded "hell ships" were drunk and inept, the officers corrupt and brutal, and death rates among the prisoners, kept huddled in chains in the dark lower decks, were appallingly high: many of those who survived the rigors of the voyage were unfit for heavy labor for months or even years after arrival, posing an economic burden on the colony. Once captains were paid a bonus for every prisoner landed fit for work, conditions on the transport ships began to improve.

Above Shortly after arriving in New South Wales, Governor Phillip ordered the settlement of Norfolk Island, lying in the Pacific some 1,500 kilometers east of the Australian coastline. It was hoped that the indigenous Norfolk pines, which had been noted by Captain Cook when he passed the island in 1774, would form the basis of a Pacific timber trade. But though the pines grew straight and to a good height their trunks snapped too easily under stress to make them suitable for ships' masts or spars, and this plan had to be abandoned. Flax production on the island proved only a little more successful.

some historians and commentators have come to term it. Though a handful of prisoners contrived to stow away or illegally commandeer a ship, the number of escapees from the colony was slight. Chains were used to prevent "bolters" from fleeing into the bush, but they were scarcely necessary. Only the very crafty or the very stupid risked moving outside the limits of settlement, to face an almost certain death, either through hunger and thirst from ignorance of what plants were safe to eat or the whereabouts of water-holes, or at the hands of hostile Aborigines. In 1791 a group of desperate Irish attempted to escape by walking overland to China – which they imagined lay some distance to the north, a persistent belief among early convicts – but perished only a few kilometers from Sydney. Windowbars were placed on colonial buildings not to confine the convicts but to keep the Aboriginals out and frustrate their "thieving ways". It was not until the 1820s and later that gangs of escaped convicts began to live as bushrangers, hunting kangaroos to sell for their skins (especially in Van Diemen's Land), cattle-rustling and sheep-stealing.

Criminals, martyrs and slaves

Between 1788 and 1868 around 160,000 convicts were forcibly shipped to Australia. In the early years, the transports all went directly to New South Wales. In 1788 Phillip, hoping to relieve pressure on the Port

Jackson colony, sent a shipload of convicts and guards on to Norfolk Island, a volcanic peak in the Pacific nearly 1,500 kilometers northeast of Sydney. He may also have wanted to forestall French claims to the island: when Cook first sighted it in 1774 he noted its fine stands of pine trees, which he thought would make excellent ships' masts (he was wrong). New Zealand flax was also found to grow there but attempts to set up a flax industry were unsuccessful, and the settlement was abandoned in 1814 (the island was used again as a prison for re-offenders between 1825 and 1856). The retransportation of convicts from New South Wales to Van Diemen's Land started in 1803; it began receiving shipments directly from Britain and Ireland in 1817. During the wars against Revolutionary and Napoleonic France (1793–1802; 1803–15), the transports arrived irregularly, and there were long periods when none came at all. Shifting villains halfway round the world was considered an extravagant use of resources in wartime; moreover, convicts could usefully be put to work building warships in the dockyards at home or made to serve as cannon fodder on the battlefields of Europe. With the coming of peace, the transports were much more systematically organized – more than 50,000 convicts arrived in the 1820s and 1830s. By the time the shipments to New South Wales ceased in 1840 it had received more than 80,000 convicts; Van Diemen's

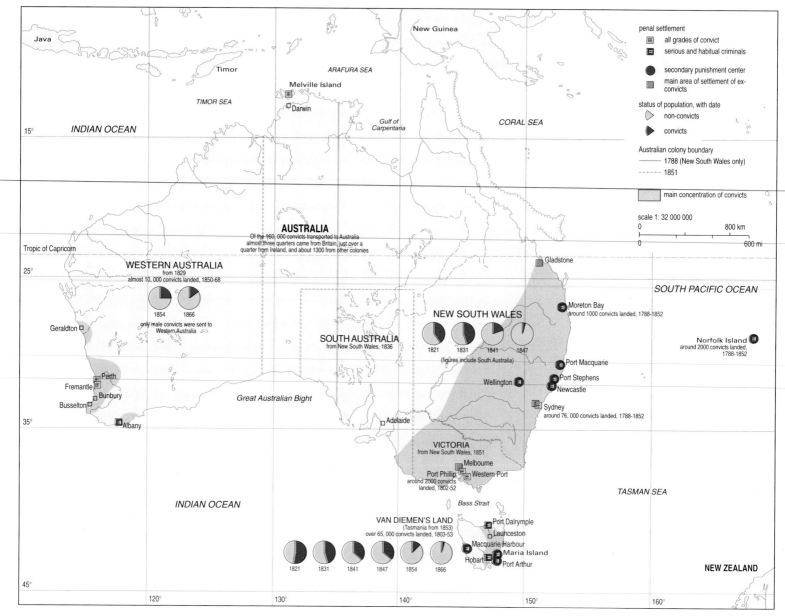

penal settlement
- all grades of convict
- serious and habitual criminals
- secondary punishment center
- main area of settlement of ex-convicts

status of population, with date
- non-convicts
- convicts

Australian colony boundary
— 1788 (New South Wales only)
---- 1851

main concentration of convicts

scale 1: 32 000 000
0   800 km
0   600 mi

Java

Timor

TIMOR SEA

INDIAN OCEAN

ARAFURA SEA

New Guinea

Gulf of Carpentaria

CORAL SEA

Melville Island
Darwin

Tropic of Capricorn

AUSTRALIA
Of the 160, 000 convicts transported to Australia almost three quarters came from Britain, just over a quarter from Ireland, and about 1300 from other colonies

WESTERN AUSTRALIA
from 1829
almost 10, 000 convicts landed, 1850-68

1854   1866
only male convicts were sent to Western Australia

Geraldton

Perth
Fremantle
Bunbury
Busselton

Great Australian Bight

Albany

SOUTH AUSTRALIA
from New South Wales, 1836

NEW SOUTH WALES

1821   1831   1841   1847
(figures include South Australia)

SOUTH PACIFIC OCEAN

Gladstone

Moreton Bay
around 1000 convicts landed, 1788-1852

Norfolk Island
around 2000 convicts landed, 1788-1852

Port Macquarie

Port Stephens
Newcastle

Wellington

Sydney
around 76, 000 convicts landed, 1788-1852

Adelaide

VICTORIA
from New South Wales, 1851

Melbourne
Port Phillip   Western Port
around 2000 convicts landed, 1802-52

INDIAN OCEAN

TASMAN SEA

Bass Strait

VAN DIEMEN'S LAND
(Tasmania from 1853)
over 65, 000 convicts landed, 1803-53

1821   1831   1841   1847   1854   1866

Port Dalrymple
Launceston
Macquarie Harbour
Maria Island
Hobart   Port Arthur

NEW ZEALAND

Land, which stopped taking in convicts in 1852, had absorbed a further 65,000.

A less ambitious, more short-lived period of transportation began to Western Australia in 1850. The western third of the continent had been annexed by Britain in 1829, when a free colony was set up on the Swan River with its main settlement at Perth and its port at Fremantle. The land proved difficult to work and labor was always short. Through the 1840s local demand grew for a convict labor force to prop up the ailing economy, and in 1850 the British government reluctantly allowed transportation to begin again. Just over 500 convicts arrived in Fremantle every year over the course of the next 18 years. The last convict ship to arrive in Australia, the *Hougoumont*, berthed at Fremantle Harbor in 1868.

What sort of men and women composed this force of unwilling migrants? Many have argued that the transportees were more sinned against than sinning, the victims of Britain's unfair judicial system, which listed more than 200 crimes as hanging offenses at the end of the 18th century. They had perhaps been sentenced to punitive exile simply for stealing a loaf of bread or poaching a rabbit from the squire's estate to feed their starving families. Others were transported for protesting against the English political system: Irish nationalists and agitators, including a number

convicted for their part in the United Irish rebellion of 1798; radicals such as the "Scottish Martyrs", Jacobins influenced by the ideas of the French Revolution and convicted for sedition in Edinburgh in 1793 and 1794; and working-class dissidents – machine-breaking Luddites, agricultural agitators such as the "Swing" rioters and hayrick-burners of the 1830s, and early trades unionists, including the Tolpuddle Martyrs, six agricultural laborers transported in 1834 for the crime of "administering unlawful oaths". Nevertheless, many of the convicts were undoubtedly habitual criminals, murderers and other violent offenders, who had been before the courts many times before being sentenced to penal servitude in Australia.

The typical convict transported to Australia was male, aged between 16 and 25, and of average height and weight. He often had a trade or was semi-skilled; around 60 percent were able to read and write – a higher rate of literacy than was to be found among those left behind in England. Such statistics have led historians to conclude that the convicts, particularly in the 1820s and 1830s, were specially selected for the transports for their intelligence and ability to work hard. It has not passed unnoticed that broadly similar physical criteria were used by those responsible for selecting immigrants to Australia in the 20th century. Whatever the nature of their crimes, it seems that the

The penal settlement of Australia
Just under half of the total number of 160,000 convicts shipped to Australia were destined for New South Wales, though Van Diemen's Land also absorbed large numbers; it continued to receive transport ships for 13 years after New South Wales refused to accept any more in 1840. No convicts were sent to South Australia, and only a few jails were established in Victoria. Western Australia received convicts between 1850 and 1868. Even after transportation ceased, large numbers of convicts remained to complete their sentences.

Above right Convicts were dressed in a distinctive yellow and black uniform known as magpie clothing; they were chained when working on road gangs and when carrying out public works – visible marks of the "convict stain".

Right The convicts who were assigned as workers to free settlers were treated as little more than slaves. With a plentiful and cheap labor force at their disposal settlers quickly adopted the style of local aristocrats. Here convict workers are pushing a railway dolly containing top-hatted and bewhiskered dignitaries.

primary purpose of the transportation system was to create a labor force to lay the foundations of a new society in the Pacific. Seen from this point of view, the convicts are just one part of a larger movement of enslaved and indentured workers that in the course of the 19th century transported as many as 5 million people from one part of the globe to another – about the same number as migrated to the new worlds of their own free will during the same period.

Several colonial administrators in the convict period – notably Lachlan Macquarie (1762–1824), governor of New South Wales from 1810 to 1821, Sir George Arthur (1784–1854), lieutenant-governor of Van Diemen's Land from 1824 to 1836, Sir Richard Bourke (1777–1855), governor of New South Wales from 1830 to 1837, and Sir George Gipps (1791–1847), governor of New South Wales from 1838 to 1846 – publicly stated that the convict system was a form of slavery. An influential inquiry into transportation completed in 1838 concluded that it "is much more than exile; it is slavery as well." Several points of similarity can be found between transportation and the African–American slave trade. For both convicts and slaves, the conditions of incarceration were often very brutal. Both groups were physically confined in chains and forcibly shipped across the sea, with enormous psychological effects of dislocation. Both were punished with whippings and beatings. Both sought what comfort there was to be had from turning to one another for support.

But there were all-important differences. African slaves were kidnapped and transported to North America and the Caribbean without even so much a pretence of having committed a crime: the fact of their

color and race alone was enough to condemn them to servitude. Moreover, unless explicitly sentenced to serve "for the term of his natural life", a convict could expect to be released after 7, 14 or 21 years. When their sentences expired, some convicts (such as the first ex-convict landowner, James Ruse) became wealthy colonists. Any children born of convicts in Australia were not, as a matter of birth, slaves. By contrast, the Afro-American slaves could not win their freedom until liberated as a class. The only real slave trade that existed in 19th-century Australia was that of the Kanaka workers forcibly removed from the islands of Melanesia to the cane fields of Queensland.

Irish rebels

The first Irish to arrive in New South Wales came with the Third Fleet in 1791. From then until the arrival of the last convict ship in 1868 approximately one in three of all transportees was Irish. Some 40,000 were transported directly from Ireland, while a further 8,000 were sent from England. In character and background the Irish convicts were very different from those from other parts of the United Kingdom. Study of court records and ships' indents show that most English convicts came from the criminal underworlds of the rapidly industrializing cities – more than 45 percent of them were from London and the surrounding area, the Midlands and the northwest. (There were of course significant exceptions, such as the agrarian rioters.) Those from Scotland were usually serious reoffenders sentenced to transportation rather than the gallows. By contrast, the Irish were very often farm laborers and peasants, mostly from Dublin and the northwest counties of Donegal, Leitrim and Sligo.

Many of the Irish were transported as thieves. The circumstances of every convict were different, and each had an individual story to tell, but Mary Talbot's was probably not untypical. After her stonemason husband was crippled in an accident at work she made her way across the Irish Sea to England in order to support her two children. There she was charged with theft, which she admitted, saying that she had needed to steal to feed her children, and was sentenced to death. A reprieve was offered in the form of transportation, but on learning that her children could not travel to Australia with her she chose the gallows instead. Once again she was offered the chance of transportation, and this time accepted on the understanding that her children would be allowed to accompany her. Several years later they still had not joined her. Her petition to the governor survives, in which she asks him to pardon her "for the sake of my motherless children, they are the only cause of my anxiety and unhappiness." We do not know the end of her story, though it is likely that Mary Talbot died in Australia without ever seeing her children again.

The authorities also despatched a steady stream of political agitators protesting against English colonial rule – the Irish made up the majority of political prisoners arriving in Australia, though not all were recognized as such, and from first to last the ships bringing the Irish to Australia could claim to have rebels on board. Among those on the *Queen* in 1791 were members of the Break o' Day Boys, one of many agrarian protest groups violently engaged against English landlords in the northwest of the country, while in 1868 the *Hougoumont* contained a number of Fenian rebels who had been sentenced to transportation for the seditious activity of singing Irish nationalist songs.

The Irish were overwhelmingly Roman Catholic, so – though not all Catholics in Australia were Irish – Catholicism and Irishness became synonymous in the popular mind. Nationalist conviction and commitment to their religion frequently brought the Irish into conflict with the colonial authorities, from which they have earned the reputation of providing the radical dynamic in Australian history. The Irish determination not to have English manners and laws perfectly reproduced in Australia, thus preventing it from becoming a new Britannia in the south seas, was central to the shaping of Australian nationalism, encouraging its development as a form of emotional resentment of authority. With their strongly felt and highly developed anti-British rhetoric, the Irish were able to articulate in political terms the grievances of many convicts. They readily provided the leadership in protest movements. Although armed uprisings in Australia were surprisingly few, the Irish were invariably identified as ringleaders. One of Irish Australia's legendary heroes is John Boyle O'Reilly, who arrived as a Fenian rebel on board the *Hougoumont*. Within a year he had managed to escape to America where he established himself as an editor and writer in Boston. In 1875, with the members of an Irish nationalist group known as Clan na Gael, he sailed a yacht, the *Catalpa*, to Western Australia and rescued the remaining Fenians from jail. A chase ensued across the Indian Ocean but the flamboyant O'Reilly eluded the authorities and was given a hero's welcome when he brought the *Catalpa* safely back to Boston. The *Catalpa* raid subsequently became celebrated in Australian folksong and literature.

Above The Reverend Samuel Marsden (1784–1838) arrived in New South Wales in 1794 to coordinate the efforts of the influential London Missionary Society throughout the Pacific. A sadistic magistrate famous for his loathing of the Irish, he became known as the "flogging parson" and was the object of considerable derision, as well as hatred, among the convict population.

The Castle Hill uprising

It was Irish nationalists from the 1798 rebellion who formed the leadership of the first and most famous armed uprising against colonial rule in Australia. This took place at Castle Hill, an agricultural settlement northwest of Sydney, in 1804. The Irish had been particularly incensed by the activities of the Reverend Samuel Marsden, assistant chaplain in the colony, as well as a magistrate and one of the richest men in New South Wales at that time. He was well-known for his hatred of Catholicism and of Irish nationals, whom he would order to be chastised on the merest suspicion of political or religious intrigue. His arbitrary use of the lash, however, actually defeated his own purpose by making cult heroes of those Irish who refused to buckle under his authoritarian pressure.

In 1800 Marsden had sentenced two Irishmen, Maurice Fitzgerald and Paddy Galvin, to be flogged on the slimmest of evidence. Each was to receive 300 lashes with the cat-o-nine tails, and two men, one left-handed, the other right-handed, were appointed to flog them in tandem. According to an eye-witness account, "During the time Fitzgerald was receiving the punishment, he never uttered a groan; the only words he said were, 'Flog me fair; do not strike me on the neck.'" Galvin "never even whimpered or flinched" and when asked to reveal others involved in his crime replied, "You may hang me ...if you like; but you will have not music from my mouth to make others dance upon nothing." The unwarranted severity of the flogging hardened Irish attitudes against Marsden in particular and the English in general. Relations between them had reached flash point when, in 1804, 300 rebels assembled at Castle Hill with the intention of sparking a widespread revolution in the colony.

Alerted to the uprising, soldiers marched against the protesters, who were armed only with a few guns, sticks, stones and pitchforks. When the troopers opened fire, several rebels were killed outright. Others were hunted down and killed in the bush. Six "ring-leaders" were hanged and the remainder sent off for secondary punishment. The Castle Hill rebels entered the Australian legend as defenders of liberty and protesters against tyranny. But Marsden did not learn his lesson. Some 18 years later an inquiry into the running of the colony singled him out for criticism. "Without, however, impeaching the moral feelings of Mr Marsden, and without stating it as my opinion that he has acted with undue severity," wrote John Bigge (1780–1843), the commissioner of the inquiry, "it is in proof, that his sentences are not only, in fact, more severe than those of other magistrates, but the general opinion of the colony is, that his character, as displayed in the administration of the penal law in New South Wales is stamped with severity."

Not surprisingly, in the wake of the Castle Hill uprising and other mutinies, the Irish developed a reputation as trouble-makers, which later reappeared in their role as active trades unionists in the second half of the 19th century. In another sense, however, they proved to be exemplary subjects. While being well represented in the annals of radical Australian nationalism, they were also builders of churches and schools and exponents of a strict moral code based on the tenets of Catholicism. Moreover, their community values were centered on the family. In the transportation period almost half the women convicts sent to Australia were Irish. This meant that the ratio of Irish men to women was as low as two to one, while it reached ten to one among the convict population in

Above Irish convicts – many of whom were transported as political prisoners – quickly developed a reputation for rebellious behavior. It was dissidents transported for their part in the 1798 Irish rebellion, marching under the Irish radical banner "Death or Liberty", who instigated the Castle Hill uprising of 1804 , the first organized protest against authority in Australia. The rebellion was swiftly put down by a detachment of the New South Wales Corps. Many rebels were killed, and the surviving organizers executed.

Right This watercolor by Augustus Earle shows the new Female Factory at Parramatta designed by the former convict Francis Greenway about 1820. It housed the female convicts who had not been assigned to settlers and was also used as a place of punishment for women who had committed crimes within the colony. On Sundays the inmates of the factory at Parramatta were lined up for inspection by male settlers looking for sexual partners. Though the practice was referred to as "courting", it was little more than a form of concubinage, with the women winning release from the grim conditions of incarceration by trading their sex in return for food and shelter.

general. Marriage and cohabitation were consequently higher among the Irish than among other convicts, with a proportionately greater number of families. At the center of the family unit was the figure of the "little Irish mother". Fiery rebels and defenders of basic freedoms the Irish might have been, but they also laid the foundations of Australia's class of respectable poor.

Women convicts

The image of the Irish "little mother" notwithstanding, the character most commonly attributed to women convicts in Australia was that of a prostitute. No doubt there were prostitutes among their number, but as soliciting was not a transportable offence, they would have to have been sent down for a crime other than this. This did not stop a commission of inquiry into the convict system carried out in 1838 from reporting that women convicts "are all of them, with scarcely an exception, drunken and abandoned prostitutes." Many women convicts were called whores simply because they cohabited with men. So-called common-law marriages were widespread among working-class men and women in Britain at this time, but the practice was beginning to offend the sensibilities of the middle classes. As more and more free settlers, drawn mostly from the middle classes, or aspiring to belong to them, made their way to Australia, their protests against the supposed sexual promiscuity and moral laxity of the colony had a profound impact on moral attitudes.

Officers and sailors on board the convict ships assumed it was their right to "have their way" with the female convicts. Today we would call this rape, or at the very least sexual harassment. In practical terms it meant that a number of the women arrived pregnant and were immediately sent to the female factory at Parramatta, today a suburb of Sydney, to give birth. Here they were employed making blankets. With no means of contraception, abortion and infanticide were common means of getting rid of unwanted children. Within the routine of factory life, women were required to set Sundays aside for "courting" – in effect, a parade to which free settlers would come to select a sexual partner. The chosen woman would then be released into the man's custodial care. Despite becoming his responsibility, the tag "whore" invariably stuck. It was commonly accepted that men could do as they pleased with the women convicts under their care, who lived under constant threat of being returned to the factory or to some other place of incarceration. Women were sometimes accused of coercing men by threatening to move to another partner if their conditions were not satisfactory, but their dependence left them ultimately powerless; who was to say that the next man would be any better than the one they had left behind?

In a society where men were starved of opportunities for heterosexual activity the demand for women was high; men also raped or took Aboriginal women and girls into concubinage. Wild scenes habitually greeted the arrival of a new contingent of women convicts, and unofficial quayside auctions would be set up to bid for the newcomers. On sighting the cargo on board the *Lady Juliana* which was carrying 200 women to New South Wales in 1790, an officer was heard to exclaim, "No, no – surely not! My God – not more of those damned whores. Never have I known worse women." Homosexuality, though punishable by death, was commonplace among the prison population. The norm of homosexual men was to be found among the convicts, but habitual heterosexuals also turned to homosexual relationships for comfort in a world where brutality was routine and tenderness the rarest of all human qualities.

Women had few rights in British society at that time, but the convict women of Australia had fewer still, lacking both the power and the weight of numbers to alter their situation or effect any change in attitude. Perhaps this is one reason why Australia today has a reputation for being a "man's country". In the convict period as a whole, women accounted for around 16 percent of the total convict population, a ratio of one to six. But the ratios were never fixed. In the first 27 years of the settlement to 1815 women comprised about one third of the convict population. This rate dropped when the circumstances of peacetime condemned more men to the transports, and in the 1820s and 1830s women were outnumbered by as many as ten to one.

For historians of the transportation period, the story of Mary Wade and her even more unfortunate companion Jane Whiting, girls aged 11 and 14 who were committed to trial at London's Old Bailey in 1789, has acquired iconic status. Their crime was to have stolen from 8-year-old Mary Phillips, "putting her in fear, and feloniously taking from her person, and against her will, one cotton frock, value three shillings, one tippet, value two pence, one linen cap, value two pence." In his summing up Lord Chief Justice Barron entreated the jury to find guilty and make an example of the two girls. The jury took his instruction seriously; both girls were convicted of bullying and stealing goods to the value of two shillings and fourpence, and sentenced to death. Jane Whiting was duly hanged; Mary Wade had her sentence commuted to exile "for the term of her natural life to the east coast of New South Wales or some island adjoining".

Mary Wade was one of just over 24,000 women transported to New South Wales and Van Diemen's Land between 1788 and 1850 (none were sent in the later transports to Western Australia). More than 96 percent were convicted of crimes against property – most commonly of theft while in domestic service – in which the value of the goods or money stolen was usually insignificant. In less than two percent of cases was violence involved, and more than 60 percent of women transported to New South Wales were first offenders. But if the system that condemned Mary Wade and her companions was unconscionably severe, and if the conditions of their incarceration were intolerably brutal, the gin alleys of London or Liverpool offered women barely more comfort, with an early death from violence, child-bearing or disease predicated for most, while domestic service at that time was essentially a form of indefinite servitude.

Convict labor

One of the principal arguments in favor of transporting convicts to Australia was that they would ultimately pay for themselves through the work they performed. Among the chief proponents of the New South Wales scheme was the British Home Secretary of the day, Viscount Sydney, for whom Sydney Cove was named in 1788. He maintained that "the very heavy expense Government is annually put to for transporting and otherwise punishing felons, together with the facility of their return, are evils long and

Above John Thomas Bigge (1780–1843) was commissioned in 1819 to investigate the convict system in New South Wales and Van Diemen's Land. His three-volume report found that the convicts were treated too leniently, that reform did not work and that greater punishment should be meted out. His criticisms brought about a number of changes, including the setting up of a legislative council and the establishment of Van Diemen's Land as a separate colony.

Above Bigge singled out for criticism the reforms of Lachlan Macquarie (1762–1824) who had succeeded William Bligh as governor of New South Wales in 1810. He introduced many changes to alleviate the harshness of the convict system, including the granting of emancipist (or free) status to convicts for good behavior; his treatment of the Aborigines was also more sympathetic than that of his predecessors. Macquarie returned to England in 1822 under the shadow of the Bigge inquiry. Among the particular charges made against him was that he wasted prison resources on building public works.

Above In the 1830s, when schemes for assisted immigration were set up to boost the number of free settlers, particular efforts were made to attract women immigrants in order to restore the balance of numbers between the sexes. This allegorical cartoon of 1832 shows a swarm of butterfly women being lured across the ocean ready to be netted by the men waiting on the shoreline – an image of womanhood that is in stark contrast to that commonly accorded the female convicts. Active in promoting women as the agents of civilization in the young colony was Caroline Chisholm (1808–77), the wife of an East India Company officer. In 1841 she founded a Female Immigrants' Home in Sydney, and in order to alleviate the loneliness of the bush workers' lives accompanied the girls to outlying country areas where she arranged employment for them.

much lamented. Here is an asylum open that will considerably reduce the first and for ever prevent the latter." The annual cost to the Colonial Office of keeping a convict in Australia was £120. A large number of convicts were directly employed on public works, as laborers, engineers, architects and public servants. But great savings could be made in costs of maintenance by allowing convicts to work for free settlers.

This could be done in one of two ways. A convict could be directly assigned to a free settler, usually a landholder, in return for food and shelter, which in essence meant that he or she passed into his ownership. Such employers cared little about the welfare of their assigned convicts, whose upkeep was seen merely as an item of expenditure on their account books. Accommodation was uniformly substandard and assigned convicts were often thrashed. Legal restraints on the form of punishment that could be meted out were little observed since the Australian magistracy was principally made up of landowners and charges of illtreatment were rarely upheld in the courts. Many landholders built small prisons where a convict worker who committed a misdemeanor could be held in solitary confinement. Recalcitrant convicts might also be threatened with retransportation to places of secondary punishment: if a worker did not fully cooperate with the landholder, local magistrates had it in their power to order three years' detention at one of these notorious penal settlements. Superior courts could hand down more severe penalties, but the threat

of even three years' confinement at Port Macquarie, Norfolk Island or Moreton Bay was enough to make even the most hardened convict think twice before disputing the authority of a landholder or his overseer.

Free settlers could also employ convicts who had been granted tickets of leave. These were certificates awarded for good conduct that gave their holders an early release, on the proviso that they did not reoffend, and allowed them to work for wages for an employer of their choice – the closest thing to a full pardon. The system, introduced by Governor King in 1801, proved effective. The heavy penalties exacted against reoffenders ensured the continued good behavior of many of those released early. In times of economic stringency tickets of leave were widely resorted to as a means of reducing expenditure on convicts' upkeep.

Among early governors noted for their liberal attitudes toward convicts and ex-convicts (often referred to as emancipists) was Lachlan Macquarie. He arranged for convicts' families to be brought to Australia in the hope that it would help their rehabilitation. This led to conflict with those, such as Samuel Marsden, who argued that the purpose of incarceration was to punish rather than rehabilitate criminals, and the colonial administrators became concerned. The Bigge inquiry into the running of the colony published its findings in 1822, a year after Macquarie's resignation; it criticized the leniency of his reforms, maintaining that convicts ought not to look forward to privileges to facilitate their return to civil society.

Secondary punishment

Those who succeeded Macquarie in the 1820s, in particular Sir Ralph Darling (1775–1858), governor of New South Wales from 1825–31, and Sir George Arthur in Van Diemen's Land, applied themselves to carrying out the recommendations of Bigge's report. In their efforts to ensure that convicts' conditions were not made too easy, places of secondary punishment became islands of punishment in which floggings were endemic. The most notorious were at Port Macquarie, on the coast north of Sydney (1821–30), Macquarie Harbor in Van Diemen's Land (1822–33), Moreton Bay, close to the site of present-day Brisbane (1824–39), Norfolk Island (1825–56) and Port Arthur, which succeeded Macquarie Harbor and continued in use as a prison after transportation ended, before being finally abandoned in 1877. The commandants of these penal settlements, in particular Captain Patrick Logan of Moreton Bay and Lieutenant-Colonel James Morisset of Norfolk Island, acquired reputations as pathological sadists who reveled in the high mortality rates among their charges.

Many of the more brutal images of convict life in Australian literature and folksong derive from these places. Prisoners were kept permanently in irons and put to work building roads, dragging behind them the wheeled huts in which they were confined for the night in groups of 16 or 24 – the infamous "iron-gangs". It was commonly rumored that conditions were so

Above These photographs of convicts were taken at Port Arthur in 1874. Though transportation had ended 12 years earlier, some of the men in these portraits were transportees, repeat offenders serving secondary sentences for crimes such house-breaking and sheep-stealing. Some had been convicted for sex offenses, crimes that are rarely discussed by those who argue that the Australian convicts were more sinned against than sinning, the victims of an unjust system that transported men for stealing loaves of bread to feed their starving families.

Above left In 1801 Governor King (1758–1808) introduced the system of tickets of leave that enabled convicts on good behavior to leave the chain gangs and find work as independent wage-earning laborers. The tickets were issued under strict conditions and could be revoked at any time. The system provided a much more flexible workforce suited to the needs of the young colony, and removed the costs of paying for convicts' upkeep from the central administration.

Left The convict workforce was responsible for laying the foundations of Australia's roads and other public works. This three-span bridge over the Ross River in Tasmania was built by convicts in 1836. Made of well-finished ashlar and rusticated stone blocks, it is a typical product of convict labor.

appalling that hardened convicts would make death pacts with each other – one would agree to release the other from the relentless flogging and repetitive work by murdering him, thereby bringing on himself a sentence of death. Commissions of inquiry into the convict system more than once heard evidence of men weeping bitterly on learning that they had been granted a reprieve from the death sentence, while others who were condemned to death "went down on [their] knees, with dry eyes, and thanked God". Sir Francis Forbes (1813–51), who was appointed the first chief justice of New South Wales, declared after observing the conditions on Norfolk Island that he too would rather die "under any form that could be presented" than become a prisoner there.

Not surprisingly, convicts were driven to desperate attempts to escape from these dreadful places of incarceration. It was almost impossible to survive alone in the bush, so several men would breakout together. In the legends of convict life that sprang up at the end of the 19th century it was said that escapes were organized in groups of three so that when food ran out the two strongest could murder the weakest and feed on his corpse. But the details of such incidents are sketchy and it is likely that the rumors of cannibalism are exaggerated, deriving in large part from the famed exploits of Alexander Pearce who escaped from Macquarie Harbor in 1822 with seven other convicts. When he was picked up several months later he confessed to having eaten all his companions, and boasted that the flesh was sweeter than either fish or pork. He was not believed, and so avoided hanging, but he escaped again with a single mate whom he also killed and ate. This time when the self-confessed cannibal was captured the mutilated body of his companion was discovered, and Pearce was duly hanged.

The most horrifying image of human degradation that emerges from the dark archives of Australian convictry is that of Charles Anderson, a brain-damaged ex-soldier originally transported for burglary who proved impossible to restrain and was taken to Goat Island, a rock in Sydney Harbor. After repeated efforts to escape by swimming from the rock he was tethered to a chain and at night was bundled into a small, grave-like pit, cut into the sandstone, over which a timber door was placed, which admitted no light except through small holes made for breathing. His food was passed through on a stick. Maggots infested the wounds left on his body by repeated lashings as he

lay, unable to move, in his own filth. Other prisoners could hear his screams, especially when it rained and his pit filled with water. Eventually, after he had become a public spectacle for the people of Sydney, the governor of New South Wales was shamed into releasing him and he finally finished up on Norfolk Island.

He was still there when Alexander Maconochie (1787–1860) was appointed superintendant of the settlement in 1840. Maconochie was a penal reformer. He had originally arrived in Australia to take up an appointment as secretary to Sir John Franklin, the lieutenant governor of Van Diemen's land, with a view to becoming his successor. However, the two had fallen out over Maconochie's views, in particular that the purpose of punishment should be rehabilitation rather than retribution, and that convicted felons should be released when it was believed they had reformed. Out of favor, he was sent as superintendant to Norfolk Island where, undaunted, he put his ideas into practice. Arguing that prison discipline would be better secured through providing incentives than by inflicting violent punishment, he introduced a system that awarded marks for work and good behavior. The accumulution of sufficient marks would allow convicts to buy their freedom. Maconochie dismantled the gallows, threw away the cat-o'-nine tails, allowed headstones to be placed on the convicts' graves and set up classes in vegetable and fruit growing. His methods, which were far in advance of their time, achieved a number of promising results (including the partial rehabilitation of Anderson, who he put to work managing the settlement's signal station) but they did not survive his recall to Britain in 1844. He became superintendent of Birmingham jail in 1849 but was dismissed in 1851, his reforms having once again failed to impress the authorities.

Policing the state

Not only the jailed, but also the jailers, exerted a powerful influence on the Australian imagination. From the beginning, the tight control exercised by the military gave the settlement many of the aspects of a police state. The detachment of marines sent out with the First Fleet under the command of Major Robert Ross (who was also Phillip's lieutenant governor, or second in command) was charged with guarding the convicts and with general administrative and policing duties. Ross was an egotist who found it difficult to act in a subordinate role; a senior officer in the marines

Islands of Punishment

It was as a direct consequence of John Bigge's three-volume official report on the *Judicial Establishments in New South Wales and Van Diemen's Land* (1823), in which he severely criticized the leniency of the penal system under Macquarie's governorship, that the places of secondary punishment were created – islands of punishment within the prison colony for the incarceration of the most hardened criminals. Some of these places were literally islands. By far the most remote was Norfolk Island. Some 1,500 kilometers away in the Pacific Ocean, it had failed its early promise as a supplier of timber and flax to the colony and the first settlement there had been abandoned in 1814. In 1825 a penal colony for reoffenders was started on the island. The green meadows and wooded hills of Norfolk Island, whose basalt cliffs rise sheer out of the Pacific, gave it the appearance of paradise, but under the rule of James Morisset (1780–1852), commandant from 1829 to 1834, it soon became notorious as a place of sadistic punishment.

Van Diemen's Land, too, was a potentially idyllic setting, but despite its obvious charms the island soon became a dumping place for criminals: penal settlements were set up at Hobart in 1804 and at Launceston in 1806. Convicts sent to Van Diemen's Land were considered "incorrigibles" and the island rapidly acquired a repugnant reputation. In 1822 a place of secondary punishment was established at Macquarie Harbor. It was later replaced by Port Arthur, the most infamous prison of all. Terrible stories were told of the punishments and lashings inflicted on the prisoners, and through the writings of Marcus Clarke, Price Warung and others Port Arthur came to hold a sinister place in Australian legends of convict life. It was to escape the stain of convictry that the inhabitants opted in 1855 to rename the island Tasmania.

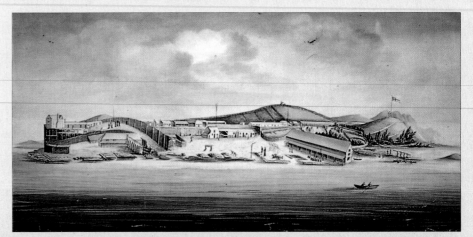

Below This sketch by a convict artist, William Buelow Gould, shows the penal settlement at Macquarie Harbor, the first of the secondary places of punishment to be set up in the wake of Bigge's criticisms. Convicts were employed in timber felling and ship building, and it soon acquired a notorious reputation. The prison was abandoned in 1833.

Above Many of the prison buildings on Norfolk Island were pulled down for building stone by the Pitcairn Islanders, descendants of the Bounty mutineers, who were relocated here in 1856 after the penal settlement had been closed down. Among the graves in the island's small cemetery are some that commemorate convicts – relics of the reforms of Alexander Maconochie, whose measures did much to alleviate the worst excesses of Morisset's regime; alone among prison governors, he accorded the convicts the dignity of a carved headstone to remember them in death.

Left Modest chapels, like this one at Port Arthur, were built within the prison walls in the hope that redemption might be granted to even the most blighted of souls. The religious care of prisoners was in the hands of hellfire, protestant ministers such as the Reverend Samuel Marsden, who was renowned for the severity of the sentences he handed down as magistrate. Though most of the Irish convicts were Roman Catholics, including a number of priests, public celebration of the mass was forbidden until 1821.

Left The abandoned buildings of Port Arthur present a tranquil aspect today, in marked contrast to the prison's violent past. Port Arthur was opened in 1832 after a follow-up report to the Bigge commission had found that the convict system was still too lenient. Brutal punishment and harsh discipline, however, did not apparently curb the incidence of crime: in 1835 it was reported to be eight times higher in New South Wales than in Britain.

Above When, in 1853, the French annexed the islands of New Caledonia they had in mind their possible use as a penal colony and in the 1860s the Isle of Pines began to be used as a place for the incarceration of French criminals. This monument commemorates the 4,000 *deportés* of 1871, political dissidents who were exiled for their part in the Paris *communard* uprising.

described him as "without exception the most dis-agreeable commanding officer I ever knew." He got on very badly with Phillip, and was unwilling to cooper-ate with him so that the force effectively functioned independently of the governor. Within a year of set-tlement individual officers and men were being given grants of land, thereby laying the foundations of the system of favors and patronage that was to flourish within the Australian service.

In 1789 the Second Fleet brought the first units of the New South Wales Corps, raised in Britain specifi-cally to police the settlement and to defend it in case of French attack. Many of those enlisted in this new force were little different from the criminals they were set to guard, and their officers were scarcely better; a large number (both non-commissioned officers and men) had been offered the option of joining the Corps rather than serve sentences imposed by the military courts. In 1792 ill-health forced Phillip to return to Britain leaving Francis Grose, the commandant of the Corps and lieutenant governor, as the most important officer in the colony. Phillip's successor was not appointed until 1795 and the Corps took advantage of this interregnum to seize even greater powers for itself. In 1794, Grose – incensed by an incident when the naval governor of Norfolk Island set armed civilians to quell a mutinous body of corpsmen – wrote that civilian constables and magistrates "are to understand

that they are not on any pretence whatever to stop or seize a soldier, although he should be detected in an unlawful act." In other words, the officers and men of the Corps (whose ranks were not infrequently filled by ex-convicts) were answerable to no authority except their own military courts, and had virtual carte blanche to carry out their business free from any con-straints imposed by the governor. Exasperated by this situation, Governor Philip Gidley King (1758–1808) complained in 1803: "How far ought I to expect impartiality when those officers [in breach of the law] were tried by other of their own Corps?"

There were plentiful opportunities for corruption and self-enrichment. The wife of Captain John Macarthur (1767–1834), an influential officer in the New South Wales Corps, wrote in 1798: "This coun-try possesses numerous advantages to persons holding appointments under the government," noting that her husband, who enjoyed the position of inspector of public works in the colony, had a "handsome addition to his income by having the payment of a company and transacting the business of Paymaster to the Reg-iment." Officers exercised a lucrative monopoly over most of the goods imported into the colony. The most significant of these was rum, which was the primary means of barter and exchange. By controlling its importation, local distillation and distribution, the New South Wales Corps (which as a result became

Above This aquatint of 1825 by Joseph Lycett shows Elizabeth Farm at Parramatta, the property owned by John Macarthur. Arriving in New South Wales as a lieutenant in the New South Wales Corps, Macarthur was one who rapidly enriched himself through corrupt dealings in the colony's affairs. When he was forced to leave New South Wales from 1808 to 1817 his wife Elizabeth remained behind to oversee his farming interests. Together they are credited with laying the foundations of the Australian fine wool industry, having introduced merino sheep to the 2,025 hectare farm at Parramatta.

known as the Rum Corps) was able to exert a tremendous influence over the early economy of the colony.

Though he tried hard to break the influence of the Corps and end corruption, King found in the end that it was easier to tolerate its excesses. Like Phillip before him, King eventually asked to be recalled. In 1806 William Bligh, the authoritarian captain of HMS *Bounty*, was appointed governor – an indication of the Colonial Office's determination to take stern measures against the Corps. His attempts to limit the power of the rum traders, however, provoked the second mutiny of his career and in 1808 officers of the Corps led a rebellion that overthrew his government. (Legend has it that Bligh attempted to avoid arrest by hiding under his bed; though probably untrue, the event has become enshrined in Australian folklore and is the subject of a famous painting by Sidney Nolan.) Bligh eventually returned to England in 1810, having failed to reestablish his authority in New South Wales, and was succeeded as governor by Macquarie. The Corps was recalled to England and the ringleaders tried at a court martial that virtually exonerated Bligh from any blame.

Among those implicated in the rebellion was John Macarthur. In 1801 Macarthur had been sent back to England by Governor King after he had wounded the then lieutenant governor in a duel, but he resigned his commission from the army in 1805 and returned to New South Wales to pursue his trading and farming interests. His actions against Bligh again forced his exile to England, where he remained until 1817 when he was allowed to return on condition that he did not involve himself in public affairs. His wife Elizabeth had stayed behind in New South Wales, building up a fortune based on the developing wool trade from her farm at Parramatta, and for the rest of his life Macarthur concentrated on enlarging his agricultural wealth, taking control of the Australian Agricultural Company in 1827.

Macarthur typified the new landed class of the colony, which was made up of serving and former officers who exploited their position and contacts to tap supplies of assigned convicts, tools, seeds and livestock to build up their estates. Their control of the magistracy virtually placed them outside the law and gave rise to the system of corruption and mutual support that later came to be known as "cronyism". By the time the first free settlers began to arrive in substantial numbers in the 1830s, this officer class had entrenched itself as a local aristocracy that ruthlessly abused power, title and privilege to defend and enlarge its interests. After the Napoleonic wars, it had been swelled by numbers of supernumerary officers from Britain who sold their commissions to finance their settlement in Australia. Many insisted on using their former title of military rank in the new world, though not entitled to do so. While clearly signaling their membership of the landed gentry, this clinging to the vestiges of rank became the object of contempt and ironic humor in the folklore of the convicts and working people. The original landed class in Australia was at one and the same time powerful and despised. It is this that gave rise to the skepticism of social privilege and presumed status that remains characteristic of Australians to this day.

Reclaiming the convict past
By the late 1830s the non-Aboriginal population of New South Wales had risen to 75,000. Convicts were outnumbered by two to one, but of the free population of 50,000, approximately 17,000 were former convicts and an unknown but considerable number were the sons and daughters of convicts. Nevertheless, free settlers were now in the majority in the colony as a whole. The population of Sydney was around 60,000 and here the number of convicts and non-convicts was roughly even. About 3,500 new convicts arrived each year but while some remained in the city, Sydney also acted as a clearing station from which convicts were assigned to landowners in rural districts and others

Right Macarthur played a leading role in the Rum Rebellion of 1808 when the New South Wales Corps arrested and imprisoned Governor William Bligh. For the second time in his life Bligh faced a mutiny, and on this occasion is popularly supposed to have tried to avoid detection by hiding under his bed – an event portrayed in this contemporary sketch by an unknown artist. Bligh had attempted to curb the excessive power and corruption of the Corps but his authoritarian ways had invited derision and contempt.

were sent on to places of secondary punishment. By this time the free settlers were bringing increasing pressure on the colonial administration to end the transport system, which they felt reflected badly on the reputation of New South Wales, and after 1840 no more convict ships were sent to Sydney.

A vast, unbridgeable gap separated convicts and free settlers. In the first decade of the settlement, when forced migrants easily outnumbered voluntary, it was officially stated that "Persons who have been once convicts can never be restored to full participation in the Rights and Privileges of Free British subjects." Since then it had been constantly reiterated that "a line of demarcation has ever existed between convicts and free persons, which the future acquisition of their freedom has never enabled them to overstep." To be a convict or to be of convict stock was to be forever a second-class citizen. "The community is composed of three classes," reported the *Colonial Times* in 1844, "the free, the freed and the bond."

Throughout the 19th century and for a good part of the 20th century, Australia tried to deny its convict past. The history books emphasized the founding role of the free pioneers in establishing Australia's respectable colonial society, while the transportation era was glossed over as an unfortunate aberration; the convicts themselves were given scarcely a mention. The government was suspicious of anything that played up the country's convict past, fearful that it might undermine the authority of the law and the law-keepers, and in the early years of the 20th century movies featuring convicts and bushrangers were frequently censored. But though officially ignored, the convicts remained firmly rooted in the collective folk memory of white Australia. In the oral tradition, in folksongs and in literature, they were celebrated as the heroes of Australian nationalism in defiance of British imperialism.

From the very beginning the convict experience provided a rich vein in Australian imaginative writing. Artists by contrast tended to be more interested in recording scenes from pioneer and working life. The first novel to be published in Australia – the partly autobiographical *Quintus Servinton* (1831) – was written by a convict, Henry Savery (1791–1842), who had been transported for life to Van Diemen's Land for forgery in 1825. As convicts were not allowed to publish their own work (though they ran the government printing presses) it appeared anonymously. Another early novel of convict life, *The Adventures of Ralph Rashleigh*, was written in the 1840s but remained unpublished until the late 1920s. The identity of its author was not revealed until the 1950s when handwriting analysis showed it to be the work of a convict called James Tucker (the writing of the manuscript was matched to Tucker's signature on a convict indent). The central character of *The Adventures of Ralph Rashleigh* was a man "sent down" because of the unscrupulous action of others – a theme of unjust victimization that was to recur constantly in Australian convict literature.

This, indeed, was the formula adopted in Marcus Clarke's *For the Term of His Natural Life*, by far the best-known narrative of convict life, which first appeared as a serial between 1870 and 1872 and was published as a three-volume novel in 1874 (it was later condensed into a single volume). It is a forceful, dramatic work that chronicles in gory detail the brutality of the penal settlements and the pathological men that

ran them. Clarke, who had migrated to Australia in 1863, was a journalist and he based his novel on the documents and records of the convict system. Despite his melodramatic effects, Clarke gives an honest account of many aspects of convict life, such as the homosexuality practiced between the inmates, then a taboo subject. The enormous popularity of his work meant that many of his fictionalized stories entered the popular canon of convict history as "true" fact. *For the Term of His Natural Life* was instrumental in making Port Arthur a tourist attraction for trippers from Hobart in the late 1870s and 1880s, and Clarke had many imitators. His novel, which has rarely been out of print since its first publication, has been adapted as a stage play, a musical, several movies, and at least one television mini-series.

One of the most prolific writers of the late 19th century was William Astley (1855–1911), who wrote under the pseudonym of Price Warung. His numerous stories of convict life were in the mold of Marcus Clarke and he claimed to have spent more than two decades researching convict indents and interviewing "old lags". His overt sympathy for the jailed and harsh criticism of the unjustness of the convict system incurred the wrath of the censor. Astley was a strong supporter of workers' rights and republicanism, and many of his stories appeared in the pro-republican *Bulletin*. Writing in the same journal in the 1890s, the poet and short-story writer Henry Lawson (1867–1922) began to claim the convicts as the folk heroes of Australian history, representatives of an oppressed class. Thus it was that, in the absence of serious historical study, the novelists and journalists kept the memory of the convicts alive.

Gradually the academics began to enter the field. In the 1920s, the historian Professor George Arnold Wood (1865–1928) stated in a famous phrase that "the real criminals" – by which he meant the landed gentry, the law-makers and the judiciary – "had remained in Britain," so adding scholarly weight to the nationalist view of the convict system. In 1958 Professor Russel Ward (b. 1914) published *The Australian Legend*, perhaps the most important and influential thesis on the Australian character to emerge from the radical nationalist tradition. In it Ward argued that Australia owes its egalitarian spirit to the

Left The best-known novel of convict life is Marcus Clarke's *For the Term of His Natural Life*. Set in the infamous jails of Van Diemen's Land it is responsible for many of the most enduring legends of the repressive convict system. It has rarely been out of print since its publication in1874. This poster is for a movie version of the story, made in 1908.

Below Convict life has given rise to what commentators have termed the "Australian Legend", distinguished by qualities of mateship and egalitarianism. The easy-going comradeship that existed among the nomadic workers who roamed the outback in search of seasonal employment is held to derive from convict traditions of fraternity . The apotheosis of the legend was in the 1890s, when this gang of itinerant workers was photographed harvesting tobacco on a remote bush property in New South Wales.

convicts, and that the spirit of "mateship" in contemporary society is directly attributable to its convict origins. Ward described the Australian male as a rough diamond, a worker and a socialist, practical and handy in the bushcrafts, a doer rather than a thinker who accepts that near enough is good enough. Capable of great exertion in an emergency, he paces his work and does not over-exert himself. His attitude is that Jack is not only as good as his master but, in some matters, considerably better. In the history of the 20th century this typical Australian was to be found arguing for trades union rights against the employers, serving with courage in two world wars as a common soldier, pitting himself against the blows of economic depression, and was idolized by the nation for his feats on the sports field and in the sports arena. Underlying the thesis is the assumption that the convicts were the products of an unjust system.

Folk culture and literature alike have celebrated the peculiarly Australian virtues that are said to emanate from the convicts. Les Murray (b. 1938), one of Australia's most highly regarded poets of the late 20th

century, has referred to the convicts as "the working-class who got away" to make a new life for themselves in Australia. The novelist Patrick White (1912–90), winner of the Nobel Prize for Literature in 1973, wrote directly about the convict system in *A Fringe of Leaves* (1976). The Australian novels of Thomas Keneally (b. 1935) are similarly informed by consciousness of the convict experience. Little by little the convicts have been reclaimed and Australians have come to acknowledge and take some pride in their convict origins. In the 1980s – particularly in the period leading up to Australia's bicentennial celebrations in 1988 – the tracing of family histories became something of a national pastime. But many are still reluctant to admit that their convict ancestors were anything other than the victims of an unfair penal system that oppressed people for the mere act of stealing a loaf of bread to feed their own. Murderers, habitual criminals, pimps and sexual offenders are excluded from the record. And so the folk memory of the convicts as more sinned against than sinning survives among the Australians.

THE WHITE TRIBES OF THE ANTIPODES

Questions of identity

Most societies feel the need at one time or another to identify and articulate a common sense of belonging. Relatively young societies, more than longer established nations and communities, are particularly prone to periods of prolonged and often intense cultural self-examination when the questions "Who are we?" and "What are we?" are recurrently asked, and there is an overarching desire to reconcile self and community with place. Such is the case in both Australia and New Zealand. Their settler societies and cultures were built in a very short period of time. Other European nationalities were present almost from the start, as later too were Asians and other ethnic groups, but it was the British and Irish – immigrant fragments from the old world – who dominated these new societies as they transformed themselves from settler communities to nations. Myths and legends were evolved to explain their origins, to find common linkages and build up a sense of belonging, and even in the multicultural societies of today these still contribute powerfully to the way Australians and New Zealanders regard themselves and the places where they live.

One consequence of being a colonial society was that the settlers were always glancing over their shoulders to "home": Australia and New Zealand were perceived to be peripheral societies, and the inadequacies of the margins were habitually held up for comparison with the achievements of the center. This sense of cultural insecurity, derived from a feeling of colonial dependence on Britain, realized itself in two ways. On the one hand, there was the tendency to extol the positive value of things Australian and New Zealand. Termed the "God's own" or "God's Zone" mentality, this found expression, among other things, in the habitual denigration of the colonizing nation: the derogatory term "Pom" or "Pommy" for an Englishman (the derivation of which is uncertain) was already widespread at the beginning of the 20th century. On the other hand, there was embarrassment about the antipodean condition because it was not metropolitan. These responses – in effect, opposite sides of the same coin – were identified as the colonial "cultural cringe" in a famous essay of the 1950s by the Australian critic A. A. Phillips (1900–85).

The white tribes that made up the new settler societies were simultaneously strutters and cringers, boasting proudly of their differences from the rest of the world, particularly Britain, but suffering considerable insecurities that the civilizations they had built were insubstantial. For this reason, up until the 1960s, many artists, writers and intellectuals left Australia and New Zealand for Europe or the United States in the belief that only there would their talents flourish and they would win an international reputation. Among those who spent the greater part of their working lives abroad were novelists such as the New Zealand-born Katherine Mansfield (1888–1923), Henry Handel Richardson (the pseudonym of Ethel Robertson, 1870–1946), Christina Stead (1902–83), artists such as Sidney Nolan (1917–91), Arthur Boyd (b. 1920) and the New Zealand painter Frances Hodgkins (1869–1947), the composer Percy Grainger (1882–1961), the ballet dancer and choreographer Robert Helpmann (1909–86), and the opera singers Dame Nellie Melba (1861–1931), Dame Joan Sutherland (b. 1927) and Dame Kiri Te Kanawa (b.1944), as well as scores of actors, journalists, academics, scientists and doctors. The ease of air travel since the 1960s means that writers can now keep in touch with audiences at home and around the globe: a trip overseas no longer involves an extended period of stay abroad. Among the list of contemporary globe-trotting antipodean writers are Peter Carey (b. 1943), Shirley Hazzard (b. 1931) and Janet Turner-Hospital (b. 1942).

Though Australia and New Zealand were both settler societies and possess many cultural similarities, their histories are quite unalike and they developed along very different lines. This markedly affects the way each conceptualizes its national identity. Yet all too often outsiders regard them as a single entity – on the dubious grounds that since they are so far from anywhere else, they must be close to each other. Visitors from Europe and the United States today may be as ignorant as Mark Twain was a hundred years ago of the distance and differences between them. "All people think that New Zealand is close to Australia or Asia, or somewhere, and that you cross it on a bridge," he wrote in 1897. "It is nearest to Australia, but still not near. The gap between is very wide. It will be a surprise to the reader, as it was to me, to learn that the distance from Australia to New Zealand is really twelve or thirteen hundred miles and that there is no bridge." This misapprehension is particularly irritating to New Zealanders, who resent being overshadowed by their larger neighbor on the other side of the Tasman Sea, just as Canadians resist the overbearing cultural influence of the United States.

The free settlers

By the early decades of the 19th century there was a growing movement to establish settlements in Australia that were not reliant on convict labor. At the same time, New Zealand was rapidly being opened up to colonization. For both enterprises to succeed, it was clearly necessary to find the means of attracting a flow of free emigrants who were prepared to take on the challenge of making a new life for themselves in the antipodes. Few people would travel voluntarily halfway round the world without an incentive when the forests and plains of North America, much closer to Europe, offered far greater attractions for pioneering spirits. So both Australia and New Zealand developed forms of assisted migration.

The first organized attempt to establish a convict-free society in Australia took place under the auspices of the Swan River Colony scheme. Fears that the French were about to claim the western third of the Australian continent prompted the British move to annex it in 1829. Almost immediately plans were

Above Exile from the old world was a traumatic experience even for those who traveled out as free settlers. This illustration of 1858 depicts the arrival in Australia of a primrose from England – a poignant metaphor of transplantation. The faces of the women are transfigured by an almost spiritual fervor as they contemplate this familiar object from the past, which will flourish as a tangible reminder of home in the soil of the new world.

Left Katherine Mansfield is one of New Zealand's most respected authors. Born in Wellington, she completed her schooling in London and returned to Britain in 1908, where she became a leading figure in the modernist literary movement. An expatriate, many of her delicate and impressionistic short stories such as "Prelude" and "The Garden Party" are set in the New Zealand of her childhood. She died from tuberculosis in Paris at the age of 34.

drawn up to establish the Swan River Colony on the western seaboard as a free society that would thrive untainted by convictry. The scheme was simple and efficient. Land would be given out freely in proportion to the amount of capital brought out by immigrants. Would-be colonists paid their own passage in return for the promise of land when they arrived. The scheme initially received a favorable press throughout Britain, but the planned settlement area had not been properly surveyed and corrupt speculators in London soon tarnished its image. The grand plans for Swan River foundered after only a short period of time, and the land-grant system was abandoned. Western Australia was to labor for more than half a century with the reputation of being an unreliable settlement. Among the schemes that failed was that for a model settlement at Australind, about 145 kilometers south of Perth, set up by the Western Australia Company in 1840. The settlement collapsed within three or four years, its hopes dashed by lack of labor, farming inexperience and financial mismanagement.

The failure of the Swan River Colony was South Australia's and New Zealand's gain. Edward Gibbon Wakefield absorbed the lessons of its failure to develop his scheme of direct assisted, or systematic, migration, which were put into practice first in the settlement of Adelaide in South Australia in the late 1830s and then of Wellington, Wanganui, New Plymouth and Nelson in New Zealand. In New Zealand, it happened that emigrants from one particular area in Britain would congregate together to form whole communities in the new world. On a visit to New Plymouth in 1850, Lady Grey, wife of the governor Sir George Grey, commented: "This is a lovely country, the finest agricultural country you can imagine with the nicest quietest, most simple, rural population you can imagine out of dear old England, and almost all of them from my own West Country and it is a pleasure to hear the old Dorsetshire farmers speak of my own dear father." The new townships thus acquired different, lasting characters, evidenced in their architecture and social organization: Dunedin on the South Island, founded by Scots Presbyterians, for example, was in marked contrast to Christchurch, 300 kilometers to

167

Sporting Nations

The white tribes of the antipodes took to the sports-field with gusto. Sporting success was proof that colonial sons could flourish in their adopted environments. The sportsman was composed of the stuff that made settlement possible and the sporting hero later came to be identified with Australia's and New Zealand's emergent national identities. Sport taught masculine qualities of discipline, team spirit, loyalty. The first organized sport to be played in both countries was cricket. The first test series was played between Australia and England in 1876–7, and the "Ashes" (as the competition came to be called) was soon the focus for keen international rivalry: feeling against the Poms never ran higher than during the 1932–3 series, played in Australia, when the English team employed the notoriously aggressive "bodyline" style of bowling. In New Zealand, Rugby Union football, first played in 1870, is the sporting obsession, regarded almost as a national religion. Both countries participate strongly in Olympic competition – Australia is one of only four nations to have sent representatives to every Olympic games since 1896. Its most successful Olympian ever is the swimmer Dawn Fraser (1937–) yet Australia, like New Zealand, continues to link sport to a mystique of masculinity. While their sportswomen achieve wide international success, women's sport occupies a mere 2 percent of sports coverage in Australian and New Zealand newspapers.

Left Donald Bradman (1908–), seen here on the right striding to the wicket against England in 1934, is probably the bestknown sports personality Australia has ever produced. He dominated the international game for more than two decades and many of the batting records he set have yet to be bettered.

Right More than half a million registered cricketers play the game each summer, making it still the most popular sport amongst Australian men. Millions more follow the professional game. Here Australia's batsmen take on South Africa in a World Cup one-day international competition at the Sydney Cricket Ground. The introduction of one-day matches in the 1970s, played in the evening under floodlights and staged especially for television, transformed the traditional sport into a modern media event. In Australia and New Zealand, all sports are passionately followed. When Australia (1983) and New Zealand (1995) snatched yachting's coveted America's Cup, there were massive outpourings of national pride. The announcement in September 1995 that Sydney would host the Olympic Games in 2000 was greeted by an estimated one million people who congregated at the harbor to hear the news via specially constructed television screens.

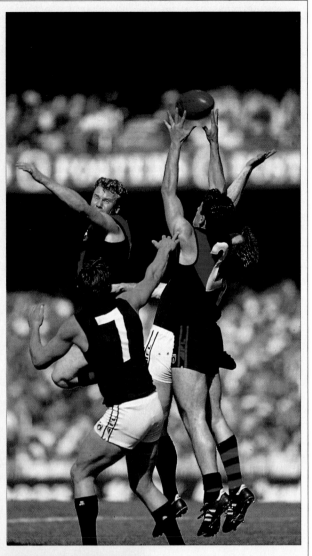

Above left The famous Maori wardance the Haka is performed by the New Zealand All Black Rugby Union team before every international competition. Here the Australians are their opponents. With its chant "Ka mate! Ka mate!" (It is death! It is death!), the Haka is a gesture of aggression and defiance; the rhythmic chants are coupled with the slapping of hands and stamping of feet. Today many of the All Blacks are Polynesian, particularly Samoan. New Zealand is the most successful Rugby Union nation in the world.

Above Players strive to outdo each other in the air as they reach for the ball in Australian (or Aussie) Rules, the most popular of the three codes of football played in Australia: the others are Rugby Union and Rugby League. The sport grew up on the goldfields of Victoria in the 1850s, and may have been based on a similar game played by Aborigines, with influences from Irish gaelic football. It is a fast-moving, close-contact game, played on a large oval field. There are 20 players on each side.

the north, predominantly English and Anglican. This was not the case in Australia, where immigrants would stick together for assurance when they first arrived but disperse as soon as they had got their bearings. They were driven to go where the work was, and as there were fewer opportunities for close agricultural settlement than in New Zealand, the population as a whole was more mobile. There were a few settled communities, however. Southwestern New South Wales, for example, was dominated by farmers from Tipperary in western Ireland.

Only fragments of the old world came to the new. The full range of British society was never completely represented in Australia and New Zealand. These fragments formed the cultural and social basis of their new colonial societies. While Australia was shaped by the continuing influence of the convicts, New Zealand self-consciously constructed itself as a society of the respectable poor and middling classes. To this end, immigration agents were instructed to weed out undesirables. A mid 19th-century commentator identified four such categories: the "too lates" who lacked financial independence; the "fastidious genteel people of feeble intellect" known as the "De Smythes"; the "grumblers"; and the "fast gents" or ne'er-do-wells. New Zealand's immigration agencies positively discriminated in favor of families, and the family unit was the basis of settlement. This contrasted strongly with Australia, which remained a male-dominated society throughout the 19th century.

Rural myths

Though New Zealand – almost the exact antipodes to Britain – was the farthest removed from home of all the British colonies, to its first immigrant settlers it presented perhaps the closest mirror-image of the old world. Like Britain, New Zealand was an island country, and though its native fauna and flora were unfamiliar, its climate was temperate and its landscapes pleasing, encompassing snow-capped mountains, grass-covered foothills, fast-flowing rivers and majestic harbors. An influential late 19th-century artist and critic, William Mathew Hodgkins (1839–98), claimed that New Zealand had all the "special features of every country which is remarkable for its scenery, the English lake, the Scottish mountain and glen, the snow peaks of Switzerland, the fiords of Norway". New Zealand, then, was seen as the Arcadia of the south seas, a place where the traditional values of British rural life could take root. Farmers were encouraged to migrate there, and most settlers came from rural backgrounds. Mixed farming communities flourished in the hinterlands of the coastal townships. "The Heavens look benignly upon it", wrote a visitor in 1876, "by universal consent, [it] is called the "Garden of New Zealand."

In reality, of course, pioneer life was much more rigorous than these impressions conveyed. The early days of the New Zealand Company settlements were dogged by a chronic shortage of capital, irregularity of supplies and administrative ineptitude. The propaganda literature put out by the Company and other emigration bodies gave little idea of the physical challenges the pioneers would have to face – dense bush, rugged terrain, frequent heavy rains and gale-force winds. They had to adapt to living in a geologically unstable landscape, learning to build in wood rather than stone to withstand earth movements (the Cook Strait region suffered a substantial earthquake in

Francis Greenway: Australia's First Architect

The colonial response to make familiar the unfamiliar is reflected in the early architecture of Australia: from the start, army barracks, prisons and other official government buildings were designed in the neoclassical styles of the old world. Francis Greenway (1777–1837), the first architect to work in Australia was, like its earliest writers and artists, a convict – an architect from Bristol sentenced to 14 years' transportation for forgery. He owed his commissions to New South Wales' reforming governor, Lachlan Macquarie, who was subsequently criticized by the Bigge commission of enquiry for wasting public money on his attempts to build a civil society with adequate roads and suitable public buildings. Macquarie granted Greenway ticket of leave in 1814, two years after his arrival in the colony, and made him his adviser on public works, later appointing him civil architect and assistant engineer. Greenway was an able though not outstanding architect. With a large workforce at his disposal, he was able to see his plans converted into buildings of substance, setting the standard for public architecture for the next half century. Among them were numerous churches, the female factory at Parramatta, the convict barracks in Sydney, the Liverpool hospital and the supreme court. Many still stand today, though converted to different uses.

Left One of the first commissions Greenway was given after being appointed civil architect in 1816 was to supervise Macquarie's extensions to the government house at Parramatta. The original timber-framed, wattle-and-daub building erected by Governor Phillip had been rebuilt in brick in 1800, and now Macquarie wanted a more spacious and elegant building fit for entertaining. Greenway was responsible for the building of the fine entrance portico.

Below left Greenway's most impressive building is undoubtedly St Matthew's Church at Windsor, designed in the neoclassical style then fashionable in England: the finely proportioned windows and tower surmounted by classical urns and an octagonal lantern recall the "Waterloo churches" that were commissioned to celebrate Wellington's victory and provide places of worship for England's burgeoning industrial cities. The foundation stone was laid on 11 October 1816, but the ceremony had to be repeated two days later when it was discovered that the silver dollar Macquarie had placed beneath the stone had been stolen.

Above This portrait hints at the arrogance of Francis Greenway's character – the building needs of the colony exaggerated his otherwise competent architectural skills and he became correspondingly self-important; an inefficient administrator, he was noted for his irascibility and made many enemies. He received few private commissions and government patronage dried up after Macquarie's replacement by Governor Brisbane in 1822. Greenway, with more than forty colonial buildings to his credit, died in relative poverty.

Above Sheep farming has dominated the New Zealand economy since 1834 when the first flock of around 100 animals was introduced. The creation of grazing land through forest clearance to support intensive pastoralism has had dramatic impact on the landscape.

Right The harsh Australian landscape did not lend itself to the close agricultural settlement that flourished in New Zealand. While powerful graziers extended their vast pastoral ranges, small-time farmers known as "cockies" scratched out meager livings on marginal land, living in rudimentary cabins.

1848), and to cope with drought, floods and mudslides. The introduction of European species – especially birds and rabbits, which decimated crops and grasslands – brought other environmental hazards, while the clearance of forest slopes for farming leached fertile soils from the land. Farms and areas of forest were frequently destroyed by fire when scrub-burning ran out of control. The daily labor of pioneer life was punishing for the farmers-cum-frontiersmen and women who became the heroes and heroines of New Zealand's national mythology.

But if life in New Zealand was rigorous, in Australia it was harder still. The New Zealand landscape, hazardous though it was, was of manageable proportions. New South Wales stretched for unimaginable distances and was a landscape to be endured rather than cultivated. Some Australian settlers may have deluded themselves into thinking that the thin southeastern coastal strip was a new Arcadia, but just beyond sprawled the arid deserts of the continent's interior. The environment was so profoundly different that it exaggerated the settlers' sense of exile and made British ways of life seem irrelevant.

The very landscape was a spur to radical nationalism. By the 1850s most of the land was in the hands of large landowners and squatters (a term originally applied in New South Wales to ex-convicts who occupied land without authority, but which was later the name given to the pastoralists who secured grazing rights over large tracts of land). The Land Act of 1861 tried to encourage more close settlement by making land available for small farmers, who could select areas of between 16 and 129 hectares (40 and 320 acres) on payment of a quarter of the price; thus they became known as selectors. The move was not a success. The squatters made dummy claims to keep their hold over the best land, forcing the selectors onto marginal lands, where dust bowls were created and the soil become salinated. In the aftermath of selection, hostility between the large landowning interests and rural workers increased. For many, the outlaw Ned Kelly (1855–80) and his gang of primitive rebels, who outwitted the authorities and evaded police capture for two years in rural New South Wales, personified the struggle of the rural worker against the exploitative landowner, while in the biting humor of his Dad and Dave stories, written under the pseudonym of Steele Rudd, Arthur Hoey Davis (1868–1935) carried the memory of the selector's self-reliance and toil into the 20th century. The myth of Arcadia could not be sustained; instead, the Australian myth focused on the contrast between town and country, stressing the virtues of physical labor in the outback.

In their shared propensity to work hard in order to "civilize" the environment by bringing it under cultivation, both Australian and New Zealander pioneers imagined far greater riches than their countries were able to deliver. Both societies set great store by the qualities of the working man, and the cult of masculinity still looms large in their national mythologies. But while New Zealand became a land of peasant farmers and of small rural communities and townships, the Australian countryside came to be dominated by large landowners whose vast holdings were tended by armies of itinerant workers – the stockmen, shearers, cane-cutters and swagmen who recur in the literature, art and film of Australia. The irony was that, unlike New Zealand, Australia was a predominately urban society. Like the convicts, the free settlers

Ned Kelly

Bushrangers are the Australian equivalent of highwaymen or outlaws. Many have been mythologized in ballad and story, but none is so famous as Ned Kelly (1855–88). The first of the bushrangers were convict "bolters" who took to the bush and lived by raiding and terrorizing settlements – they were particularly rife in Van Diemen's Land in the early 1800s. A second type of bushranger, more strictly a highwayman, emerged in the early goldrushes. Then, during the agrarian unrest of the 1860s and 1870s that resulted from friction between the rich squatters and the small-time farmers or selectors, the bushranger evolved yet again, becoming in the popular imagination a Robin Hood-like figure, a social bandit. It is to this period that the Kelly gang belongs. The bushrangers evaded the law for so long because they were able to call on the support of smallscale farmers who sympathized with their stand against the powerful landowners. Many have seen the exploits of the Kelly gang, and others like them, as a form of political protest against colonial authority. Ned Kelly himself claimed in his famous Jerilderie Letter that the "Kelly outbreak" was a response to the corruption of the police.

Ned Kelly and his brother Dan had been involved in cattle stealing in northeast Victoria for some years before they formed the Kelly gang with Joe Byrne and Steve Hart. The first of their many raids was in April 1878. A series of robberies followed over the next two years and in June 1880 they captured the town of Glenrowan . In the ensuing shootout with the police the other members of the gang were killed (though some said Dan escaped to Queensland) and Ned was wounded in the leg and captured. He was tried later in the year and hanged at Melbourne on 11 November.

Bottom left The story of Ned Kelly has been retold countless times in poetry and prose, plays and movies. *The Trial* (1947) is one of a famous series of paintings by Sidney Nolan that depict Kelly as a natural rebel disdainful of authority. Even in court he wears his armor and his famous iron helmet with its narrow eyeslit. In some of his abstractions Nolan has left the slit empty, but here two glaring eyes survey the court as Judge Redmond sentences Kelly to death.

Far left Ned Kelly, sporting a long beard, was photographed in prison after his capture. Wearing chains, he is seemingly resigned to his fate. There is a self-assuredness in his hands-on-hip pose that is consonant with the remark he is supposed to have made to the hangman before his execution, "Such is life".

Left A magazine depicts Kelly making his last stand at Glenrowan in northeastern Victoria. Ned and Dan Kelly inherited their fiery temperament from their father, John "Red" Kelly, an Irish patriot and former convict. When he died in 1866 their mother took up a selected plot of land between Greta and Glenrowan, an area that is now popularly known as Kelly country, and here they eked out a living as smalltime farmers and cattle stealers. It is part of the legend that the brothers were devoted to their mother and sister Kate. They claimed to have formed their gang as an act of revenge against police corruption after their mother had been arrested for attempted murder and Kate sexually harassed by one of the arresting officers.

Below The last bushrangers in Australia, the Kellys have endured in the public imagination partly on account of their ingenuity in evading police capture for so long, and partly on account of their home-made armor, displayed here after Ned Kelly's arrest, which was crudely made from plowshares.

came mostly from Britain's towns and cities. Few took naturally to farming. By the mid 19th century, six Australian states (then known as colonies) had been established: New South Wales, Tasmania (1825), Western Australia (1829), South Australia (1836), Victoria (1851) and Queensland (1859). In each of them, the place of initial settlement – Sydney in New South Wales, Hobart in Tasmania, Perth in Western Australia, Adelaide in South Australia, Melbourne in Victoria and Brisbane in Queensland – grew rapidly as the colony's principal center of commercial, economic and political activity, providing numerous opportunities for migrants. Wool, cereals, minerals and other commodities flowed into them from their coastal hinterlands for onward shipping, and each maintained its separate lines of communications with Britain and the outside world. By the 1890s an observer noted that "The abnormal aggregation of the population into their capital cities is a most unfortunate element in the progress of the colonies."

Here to stay

The early settlers of Australia and New Zealand had few doubts about their identity – they were British. The concept of being an Australian or a New Zealander did not yet exist, and children born to these settlers were considered to be Britons born overseas, or colonials, at least by their parents. The term "home" – meaning Britain – survived in the language and in the emotions of Australians and New Zealanders until well into the 20th century. Writing as late as the 1930s the Australian historian William Keith Hancock (1898–1988) referred to the white settler Australians as "Independent Australian Britons", an ambiguous label that embodied the shared loyalty that many felt for both nation and empire (settler New Zealanders

Above An early settler in his bark shanty, surrounded by his tools and few possessions. Clearing the land was back-breaking work, and many failed in their efforts. Not for nothing were the unyielding hardwoods of the Australian bush given such names as ironbark.

might have similarly have been designated "Independent New Zealander Britons"). Yet significant minorities in both societies – the Australian Aborigines, the Maori, other ethnic groups such as the Chinese, for instance – did not fit these descriptions.

At some point in the 19th century an important semantic shift occurred: new arrivals stopped being emigrants and became immigrants. In other words, the emphasis had shifted toward the new place, though the link with the old was always still implied. Gradually the term migrant became an accepted usage. This emphasized neither the place of origin nor the destination but, as it was widely understood, still carried an overtone of transience. Apart from the convicts, who had little choice but to remain where they had been sent, others came to the colonies in the hope of making a fortune that would allow them to establish themselves in an affluent lifestyle back home. Though a substantial number of successful colonists did return to Britain, a much greater number stayed, usually out of necessity, and life in Australia and New Zealand was often regarded as an exile born of failure. Traces of this attitude, given frequent expression in colonial novels and works of art, still survive in some aspects of contemporary society.

Only gradually did people come to see that there were positive reasons for becoming Australians and New Zealanders, that there was something special or different about the generations "born into the soil", as the expression went, that distinguished them from the British. Once arrived, the vast majority of immigrants

Exploring Australia

When Arthur Phillip declared New South Wales a British possession in 1788 he laid claim to all the land between latitude 40° 49′ south and 10° 37′ south and extending westward to longitude 135° east – a vast area that covered almost half the continent. However, European settlement moved out only gradually into the interior from the narrow coastal strip around Sydney. As the population grew there was pressing need to take over more land for agriculture but the Blue Mountains, part of the Great Dividing Range, proved a formidable barrier to westward expansion until a route was found across them in 1813. In the next quarter of a century expeditions led by John Oxley, John Mitchell and others "unlocked" the southeastern corner of the continent, revealing its potential for grazing and agriculture. In the late 1820s Charles Sturt (1795–1869) began to explore the rivers of the Murray-Darling system.

By the 1840s coastal settlements had been founded at Perth, Moreton Bay (later Brisbane), Melbourne and Adelaide. A second phase of exploration now began into Australia's inhospitable interior. These often privately funded expeditions were undertaken by scientists and adventurers with the aim of adding to geographical knowledge and filling in the empty spaces on the map. After two unsuccessful attempts to find a route north from Adelaide, Edward John Eyre (1815–1901) became the first European to cross the Nullarbor Plain in 1841. In 1844 Sturt headed into central Australia in search of a great inland sea. The same year Ludwig Leichhardt (1813–48) led an expedition from Moreton Bay to the area around the Gulf of Carpentaria in the north; he disappeared in 1848 in his second attempt to cross the continent. The first south–north crossing of Australia was made by Burke and Wills in 1860-1. It was the largest and best-equipped expedition yet to have taken place, but both perished (with five others) on the return journey.

Above Charles Sturt's pioneering expedition down the Murrumbidgee and Murray rivers in 1829–30 was instrumental in the choice of South Australia as the site of a new settlement.

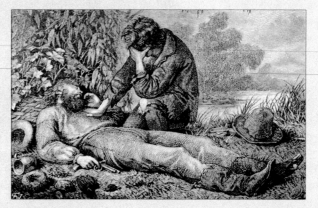

Left John King, sole survivor of the team that made the first illfated south–north crossing of Australia, weeps beside the body of Robert Burke. This sentimental drawing is typical of the public reaction to the tragedy, but a committee of enquiry blamed Burke for the disaster.

Below It was endurance rather than heroism that conquered the "unforgiving continent". This did not prevent popular myths emerging about encounters with huge beasts and hostile "natives". Thomas Baines is depicted in heroic pose subduing a monster crocodile in the north of Australia.

Left John McDouall Stuart (1815–66) crossed the continent from Adelaide to Darwin in 1862. As a result, the Northern Territory was annexed by South Australia the following year. The Overland Telegraph Line, completed in 1872 and paid for by the South Australian government, followed the line of Stuart's pioneering route.

Right By the late 19th century expeditions had become major, well-funded operations. Ernest Giles (1835–97) is seen here striding ahead of a camel caravan (complete with Afghan driver) as he sets out from Beltana, north of Port Augusta in South Australia, to cross the Nullarbor Plain to Perth in 1875 .

The exploration of Australia *(below)*
Flinders' circumnavigation of 1802/3 confirmed the extent and shape of Australia but exploration of the interior was slow. Oxley and Mitchell, among others, opened up the southeastern corner. Sturt was one of the first to penetrate the continent's center, but like Eyre, who completed the first east–west crossing, found little to recommend it. Leichhardt and later Gregory mounted expeditions into the northeast and north. After the south–north crossings by Burke and Wills (1861) and Stuart (1862), the attention of explorers such as Warburton, Forrest and Giles turned to the center and western half of the continent.

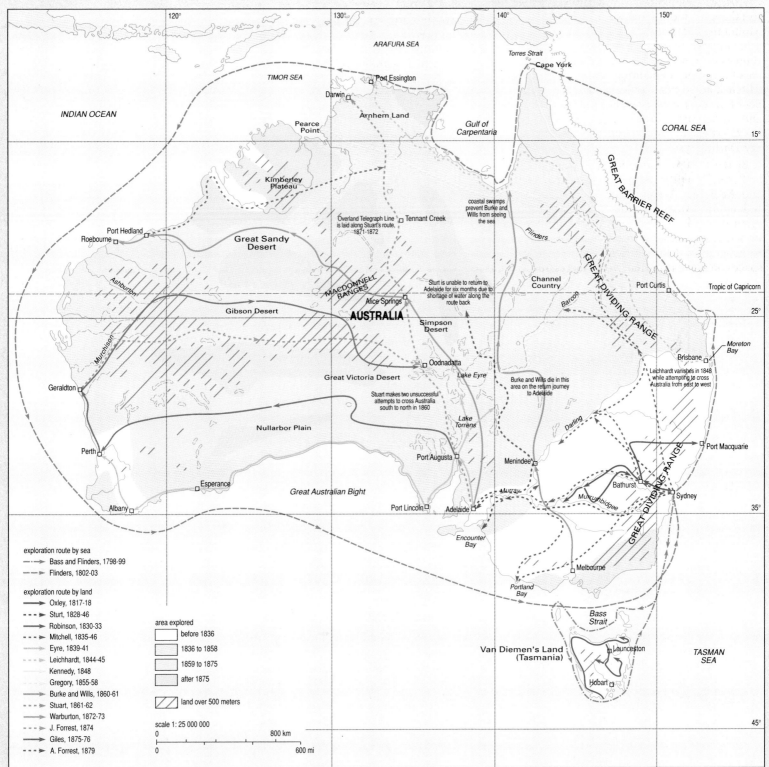

exploration route by sea
- – · – Bass and Flinders, 1798-99
- – – – Flinders, 1802-03

exploration route by land
- ▬▶ Oxley, 1817-18
- ▪▪▪▶ Sturt, 1828-46
- ▬▶ Robinson, 1830-33
- ▪▪▪▶ Mitchell, 1835-46
- ▬▶ Eyre, 1839-41
- ▬▶ Leichhardt, 1844-45
- ▬▶ Kennedy, 1848
- ▬▶ Gregory, 1855-58
- ▬▶ Burke and Wills, 1860-61
- ▪▪▪▶ Stuart, 1861-62
- ▬▶ Warburton, 1872-73
- ▪▪▪▶ J. Forrest, 1874
- ▬▶ Giles, 1875-76
- ▪▪▪▶ A. Forrest, 1879

area explored
- before 1836
- 1836 to 1858
- 1859 to 1875
- after 1875

land over 500 meters

scale 1: 25 000 000
0 ——— 800 km
0 ——— 600 mi

to the antipodes would never travel outside Australia or New Zealand again, save in the imagination. The power of this imagination transformed antipodean environments into old-world shapes, into English cities with English gardens, small Welsh hamlets, Scottish villages and Irish towns. Agriculture and pastoralism at first followed old-world patterns, even when these were highly inappropriate to Australian and New Zealand conditions. Only slowly did stone cottages give way to bungalows and verandahs, only slowly did fields and meadows become paddocks and runs, only slowly were old-world practices changed in the light of the new agricultural environments.

This hankering for the old country was a powerful and commonly shared emotion, but it ultimately proved to be a transitory phase in the development of new national identities. Though language and story-telling still connected the new Australians and New Zealanders to the worlds of their forebears, the physical sensation of living under southern skies provided new and different cultural experiences. With each generation, the Diggers (a name first applied to the miners of the Australian gold-rushes) and Kiwis, as Australians and New Zealanders came to call themselves, identified increasingly with the land of their birth. These second-, third- and fourth-generation inhabitants enjoyed the additional nickname of Cornstalkers in New South Wales, Cabbage Patchers in Victoria, Apple Islanders in Tasmania, Banana Benders in Queensland, Crow Eaters in South Australia and Sandgropers in Western Australia – all serving to emphasize the separate identities of the colonies.

In 1852 the Constitution Act of New Zealand divided the country for administrative purposes into six provinces – Auckland, New Plymouth (Taranaki), Wellington in the North Island; Nelson, Canterbury and Otago in the South Island. This was done to satisfy the demand of the white settlers for a greater voice in their affairs, but the central government (consisting of a governor and a two-chamber General Assembly) remained the overriding authority. The provinces never had the sharp regional distinctions of the Australian colonies: people tended to see themselves as New Zealanders first, belonging to either the North Island or the South Island.

Gold fever

In 1851, hot on the heels of the Californian goldrush, came the first of the Australian goldrushes, to the newly discovered goldfield near Bathurst in New South Wales. Soon afterward the much richer fields of Ballarat and Bendigo in Victoria were opened up. Though prospectors continued to find gold among Australia's mineral-rich deposits throughout the 19th century, sparking off rushes to Queensland in the 1860s and 1870s and to Western Australia (Kalgoorlie) in the 1890s, none were so spectacular as the Victoria rush. More than 1,000 tonnes of gold were unearthed there in the 1850s, when Victoria alone was responsible for more than a third of the world's output of gold. Though not as dramatic as in Australia, gold fever also struck New Zealand in the 1860s. The discovery of gold in Otago in 1861 more than doubled the population of Dunedin to 30,000. Australian miners crossed the Tasman Sea in quite large numbers in search of riches (around 6,000 hopeful prospectors were attracted to a find on the Wakemarina River, for example) but by the end of the decade most had left disappointed.

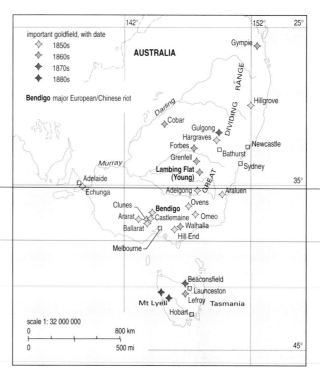

The southeast Australian goldrush
The discovery of gold near Bathurst in New South Wales, followed by other, more valuable finds in Victoria, sparked off the first Australian goldrush in 1851. The flood of prospectors continued throughout the decade, increasing by more than two-thirds the population of the area, but by the end of the 1850s these fields, which in a single six months yielded nearly £3 million worth of surface gold, had been virtually worked out. Though goldfields continued to be opened up in southeastern Australia in the 1860s and 1870s, none was so valuable as the first diggings, and the impetus shifted to the goldfields of Queensland and, later in the century, Western Australia.

The goldrushes had enormous impact on Australia's development. For the first time a flood of people were attracted to the country who were neither convicts nor assisted immigrants. In just 10 years, the population of Australia doubled, to reach one million by 1861: the population of Victoria increased from 77,000 to 540,000 in the same period. By 1871 the population had doubled again. But the rush to the fields left huge labor shortages in the cities and rural areas, so assisted immigration was stepped up to make good the shortfall. The diggers were a rough, nomadic tribe. They may have had families elsewhere, but they traveled to the diggings as single men. In rural Victoria there were twice as many men as women, and the figure on the goldfields can be assumed to have been very much greater: some estimates put the ratio at as much as 100 to one. Certainly, in the absence of reliable statistics, anecdotal evidence in the form of letters, diaries and newspaper articles points to a high concentration of men on the diggings and very few women. This description, from a 19th-century journal, is typical:

> Those readers who have visited an extensive goldfield with thousands of migratory gold-diggers vigorously at work cannot realize the scene. There are to be seen broken down gentlemen, graduates, young men from the upper classes, all such who previously had never handled pick or shovel, working on the same level as to their present station not only with honest but rough men, ordinary laborers and seamen of all nations, but also with men whose previous careers had been stained by long-continued criminal actions. Let my gentle readers fancy such a mixture of men almost without the presence of women, and of the few of those softeners of men's lives (say one in a hundred of men) could be found a small proportion only whose influence would be beneficial – the conclusion would naturally be that such a community would represent a "hell upon earth". But such a conclusion would be erroneous.

As well as Europeans, Asian and American immigrants swelled the Australian population during the goldrushes. The number of Chinese increased tenfold to 20,000 and they made up approximately 20 percent of the male population on the diggings. The Chinese

Right A goldminer poses at the entrance to a shaft. Though the lone prospector, or fossicker, has become the stuff of Australian legend, the independent diggers came to be replaced by large mining companies, which possessed the capital and machinery to dig deep beneath the surface.

miners were resented, and immigration restrictions in the form of entry and residential taxes were imposed. Violent riots against the Chinese were not uncommon, nor were beatings and the ritual of cutting off of pigtails. The most notorious act of aggression happened at Lambing Flat in New South Wales in 1861, when 4,000 white miners descended on the camps of 3,000 Chinese miners and burned them to the ground. Such riots sent shock waves through the colonial society: "Britons would take the Chinese pigtails with the scalp attached" ran a typical headline. The solution was to restrict Chinese immigration still further. New Zealand did not legislate for immigration restriction until the 1880s, but here, too, the Chinese were actively discouraged from entering the country.

Democratic rumblings

The discovery of gold speeded up the introduction of "responsible government" – the contemporary term for self-government – to the antipodean colonies. In 1849 a committee of the Privy Council in England recommended that the means be investigated whereby the colonies of Australia and New Zealand might move in this direction, but nobody seriously thought this would happen in the short term. But as the goldrushes brought economic confidence to Victoria and New South Wales, dramatically altering colonial Australia from a prison to a land of opportunity, so came the desire for a new national identity. In 1853, Gilbert Wright, an early advocate of Australian independence, wrote to the editor of the *Sydney Morning Herald*: "We should aim at nationality – at individuality – at character. We should not blend our associations with the histories of the Old World! Why not have an era – a chronology of our own?"

The movement for self-government was given strong emotional impetus by the Eureka uprising of 1854. To raise revenue from the goldmines, the colonial administration in Victoria levied a license fee. This was resented by the miners, especially when

troopers were sent to the diggings to inspect the payment of licenses. The troopers were badly trained and ill-disciplined, and many took kickbacks in return for protecting illegal operations. Miners were often dragged away from their claims to spend time in prison for non-payment of the license, and this fed the growing discontent. Eventually, miners in Ballarat were led to rebel. The uprising took its name from the Eureka Hotel which was burnt to the ground during the protests. A flag depicting the Southern Cross constellation against a blue ground (which, often called the Eureka Flag, was to become the symbol of Australian republicanism) was hoisted at a mass meeting. The miners, inspired by the fiery speeches of their leader Peter Lalor, drafted a program of radical reform which stated "That it is the inalienable right of every citizen to have a voice in making the laws he is called to obey. That taxation without representation is tyranny." The manifesto went on to call upon democrats to "resist and if necessary remove the irresponsible power which so tyrannises them" and additionally demanded "full and fair representation; manhood suffrages; no property qualifications of members of the Legislative Council; payment of members [of parliament]; short durations of parliaments." The end came when troopers and police overran a stockade raised by the miners; 45 deaths were reported. The stand-off was over, but the democratic mood it had ignited became so irresistible that within a year Victoria and New South Wales had their own parliaments. New Zealand, Tasmania and South Australia followed suit the following year, and in 1860 Queensland also opted for self-government. Western Australia was the last of the 19th-century colonies to achieve self-government in 1890, and here too it coincided with the discovery of gold. The Eureka uprising subsequently became enshrined in Australian legend as one of the most significant moments in the country's history, and the story has been told again and again in poetry, prose, art and film.

Above Lower High Street, Dunedin, photographed in 1907. Dunedin's early growth was fueled by the Otago goldrush and for a time in the 1860s and 1870s it was New Zealand's largest city. It was the site of New Zealand's first university and medical school but by the end of the century had been overtaken by Auckland and Christchurch. Its fine stone buildings are among the finest antipodean examples of Victorian colonial architecture, second only to Melbourne. Shown here is the Telegraph Building with the tower of the Exchange Building behind.

Right Melbourne's boom years, founded on the sudden wealth of the Victorian goldrush, ended as quickly as they had begun in the 1890s when banks closed, businesses were bankrupted and unemployment soared. Much of the blame was placed at the hands of disreputable land speculators. Beyond the elegant boulevards of Collins and Burke streets in the city's commercial center were rows of cheaply built wooden houses, which became the slums of the urban poor. A century later many such rows, as here, were in the process of gentrification.

Above Camels, horses and bullocks were long used to transport wool, grain, timber and other raw materials along the trunk routes of the interior to depots and terminals that could be tens, sometimes hundreds, of kilometers away. Katherine Susannah Prichard's novel *Bullocks* (1926) captures the last days of the bullock teams that worked in the timber industry.

Popular culture

One particular form of performance art that emerged from the goldrushes was the ballad, now readily identified with Australian and New Zealand culture. New words to fit their new environment were added to the tunes that immigrants had brought from the old world. The ballad thus became a narrative form by which Australian and New Zealand myths and stories were transmitted, and the more they were sung, the more they became embellished with local lore and language. Closely allied to the ballad were verse and lyric poetry, which became the favored literary forms in both societies in the second half of the 19th century. Short fiction grew from the propensity of the Australians and New Zealanders to "tell yarns".

Popular culture flourished in the diggers' encampments on the goldfields. Bars were commonplace, and often doubled as brothels. Vaudeville, minstrel shows, opera and theater were palliatives to days spent in hard toil and nights in the most rudimentary accommodation. Touring companies, many of them originally from Europe and America, visited the goldfields from the cities, but they often made use of local performers who incorporated local references in their material, and a few returned to Melbourne and Sydney with good material for stage productions there. For the most part, however, the goldfields' entertainments were too vulgar for Australia's metropolises, whose plays and operas imitated the latest shows from London's West End or from Broadway.

With the concentration of more and more gold-generated wealth in the cities, elements of urban society were becoming bourgeoisified. Australia's first university, Sydney University, was inaugurated in 1851, followed soon after by Melbourne in 1853. Like the University of New Zealand, founded in 1883, these institutions were modeled on the English universities, and were the preserve of the new "respectable" classes. The most magnificent expression of Australia's new prosperity was Melbourne. In the 1850s it rose to become Australia's financial capital, and for a time it overtook Sydney both in terms of population and political importance. "Marvelous Melbourne", as the city became known, developed as one of the truly splendid Victorian cities of the world. But it lived up to its name of "the London of the south", for its architecture was closely modeled on that of the British metropolis. Australia had yet to establish an artistic vision that was truly its own.

Radical nationalism

This did not begin to emerge until the end of the century. It was in the pages of the *Bulletin*, founded in 1880 by Jules Francois Archibald (1856–1919), that Australian writers and artists, together with intellectuals, union leaders and some politicians, began to find a distinctly Australian voice. The *Bulletin*'s motto was "Australia for the Australians" and it became the leading vehicle for the radical nationalism of the 1890s, when it was at the height of its popularity. Among the writers it fostered were Australia's proletarian poet Henry Lawson, Andrew Barton ("Banjo") Paterson (1864–1941) and Joseph Furphy (1843–1912). Banjo Paterson was best-known for his bush ballads, including "The Man from Snowy River" (1890) and "Waltzing Matilda", to this day the most widely sung song in Australia and the nation's unofficial national anthem. Though "Waltzing Matilda" tells the story of the swagman (itinerant laborer) who takes his own life rather than face arrest, Paterson was not in fact especially radical – he was reputed to be more friendly to the squatters, Australia's landed class, than to the working man. In popularizing types such as the man from Snowy River, the best rider in the mountains who recaptured a colt "worth a thousand pounds", Paterson gave literary form to characteristics that Australians had come to believe to be distinct to themselves. The new Australians saw themselves as sons of the saddle, practical working men, more than able to hold their own against the large landowner.

The term radical nationalist belongs more accurately to Lawson and Furphy, both socialists who strove to fit Australian working-class culture into a socialist model. Lawson's radical politics included support for an Australian republic. He was enormously popular in his day, and his poems and short stories, many of them about the bush and bush workers, were known the length and breadth of Australia. Furphy, the son of a tenant farmer who had worked on cattle stations and as a foundry worker, wrote in the *Bulletin* throughout the 1890s under the name of "Warrigal Jack". As "Tom Collins" he published *Such is Life*, the novel for which he is best known, in 1903. In it he declared his literary manifesto: "temper, democratic; bias offensively Australian." The egalitarian spirit of the Australians, Furphy maintained, was the spirit of practical socialism, the commune of Australian mateship. Visiting left-wing intellectuals from Europe supported this view, claiming Australia to be a social laboratory where socialism existed without a doctrine.

Where the radical nationalist writers of the 1890s found a distinctively Australian voice that captured the mood of Australian nationalism, the artists of the Heidelberg school created the first truly representative paintings of Australia. Its principal members were Tom Roberts (1856–1931), Arthur Streeton (1867–1943), Frederick McCubbin (1855-1917) and Charles Conder (1868–1909). At artists' camps outside Melbourne at Box Hill and Heidelberg (from which the school took its name) the group worked together out of doors, developing an impressionistic style. They were supremely successful at capturing the southern light and colors of Australia that had evaded earlier painters. "An effect is only momentary," ran the manifesto of their controversial *Exhibition of 9 x 5 Impressions*, consisting of works painted on cigar-box lids, held in 1889. "Two half hours are never alike,

Left The 1890s were years of severe depression and high unemployment in southeastern Australia. Class attitudes hardened as striking workers were locked out by employers; out-of-work men, made desperate by their situation, were forced to accept the lower rates of pay offered them to return. Writers, artists and intellectuals championed the workers' cause: this illustration appeared in the *Bulletin* in 1891.

Below The central hero of the Australian legend is the swagman or swaggy, an itinerant worker who wandered the outback in search of seasonal work carrying his personal belongings on his back in a swag or pack. In most other western cultures such men, known as tramps or hoboes, are objects of contempt. The swagman – immortalized in the words of "Waltzing Matilda" – seized the Australian imagination during the 1890s when armies of unemployed men, refusing to accept the employers' harsh terms, chose the freedom of the bush track. Swaggies gradually disappeared with changes to transportation in the 20th century, but a few were still in evidence in the 1950s.

most appropriate idioms for the presentation of what were distinctively Australian themes, as opposed to what were merely derivative of styles and subjects from overseas, the artists and writers of the 1890s gave confidence to those that followed them, though the emphasis on nationalism gradually gave way to social realism. One popular work of the next generation that explored the heroic nature of the Australian pioneering spirit was *My Brilliant Career* (1901), the fictitious autobiography of Miles Franklin (1879–1954). Henry Handel Richardson's trilogy *The Fortunes of Richard Mahony* (1917–29), which she modeled on her father's life, was a closely researched study of immigrant life in the mid 19th century. The influence of the 1890s' writers can be traced through to the present, especially in popular representations of Australia. Though art and literature have moved into a greater diversity of genres and styles, film and television in particular now utilize a number of motifs that emanate from that period. The visual style of a number of period movies such as Peter Weir's hauntingly beautiful *Picnic at Hanging Rock* (1975) and Gillian Armstrong's adaptation of *My Brilliant Career* (1979) owes a great deal to the imagery of the 1890s impressionists, while the laconic hero of Paul Hogan's two *Crocodile Dundee* films of the 1980s can be traced directly back to the literature of the same period.

The political and cultural mood of New Zealand was very different. There were some who shared the radicalism of Australia's writers and artists and expressed nationalist sentiments, but on the whole, New Zealand was more imperial-minded than Australia. When Britain opposed the Dutch Boer farmers of the Transvaal in the South African war of 1899–1902, New Zealand sent proportionately more troops to fight the Boers than any other part of the empire. Though the desire for a republic and full independence from the "Mother country" has been expressed with greater or lesser force in Australia since the 19th century, until quite recently most New Zealanders would have considered such a position a betrayal of New Zealand itself.

Above The independent man, practical, rough and ready, who drinks deeply, gambles and is liberal with his manners, has found expression in all forms of Australian culture. Laid back and generally idle, he works hard in an emergency, is loyal to his mates even when he knows they are wrong and possesses a laconic sense of humor. In the *Crocodile Dundee* movies of the 1980s Paul Hogan recreated these characteristics in the larger than life imaginary figure of Mike Dundee.

and he who tries to paint a sunset on two consecutive evenings must be more or less painting from memory. So, in these works it has been the object of the artists to render faithfully, and thus obtain first records of effects widely differing, and of a very fleeting character." The Heidelberg painters were not overtly radical in the way that the *Bulletin* writers were. But by flouting the pastoral conventions of the earlier colonial style, which still predominated in New Zealand, and by choosing scenes of Australian working life as their subjects, they were hugely influential in creating an Australian school of painting. It is ironic, therefore, that nearly all the Heidelberg painters, with the exception of McCubbin, spent a very great part of their working lives as expatriates in Europe – a significant drain of artistic talent away from Australia.

In both literature and art, however, a significant cultural breakthrough had been made. By discovering the

Right South Australian nurses in 1900 prepare to leave for the Cape. The call to support the mother country in its war against the Boer farmers in South Africa aroused deeply contradictory feelings, coming at a time when the Australian colonies were pressing for autonomy. In the radical climate of the day many identified with the Boers' quest for self-determination. Nevertheless, each of the colonies committed troops to the conflict. As sons of the saddle, the Australians proved capable soldiers, being as skilled in bush survival techniques as their Boer opponents.

Australian and New Zealand Painters

For the first hundred years or so after European settlement, the response of painters to the antipodean environment was a colonial one: the style, shapes and sensibility of their paintings reflected the values of the old world rather than the new. Arcadian landscapes, painted mostly in watercolors, were filled with the elms and oaks familiar from English paintings. The harsh light and garish colors of the outback demanded different treatment and when, eventually, a recognizably Australian school of painting began to emerge at the end of the 19th century, the bush – and especially the gum tree – became the dominating theme. Leading the way were the Heidelberg painters, whose impressionistic style was the first to capture the distinctive Australian light. The colonial tradition of pastoral painting was even more deeply entrenched in New Zealand, but here, too, a nationalist school of painting gradually evolved that took account of the special features of the New Zealand landscape. If New Zealand art tended to be more conservative than Australian, it differed also in that the Maori were seen as

suitable subjects for painting, even though from a colonial perspective.

Expatriation took its toll of painters in the early 20th century. The experiences of World War I tended to reduce experimentation: modernism was largely rejected as being decadent and defeatist. Painting in the 1920s demonstrated a vitality of mood that was in keeping with the buoyancy of the times, while responses to the depression of the 1930s ranged from social realism to surrealism. Art became more experimental after World War II, and a number of significant painters emerged in the 1960s, including Sidney Nolan, Arthur Boyd and Brett Whiteley from Australia and Toss Woolaston and Colin McCahon from New Zealand. Since the 1980s Aboriginal and Maori art has received the recognition previously denied it.

Left Frederick McCubbin's *The Pioneers* (1904), one of Australia's best-known paintings, is the center canvas of a triptych that tells the story of a pioneering family and is a metaphor for the opening up of Australia. The other two panels show the mourning parents after the child has died, and the man, now a widower, left all alone. Civilization can be seen through the clearing. McCubbin was perhaps the most strongly nationalist of the Heidelberg painters.

Above Tom Roberts was the leader of the Heidelberg painters. He shared with his contemporaries a romantic view of manual labor. *Shearing the Rams* (1889–90) was painted on the eve of the great shearers' strikes of the 1890s. But there is no sense of class conflict in his painting. In the same vein, Roberts produced other classic paintings of Australian life, such as *The Breakaway* and *Bailed Up*, which are part of the romanticization of the pioneering past.

Right Arthur Streeton, perhaps the most gifted of all the Heidelberg painters, had a long-lasting influence over Australian art. *The Purple Noon's Transparent Might* received considerable critical acclaim when it was first exhibited in 1896. Other notable Australian works include early cityscapes such as *Redfern Station* and beach scenes such as *Coogee*. During World War I Streeton devoted himself to painting patriotic subjects, but the forms are stale and tired. When he returned to live in Australia in

Far left Frances Hodgkins, a water colorist with no formal training, taught art in Europe between 1902–12. Returning to New Zealand, she began painting in oils in 1915 and four years later went back to Europe where she remained until her death in 1947. Her significance as a New Zealand painter, then, lies not so much in her contribution to developments in New Zealand art or in her influence on her contemporaries, but in the inspiration her work has given younger generations of New Zealand painters. *Wings over Water* (1936), shown here, is one of her finest paintings.

Left James Nairn, a professionally trained British-born painter, started an art school in Wellington in the 1890s. Along with Petrus Van Der Velden and G. P. Nerli, he was instrumental in transforming New Zealand art, freeing it from its colonial mold. He tended to concentrate on people rather than landscape, as in this portrait of *Old Age*.

1924, after almost 20 years abroad, he found himself much revered, but his statements on art were by now quite old-fashioned. He was especially critical of modernism.

The workingman's paradise

The Workingman's Paradise: An Australian Labor Novel (1892) was the title of a popular work of fiction by William Lane (1861–1917), a journalist and trade unionist. In their romanticization of Australia's manual workers and of its pioneering stock the writers and the painters of the 1890s helped to foster the growing sense of Australia's being a workers' utopia. At the beginning of the 20th century, Australia and New Zealand were leading the world in democratic progress. Manhood suffrage had been introduced in the 1850s, and the vote was extended to women in the 1890s (New Zealand was the first to do so, in 1893). This was well ahead of its time – women in the United States and Britain did not become fully enfranchised until the 1920s – and while this may seem at odds with such male-dominated societies, it is a measure of the keen sense of social justice that prevailed at the time, as it is of the strength of character of the women suffragists. The 1870s and 1880s had seen the growing influence of trade unions on both sides of the Tasman Sea. Some notable job benefits had been won, including the widespread adoption of the eight-hour day. In Australia, trade union organizations, particularly strong among miners and sheep shearers, extended across colonial boundaries: the massive Australian Workers Union (AWU), for example, represented sheep shearers in all parts of the continent in pressing demands for standard rates of pay and conditions. However, the worldwide economic depression of the early 1890s, which was particularly marked in Victoria and New South Wales, strengthened the employers' resistance and the unions were defeated in a number of industrial disputes. Thwarted, they turned instead to political representation. The first Labor parties in the world were formed in Australia and New Zealand, the first Labor members were elected to parliament in Queensland in the early 1890s, and the first national Labor government came to power in Australia in 1904. In time, the Labor parties developed their own political momentum, but retained close ties with the union movement. The formation of Labor parties in both countries checked the radicalization of the union movement, which now sought influence in parliament as a means of gaining its objectives. Though Communist parties would later exert an influence over key unions in both Australia and New Zealand, by and large it was left to the Labor parties, as the political wings of the unions, to represent worker politics.

At the beginning of the 20th century standards of living in Australia and New Zealand were among the highest in the world, and workers' rights were better protected than almost anywhere else. There was provision of old age, invalid and widows' pensions; conciliation and arbitration courts had been set up to deal with industrial disputes; and in 1907, in what is known as the "Harvester Judgement", the courts found that employers should pay wages based on the needs of the worker. Thus the nexus between the level of wages and the ability of the employer to pay was broken, and the basic wage became the cornerstone of industrial arbitration. New Zealand also established a basic wage, though in 1921 the Conciliation and Arbitration Act was changed so that "economic conditions affecting any trade or industry" were taken into account. But, as in Australia, employers were expected to pay a minimum amount to their workers based on the needs of a man to support a wife and family.

Left Australia and New Zealand led the world in extending the franchise to women. But voting power did not translate into political representation. In 1903 Vida Goldstein was the first woman anywhere in the British empire to stand for parliament when she put herself forward for election to the Australian Senate. She made four more attempts in 1910, 1913, 1914 and 1917 but was defeated on each occasion. The first women to gain election to the Australian parliament were Dorothy Tangey and Edith Lyons in 1943. Women have remained under-represented and few have held senior government portfolios. A breakthrough was made in the 1980s when Carmen Lawrence in Western Australia and Joan Kirner in Victoria were elected as state premiers.

Women were exempt from the basic wage. They earned between half and two thirds the male wage, because it was determined that men were the breadwinners and providers for family life.

Federation and sovereignty

The literary and social movements of the 1890s, that were so instrumental in defining how Australians viewed themselves, fed into the popular demand for a form of government that would bring the six Australian colonies together as a single national entity – a move that had first been raised as early as the 1840s. There was a perceived need to share the financial and administrative burdens of defense and to streamline utilities such as the postal service, while the colonies' wish to unite coincided with Britain's desire to reduce the costs of providing naval protection for Australia and New Zealand. Union would also make it less cumbersome for British businesses to trade in Australia; instead of having to go through the agencies of the individual colonies, traders could deal with one central authority. Because the colonies were powerful political units jealous of their own rights and suspicious of each other, some kind of federal compact with implicit power-sharing arrangements between the individual components and the central administration seemed inevitable. Federation would safeguard the rights of the states (as the colonies would become) and offer them the flexibility to negotiate their individual relations with the central administration.

Federation was discussed at various conferences in Australia throughout the 1890s, and by 1899 a federation constitution, which divided power between the Commonwealth, or federal, parliament and the state

Federation Australia

Nineteenth-century Australia was a loose grouping of six self-governing colonies that each maintained separate relations and communication links with Britain and the rest of the world. The distances that separated the colonial capitals hindered overland communication and encouraged the development of independent economies and political systems. Inter-colonial rivalry was great, though all were linked by a common culture. By the end of the century the advantages of some kind of political arrangement to share certain administrative responsibilities were becoming obvious. Through a series of constitutional conventions held in the 1890s the colonies decided to form a federated nation in a power-sharing relationship with a central government. Referendums in favor of federation were passed with varying degrees of support: opposition was greatest in New South Wales, which initially voted to reject it, Queensland and Western Australia, the last colony to decide to join. The Commonwealth of Australia came into being on 1 January 1901, the first day of the 20th century. The states retained their own parliaments and jealously defended their powers. The central government, located in Melbourne before moving to Canberra in 1927, was initially quite weak but in the course of time the balance of power has shifted decisively in its favor.

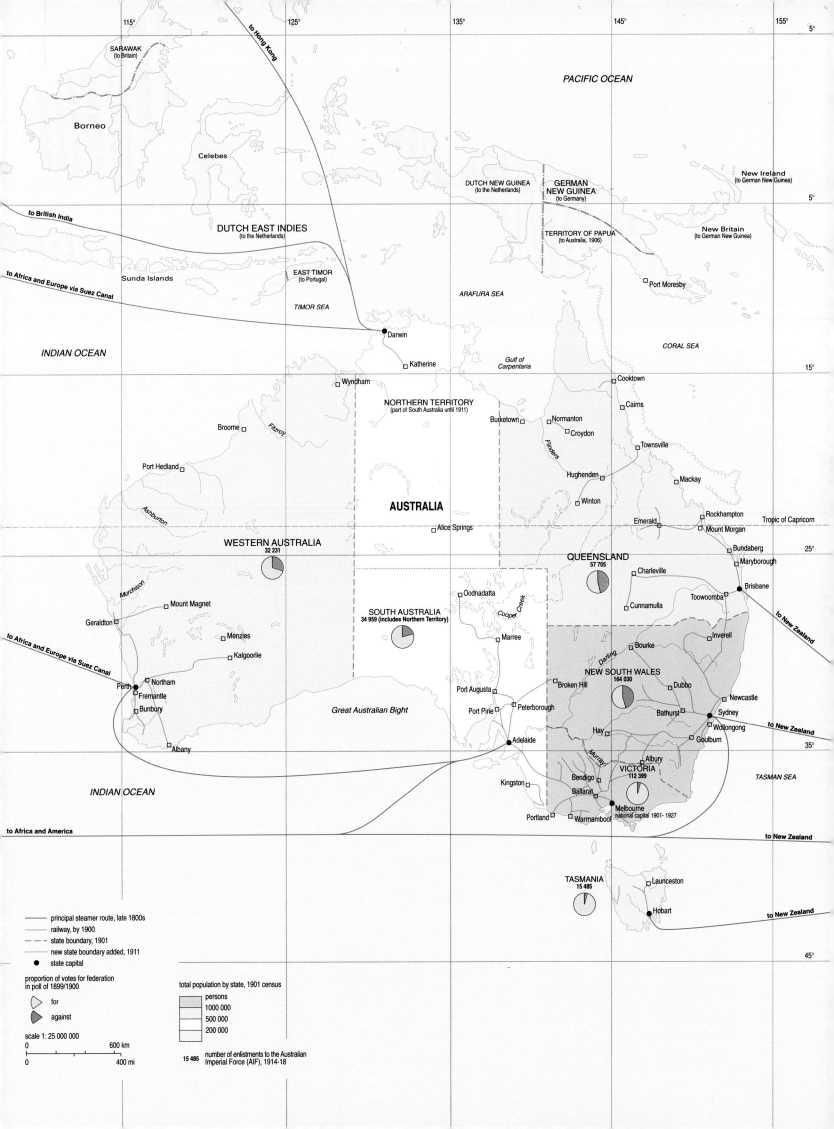

115°   125°   135°   145°   155°   5°

to Hong Kong

SARAWAK
(to Britain)

PACIFIC OCEAN

Borneo

Celebes

DUTCH NEW GUINEA
(to the Netherlands)

GERMAN
NEW GUINEA
(to Germany)

New Ireland
(to German New Guinea)

5°

to British India

DUTCH EAST INDIES
(to the Netherlands)

TERRITORY OF PAPUA
(to Australia, 1906)

New Britain
(to German New Guinea)

to Africa and Europe via Suez Canal

Sunda Islands

EAST TIMOR
(to Portugal)

ARAFURA SEA

□ Port Moresby

TIMOR SEA

INDIAN OCEAN

● Darwin

□ Katherine

Gulf of Carpentaria

CORAL SEA

15°

□ Wyndham

NORTHERN TERRITORY
(part of South Australia until 1911)

□ Cooktown

□ Cairns

Broome □

Fitzroy

Burketown □

□ Normanton
□ Croydon

Flinders

□ Townsville

Port Hedland □

□ Hughenden

□ Mackay

Ashburton

AUSTRALIA

□ Winton

□ Rockhampton
□ Mount Morgan

Emerald □

Tropic of Capricorn

25°

□ Alice Springs

WESTERN AUSTRALIA
32 231

QUEENSLAND
57 705

□ Bundaberg
□ Maryborough

□ Charleville

□ Brisbane

Murchison

□ Mount Magnet

□ Oodnadatta

Coopers Creek

□ Cunnamulla

□ Toowoomba

to New Zealand

Geraldton □

SOUTH AUSTRALIA
34 959 (includes Northern Territory)

□ Inverell

□ Menzies

□ Marree

□ Bourke

Darling

□ Dubbo

to Africa and Europe via Suez Canal

□ Kalgoorlie

Broken Hill □

NEW SOUTH WALES
164 030

□ Newcastle

□ Northam

Port Augusta □

□ Bathurst

● Sydney

Perth ●
□ Fremantle

□ Peterborough

□ Hay

□ Wollongong
□ Goulburn

to New Zealand

□ Bunbury

Port Pirie □

35°

Great Australian Bight

□ Albury

Murray

□ Bendigo

VICTORIA
112 399

TASMAN SEA

□ Albany

● Adelaide

□ Ballarat

INDIAN OCEAN

□ Kingston

● Melbourne
national capital 1901- 1927

Portland □
□ Warrnambool

to Africa and America

to New Zealand

TASMANIA
15 485

□ Launceston

45°

● Hobart

to New Zealand

principal steamer route, late 1800s

railway, by 1900

state boundary, 1901

new state boundary added, 1911

● state capital

proportion of votes for federation
in poll of 1899/1900

◐ for

◑ against

scale 1: 25 000 000

0   600 km

0   400 mi

total population by state, 1901 census

persons

1000 000
500 000
200 000

15 485 number of enlistments to the Australian
Imperial Force (AIF), 1914-18

parliaments had been approved by referendums held in five of the six states. In Western Australia, which had been the last colony to enter the discussions, the referendum that confirmed approval was delayed until 1900. There were a number of reasons to explain this. Perth is farther from Sydney and Melbourne on the eastern seaboard of Australia than Auckland and Wellington in New Zealand are. To the Sandgropers of Western Australia (a name they were proud to call themselves) all other Australians were "t'othersiders". Western Australia had been proclaimed as a free colony and settled separately, without any form of dependence on New South Wales. In addition, it was economically self-sufficient; the discovery of gold protected it from the effects of economic depression in the early 1890s. It was only when the population of the goldfields threatened to secede from Western Australia in order to join the federal movement that the Western Australian government began seriously to consider joining the union. Western Australians continued to see themselves as different; as late as the early 1930s, they voted by a two to one majority to leave the federation, but the Privy Council in London did not recognize the referendum as constitutional.

With the inauguration of the Commonwealth of Australia on 1 January 1901 the Australian nation-state was officially born. New Zealand had originally been part of the negotiations for a centralized Australian administration, but the Tasman Sea had proved too great a psychological barrier to political integration. Though the way was left open for New Zealand to join the federation at a later date, the talks

were only ever half-hearted. There was no apparent will to join; "a close relationship but a safe distance" was the motto. In the process of defining themselves as not being Australians, the white tribe of New Zealand emerged as an independent people and in 1907 an act of the British parliament granted New Zealand sovereignty. Australia and New Zealand became nation-states without much fanfare, and within a colonial setting. Since they also had dominion status within the British empire, dual loyalty to nation and to crown was no contradiction, and Australians and New Zealanders were able to define themselves as nationalists and colonials at one and the same time.

Political culture

For New Zealand, which had had responsible central government since the 1850s, the transition from colony to dominion, or nation-state, was a relatively smooth process. But an entirely new structure of central government had to be created for Australia. Under the terms of the federation, the states conceded only limited and specified powers to the Commonwealth government, including management of defense, external affairs, immigration policy and customs. The lower house of the two-chamber legislature, the House of Representatives, was elected by single-member constituencies of roughly equal size. This was, and is, the main legislative body, and elects the prime minister. The upper house, or Senate, became the states' house, based on the US model. Equal numbers of senators were elected from each of the states, irrespective of size. Like the House of Representatives, the Senate

Above Canberra was chosen as the site of the future Australian State Territory in 1909. An international competition to find a design for the new capital was won by an American, Walter Burley Griffin (1876–1937). His plan incorporated an artificial lake and parks, broad avenues and sweeping vistas, but World War I delayed development. A temporary Parliament House was opened in 1927, and then economic depression and another world war intervened to hold up work on the city yet again. It was not until the 1950s that the Australian government committed itself to spending the money needed to develop Canberra. At its heart is the new Parliament House, opened during the Bicentennial in 1988, surrounded by a cluster of public buildings including the National Library and the National War Memorial.

sovereign nation-state, it was still dependent on the links of empire. Though these links would gradually dissolve in the course of the 20th century, they would have profound impact on Australian political culture. Moreover, as time went on, the central government would become more powerful, and the states less so, in the power-sharing arrangements.

The political divide in the first two national parliaments lay between the protectionists, who sought to impose tariffs on imported manufactures to allow Australia to develop an industrial base, and the free traders, who opposed restrictions of all kinds. The weight of the argument went to the protectionists, and Australian governments since have generally pursued protectionist policies. It was the formation of the shortlived Labor government of 1904 that signalled the birth of modern party politics in Australia. The Labor Party has continued to play a major role in politics ever since, holding power from 1910–17, 1929–32, 1941–49, 1972–75, and 1983–. The majority of governments, however, have been formed by non-Labor parties. The chief party of opposition to the Labor Party went under a number of labels – Liberal, Fusion, Nationalist, United Australia Party – before returning to the Liberal name in the 1940s. It dominated Australian government between 1949 and 1972 and produced the country's longest-serving prime minister, Robert Menzies (1894–1978), whose two ministries ran from 1939–41 and from 1949–65. Australia's other "conservative" party is the Country Party, which changed its name to the National Party in the 1970s.

The most important force in New Zealand's early political history was the Liberal Party. Holding power between 1891 and 1912, it oversaw New Zealand's transformation to sovereign state and initiated a far-reaching program of social legislation and economic development, building roads and railways and expanding the dairying and meat-producing industries. During its term of office, and especially during the premiership of the popularist politician Richard Seddon ("King Dick", 1845–1906) from 1893 until his death, politics became organized along modern party lines. The Reform Party was in power from 1912 to 1930, when it formed a coalition with the United Party from which it emerged as the National Party. It was more narrowly sectional than the Liberal Party, gaining its support from the farmers. By the 1930s its main opposition was the Labor Party, which became the controlling power in government for the period from 1935 to 1949. Since then the National Party has been the dominant party of government, interrupted by Labor governments from 1957–69, 1972–75 and 1984–90.

Though the parliamentary systems in Australia and New Zealand are heavily influenced by British models, there are substantial differences. For a start, there is no conservative force in either country. The non-Labor parties have tended to be an amalgam of economic interests such as farmers, manufacturers and merchants. Like their Labor opponents, they have seen the state as being central to the well-being of the people, and have supported significant social reforms. However, despite Australia's and New Zealand's reputations for being progressive societies, their governments have been reluctant to pursue constitutional reform, especially in relation to citizenship. Australia and New Zealand did not have formal citizenship until after the World War II; before this, nationals of

Above Richard John Seddon was New Zealand's longest serving prime minister, from 1893 to 1906. He had worked as a miner, storekeeper and publican before entering politics with solid working-class credentials. Possessing both a flair for publicity and a commanding platform style he transformed New Zealand's politics, presiding over the Liberal Party at the time that its program of social reform was leading the world. Assuming responsibilities for finance, education, defense and public works, his style of government became increasingly autocratic. The close association of the Liberal Party with his personality contributed in no small way to its decline after his death in office.

soon became dominated by party politics.

To avoid fears that New South Wales, and especially Sydney, would become too dominant in the federation the Commonwealth parliament at first convened at Melbourne, but in order to solve the problem of interstate rivalry it was soon decided to build an entirely new national capital. In 1911 land was acquired for this purpose at Canberra, and in 1927 the Duke of York (later King George VI) officially opened the parliament building here. This remained the home of the Australian national parliament until 1988 when it was replaced by a magnificent new Parliament House, officially opened during the Bicentennial celebrations. These changes are something of a metaphor of the changing nature of Australia itself. The constitution, written in the solemn legal language of the late 19th century, is a solid document that outlined the relationship between the six states and the commonwealth government. It also stressed the central role of the monarchy and of Britain in Australian political life. So, while Australia was a

Gallipoli: the Making of a Legend

Every year Australians and New Zealanders observe 25 April as Anzac Day, a national day of commemoration for the Gallipoli landings in 1915 when an expeditionary force, consisting mostly of Anzacs (members of the Australian and New Zealand Army Corps), was put ashore on a narrow beach in Turkey. The aim was to force the Turks out of the war and open up the searoute to Russia through the Dardanelles and the Black Sea. After nine months of fierce fighting the attempt was abandoned. The Allied force was withdrawn in the middle of the night, leaving behind 12,000 dead, of whom more than 8,500 were Australian and 2,700 New Zealanders. Paradoxically, it was out of this defeat, and out of the conflict in Europe, that Australian and New Zealand nationhood was forged. Though interpretations of the Anzac myth are complex, the story itself is simple: a generation of brave young Australians and New Zealanders went off to war, and from their blood-letting the Australian and New Zealand nations emerged. The annual Anzac commemorations keep the myth alive; many Australians and New Zealanders, most of them around the same age as the fallen soldiers, make the pilgrimage each year to Anzac Cove where the first landings were made. Very few can name the officers in charge, nor any individual heroes. It is the common soldier, the anonymous "digger", that this moment of national remembrance commemorates.

Below left The Australian soldier, the "digger" in his slouch hat, became an enduring icon of Australian nationalism. *Kenneth Soldier* (1958) is one of many war paintings by Sidney Nolan. Its reference is probably to Kenneth Slessor, the poet turned World War II war correspondent, but its motif is recognizably that of the Anzac of both world wars.

Below For three weeks following the landing at Gallipoli, John Simpson Kirkpatrick (1892–1915), serving as a private with the Australian Army Medical Corps, ferried wounded men from the front across the beach to the waiting hospital ships, carrying them on a donkey. He was killed on 19 May 1915. Almost immediately the story of Simpson or the "Man with the Donkey" became a central legend of Australian nationhood, embellished with biblical qualities of service and self-sacrifice. Little was known about the man himself who – it is now established – was an Englishman who had migrated to Australia before the war and worked as an itinerant laborer.

both countries were British subjects. Though the Maori had been included in New Zealand's political system since the 19th century, returning candidates from four Maori constituencies to parliament, Australian Aborigines were not even granted citizenship until 1967. This reluctance to express full national sovereignty featured in the slowness of both countries to adopt the Statute of Westminster of 1931, the constitutional instrument whereby the British Parliament gave equal status to the self-governing dominions of the empire, and extended the sovereignty of the individual countries while diminishing British influence. The statute was not ratified by Australia until 1941 and by New Zealand until 1949.

World War I

It is perhaps ironic that what proved to be one of the most formative events in the forging of Australian and New Zealand nationhood should be a war fought between European powers on the other side of the world. When Britain entered World War I in 1914, Australia and New Zealand, along with the other dominions and dependencies of the British empire, immediately sent volunteers to join the fighting and turned their factories to making munitions. Recruitment figures in both countries were high: about half the men eligible to do so went off to fight. Critics of the part played in the war by the Australian and New Zealand Army Corps (ANZAC), and of the later mythologizing that surrounds its campaigns, particularly Gallipoli, argue that Australians and New Zealanders served as mindless colonials in a war that had little or no relevance to them. But public opinion almost unanimously considered the war against Germany to be a just one. Moreover, the involvement of Australia and New Zealand was seen as a repayment of a deep cultural debt owed to Britain. Australia was only 14 years old, and New Zealand half that age, when the Anzacs went into battle. Pictures, newspapers and letters sent back from the front that depicted and described Australians and New Zealanders fighting for the first time under their national colors had profound psychological impact in arousing truly national emotions among the population left at home.

It should not be forgotten that the engagement in the war was undertaken in partnership. When it was recommended that Australian units be broken up and placed under British command, the troops went on strike. Moreover, when politicians in Australia tried to introduce conscription, violence broke out on the streets. Two referendums were held, and on both occasions the population refused to send conscript soldiers overseas. As if to stress the independence of the Anzacs, soldiers at the front also voted against compulsory military service, which had been adopted by all the other combatant nations.

Australia and New Zealand suffered disproportionately high casualties in the war. Of 100,000 New Zealanders who enlisted, 16,000 died and 45,000 were wounded, and of 333,000 Australian recruits, almost 70,000 were killed and 100,000 were wounded – a higher percentage of loss than that suffered by Britain or any other part of the British empire. A further 30,000 died as a result of war service in the decade following the Armistice of 1918. Such losses had a dramatic impact on life in both countries. For the first time since the colonial settlement there were more women than men in the population. Moreover, the majority of those men who had been killed or

Left The painter George Lambert (1872–1930) became the official Australian war artist in 1917. He is remembered for many enduring images of Gallipoli, in particular for his resplendent pictures of Australian light horsemen. Less celebratory is his *Anzac - the Landing* (1920–22), which records with somber and topographical exactitude the steep ascent the Anzacs had to make from the beach, and forms part of the national war memorial collection.

Above left Most casualties occurred in the first three days of the landing when the Anzacs were deployed to make a series of diversionary attacks ahead of the British advance, which never came. Those who survived endured nine months pinned down in the Gallipoli trenches. Letters home told a story of courage and camaraderie; the reality of trench warfare – lice, disease, death, boredom and desertion – was very different; a foretaste of the Western Front.

Below In his 1960 play of that title Alan Seymour called Anzac Day *The One Day of the Year*. In every city and country town in Australia it begins with a dawn service, followed by a march past of former soldiers and the laying of wreaths. But, the solemn commemorations completed, Anzac Day is also noted for the rowdiness of the afternoon "booze-up" when the men congregate to drink. It is the one day of the year when the gambling game "two-up" is legal.

wounded were in the 18–25 age group. The response to the war was something of a stunned silence. The author Eleanor Dark (1901–85) summed up the general mood when she wrote that people did not want to see the dead as "manpower wasted, as genius flung far away, as potential fatherhood most tragically sacrificed. They did not want to probe too deeply into causes, and still less to ultimate effects."

Both Australia and New Zealand produced a sizable war literature, but it is local in its preoccupations. A few works, such as John A. Lee's New Zealand novel *Citizen into Soldier* (1937) and Australian Leonard Mann's *Flesh in Armor* (1939), deal directly with the battlefields that claimed so many lives from the antipodes. It was not until the Great Depression of the 1930s that Australian and New Zealand writers and artists began directly to criticise the war in Europe – though significantly, the heroism of the Anzacs remained untouched. One consequence of the war was that, with so many men killed or wounded, an outstanding generation of women writers including H. H. Richardson, Katherine Susannah Prichard (1883–1960), Eleanor Dark and Marjorie Barnard (1897–1990) was given room to flourish. Even before this, women writers had featured prominently in the literatures of both Australia and New Zealand and continued to do so, possibly because their male-dominated settler societies considered writing an unfit occupation for men. Also, with other professions virtually closed to them until recently, women turned to writing as a channel for their energies.

The depression years

Australia and New Zealand – heavily dependent on export revenue from agriculture and pastoralism – were both badly affected by the fall in international prices that led to the great depression of the 1930s. Only in Germany was unemployment proportionately higher than in Australia where around 30 percent were thrown out of work; in New Zealand the rate was around 20 percent. Both countries had borrowed heavily during the 1920s to provide public works and expand infrastructure for farming and industry. When the loans were called in, the impact of the downturn in prices was magnified. With no central unemployment scheme, nongovernment agencies such as church groups were incapable of dealing adequately with the victims of the crisis, and there was widespread social deprivation. Amid growing class dissension there was strengthening support for radical working-class politics, while right-wing paramilitary organizations modeled on those of Italy and Germany also found some following.

Among writers and intellectuals the years of the depression released a mood of anger and tough social analysis. In New Zealand the writings of Frank Sargeson, with his portrayal of social misfits, and others such as John Mulgan were particularly influential. In Australia many writers were radicalized by the depression. Katharine Susannah Prichard, Jean Devanny (1894-1962, a New Zealander who moved to Australia in the 1920s) and J. M. Harcourt (1902–71) whose novel *Upsurge* was banned as encouraging a proletarian revolution, were communists; others such as Frank Dalby Davison (1893–1960) and Kylie Tennant (1912–92) were "fellow travelers" with the cause. Their books tended to be set in urban environments – a significant move away from the rural themes that had been favored by earlier Australian writers.

Above The economic depression of the 1930s strained Australia's social initiatives to the limits. With one in three out of work, unemployed men drifted into the cities, filling the parks and public spaces. In an attempt to clean up the streets, the authorities opened up a number of camps for the unemployed. These were located far from urban centers so as to minimize the risk of social discontent spreading and hardening into political action.

Left An antidote to the ills of the depression was Phar Lap, the racehorse who became the working-class "punters' friend". Bred in New Zealand but sold cheaply to a battling Australian trainer, Phar Lap lacked the thoroughbred credentials of the champions sponsored by the snobbish Australian Jockey Club. He delighted his supporters by overcoming all the obstacles placed in his way to win the prestigious Melbourne Cup in 1930. He died two years later in Mexico, probably of colic though foul play was suspected. The nation mourned. His carcass was returned to Australia, stuffed and put on display. Even today Phar Lap represents qualities of perseverance, determination and courage for Australians.

The experiences of the depression seemed to require an extended narrative form to encompass its many effects, and the novel came to replace short fiction, verse and lyric poetry as the most usual literary form.

In terms of international copyright, Australia and New Zealand were locked into regions defined by the limits of the British empire – limits that remained in place until 1975. Most British publishers were in the habit of printing what were called "colonial editions", which were sold in Australia and New Zealand at between half and two-thirds of their cost in Britain. As a result, they were flooded with cheap books. Australians and New Zealand became, per capita, the greatest purchasers of books in the world, consuming around a third of all British exports, but local publishers found it virtually impossible to print and distribute Australian and New Zealand books at competitive prices. In order to be published, therefore, Australian and New Zealand writers had to send their manuscripts overseas. More than two-thirds of Australian and New Zealand novels published during the depression appeared under the imprint of British publishers. Australian and New Zealand authors who sold their British-published books in their own countries were paid royalties at one-third the rate paid for sales in Britain. This alone distinguishes the writing of the 1930s onwards from that of the 1890s – authors had now to take into account the tastes of a British reading public, representing more than two-thirds of their sales, and their themes became less narrow. Many writers felt compelled to travel to Britain to put themselves in touch with the market place and with the world of publishers and literary agents.

The depression generally had long-lasting effect in Australia and New Zealand, influencing a whole generation of politicians and social commentators until the 1960s. The Labor governments in New Zealand (1935–49) and Australia (1941–49) were the survivors of the economic conditions of the 1930s, and they were determined to renew a social contract with the people, believing that the role of government was to place a buffer between the excesses of world capitalism and the people. Australia and New Zealand's claim to be the social laboratories of the world was given fresh impetus in the welfare states they built in the 1940s and 1950s. But first both societies had to survive another world war.

War in the Pacific

As they had in 1914, Australia and New Zealand responded loyally when Britain again called upon the dominions for military support against Germany in World War II. Prime Minister Robert Menzies did not consult parliament before declaring war, announcing on the radio that "Britain is at war, therefore Australia is at war." But when Japan entered the war with the bombing of Pearl Harbor in December 1941, the fighting was brought to Australia's doorstep. After the Japanese overran the British garrison in Singapore in February 1942, relations between Britain and Australia worsened. John Curtin (1885–1945), leader of the Labor Party which had succeeded the Liberals in 1941, demanded the return of Australian troops from the Middle East to defend Australia, but Churchill dismissed his fears as groundless. A public statement issued under Curtin's name declaring that "Australia looks to America, free of any pangs as to our traditional links with the United Kingdom" did not do much to improve matters.

The novelist and social commentator Vance Palmer summed up the urgency felt by Australians early in 1942 when he wrote: "The next few months may decide not only whether we are to survive as a nation, but whether we deserve to survive. As yet none of our achievements prove it, at any rate in the sight of the outer world. We have no monuments to speak of, no dreams in stone, no Guernica, no sacred places. We could vanish and leave singularly few signs that, for some generations, there had lived a people who had made a homeland of this Australian earth." Australians had real cause for fear. Japanese planes bombed Darwin and other northern ports; a Japanese submarine appeared in Sydney Harbor in May 1942, causing 19 deaths. A major naval battle was fought between US and Japanese fleets in the Coral Sea. When the Japanese invaded Papua, Australian troops successfully held Port Moresby against them and helped force their retreat at the end of 1942. A long-drawn out battle was fought for control of Guadalcanal in the Solomon Islands. Invasion fever swept through Australia and New Zealand. The introduction of blackout regulations and the building of air-raid shelters made everyone aware of the danger, and if New Zealanders appeared a degree less panicky than Australians, it was only because Australia was their buffer and forward defense. Out of self-preservation as much as emotional ties, New Zealand fought alongside the Australians in all the Pacific theaters of war.

Ultimately the war in the Pacific was settled without the intervention of either the Australians or New Zealanders, after the biggest naval battle of all time, the Battle of Midway, was won by the United States. Australia and New Zealand were invaded all the same, though not by the Japanese: more than a million American servicemen were based there during the war. The impact was enormous. Australians were addicted to the glamor of Hollywood – since the 1920s they had attended at least three movies per capita a week, more than anywhere else in the world. American servicemen were able to bask in this glory, often passing themselves off as movie stars. More than 10,000 wartime brides went back to the United States from Australia. The Americans also brought jazz. It caught on fast, and jazz clubs soon sprang up around the country. The arrival of American culture was the first external threat to British hegemony in the antipodes since the arrival of the First Fleet in 1788.

Changing allegiances

Australia emerged from World War II with its loyalty to the old imperial ties loosened. Once again it had made a large contribution of men to the fighting – more than 550,000 (out of a population of 7 million) had served overseas, 23,000 of whom had been killed in action and 8,000 died in Japanese prisoner of war camps. But it was much more critical of British policies than before. Proportionately, New Zealand's contribution to the war was even greater – a quarter of all males were called up, and the casualty rate was higher. Yet even though deprived of manpower, New Zealand achieved the highest agricultural productivity of any combatant nation, sending all the food it could to the UK. It still stood foursquare behind king and empire.

However, the rapidly changing world situation of the 1940s and 1950s would force both Australia and New Zealand to reappraise their traditional loyalties, bringing about a new questioning of national identity. The Pacific war had brought home the paramountcy

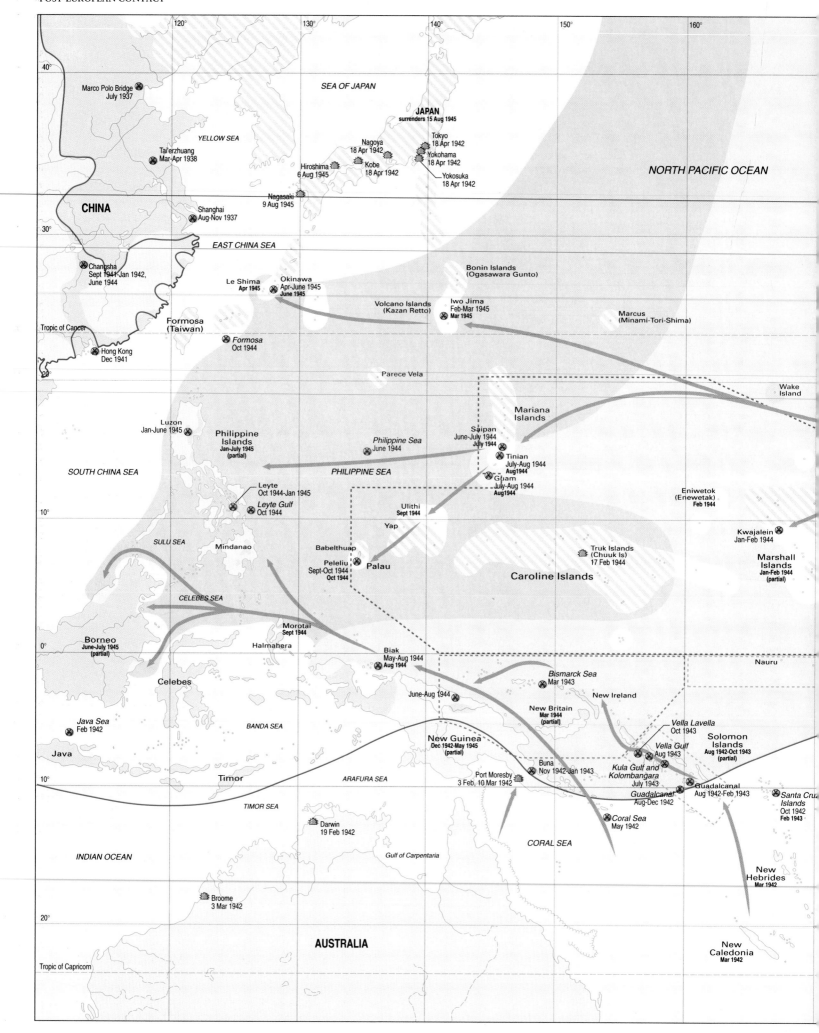

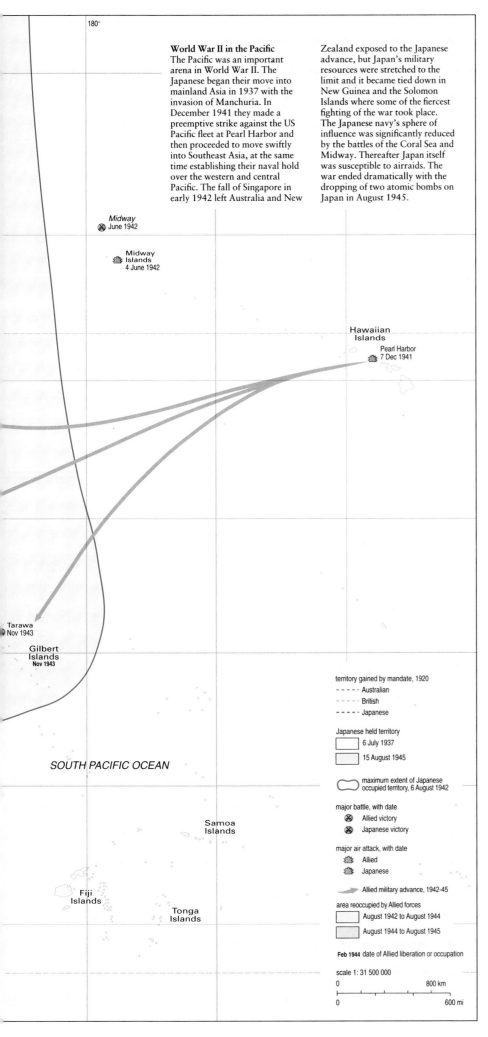

World War II in the Pacific
The Pacific was an important arena in World War II. The Japanese began their move into mainland Asia in 1937 with the invasion of Manchuria. In December 1941 they made a preemptive strike against the US Pacific fleet at Pearl Harbor and then proceeded to move swiftly into Southeast Asia, at the same time establishing their naval hold over the western and central Pacific. The fall of Singapore in early 1942 left Australia and New Zealand exposed to the Japanese advance, but Japan's military resources were stretched to the limit and it became tied down in New Guinea and the Solomon Islands where some of the fiercest fighting of the war took place. The Japanese navy's sphere of influence was significantly reduced by the battles of the Coral Sea and Midway. Thereafter Japan itself was susceptible to airraids. The war ended dramatically with the dropping of two atomic bombs on Japan in August 1945.

of American influence in the region, and Britain's obvious inability to maintain an influence east of Suez called for a reassessment of Australian and New Zealand foreign policy. While Menzies said of himself that he was "British to the bootstraps" and stressed his continuing commitment to close relations with Britain, he nevertheless presided over the period of transition when Australia tied its foreign relations much more firmly to those of the United States. In 1951 the ANZUS security pact between Australia, New Zealand and the United States was signed, the first time in history that the two former colonies had entered into an alliance that did not include Britain (it remained in place until 1987, when New Zealand's decision to refuse access to nuclear ships led the United States to designate it a "friendly" rather than an "allied" state). Both Australia and New Zealand committed troops to the US-led United Nations' force in the Korean war (1950–53) and to the Vietnam war (1964–73), though Britain did not participate in the latter conflict. And when American students began protesting their country's involvement in the Vietnam war, students in Australia and New Zealand led similar anti-war protests in their countries. What began as a minority cause soon developed into a mass movement, with the result that Australia had withdrawn all its soldiers by 1972. Relations with Britain became still more strained after its entry into the European Community in 1972, thus bringing to an end the policy of imperial preference that gave favorable terms to Australian and New Zealand exports into Britain. This was regarded as a betrayal of former ties, particularly in New Zealand, whose economy had not diversified to the same extent as Australia in the postwar period and which remained heavily reliant on agricultural exports to Britain. Australia, on the other hand, had established robust trading relations with Japan, China and the United States.

In economic and social legislation, both Australia and New Zealand have changed their traditional stance in response to world trends. Both countries ended gender inequality in wage settlements in the 1970s. At the same time, the concept of the basic wage was officially abandoned, though worker needs, as opposed to employer capacity, still tend to be the criteria upon which wages and conditions are established. In the 1980s and 1990s, both countries moved away from notions of centralized wage fixing, and embraced enterprise bargaining in the workplace. Republicanism once again became a major issue in Australia, and to a lesser extent in New Zealand, in the 1990s. By this time, only a residual connection remained with the British monarch as the ceremonial head of state, represented by the office of the governor general, and in both countries there was lively debate as to whether they should cease to be monarchies and have an elected president instead.

As predominantly English-speaking cultures, Australia and New Zealand make up a little over 21 million people in a world that is estimated to have between 750 million and one billion English speakers. As colonial societies, the cultural elites of both felt overwhelmed and inadequate in the face of the massive corpus of English literature and the burgeoning American one. More recently, however, both countries have been acknowledged for their distinctive literatures. In 1973 the status of Australian letters was confirmed by the award of the Nobel Prize for Literature to Patrick White, while Thomas Keneally, Peter

193

Carey and, among New Zealand writers, Keri Hulme have all won international prizes for their work. Australian and New Zealand educational units have become among world leaders in teaching English as a second or foreign language. Once the bane of cultural life, the English language has turned out to be one of the greatest cultural assets possessed by the white tribes of the antipodes.

Successive governments have supported the arts in Australia and New Zealand, whether in the form of public sponsorship of broadcasting, galleries, museums, libraries, educational institutions or through direct patronage. No substantial private arts foundations exist in Australia or New Zealand. Patronage, therefore has traditionally fallen to the government. In 1908, the Commonwealth Literature Board (Australia) was founded as a means of providing pensions for destitute writers. In 1973 it became the Literature Board of the Australia Council, with a program of greatly increased funding for the arts. Arts councils in both countries support dance, drama, film and televi-sion, literature and the visual arts. One very positive result of this state patronage has been the renaissance of Australian and New Zealand culture in all fields of the arts since the 1970s. Its success has been most marked internationally in cinema. In the 1990s Australian movies moved away from period themes to concentrate on cosmopolitan life, as in the highly regarded *Strictly Ballroom* (1992), though Stephan Elliot's *Priscilla: Queen of the Desert* (1994), which told the story of a drag-queen revue touring the outback, gave a startling new twist to the Australian legend. New Zealand cinema underwent a significant metamorphosis in the 1990s, led by Jane Campion. Lee Tamahori's *Once Were Warriors* (1995), based on Alan Duff's novel of the same name, is brutally frank in its reassessment of Maori society and values.

Multicultural societies

By far the most important change in both countries has been in their immigration policies. Before World War II Australia and New Zealand had virtually

Land use in Australia and New Zealand

Both countries developed as agricultural societies, but with important differences. In Australia, most agricultural land is suitable only for rough grazing, and so vast ranches developed, with few settlements. Less than 10 percent can support arable (mainly wheat) farming, mostly in the southeast. By contrast, New Zealand's temperate climate makes it more suitable for close agricultural settlement. Sheep and dairying are the chief types of farming, though fruit is increasingly important. With the exception of the 19th-century goldrushes, exploitation of Australia's mineral wealth did not begin until after World War II. Most of its resource-based industries are confined to coastal areas. Since the 1980s Australia has diversified into areas such as aerospace, avionics and information technology, while New Zealand has developed new food-processing technologies.

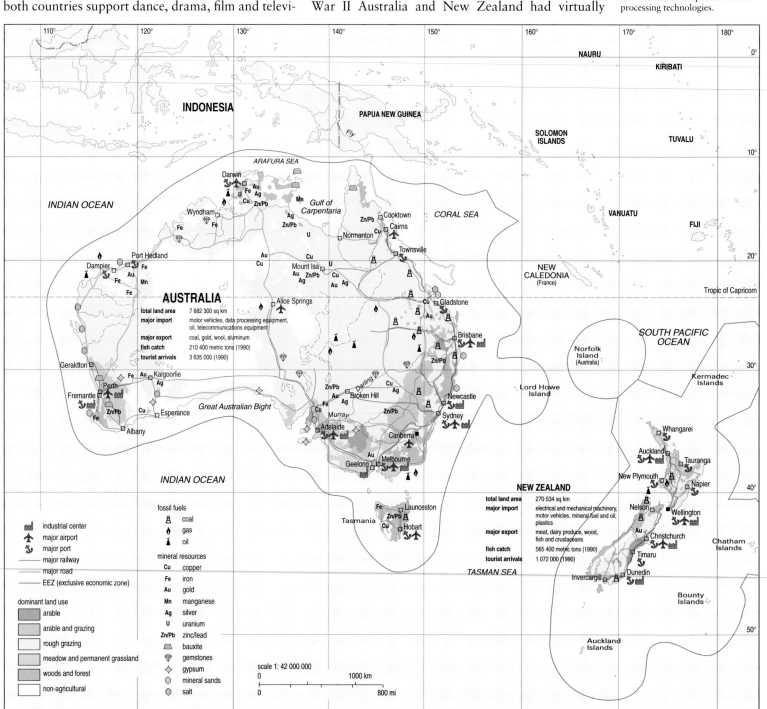

Above For long, a commonly voiced complaint was that Australia had no great monuments or buildings of architectural distinction. But when plans for a new opera house to be built on the harbor front in Sydney were unveiled in the 1950s, a huge furore erupted, many claiming that it was a vast waste of public funds. The Danish architect Jørn Utzon left before the construction was completed, but today his building is recognized as one of Australia's best-known landmarks. Opened in 1973, Sydney Opera House , which houses two theaters, a cinema, rehearsal and recording studios, has been the focus for cultural achievement in all spheres of the performing arts.

Right Holly Hunter and Anna Paquin in *The Piano* (1993). Made in Australia by New-Zealand born Jane Campion, this is one of the most highly regarded movies to be shot in the antipodes. Set in early colonial New Zealand, it was the Australian entry at the Cannes film festival where it won the prestigious Palme d'Or. It also won three Academy Awards.

excluded migrants from all countries except Britain. Though there were significant minorities of Germans and Italians in Australia, and Germans and Scandinavians in New Zealand, both countries passed legislation to discourage non-British migrants, especially Asians. In the 1940s and 1950s, however, this began to change: the slogan was "populate or perish". Both Australia and New Zealand feared that they would be overtaken economically by Asia's rapidly growing societies if they did not build up their numbers. And their populations were not increasing fast enough. At the end of the World War II, both countries committed money to assisted migration, and Australia and New Zealand took sizable numbers of displaced persons from the conflict in Europe. Immigration policies were extended to accommodate non-English speaking Europeans, profoundly changing the cultural identities of both countries: in particular, large numbers of Greeks and Italians settled in Australia in the 1950s. In the 1970s Australia officially abandoned the White Australia Policy – though it had been a dead letter for more than two decades – and removed all racist restrictions from its immigration policies. In the prewar years, between 96 and 98 percent of the Australian population was held to be of British descent, and politicians often boasted of the country's racial purity. By the 1990s Australia had become the second

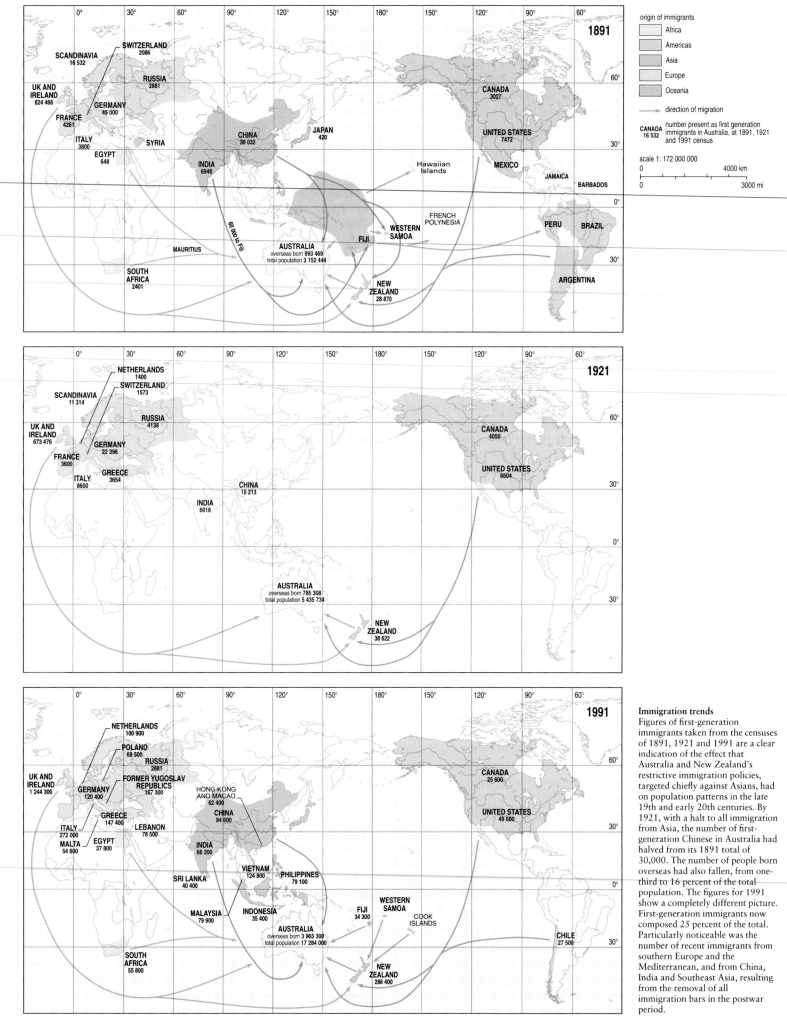

1891

origin of immigrants

- Africa
- Americas
- Asia
- Europe
- Oceania

→ direction of migration

CANADA
16 532   number present as first generation immigrants in Australia, at 1891, 1921 and 1991 census

scale 1: 172 000 000

0   4000 km

0   3000 mi

SCANDINAVIA
16 532

SWITZERLAND
2086

RUSSIA
2881

UK AND
IRELAND
824 466

GERMANY
45 000

FRANCE
4261

ITALY
3800

SYRIA

EGYPT
648

INDIA
6948

CHINA
30 032

JAPAN
420

CANADA
3027

UNITED STATES
7472

MEXICO

JAMAICA

BARBADOS

Hawaiian
Islands

FRENCH
POLYNESIA

PERU

BRAZIL

MAURITIUS

60 000 to Fiji

AUSTRALIA
overseas born 993 469
total population 3 152 444

FIJI

WESTERN
SAMOA

SOUTH
AFRICA
2401

NEW
ZEALAND
28 870

ARGENTINA

1921

NETHERLANDS
1400

SWITZERLAND
1573

SCANDINAVIA
11 314

RUSSIA
4138

UK AND
IRELAND
673 476

GERMANY
22 396

FRANCE
3600

GREECE
3654

ITALY
8600

CHINA
15 213

INDIA
6918

CANADA
4050

UNITED STATES
6604

AUSTRALIA
overseas born 785 308
total population 5 435 734

NEW
ZEALAND
38 622

1991

NETHERLANDS
100 900

POLAND
69 500

RUSSIA
2881

UK AND
IRELAND
1 244 300

GERMANY
120 400

FORMER YUGOSLAV
REPUBLICS
167 300

HONG KONG
AND MACAO
62 400

CANADA
25 600

GREECE
147 400

CHINA
84 600

ITALY
272 000

LEBANON
78 500

UNITED STATES
49 500

MALTA
54 600

EGYPT
37 800

INDIA
66 200

SRI LANKA
40 400

VIETNAM
124 800

PHILIPPINES
79 100

MALAYSIA
79 900

INDONESIA
35 400

FIJI
34 300

WESTERN
SAMOA

COOK
ISLANDS

CHILE
27 500

AUSTRALIA
overseas born 3 965 300
total population 17 284 000

SOUTH
AFRICA
55 800

NEW
ZEALAND
286 400

Immigration trends

Figures of first-generation immigrants taken from the censuses of 1891, 1921 and 1991 are a clear indication of the effect that Australia and New Zealand's restrictive immigration policies, targeted chiefly against Asians, had on population patterns in the late 19th and early 20th centuries. By 1921, with a halt to all immigration from Asia, the number of first-generation Chinese in Australia had halved from its 1891 total of 30,000. The number of people born overseas had also fallen, from one-third to 16 percent of the total population. The figures for 1991 show a completely different picture. First-generation immigrants now composed 25 percent of the total. Particularly noticeable was the number of recent immigrants from southern Europe and the Mediterranean, and from China, India and Southeast Asia, resulting from the removal of all immigration bars in the postwar period.

alcohol with an Aboriginal friend (it was then illegal for peoples of Aboriginal descent to buy and consume alcohol). The first Aboriginal poetry and fiction did not appear in print until the 1960s. As the Aboriginal assertion of cultural identity became increasingly politicized, protest centered on the issue of land rights, but Aboriginal title was not recognized until 1977, when certain tribal groups were granted land rights in reserves under government control in the Northern Territory. It was not until 1993 that the rule of *terra nullius* was overturned and the Aborigines' prior ownership of Australia legally acknowledged.

New Zealand is not as ethnically diverse as Australia, though its population base has changed considerably in the second half of the 20th century with the arrival of more and more migrants from continental Europe. For many years there has been a free movement of populations across the Tasman Sea. Sydney contains a population of several thousand New Zealanders, most of them living in the eastern suburbs; New Zealand politicians campaign vigorously for their support at election time. The drift of young New Zealanders to Australia was particularly marked in the 1970s and 1980s, when it had significant psychological impact on the nation. For the first time in its history, the population not only began to fall but at the same time it aged.

As labor shortages worsened in New Zealand, more and more migrant workers were attracted to the country from the Pacific islands – in particular the Cook Islands, Samoa, Tonga and Fiji. Most settled in the cities, particularly Auckland which has become "the largest Polynesian city in the world". There has been a strong revival of Maori, and more generally, of Polynesian culture. Among the Maori, this increasingly took the form of political action. In the 1960s a strong movement developed that sought to redress the wrongs of the Treaty of Waitangi. Within parliament, a Maori party – the Mana Motuhake – was formed to advance a tougher nationalist line. The New Zealand government established the Waitangi tribunal to hear Maori claims to wrongful dispossession of their lands and proposed a fund to make "full and final" reparation for illegal confiscations and unfair land purchases. But many Maori rejected these offers, wanting nothing less than sovereignty over their own lands and their own laws, which they claim the clause *te tino rangatiratanga* guaranteed them in the treaty. Militancy is particularly strong among urban Maori, where levels of unemployment are especially high. There is a strong demand for a return to the Maori name of Aotearoa for New Zealand.

By the last decade of the 20th century, many in New Zealand had come to regard the country as an integral part of the emerging regional economy and society of the Pacific, rather than as a European outpost. In the 1980s, the then prime minister David Lange said: "We...accept what the map tells us, that we are a South Pacific nation." By contrast, for many Australians the future lay in closer cooperation with the prosperous economies of Southeast Asia and Japan. Where it once described itself as the "odd country out in Asia", Australia now wanted to be the "odd country in". New Zealand's increasingly Pacific identity and Australia's greater willingness to integrate economically with Asia may ultimately prove to be the emotional parting of the ways for the white tribes of the antipodes, though their histories still bind them closely together.

Above The bicentennial celebrations of European settlement in Australia in 1988 were met with protests by many Aborigines. Thousands marched in Sydney on Australia Day, 26 January, as leading politicians and guests, including Queen Elizabeth, gathered for an official ceremony at the site of the first settlement. Similar protests were held in all Australian cities. Here, at Brisbane, a banner proclaims that "White Australia has a Black History". The demonstrations were instrumental in helping to bring about recognition of Aboriginal rights, for so long ignored by white Australians.

most ethnically diverse society in the world, after Israel. Anglo-Celtic values still hold a central place in the "imagined community" of Australians, but multiculturalism is now the nation's official doctrine.

This embraces the Aboriginal population who, until the last quarter of the 20th century, were all but forgotten by Australia's official policy-makers. In 1988 commemorations were held to mark the 200th anniversary of the founding of white Australia. Some 15,000 Aborigines marched in Sydney to protest against the celebratory nature of these events, a powerful reminder to white Australians that for these same 200 years the Aborigines had been almost entirely excluded from the nation's self-image. This extended even to the artistic imagination. Though the Anglo-Australian artist Margaret Preston became known in the 1920s and 1930s for her paintings of Aboriginal motifs, and in the 1940s a group of Anglo-Australian poets calling themselves the Jindyworobaks (based on an Aboriginal term meaning "to join") sought to include Aboriginal myths, beliefs and some language into their poetry, by and large the Aboriginal culture of Australia had been marginalized and ignored. Albert Namatjira (1902–59), a member of the Aranda peoples of central Australia achieved fame in the 1950s and 1960s as a watercolorist and landscape painter. Yet he possessed no citizenship rights until specially granted them in 1957, and a scandal occurred when he was jailed for sharing a drink of

THE SOUTH PACIFIC TODAY

Independent Pacific states

One effect of World War II in the Pacific was to hasten the end of old-style colonialism: the war itself had exposed many of the Pacific islands to greater external influences, and in the changed political climate of the postwar world there was international pressure to decolonize. On the region's very doorstep, in the former territories of the Dutch East Indies, a bitter nationalist war was being fought. There was an acceptance among the colonial powers in the Pacific that constitutional arrangements should be altered to give the islands a greater say in their own affairs and greater resources made available to promote their economic development as they made their way toward full independence or self-government.

Western Samoa was the first Pacific state to gain full independence – from New Zealand – in 1962, and by 1980 eight others had followed: Nauru (1968), Fiji (1970), Tonga (1970), Papua New Guinea (1975), Solomon Islands (1978), Kiribati (1978), Tuvalu (1978), Vanuatu (1980). These were all formerly British territories or Australian or New Zealand colonies or protectorates. The Cook Islands and Niue are self-governing in a relationship of free association with New Zealand. By mutual agreement the latter has responsibility for their external affairs and defense, while the islanders effectively have dual citizenship and the advantage of free access to New Zealand. All these Pacific island states have adopted forms of parliamentary government that are based on the British model. There is, however, considerable variation in their political systems, which – to a greater or lesser degree – reflect elements of traditional social and political structures.

At the top end of the scale is the kingdom of Tonga. Though a British protectorate from 1901 it was never fully annexed to a colonial power and maintained a unique degree of political continuity and autonomy. Tonga has been a monarchy since 1845, its rulers drawn from the high chiefly line that emerged dominant from the civil wars of the first half of the 19th century. The first of these rulers, Taufa'ahau, was converted to Christianity and ruled as King George Tupou I; the constitution he introduced in 1875 is still in force today. Substantial power rests with the monarch: Tonga's legislative assembly is made up of a cabinet of about 12 members appointed by the monarch, 9 noble members elected by the 33 hereditary nobles of the kingdom, and 9 members elected by the adult population at large. The monarch appoints one of the noble members of the assembly as Speaker. Until recently there were no political parties.

While it would be an oversimplification to view the Tongan political system as just a continuation of a Polynesian system of chiefly rule, it is nonetheless rooted in the Polynesian culture that gave great emphasis to social hierarchy, and this – together with the Tongans' respect and affection for the royal family – has helped to maintain it. In recent years, however, there has been growing pressure for change. An

Above left Brownies carrying Papua New Guinean and British flags greet Queen Elizabeth II as she visits Port Moresby, the national capital. Papua New Guinea became an independent parliamentary democracy within the British Commonwealth in 1975. The Queen as titular head of state is represented by a governor-general who is nominated by parliament.

Above Indian sugar cane workers in Fiji at the time of the 1987 coups. The first indentured workers were brought from India to Fiji in 1879. More than 60,000 had followed before the ending of the indenture system in 1916. Many remained in Fiji after their contracts had expired, and by 1945 the Fijian Indian population slightly outnumbered the ethnic Fijians. Since the constitutional changes in favor of ethnic Fijians that followed the 1987 coups there has been an increase in the outflow of Indo-Fijian people and capital from the country.

Left King Taufa'ahau Tupou IV of Tonga takes a bicycle ride, his escort jogging alongside. The king was the first Tongan to gain a university degree. He succeeded his mother, Queen Salote, in 1965 and in 1970 oversaw Tonga's transition to full independence from Britain. Strongly identified with the reforms of his mother's reign, King Taufa'ahau has steered a path between further reform and a basically conservative stance toward the traditional structure of power in Tonga. Respect for him has been a moderating factor in the pressures for constitutional change in that country.

informal opposition movement arose in the 1980s pressing for the extension of democracy and for action to reduce ministerial privilege and secrecy. The movement originated among university graduates and civil servants, but its efforts helped to push issues of democracy firmly up the Tongan political agenda. Election results in the 1990s showed the spread of popular support for political reform. Even this most traditional of Pacific states appeared to be set for some constitutional change.

After Tonga, Western Samoa has probably the strongest links with traditional political structures. The head of state is chosen by the *Fono*, the legislative assembly, from among four paramount chiefs, the *tama ainga*. The head of state at independence in 1962, Malietoa Tanumafili II, was elected for life; thereafter the constitution lays down that the head of state will be elected for a five-year term. In the pre-independence discussions, it was decided by plebiscite that the majority of votes for the *Fono* should be cast by the *matai*, the titled heads of extended families elected to their position by all the heirs to their particular titles. As in Tonga, however, there has been pressure for limited reform, and in another plebiscite in 1990 a narrow majority voted in favor of changing to adult suffrage. The new electorate consists of all those over 21, though only *matai* can occupy seats in the assembly. One effect has been substantially to increase the percentage of women voters. However, the limited registration for the 1990 plebiscite and the small margin of votes by which it was passed did not suggest a wholesale rejection of the earlier arrangements.

In Fiji, the Great Council of Chiefs retains considerable influence within the parliamentary and party system. Under the 1970 constitution it appointed a majority of members to the Senate, the upper house of

parliament, and its influence appeared to increase after 1987, which saw two military-led coups. At the heart of the crisis were shifts in the balance of power affecting relations between ethnic Fijians (accounting for 43 percent of the population in 1970) and Indo-Fijians (51 percent), who were descended from the indentured laborers brought from the subcontinent to work in the sugar plantations during the colonial period. Under British rule, separation between the two communities had been fostered not only by differences of language, religion and custom, but also by colonial policy. The independence constitution ensured representation for both communities, but gave considerable protection to ethnic Fijian interests. There seemed at first to be a successful working accommodation: ethnic Fijians maintained rights over land, while sections of the Indo-Fijian community found success in commerce and industry. In 1987, however, the Alliance Party, which had held power since 1970, was defeated by a political party which had significant Indo-Fijian support. Ethnic Fijian nationalists began to fear a loss of political control, and the army intervened to remove the elected government from office. The constitution was subsequently amended to emphasize the "traditionally Fijian" nature of the state and ensure ethnic Fijian political predominance.

Vanuatu has a national council of chiefs to advise the government on matters of custom and tradition, but elsewhere in Melanesia the influence of indigenous political leaders may be strongest at the local level, where they have a role in mediating on behalf of their community with both national and provincial governments. However, while the mobilization of wealth has always had a part in Melanesian leadership, changing political and economic circumstances have caused shifts in the recognized distribution of power and

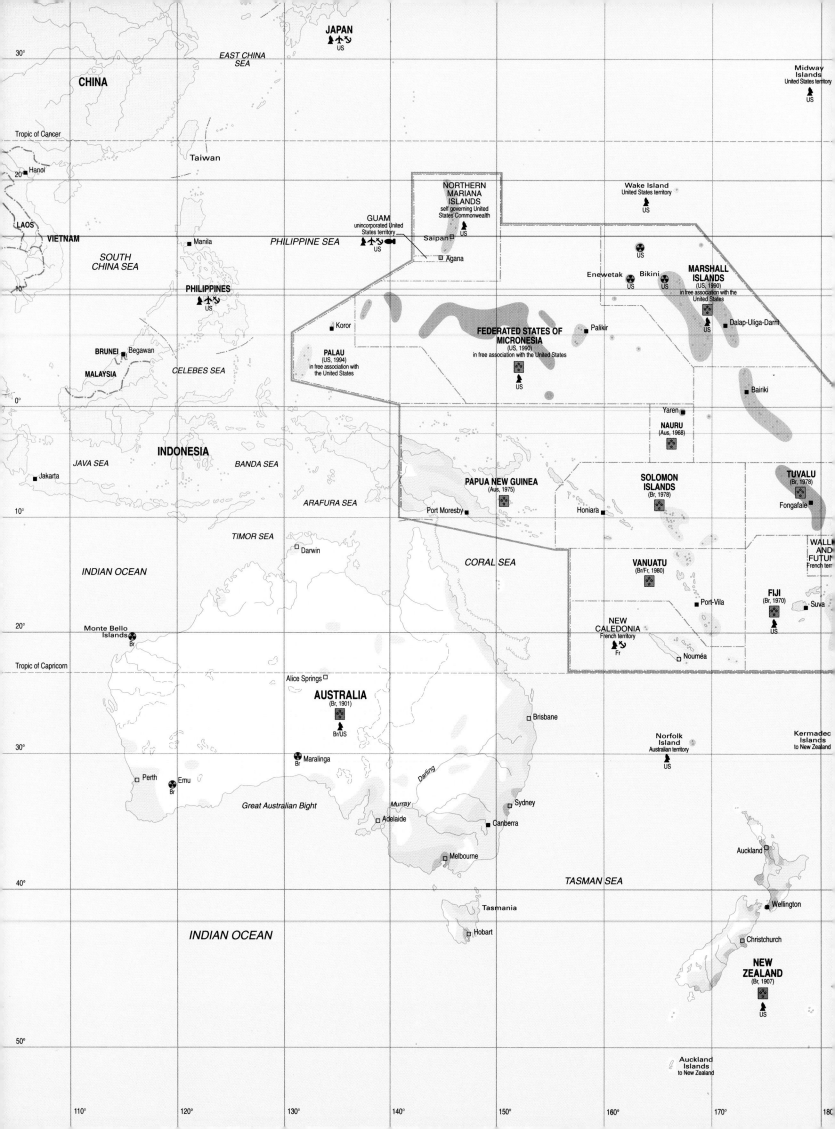

30°

JAPAN
US

EAST CHINA
SEA

Midway
Islands
United States territory
US

CHINA

Tropic of Cancer

20°   Hanoi

Taiwan

Wake Island
United States territory
US

LAOS

VIETNAM   Manila

NORTHERN
MARIANA
ISLANDS
self governing United
States Commonwealth
US

SOUTH
CHINA
SEA

GUAM
unincorporated United
States territory
US

PHILIPPINE SEA

Saipan
US

Enewetak   Bikini

MARSHALL
ISLANDS
(US, 1990)
in free association with the
United States

10°

PHILIPPINES
US

Agana

Koror

FEDERATED STATES OF
MICRONESIA
(US, 1990)
in free association with the United States

Palikir

US

Dalap-Uliga-Darrit

BRUNEI   Begawan

MALAYSIA

CELEBES SEA

PALAU
(US, 1994)
in free association with
the United States

US

Bairiki

0°

Yaren

NAURU
(Aus, 1968)

INDONESIA

JAVA SEA   BANDA SEA

Jakarta

ARAFURA SEA

PAPUA NEW GUINEA
(Aus, 1975)

SOLOMON
ISLANDS
(Br, 1978)

TUVALU
(Br, 1978)

Fongafale

10°

TIMOR SEA

Port Moresby

Honiara

WALL
AND
FUTUN
French terr

Darwin

CORAL SEA

VANUATU
(Br/Fr, 1980)

INDIAN OCEAN

FIJI
(Br, 1970)   Suva

20°

Monte Bello
Islands
Br

NEW
CALEDONIA
French territory
Fr

Port-Vila

US

Tropic of Capricorn

Alice Springs

Nouméa

AUSTRALIA
(Br, 1901)

Br/US

Brisbane

Norfolk
Island
Australian territory
US

Kermadec
Islands
to New Zealand

30°

Maralinga
Br

Perth   Emu
Br

Great Australian Bight

Darling

Murray

Sydney

Canberra

Adelaide

Auckland

Melbourne

TASMAN SEA

40°

Tasmania

Wellington

INDIAN OCEAN

Hobart

Christchurch

NEW
ZEALAND
(Br, 1907)

US

50°

Auckland
Islands
to New Zealand

110°   120°   130°   140°   150°   160°   170°   180°

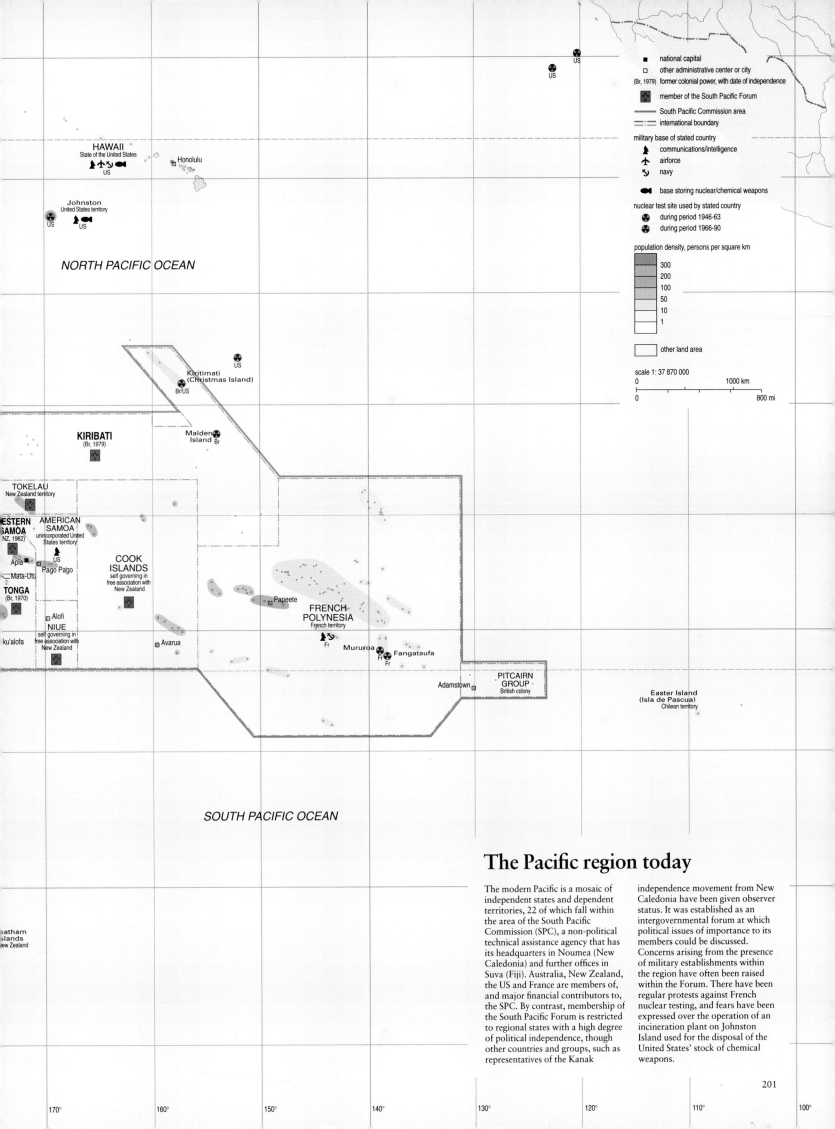

Legend

- ■ national capital
- □ other administrative center or city
- (Br, 1979) former colonial power, with date of independence
- ⬚ member of the South Pacific Forum
- ―― South Pacific Commission area
- ═══ international boundary

military base of stated country
- ☘ communications/intelligence
- ✈ airforce
- ⚓ navy

- ◗ base storing nuclear/chemical weapons

nuclear test site used by stated country
- ☢ during period 1946-63
- ☢ during period 1966-90

population density, persons per square km
- 300
- 200
- 100
- 50
- 10
- 1

- other land area

scale 1: 37 870 000
0 — 1000 km
0 — 800 mi

HAWAII
State of the United States
☘ ✈ ⚓ ◗
US
□ Honolulu

Johnston
United States territory
☢
US
☘ ◗
US

NORTH PACIFIC OCEAN

☢
US

☢
US

☢
Kiritimati
(Christmas Island)
Br/US

KIRIBATI
(Br, 1979)
⬚

Malden ☢
Island Br

TOKELAU
New Zealand territory
⬚

ESTERN SAMOA
(NZ, 1962)
■ Apia

AMERICAN SAMOA
unincorporated United States territory
☘
□ Pago Pago
US

—Mata-Utu

COOK ISLANDS
self governing in free association with New Zealand
⬚

TONGA
(Br, 1970)
⬚

□ Alofi

NIUE
self governing in free association with New Zealand
⬚

ku'alofa

□ Avarua

□ Papeete

FRENCH POLYNESIA
French territory
☘ ✈
Fr

Mururoa
Fr ☢ **Fangataufa**
Fr

PITCAIRN GROUP
British colony
Adamstown □

Easter Island
(Isla de Pascua)
Chilean territory

SOUTH PACIFIC OCEAN

atham
slands
ew Zealand

The Pacific region today

The modern Pacific is a mosaic of independent states and dependent territories, 22 of which fall within the area of the South Pacific Commission (SPC), a non-political technical assistance agency that has its headquarters in Noumea (New Caledonia) and further offices in Suva (Fiji). Australia, New Zealand, the US and France are members of, and major financial contributors to, the SPC. By contrast, membership of the South Pacific Forum is restricted to regional states with a high degree of political independence, though other countries and groups, such as representatives of the Kanak

independence movement from New Caledonia have been given observer status. It was established as an intergovernmental forum at which political issues of importance to its members could be discussed. Concerns arising from the presence of military establishments within the region have often been raised within the Forum. There have been regular protests against French nuclear testing, and fears have been expressed over the operation of an incineration plant on Johnston Island used for the disposal of the United States' stock of chemical weapons.

authority, leading to the emergence of new elites. In Papua New Guinea, for example, the layers of government – national, provincial and local – allow some expression of diversity and provide scope for customary leadership styles within an overarching national identity. But new economic opportunities have opened up new pathways to personal wealth, and so perhaps to political office. It has been suggested that lack of access to sources of wealth may have helped to ensure that no woman candidate had been elected to the national parliament by 1992.

The political boundaries of the state of Papua New Guinea are the legacy of the carving up of the island of New Guinea by three European colonial powers in the 19th century. The western half of the island, formerly part of the Dutch East Indies, was transferred in 1963 to Indonesia under the auspices of the UN and forms the Indonesian province of Irian Jaya today. The eastern half of the island had been divided between Germany in the north and Britain (later Australia) in the south. After World War I the German sector was mandated to Australia. This included the North Solomons, though their cultural and historical links lay with the rest of the Solomon Islands, then a British colony.

As Papua New Guinea moved toward independence in 1975, a strong secessionist movement developed in Bougainville, the main island of the North Solomons, where one of the world's largest open-cast copper mines, the Con-Zinc Rio Tinto mine at Panguna, is situated. Ore mined at Paguna provided a very large part of Papua New Guinea's exports, and by 1989 tension on Bougainville were running high as local succesionist demand was joined by anger about the environmental effects of the mine and the brusque dismissal of local landowners' demands for compensation. Sabotage halted mining, and a group identifying itself as the Bougainville Revolutionary Army (BRA) challenged the government for control of the island. Perhaps as many as 6,000 people may have died as a direct or indirect result of the conflict that followed. By 1994 much of the island was again under government control, though not the mine itself. The troubled history of Bougainville points up many of the problems facing the Pacific states in the post-colonial period: difficulties brought about by inherited colonial boundaries; questions of how, and to whose advantage, natural resources should be developed; conflicts of interests between the multinational companies, central and provincial governments, and local people.

American interests in the Pacific

In the US-administered states of the Pacific, progress toward full independence was more protracted. In 1947 the Caroline Islands, Palau, the Northern Marianas and the Marshall Islands were brought together in a UN trust territory under the jurisdiction of the United States, which pledged to "promote development ... toward self-government or independence as may be appropriate"; in return, the United States was granted the right to establish military bases in the area. Discussions to give the islands full self-government began in 1969, but subsequently Palau, the Northern Marianas and the Marshall Islands voted to leave the proposed federation of Micronesian states and to negotiate their future constitutional arrangements separately. In 1983 the Federated States of Micronesia (comprising the Caroline islands of Yap, Truk, Kosrae and Pohnpei) and the Marshall Islands voted to enter into free association with the United States.

Free association involves a commitment that foreign policy initiatives undertaken by the island governments should not go against American interests; it gives them the expectation of long-term aid and allows their citizens to work in the United States. In return, the United States is entitled to maintain military bases in the islands for an agreed period. In 1990 the Federated States of Micronesia and the Marshall Islands were both recognized as full members of the UN. Understandably, their constitutions reflect American influences. The Federated States of Micronesia, for instance, has a national president and vice-president, directly elected for 4-year terms, and a 14-member National Congress, while the four component states have their own state governors and legislatures.

Moves toward free association for Palau were prolonged by conflict over the United States' insistence on retaining the right to base nuclear weapons on the islands and to operate nuclear-weapons-capable vessels or aircraft within Palauan territory. This ran contrary to the Palauan constitution, which came into effect in 1981 after the electorate had rejected a draft more acceptable to the United States, and specifically excluded nuclear materials from its territory. Referendums held every year between 1983 and 1990 failed to win the 75 percent vote necessary to override the non-nuclear clauses and approve the compact of free association, though more than 50 percent consistently voted in favor of doing so. The UN Security Council wound up the US strategic trust over Belau in 1990, but the US Senate declined to ratify the compact without an amended constitution. A constitutional amendment passed in 1992 allowed for the compact to be approved by a simple majority at the end of 1993; Palau was admitted to UN membership in 1994.

In 1975 voters in the Northern Mariana Islands approved the establishment of a commonwealth in political union with the United States. There was concern here to maintain the economic benefits of the American presence (again partly military) and to

Above Papua New Guinea government soldiers patrol on Bougainville at the beginning of the fighting that broke out there in 1989 over ownership and exploitation of the island's valuable copper reserves. The signing of peace commitments by the prime minister and the commander of the Bougainville Revolutionary Army in September 1994 raised hopes of a satisfactory resolution of this long-standing conflict.

Above right Moruroa is the only atoll in the southeastern Tuamotu Islands of French Polynesia with an entrance that allows ships to enter its lagoon. This ensured its importance as the main site of the French nuclear testing center established in the Pacific in the 1960s. A support base was set up on the island of Hao. Between 1966 and 1974 over 40 atmospheric nuclear tests were carried out on Moruroa and the neighboring island of Fangataufa. Partly as the result of mounting international pressure, testing moved underground in 1975. Concerns continued to be expressed at international level about the leakage of radioactive material from the test sites, but the program continued until 1992, when a one-year suspension was declared. This was subsequently extended into a moratorium but in June 1995 the French government announced its intention of resuming testing with up to eight detonations between September 1995 and May 1996, after which France would sign the global test ban treaty in 1996. Increasing international objection to the tests was led by the South Pacific Forum who, after the second test on 2 October 1995, announced the suspension of all relations with France at the 50th annual meeting of the UN General Assembly.

Above Two Kanak boys in New Caledonia carry French loaves of bread. For over a century the Kanak people have been exposed to French influence in many areas of everyday life, including food and dress, but today the value of Kanak culture is being reasserted. Kanak leaders have pressed for more attention to be given to Kanak tradition, and the government has made some recognition of this by establishing an agency for the development of Kanak culture.

retain their rights to migrate to neighboring Guam, itself the site of major US naval and air bases – about one-third of the land in Guam is owned by the US armed forces. The center of heavy fighting in World War II, Guam was under the jurisdiction of the US Navy until 1950 and is now an unincorporated territory of the United States, a status it shares with American Samoa in Polynesia. In both Guam and American Samoa there are demands for greater autonomy, with some local leaders expressing a desire to move toward a looser relationship with the United States, such as commonwealth status. In both cases, however, the islands are wary of losing the economic advantages that flow from their present status.

French dependencies

A number of other dependent territories remain in the Pacific. On some islands the population is so small that full independence is unlikely; the three atoll islands of Tokelau are dependencies of New Zealand; the tiny British dependency of Pitcairn, which has a permanent population of only around 60, is administered by the British High Commissioner in Wellington, New Zealand. But by far the most substantial colonial power in the central Pacific is France. Anxious to maintain its economic and strategic interests in the region, France remained unresponsive to the general thrust toward decolonization, though there was some increase in the degree of autonomy exercised by its three overseas territories (*territoires d'outre-mer*) in the Pacific – New Caledonia, Wallis and Futuna, and French Polynesia. These are regarded as integral parts of the French state. They elect deputies and senators to the national parliament in Paris, but also enjoy limited powers of self-government, exercised through elected territorial assemblies.

Since the 1960s French Polynesia – consisting of the Society Islands, the Tuamotu Archipelago, the Austral Islands, the Gambier Islands and the Marquesas Islands – has been the center of the French military nuclear program. There are testing sites on Moruroa and Fangataufa atolls in the Tuamotus, with associated logistical support activities on other islands. The large military presence in the islands has distorted the local economy – per capita income is among the highest in the region but wealth is unevenly distributed in ways that have not benefited the Polynesian population. The territory is seeking development funds to cushion the economic effects of France's eventual scaling-down of its military presence. There are calls for increased self-government and the more extreme supporters of independence and the rights of Polynesians have sometimes fallen foul of the authorities. But popular backing for full independence from France appears to be tempered by fears about the economic

consequences of French withdrawal: electoral support for pro-independence candidates is lowest in the heavily aid-dependent outer island groups.

Opposition to French rule is more sharply defined in New Caledonia. Independence is overwhelmingly supported by the indigenous Kanak people, the largest single ethnic group, but they are outnumbered by non-Melanesians – a heterogeneous group that is made up of Europeans (including Caldoches, those of European extraction born in New Caledonia), Wallisians, French Polynesians, Indonesians and others. They now form around 55 percent of the population and have tended to support continued French control. In 1984 the Kanak Socialist National Liberation Front (Front de Libération National Kanake et Socialiste: FLNKS) boycotted the territorial assembly elections, frustrated at the lack of progress being made toward self-government despite the success of the pro-independence coalition at the previous elections. Barricades were set up, ballot boxes destroyed and a provisional Kanak government declared. Confrontations between Kanaks and settlers, military and police were marked by outbreaks of violence on both sides.

In 1988 a change of government in France, led to new attempts bring an end to the continuing political unrest and conflict. The Matignon Accord of 1988 provided for one year of French direct rule, followed by elections to three provincial councils. Funds were to be directed toward the provinces with Kanak majorities, and away from the European-dominated Southern Province on the main island, where the capital Noumea is situated. A referendum on independence would be held in 1998. Many on both sides found the terms of the Matignon Accord unpalatable. Many young Kanaks had become increasingly radicalized in the political struggles of recent years. In 1989 Jean-Marie Tjibaou, the leader who had guided the FLNKS throughout the 1980s, was assassinated by a Kanak dissident. Though Tjibaou's successors promised to carry the Matignon process forward to the 1998 referendum, a number of Kanaks left the movement because they regarded its policies as too conciliatory.

In 1986, the South Pacific Forum of independent states, dissatisfied with the progress the French authorities were making in resolving the crisis in New Caledonia, requested that the UN Decolonization Committee placed it under scrutiny. France's refusal to abandon its nuclear test program also aroused widespread international condemnation, particularly after French security agents mined the Greenpeace protest ship *Rainbow Warrior* in Auckland harbor to prevent it sailing to the area of Moruroa in 1985. Since the late 1980s France has been trying to improve its relations with the other states of the region. It has declared its intention of giving its Pacific territories greater involvement in the conduct of foreign policy by enabling them to sign regional agreements in areas such as trade, education and environmental protection, stepped up its support for regional organizations and boosted its aid contribution to countries such as Fiji and Tonga.

Patterns of population

The population of the Pacific islands today, excluding Irian Jaya and Hawaii, is around 6 million. These are spread very unevenly across the region. Papua New Guinea, with over 3.5 million people, accounts for more than half of the total, while the New Zealand dependency of Tokelau has a population of under 1,600: Papua New Guinea has a land area of 462,000 square kilometers compared with Tokelau's 11. The large Melanesian islands – Papua New Guinea, New Caledonia, Solomon Islands and Vanuatu – have population densities of between 8 and 14 people per square kilometer while Tuvalu, composed of 9 small atolls with a total land area of 24 square kilometers, averages around 375 people per square kilometer. The highest density of all – more than 430 per square kilometer – is found on the tiny single island state of

Above left The Greenpeace flagship *Rainbow Warrior* lies holed in Auckland harbor, New Zealand, in July 1985. Earlier in the year *Rainbow Warrior* had evacuated the people of Rongelap (Marshall Islands), the site of the American "Bravo" H-bomb test in 1954, to one of the islands of Kwajalein atoll because of fears of remnant radiation. The ship was preparing to leave Auckland for Moruroa to protest against the French nuclear testing program when underwater mines attached to its propeller shaft ripped through the hull, killing one man. It was later established that two French secret service agents had been responsible. The incident caused an international furore, ensuring publicity for the Greenpeace campaign against nuclear testing in the Pacific, and its protests continued undeterred. Its successor ship, *Rainbow Warrior II,* was in the waters off Moruroa when a suspension of testing was announced in April 1992 and again in 1995, together with a sister ship M.V. *Greenpeace,* when France announced a series of eight tests commencing in September. However, their efforts were thwarted and the vessels were towed out of the area, dinghies seized and divers "arrested".

Above Mining for phosphates on Nauru. The island is only 22 square kilometers in area. It is a raised coral reef with a central plateau where rich phosphate beds have formed from bird droppings deposited over the centuries. A valuable source of fertilizer, these have been mined since the beginning of the century. When Nauru – since 1945, a joint Australian, British and New Zealand trusteeship – became independent in 1968, the Nauru Phosphate Corporation took control of the mining industry. Phosphate revenues have brought Nauruans relative prosperity, but against this must be set the limited possibilities for inshore development once the deposits run out at the start of the next century, and the environmental degradation that mining has caused. Money from phosphates has been used to set up the country's airline, Air Nauru, a shipping line, Nauru Pacific Line, and the Nauru Fishing Corporation. Investments have also been made in real estate and hotel developments in a number of countries to try and ensure a future income for government and people. Not all have proved profitable.

Nauru, the world's smallest republic. It has come about as a result of the island's unusual economy: Nauru's population is supported by the comparative wealth earned from exploitation of its phosphate deposits, which involves the residence of substantial numbers of non-Nauruans.

Populations are growing at around 2.3 percent a year in the South Pacific as a whole, with the highest rates in Melanesia and Micronesia (3 percent in Papua New Guinea, Vanuatu and the Solomon Islands; 3.8 percent – one of the highest in the world – in the Marshall Islands). If growth continues at these rates, the region's population will have doubled to 12 million by about 2020. Factors in the increase are continuing high birth rates and the lowering of death rates. In Papua New Guinea, for example, average life expectancy rose from 35 years in 1950 to 49.6 years in 1994, and throughout the region it now averages about 60 years. Island governments are increasingly aware of the challenges posed by population growth, which seems set to continue at rates exceeding expected economic growth. As the proportion of the population below the age of 20 rises ever higher, increasing pressure will be placed on education systems and the numbers of those able to find paid work will fall still lower.

To a very large extent, the history of the Pacific region has been a history of migration, and it is therefore not surprising to find that the development of modern transportation has led to the widespread movement of people – from villages to towns, mines or plantations, from outer islands to ports and administrative centers, from mountains to coasts, and from small island nations to larger and more prosperous states both within and outside the region. The Pacific's expanding centers of commercial and administrative activity attract people with increased job prospects and greater access to educational, medical and other services. Some younger people from rural areas and outlying islands are drawn by the chance to distance

themselves from the restrictions of village life. In some areas there has been a tradition of circular migration, with people returning to their home communities after living and working away for a period. Elsewhere the expansion of towns indicates a more permanent shift of population. Large towns, such as Papua New Guinea's capital Port Moresby, which numbers some 150,000 people, now contain second- and third-generation migrants whose connections with a rural "home" are fast becoming tenuous.

In some of the island states, urban populations can reach very high densities. Ebeye, an islet in the Kwajalein atoll of the Marshall Islands with an area of only 33 hectares and limited water supplies and other services, is home to 7,000 people – a density of over 23,000 per square kilometer. This is an exceptional case: the population has been swelled by those seeking employment with the US military establishment on the neighboring islet of Kwajalein, and by residents from there who were relocated to Ebeye when it was converted into a missile site. But even Tarawa, the administrative center of the scattered island groups that make up Kiribati, has a population growth rate four times that of the country's outer islands, and population densities on a par with those of Hong Kong.

As elsewhere in the developing world, Pacific governments have had difficulty in providing the necessary infrastructure and services to keep pace with rapid urban growth. Shanty settlements have grown up around many of the region's expanding cities as rural migrants seek affordable housing, and the urban authorities face pressing problems of polluted water supplies, inadequate waste disposal, poor standards of health, and low wages and high rates of unemployment, accompanied by increasing crime rates. But governments are in a double-bind as any attempt to improve urban conditions is likely to encourage further migration from the rural areas. As the drift to the cities brings a shortage of rural labor, agricultural production falls and more food has to be imported to meet the rising needs of town-dwellers. The difficulty is to find rural development policies that will slow the rate of rural drift while maintaining satisfactory standards of urban living. Yet, while urbanization presents major problems, and looks set to increase still further in the next century, it should be stressed that in a large number of the Pacific islands the population remains predominantly rural. Guam and Nauru have more or less exclusively urban populations, in several other Micronesian states more than half the population lives in towns, but in most of the countries of Polynesia, between three-quarters and two-thirds of the population are rural-dwellers. In Papua New Guinea, more than 80 percent are, and the numbers are still higher in Solomon Islands and Vanuatu.

The Pacific islands have often been described as "exporters of people", and many people still emigrate outside the region in the hope of finding a better life. Excluding Papua New Guinea, more than one in 10 Pacific islanders now live in countries around the Pacific rim, forming lively communities that contribute to their ethnic and cultural mix. People from the former US Trust Territories in Micronesia, from Samoa and from Tonga have settled in the United States. New Zealand has become home to large numbers of Polynesians from Western Samoa, the Cook Islands, Niue and Tokelau – more than 100,000 of them living in the city of Auckland – and Australia has a smaller Polynesian population. New Zealand, the

Sport in the Pacific Islands

Sports and games have always been a feature of island life. One Pacific sport, surfing, has spread from its Hawaiian home across the world. In the last century, other sporting traditions were introduced into the region, and the sporting interests of particular island groups still strongly reflect colonial histories. It is not surprising, for example, that baseball is played in the former US Trust Territories of Micronesia, or that rugby is a major Pacific sport, popular where the Australian and New Zealand presence has been great. Increasing globalization means that sporting influences are becoming ever more complex, and martial arts clubs or body-building associations are now likely to be found in even quite small communities.

Across the Pacific, basic sporting facilities – the rugby field, the volleyball court, the cricket pitch – are an important part of local community life. At the same time, sports have themselves become a significant link between the nations of the region and, beyond it, with

the greater international community. When teams and individuals complete against other countries and participate in major international competitions their successes are a focus of national pride. Within the region itself, there are several regular sports meetings. The South Pacific Games are held every four years, with a Mini Games between the major meetings. Fifteen Pacific nations attended the 1993 Mini Games, competing in athletics, soccer, boxing, tennis, golf and netball. Traditional pastimes as well as international sports feature in the Micronesian Games, where the range of events extends from outrigger canoe racing, underwater spearfishing and coconut tree climbing to baseball, table-tennis and track and field events. Funding from the Olympic Sporting Solidarity Movement helps to encourage regional sporting cooperation, but the larger or wealthier nations – Papua New Guinea, Fiji and the French territories – can usually field the biggest and most successful teams.

Above right The progress of a bowl is anxiously tracked across a carefully tended bowling green in Apia, capital of Western Samoa. The sedate though skillful and fiercely competitive sport of greens bowling is played in a number of Pacific islands where British, Australian and New Zealand influences have been strong. Pacific islanders frequently take part in international bowls competitions.

Center right In Rarotonga, Cook Islands, dedication to rugby in part reflects a long association with New Zealand. It remains the major sport for men, and every weekend throughout the season club matches are enthusiastically contested at every level of the game.

Bottom right Bora Bora in French Polynesia is the setting for the French game of *pétanque*, a form of aerial bowls. In Tahiti, the Heiva i Tahiti festival, which leads up to the celebration of Bastille Day (14 July), includes many sports from cycling, *pétanque* and archery to outrigger canoe racing. The French tradition is also seen in Tahiti's keen participation in soccer.

Left Missionaries are said to have introduced cricket to the Trobriand Islands in eastern Papua New Guinea in the 19th century as an alternative to inter-village fighting and the sexuality linked to harvest dances. But the Trobrianders soon turned their cricket into something more exciting to them than the standard game. Village teams of perhaps 60 men dress, and use magical decoration, as if for a dance contest. Chants and dances are an important part of matches, in competitions that may last for weeks.

Below Throughout the region, simple equipment and an open space provide the opportunity for village sport. Here volleyball is played in Tanna, Vanuatu. But investment in sport is becoming greater as involvement in international competition increases. A new national sports complex was built in Vanuatu for the staging of the South Pacific Mini Games.

United States and Canada have seen immigration from Fiji, particularly – since 1987 – by Fijians of Indian descent. Within the French-controlled territories there have been movements of Wallis Islanders and Tahitians to New Caledonia.

Emigration can be a safety valve for population pressures in the smaller islands. In some cases it can relieve problems of low levels of employment, while overseas workers send money back to their home communities, thereby creating more resources for investment. But such remittances may fuel demand for additional, often imported, goods, so building a need for further wage employment. It is by no means always the "surplus" population that leaves the smaller islands and rural areas: migration of some of the fittest and most skilled workers can deprive countries of important human resources. One of the most extreme cases is that of the New Zealand dependency of Niue. Four times as many Niueans now live in New Zealand than on the island itself. Agricultural production has fallen, development prospects are limited, and the Niuean government is keen to encourage them to return. Even the substantially larger state of Tonga has had its population growth cut to 0.5 percent by emigration, leading to a shortage of agricultural labor.

In most of the Pacific islands indigenous peoples form the vast majority of the population, with significant minorities of Europeans and of other incomer groups such as the Chinese, who settled as laborers and merchants throughout the region in the 19th century. In both New Caledonia and Fiji, as already noted, the descendents of the incomer groups came to outnumber the indigenous population. Since the coups of 1987, however, Fijian Indians have emigrated from Fiji in increasing numbers, and now no longer form the largest population group. While the coups were probably rooted in the desire of an established political elite to retain power, their public justification was the assertion of the "Fijian" nature of the state. Elsewhere in the region, after a colonial period during which their cultures and interests were persistently undervalued or ignored, there has been an understandable desire on the part of the Pacific islanders to reassert their cultural identities. The Fijian case reveals the darker side of such ethnic self-assertion, which can be used to exclude people who have shared in much of the colonial experience.

Making links

The Pacific islands, particularly those of Melanesia, are still rich in languages. Sharing language is an important part of a sense of common identity that operates at different levels. The constitution of Vanuatu includes a pledge to protect its many languages as part of the national heritage. Nevertheless, throughout the region local languages and dialects are tending to become eroded or replaced by those that have wider currency. The need for communication within the linguistically diverse countries of Melanesia has led to the adoption of pidgins – Tok pisin in Papua New Guinea, Pijin in the Solomon Islands, Bislama in Vanuatu. Though containing differences, they are sufficiently alike to have contributed to the shared sense of Melanesian identity that has developed between these states. Elsewhere, despite their colonial connotations, English or French are used as the *lingua franca* in education and for official communications.

Local and national identity are both also expressed through the arts. As the independence of Papua New

Guinea approached, the Creative Arts Center – later the National Arts School – was formed. Among other things, it has promoted the exploration of visual arts, dance, music and drama, combining the traditional with the innovative. Workers from the center helped to create the national parliament building, notable for the way it combines the use of new materials with aspects of traditional design and decoration. Pacific island politicians frequently stress the importance of traditional arts, culture or *kastom* (custom/tradition, a Melanesian pidgin term), though unfortunately government spending on the arts does not always reflect this emphasis.

In some countries performers from different islands and cultural groups may come together in national festivals to share their diverse traditions. There are also subregional and regional arts festivals, the largest of which is the four-yearly Festival of Pacific Arts. Dance, song and music are at the heart of such festivals, but they are invariably accompanied by other arts and crafts. Though tourism has in many respects adversely affected Pacific cultural life, particularly in the way local traditions are devalued, coarsened or even invented in order to package them for visitors, outside interest and finance have in some cases assisted local revivals and brought a vitality and commitment to the arts that goes beyond any simple response to tourist demand. New areas of creativity have been opened up. Since the 1970s a body of Pacific literature has begun to emerge. Novelists, short story writers and poets such as Vincent Eri from Papua New Guinea, Albert Wendt from Samoa and Epeli Hau'ofa from Tonga offer their distinctive views of the modern Pacific to an international readership.

The expansion of communications and the media have opened the Pacific Islands to a new intensity of outside cultural influences. Radio has largely been locally based but the capacity for receiving foreign broadcasts has increased. Television was first established in the American and French-influenced territories but by 1991 Papua New Guinea and Fiji both had television services, and it will soon have expanded into most of the island countries; video has preceded television into many areas. Satellite broadcasting is currently only available for a well-off minority. Satellite systems such as INTELSAT or PEACESAT have improved the quality of communications between island states and with the world at large. PEACESAT has made it possible for the University of the South Pacific, which has its main campus in Fiji, to link up with students right across the island states.

There is nearly universal provision of both primary and secondary education in Polynesia and Micronesia, though schooling is more unevenly provided in Melanesia. The number of tertiary education institutions in the region has grown considerably since the 1970s, and there are now 10 full universities. In most of these English is the main teaching language, but the French-language Université Française du Pacifique, based in New Caledonia and Tahiti, was established in the 1980s.

Christianity continues to have a substantial role in the Pacific islands. Many denominations are represented, their comparative strength in different islands reflecting the history of missionary activity in the region, and the churches remain an important factor in organizing community life. Free Wesleyans form the largest group in Tonga, Methodists in Fiji and Congregationalists in the Cook Islands. Recent years

have seen a rise in the number of new denominations and sects, and evangelical missionary groups are becoming increasingly involved in broadcasting. The Pacific Conference of Churches is a significant regional body that links the churches and promotes a variety of social programs.

Island economies
Though the traditional village economy remains important, the steady drift away from agriculture as the main livelihood of the Pacific islands and the growing demand for imported goods, including foodstuffs, have created a need for cash incomes. The opportunities provided by growing cash crops or taking a waged job can seem more alluring than the wearisome efforts required to raise traditional food crops and livestock through subsistence farming. Self-sufficiency in food and other goods has been eroded at both local and national levels. Since most of the island nations export raw materials and import manufactured goods, few can expect to balance exports and imports.

In the past, plantation and cash crops were the Pacific islands' major source of income. Today the value of agricultural exports is declining, though coffee, cocoa and tea are still important exports from Papua New Guinea, and sugar from the plantations of Fiji. On many other islands copra (the dried meat of the coconut, which provides oils used in the making of soap, cosmetics, margarine and other products) is a valuable source of revenue. A vast range of fruit and vegetables – bananas, pineapples, citrus fruit, passion fruit, papaya, vanilla, yams and sweet potatoes – are grown for export, but face strong competition in world markets where agricultural products are subject to marked fluctuations in price beyond the control of the Pacific producers. Though there are recognized possibilities for agricultural development in a number of countries, agriculture no longer dominates the planning of national economies as once it did. Timber extraction from the forests of Melanesia has become increasingly significant, with Japan serving as a major customer for tropical hardwoods. But while it is tempting for countries faced with serious economic shortfalls to earn revenue by exploiting their timber

Above Though the older denominations that established Christianity throughout the Pacific islands in the 19th and early 20th centuries are still widely represented and remain very influential, there has been a great influx of diverse religious groups into the region in recent years. Latter Day Saints, Baptists, Apostolics, Seventh Day Adventists, Assemblies of God and Baha'i are among those that have won adherents. These Adventists are holding a meeting in Fiji, where Hinduism and Islam are also part of religious life among the Indo-Fijian population. Indigenous religions are strongest in parts of Melanesia such as Papua New Guinea and Vanuatu.

reserves, there are major concerns about the industry's reliance on non-sustainable forestry practices.

Minerals are now the biggest export earner in the region as a whole, accounting for about 46 percent of total revenues, but reserves are unevenly distributed. Nauru presents an extraordinary case. Mining of the tiny island's thick deposits of phosphates, carried out by German, British and Australian companies in the cause of the 20th century, has removed much of the land surface. Efforts are now being made to reclaim some land for agriculture, but there is nowhere like enough to support the island's population. The revenues generated by the export of the phosphates have contributed toward Nauru's excellent welfare services, but when the deposits run out (which is expected to happen by the end of the century) the islanders will have to rely on the income from government overseas investments. Melanesia has the greatest potential for mineral exploitation. In Papua New Guinea there are large reserves of gold and copper and considerable natural gas potential. However, the interests of the powerful multinational mining and extractive companies do not always work to the benefit of national interests. The conflict in Bougainville has shown that the rights of local customary landowners cannot be taken lightly; the Papua New Guinea government has conceded rights to the top six meters of mined sites to the traditional landowners.

Island states with very small land areas but numerous scattered islands and extended coastlines hold economic rights over vast tracts of ocean. International law recognizes a 200-mile Exclusive Economic Zone (EEZ) around islands, and nine Pacific island countries have EEZs of more than 1 million square kilometers. Realizing the full potential of their marine resources will clearly be of considerable importance to the economic future of these islands. This is particularly true of atoll-based states such as Kiribati and Tuvalu, whose scope for onshore development is very limited. Fisheries and seafoods already represent the region's second largest source of export income. Tuna is the greatest commercial fishery resource, with more than 600,000 tonnes being taken from the South Pacific every year, mostly by fishing trawler fleets operating from the United States, Japan, Korea and Taiwan. Small island states cannot afford to purchase and run large factory ships with their huge purse-seine nets that scoop up shoals of ocean fish; less costly (and more environmentally sound) are pole-and-line fishing vessels, though their catches are immeasurably smaller. The island states are entitled to income from foreign trawlers through licensing agreements relating to fishing rights within their EEZs, but the negotiation of fees has proved difficult for individual states acting on their own. In recent years a regional body, the Forum Fisheries Agency, has played a part in reaching regional licensing agreements with the United States and Japan. The monitoring of licensing agreements remains a problem, however – even with assistance from other countries, effective policing of vast territorial waters is an extremely expensive exercise. It is widely recognized that the preservation of inshore fisheries is vital to ensure future food needs in the region, and that they have additional economic potential in some areas: there are commercial canneries in Fiji, the Solomon Islands and American Samoa, for example. Nevertheless, the costly import of canned fish caught in Pacific waters but processed outside the region still continues.

In the more distant future, the seabed offers great

Below An area of forest in Papua New Guinea has been clear-felled for the extraction of timber. The high value of timber exports as a foreign currency earner makes it difficult for hard-pressed regional governments to resist pressure from international logging companies, despite the longterm environmental damage caused by clear-felling of forested slopes. There has been very extensive logging in the forests of Papua New Guinea, the Solomon Islands, New Caledonia, Vanuatu, Fiji and Western Samoa, while agricultural expansion, fire and cyclones also contribute to deforestation in the region. But increasingly initiatives are being made to show local people how financial returns might be had from sustainable use of forest resources and to provide practical inducements for conservation, with some degree of success.

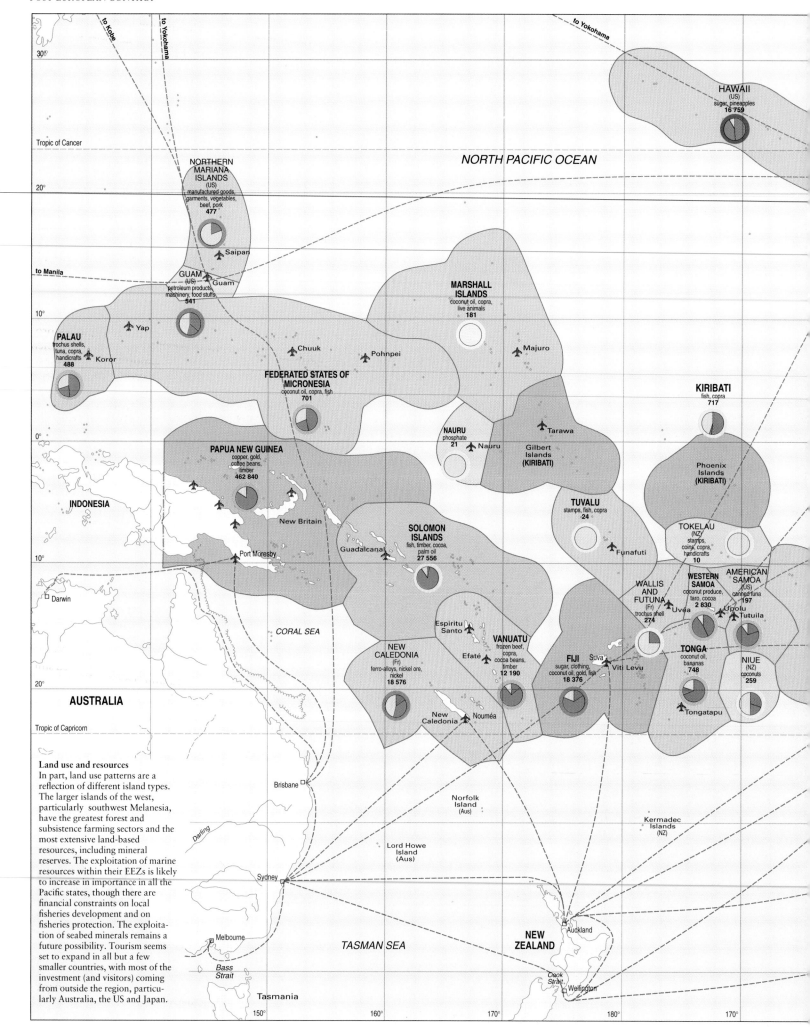

to Kobe
to Yokohama

30°

Tropic of Cancer

HAWAII
(US)
sugar, pineapples
16 759

to Yokohama

NORTH PACIFIC OCEAN

20°

**NORTHERN
MARIANA
ISLANDS**
(US)
manufactured goods,
garments, vegetables,
beef, pork
477

✈ Saipan

to Manila

GUAM
(US)
petroleum products,
machinery, food stuffs
541

✈ Guam

10°

✈ Yap

**MARSHALL
ISLANDS**
coconut oil, copra,
live animals
181

✈ Majuro

PALAU
trochus shells,
tuna, copra,
handicrafts
488
✈ Koror

✈ Chuuk

✈ Pohnpei

KIRIBATI
fish, copra
717

**FEDERATED STATES OF
MICRONESIA**
coconut oil, copra, fish
701

0°

✈ Tarawa

NAURU
phosphate
21
✈ Nauru

**Gilbert
Islands
(KIRIBATI)**

INDONESIA

PAPUA NEW GUINEA
copper, gold,
coffee beans,
timber
462 840

**Phoenix
Islands
(KIRIBATI)**

New Britain

TUVALU
stamps, fish, copra
24

10°

Port Moresby

Guadalcanal

**SOLOMON
ISLANDS**
fish, timber, cocoa,
palm oil
27 556

✈ Funafuti

TOKELAU
(NZ)
stamps,
coins, copra,
handicrafts
10

☐ Darwin

✈

**WALLIS
AND
FUTUNA**
(Fr)
trochus shell
274
✈ Uvea

**WESTERN
SAMOA**
coconut produce,
taro, cocoa
2 830

**AMERICAN
SAMOA**
(US)
canned tuna
197
✈ Upolu
✈ Tutuila

CORAL SEA

Espiritu
Santo

VANUATU
frozen beef,
copra,
cocoa beans,
timber
12 190

TONGA
coconut oil,
bananas
748

NIUE
(NZ)
coconuts
259

Efaté ✈

**NEW
CALEDONIA**
(Fr)
ferro-alloys, nickel ore,
nickel
18 576

FIJI
sugar, clothing,
coconut oil, gold, fish
18 376
Suva
✈ Viti Levu

20°

AUSTRALIA

New
Caledonia
✈ Nouméa

✈ Tongatapu

Tropic of Capricorn

Land use and resources
In part, land use patterns are a
reflection of different island types.
The larger islands of the west,
particularly southwest Melanesia,
have the greatest forest and
subsistence farming sectors and the
most extensive land-based
resources, including mineral
reserves. The exploitation of marine
resources within their EEZs is likely
to increase in importance in all the
Pacific states, though there are
financial constraints on local
fisheries development and on
fisheries protection. The exploitation of seabed minerals remains a
future possibility. Tourism seems
set to expand in all but a few
smaller countries, with most of the
investment (and visitors) coming
from outside the region, particularly Australia, the US and Japan.

☐ Brisbane

Norfolk
Island
(Aus)

Kermadec
Islands
(NZ)

Darling

• Lord Howe
Island
(Aus)

☐ Sydney

✈ Auckland

☐ Melbourne

TASMAN SEA

**NEW
ZEALAND**

Bass
Strait

Cook
Strait
☐ Wellington

Tasmania

150° 160° 170° 180° 170°

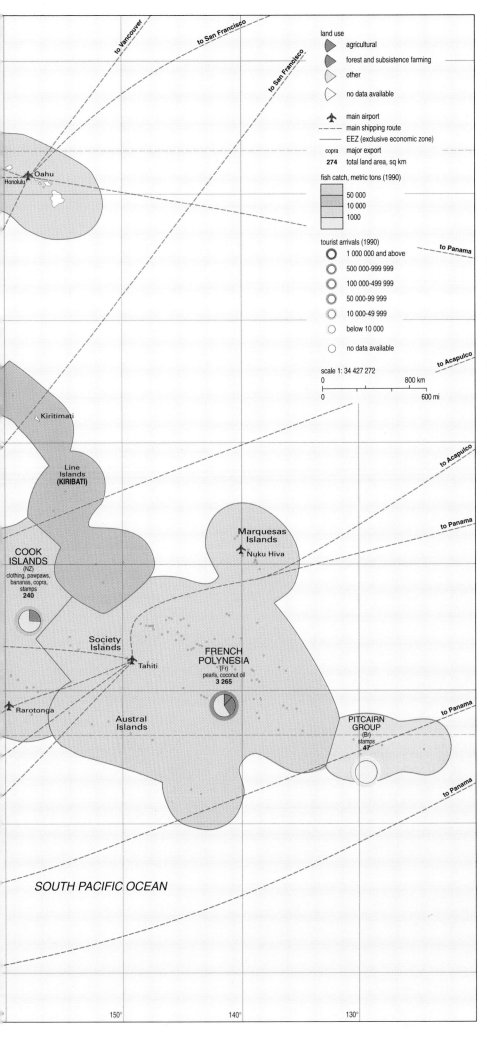

potential for mineral exploitation in the form of vast areas of metal-rich nodules. Some deposits lie within EEZs, including those of Kiribati and the Cook Islands. Full international agreement has yet to be reached to decide how the benefits from extracting minerals from the seabed outside the area of EEZs might be distributed. Whatever agreement is reached in the future, the massive investment in technology and skills that will be needed to extract the minerals from the seabed is likely to limit the extent to which the island economies will be able to participate in and profit from their exploitation.

Trade, services and tourism

The heavy costs of imported materials and fuels and of long-distance transportation, together with the small size of local markets, have tended to reduce the scope for manufacturing, though there is some food processing and attempts have been made recently to develop manufactures for export. Clothing represents a significant section of Fiji's exports and Tonga has created a small industries center for companies producing a varied range of goods from yachts to woolen garments. The success of such export ventures relies to some considerable extent on the continued existence of privileged access to markets. The South Pacific Regional Trade and Economic Cooperation Arrangement (SPARTECA), for instance, provides favorable entry to the Australian and New Zealand markets. Such agreements may prove vulnerable as the world moves toward free trade, and there are fears that increasing competition from Asia will compromise wages and conditions. Australia and New Zealand remain important trading partners, though the balance of trade is firmly against the islands. Large volumes of trade take place with the countries of the European Union and the United States, while the importance of Japan and other countries of the Pacific rim to the island economies is rising steadily.

A number of island states have sought to reduce their dependence on agricultural exports by diversifying into areas of the service industries. Vanuatu was the first Pacific island country to become involved in offshore banking, since when the Cook Islands, Tonga, Nauru and Western Samoa have followed suit. Vanuatu, the Cook Islands and Tonga also provide flags of convenience for foreign ships. A less controversial source of government revenue has been the issue of postage stamps. Though the philately market has passed its peak, governments such as Tuvalu and the Cook Islands still profit from the regular issue of new and highly decorative sets of stamps.

An area of the economy that offers great potential for growth is tourism. The Pacific states have no difficulty in promoting their island landscapes and cultures. Tourism is already well established in countries like Fiji, Tonga, and the Cook Islands and is developing rapidly elsewhere. The annual number of visitors to Guam – largely from Japan – exceeds the local population by four to one, while American and other visitors outnumber the permanent residents of the Northern Marianas by nine to one. These are exceptional cases; nevertheless, more than 1.25 million people visit the islands every year. The care and entertainment of tourists, and the sale of handcrafts and other goods, provide badly needed employment and sources of income. Around 20 percent of paid jobs in Vanuatu are now generated by tourism; the figure is higher in Fiji.

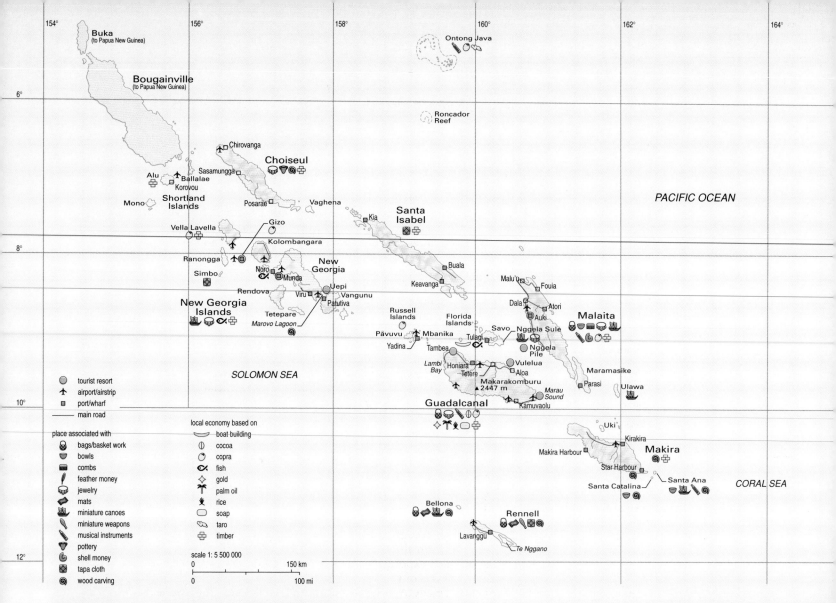

154° 156° 158° 160° 162° 164°

Buka
(to Papua New Guinea)

6° Bougainville
(to Papua New Guinea)

Ontong Java

Roncador
Reef

PACIFIC OCEAN

Chirovanga
Choiseul
Alu Sasamungga
Ballalae
Korovou
Mono Shortland Vaghena
Islands Posarae
Santa
Kia Isabel
Vella Lavella Gizo
8° Kolombangara
Ranongga Buala
Noro New Keavanga
Simbo Munda Georgia
Rendova Viru Uepi Malu'u Fouia
New Georgia Vangunu Dala Atori
Islands Patutiva Russell Florida Auki
Tetepare Islands Islands Savo Nggela Sule Malaita
Marovo Lagoon Pavuvu Mbanika Nggela
Yadina Tulagi Pile
Tambea Maramasike
SOLOMON SEA Lambi Honiara Vulelua Parasi
Bay Tetere Aloa Ulawa
Makarakomburu
▲ 2447 m Marau
Sound
Guadalcanal Kamuvaolu Uki
Kirakira
Makira Harbour Makira
10° Star Harbour Santa Ana
Santa Catalina CORAL SEA

○ tourist resort
✈ airport/airstrip
▣ port/wharf
── main road

place associated with local economy based on
🧺 bags/basket work ⌣ boat building Bellona
🥣 bowls ◗ cocoa Rennell
▭ combs ◐ copra Lavanggu Te Nggano
⸾ feather money ✂ fish
🏺 jewelry ◇ gold
mats 🌴 palm oil
◗ miniature canoes ⚘ rice
miniature weapons ◡ soap
musical instruments ∾ taro
🏺 pottery ✚ timber
◐ shell money
⊞ tapa cloth scale 1 : 5 500 000
◎ wood carving
0 150 km
0 100 mi

12°

212

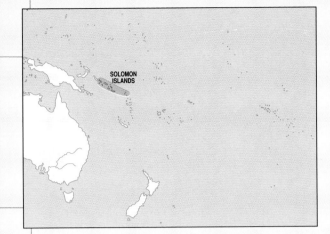

166°

SOLOMON
ISLANDS

Solomon Islands

Solomon Islands is composed of a double chain of islands with mountainous interiors and extensive forest cover, but there is diversity within the country's seven provinces, some of which include atolls and raised coral islands. Most of its population, now above 300,000, are Melanesian, though some outlying islands such as Rennell and Ontong Java are home to Polynesian peoples. While the density of population is low in comparison to many of the smaller Pacific nations (approaching 12 per square kilometer), the population growth rate is among the highest in the region. Solomon Islanders speak some 90 different languages. However, pidgin offers a bridge between language groups and English is the nation's official language.

A traditional village economy of horticulture and fishing continues to provide the basics of life for most Solomon Islands families. Less than 10 percent of the population are in paid fulltime employment. But there is a substantial commercial fishing industry, with onshore canning and freezing facilities. Timber is also a major export, with serious impact on the nation's rainforests. The need for more sustainable logging practices is recognized, but economic pressures work against their realization. Commercial agriculture provides other exports, including copra, palm oil and cocoa. Levels of tourism are, so far, low, but efforts are being made to stimulate the growth of the industry.

Below far left Villagers, banana leaves in hand, make use of a river crossing. Well over 80 percent of Solomon Islanders live in village communities – among the highest proportion of rural-dwellers in the Pacific region. Nevertheless, urbanization is increasing, with more and more people being drawn to settle around the capital Honiara, on Guadalcanal, the center of government and commerce.

Below left A wedding party sets off across the waters of the Lau lagoon in northeastern Malaita. The lagoon is noted for its artificial islets built from coral, sand and earth, which have been inhabited for many centuries. The people who live on them grow crops on the mainland, but there are long traditions of exchange in fish and garden produce between the "saltwater people" of the coast and the "bush people" living inland.

Below A pig is urged along in preparation for a feast. The pigs kept by villagers are likely to provide food for special occasions rather than supply daily needs. Today the traditional subsistence crops of yam, taro, sweet potato and cassava are supplemented by more recently introduced foodstuffs. Fish and many kinds of seafood are a major resource of coastal communities. Though few rural-dwelling people are wage-dependent, growing purchases of imported foods reflect their increased involvement in the money economy.

Duff Islands

Reef Islands

Tinakula

Nendo

Lata

Santa Cruz
Islands

Utupua

Vanikoro

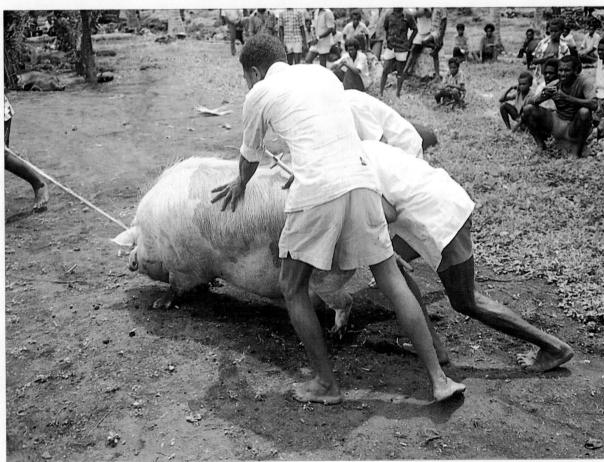

ISLAND PROFILE Fiji

Fiji is made up of two large and over 800 smaller islands, around 100 of which are inhabited. The bigger islands have rugged interiors with river valleys coming down to coastal plains. The small islands include coral atolls and reefs. About 75 percent of the population of more than 750,000 live on the largest island, Viti Levu. About one-fifth of all Fijians live in the capital, Suva. The population is balanced between Melanesian Fijians and Fijians of Indian origin, with much smaller minorities of Chinese, Europeans and others. The people of Rotuma are Polynesian, while Rabi was purchased to accommodate people from Banaba in Micronesia, displaced by phosphate mining.

In October 1970 Fiji became an independent member of the British Commonwealth. Following two military coups in 1987, it was declared a republic with a president as head of state. The new constitution was biased toward ethnic Fijians, and in elections held in 1992 the coup leader, Sitiveni Rabuka, became prime minister. Though no longer in the Commonwealth, Fiji remains a prominent member of Pacific regional councils. The sugar production that was at the heart of Fiji's colonial economy still accounts for the largest part of its visible export earnings, but today there is greater diversity. Tourism is now the country's single biggest money earner.

Below Gold mining in Fiji is centered on Vatukoula in northern Viti Levu, where the discovery of gold in the 1930s led to the setting up of the Emperor Gold Mine, pictured here. For some time gold was second only to sugar in export earnings, and it has remained among Fiji's leading visible exports. The Vatukoula mine also produces some silver, as well as gravel from rock waste. Another mining site in the Tavua basin near Vatukoula was opened up in the 1980s, and there are also schemes to develop copper ore reserves at Namosi in south central Viti Levu. Working conditions in the mining industry have been the subject of critical attention.

Left Mangrove wetlands cover thousands of hectares in some parts of Fiji. Many such swamps have been "reclaimed" for conversion to agricultural land and other purposes. Today, however, there is much greater awareness of the important part the mangrove wetlands play in coastal protection and as breeding grounds for fish and other marine species.

Below Smaller rural enterprises such as boatbuilding provide some of Fiji's growing workforce with employment. But Fiji has the problem, shared with many of its neighbors, that job creation cannot keep pace with the rising numbers of workers. In 1987 a Tax Free Factory/Tax Free Zone scheme was introduced. This gives incentives and concessions to companies willing to establish enterprises in Fiji that will export 95 percent of their production, and has been instrumental in the rapid growth of the garment industry.

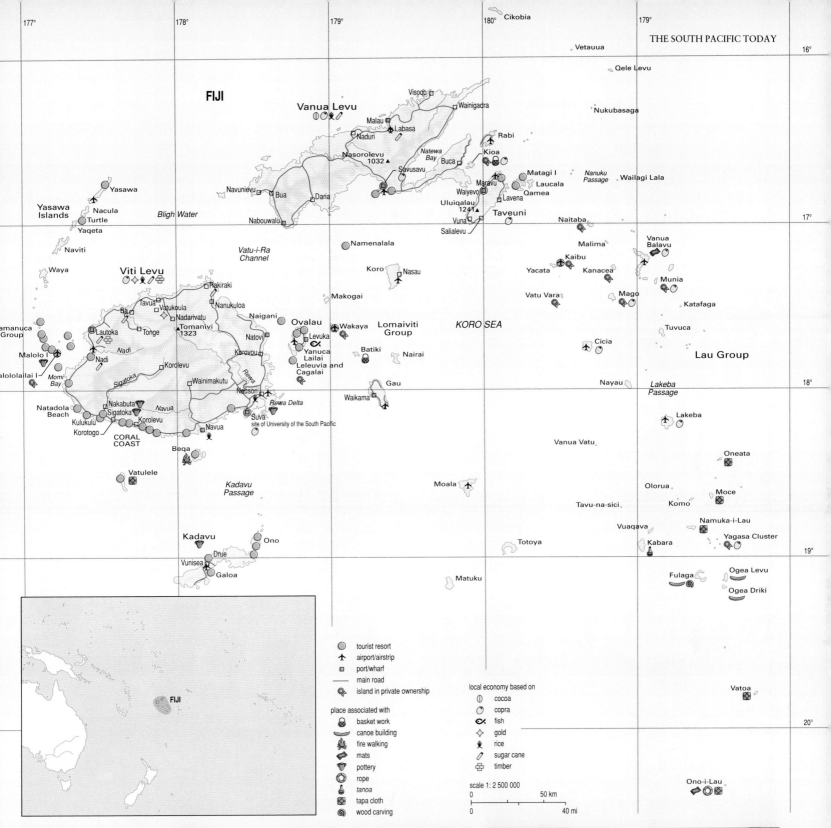

FIJI

Vanua Levu

Yasawa

Yasawa
Islands

Nacula
Turtle
Yaqeta

Naviti

Waya

Viti Levu

Yanuca
Lailai
Leleuvia and
Cagalai

amanuca
Group

Malolo I

alololailai I

Momi
Bay

Visoqp
Wainigadra

Malau
Naduri
Labasa

Nasorolevu
1032

Natewa
Bay
Savusavu
Buca

Rabi

Kioa

Matagi I
Laucala
Qamea

Maravu
Waiyevo
Lavena
Uluiqalau
1241
Vuna
Salialevu

Taveuni

Rakiraki
Ba
Tavua
Vatukoula
Nadarivatu
Tomanivi
1323
Tonge

Nanukuloa

Naigani

Ovalau
Levuka

Wakaya

Lautoka

Nadi

Korovou

Natovi

Korolevu

Sigatoka
Nakabuta
Sigatoka
Korolevu

Kulukulu
Korotogo

CORAL
COAST

Wainimakutu

Rewa

Nausori

Suva

Navua

Navua

Natadola
Beach

Beqa

Vatulele

Rewa Delta

site of University of the South Pacific

Kadavu
Passage

Kadavu

Drue

Ono

Vunisea
Galoa

Bligh Water

Navunievu
Bua
Daria

Nabouwalu

Namenalala

Koro
Nasau

Makogai

Batiki
Nairai

Gau

Waikama

Moala

Matuku

Vatu-i-Ra
Channel

Lomaiviti
Group

KORO SEA

Cikobia

Vetauua

Qele Levu

Nukubasaga

Nanuku
Passage
Wailagi Lala

Naitaba

Malima

Kaibu
Yacata
Kanacea

Vatu Vara

Vanua
Balavu

Munia

Mago

Katafaga

Tuvuca

Cicia

Lau Group

Nayau
Lakeba
Passage

Lakeba

Vanua Vatu

Oneata

Olorua
Komo
Moce

Tavu-na-sici

Vuaqava
Kabara

Namuka-i-Lau
Yagasa Cluster

Totoya

Fulaga

Ogea Levu

Ogea Driki

Vatoa

Ono-i-Lau

FIJI

	tourist resort
	airport/airstrip
	port/wharf
	main road
	island in private ownership

place associated with

	basket work
	canoe building
	fire walking
	mats
	pottery
	rope
	tanoa
	tapa cloth
	wood carving

local economy based on

	cocoa
	copra
	fish
	gold
	rice
	sugar cane
	timber

scale 1 : 2 500 000

0   50 km

0   40 mi

Right There are serious exploitation pressures on Fiji's native forests. But despite damage done by cyclones, drought and fires, the timber industry is now receiving the benefits of planting programs of both pines and hardwoods carried out by the Fiji Pine Commission and local communities in the late 1970s. Fiji has made itself an exporter of sawn timber and wood chips rather than unprocessed logs.

Far right Soap bars are packed in a Suva factory. The manufacturing export base in Fiji is diverse. Garments account for the largest part, but as well as fish canning, rice milling, steel rolling and perfumery, there is also production of music cassettes and solar water heaters.

ISLAND PROFILE Western Samoa

Below Early each morning the police band plays the national anthem as the flag is raised outside the old courthouse in Apia. Many of the capital's older buildings and institutions still reflect the influence of the years of New Zealand administration.

Western Samoa is the most populous of the independent countries of island Polynesia. More than two-thirds of its population of nearly 163,000 live on the island of Upolu, with more than 33,000 in Apia, the national capital. Though the country's overall land area is about 2,900 square kilometers, the interiors of the two large islands consist of chains of volcanic peaks and, in the case of Savaii, lava plains. Most settlement is consequently confined to villages on the coastal plains. Population growth in recent years has been moderated by steady migration out of the islands, particularly to New Zealand (which has a Samoan population of over 60,000) and to the United States, via American Samoa and Hawaii.

Western Samoa was the first Pacific island nation to regain its political independence, in 1962. Since 1991 there has been universal adult suffrage, replacing a system in which the *matai*, the chosen heads of extended families (*aiga*) were the electorate. But change in Western Samoa is balanced against the importance that is still placed upon the *fa'a Samoa*, the Samoan way of life. The *aiga* and their *matai* continue

to play crucial roles in society. Most land is owned by *aiga*. The *matai* have a responsibility for their *aiga*'s resources and for the wellbeing of their people, whom they represent in village councils. Only *matai* can be members of parliament. Complementing the role of the village councils are active and influential women's committees.

Subsistence and cash crop agriculture and fisheries remain at the heart of the Western Samoan economy. Exports include coconut products, cocoa and taro. But the proportion of export earnings from agriculture has fallen sharply. The creation of a small industries center at Vaitele, outside Apia, which includes a brewery and a plant producing electrical wiring systems, has met with some success in boosting export earnings. Nevertheless, the value of imports continues to outstrip exports by a considerable margin, and economic balance is achieved through the remittances sent home by the many Samoans living and working overseas, aid inputs and, increasingly, the income generated from tourism. Western Samoa attracts visitors from many parts of the world.

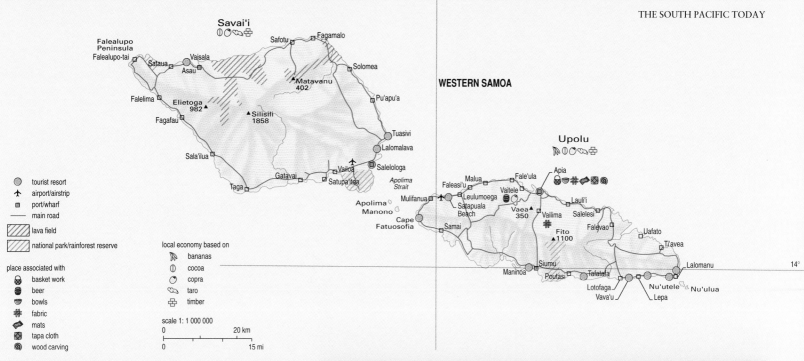

Above right Villagers make their way to Sunday church service. Christianity is an important part of Samoan life, and considerable time and money are given to church activities. About half the population belong to the Congregationalist church, which grew out of the teachings of the London Missionary Society, established here by the Reverend John Williams in 1830.

Right The town clock tower stands in the bustling commercial and administrative center of Apia. It faces the long parade strung out along the sea front where the capital's main shops, offices, hotels, places of entertainment and churches are located. A large modern government building and the Central Bank are close by. The busy bus station sees a regular flow of passengers from the villages of Upolu, many of whom come to sell produce at the covered market.

Left Schoolboys observe the annual Independence Day celebrations. These are held over the first three days of June, though independence was actually achieved on 1 January 1962. A regatta of 40-man long-boats takes place in Apia harbor, and there are many other sporting events including horse races, as well as dancing, feasting and oratorical addresses.

ISLAND PROFILE Kiribati

Makin

KIRIBATI

Marakei
Abaiang
Tarawa

Maiana
Abemama
Kuria
Aranuka

Gilbert Islands

Howland Island
(to United States)

Baker Island
(to United States)

Nonouti

Banaba

Beru   Nikunau

Tabiteuea
Onotoa
Tamana   Arorae

KIRIBATI

Winslow Reef

Phoenix Islands

Kanton Island
Enderbury

McKean Island   Birnie
Rawaki

Nikumaroro   Orona   Manra

Carondelet Reef

Nanumea   **TUVALU**
Niutao
Nanumanga

Nui   Vaitupu
Nukufetau
Funafuti

Atafu   **TOKELAU**
(to New Zealand)
Nukunono
Fakaofo

Nukulaelae

Swains
(to American Samoa)

The 33 islands of the Republic of Kiribati consist of three groups of coral atolls – the Gilbert Islands, the Phoenix Islands (uninhabited) and the Line Islands – and one isolated volcanic island (Banaba). They have a total land area of 717 square kilometers spread across some 5 million square kilometers of ocean. Formerly part of the British colony of the Gilbert and Ellice Islands, Kiribati (pronounced Kiri-bass and derived from the word "Gilberts") became independent in 1979. The people of Kiribati are known as I-Kiribati. They are predominantly Micronesian. Most of the population of 70,000 live on the atolls of the Gilbert Islands, more than a third of them in the urbanized centers of Tarawa atoll where the capital, Bairiki, and the main airport are situated. About three-quarters of the working population are engaged in agriculture or fishing – phosphate mining on Banaba, which had been the colony's main export, came to an end in 1979. Copra and fish are major exports. The income from fees paid by the fishing fleets of other nations working in Kiribati's waters are an important source of revenue, as are remittances from I-Kiribati working overseas (some in phosphate mining on Nauru). It receives significant amounts of aid. Kiribati has considerable potential for development of sea-bed mineral resources. It is one of the Pacific countries that is most at threat from the sea-level rises brought about by global warming.

Right The *maneaba* or meeting house is still an important focus for I-Kiribati communities. It is where local people come together to make important joint decisions and resolve conflicts, or for celebration. The name of one type of meeting house, *Maneaba ni Maungatabu*, has been transferred to the national parliament of Kiribati.

Far right Dance and song are part of village festivities on Kiritimati (Christmas Island). The most easterly of the three inhabited Line Islands, and more than 2,000 kilometers distant from the Gilbert Islands, Kiritimati is the largest purely coral island in the world. It makes up more than half Kiribati's total land area. In the 1950s and 60s it provided a base for British and US nuclear tests. Growing population and land pressure on Tarawa and the other Gilbertese atolls makes the development of Kiritimati an appealing option, though its isolation is a problem. It has potential for tourism.

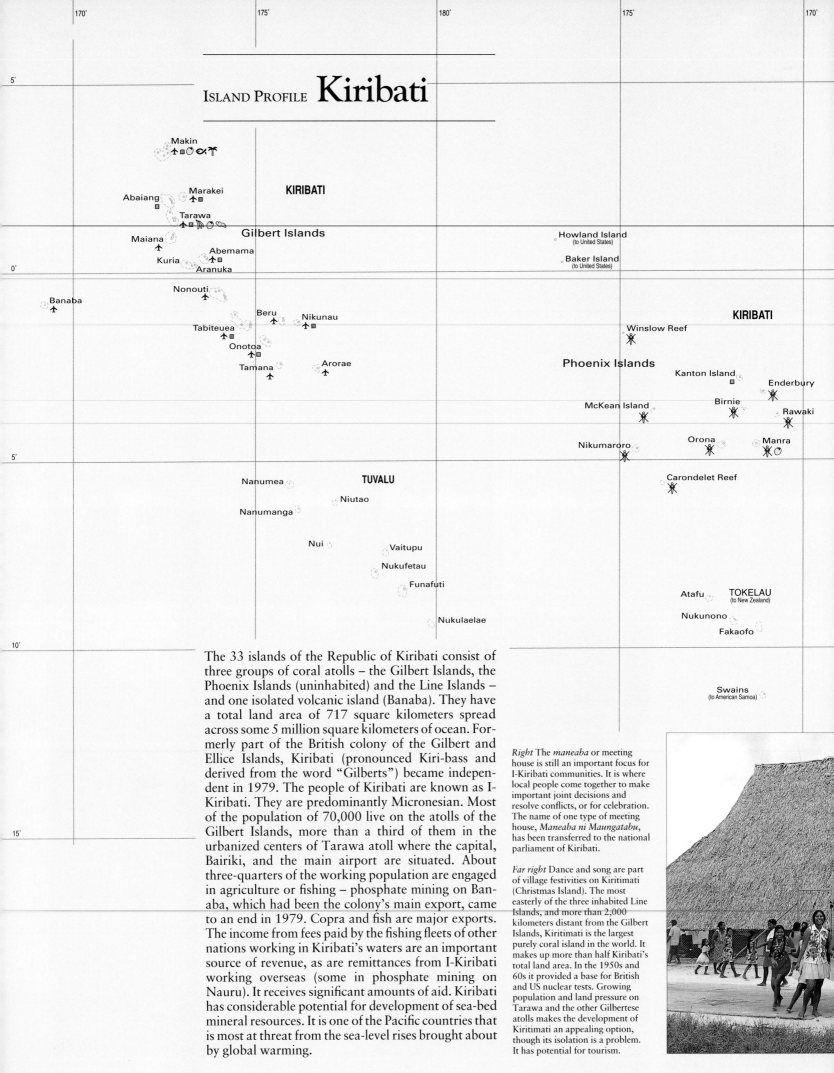

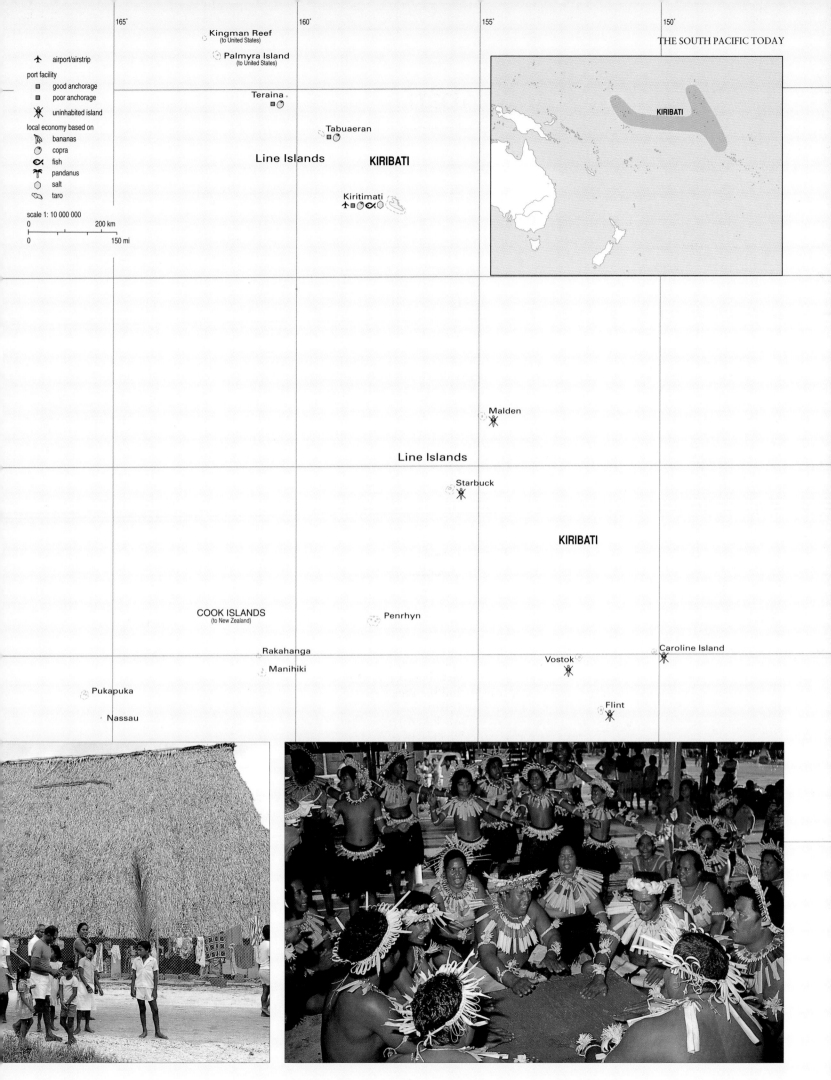

airport/airstrip
port facility
◨ good anchorage
◨ poor anchorage
✹ uninhabited island
local economy based on
🍌 bananas
🥥 copra
🐟 fish
🌴 pandanus
○ salt
🍠 taro

scale 1: 10 000 000
0   200 km
0   150 mi

Kingman Reef
(to United States)
Palmyra Island
(to United States)
Teraina
Tabuaeran
Line Islands   KIRIBATI
Kiritimati

KIRIBATI

Malden
Line Islands
Starbuck
KIRIBATI
COOK ISLANDS
(to New Zealand)   Penrhyn
Rakahanga   Caroline Island
Manihiki   Vostok
Pukapuka
Flint
Nassau

The Festival of Pacific Arts

The Festival of Pacific Arts is the region's major cultural gathering. It is held every four years when representatives from the countries of the Island Pacific, together with Australian Aboriginal and New Zealand Maori contingents, meet to share their cultural heritages in performance, demonstrations and displays. The festivals, which take place under the auspices of the South Pacific Commission, attract large numbers of visitors from outside the Pacific region. Since they began in 1972, each of the festivals has been held at a new site in one of the participating countries, so far in Fiji, New Zealand, Papua New Guinea, French Polynesia, Australia and the Cook Islands.

Taking as its theme "Seafaring Pacific Islanders", the sixth festival, which was held in October 1992 at Rarotonga in the Cook Islands, set out to celebrate the oceanic nature of Pacific cultures. Canoes from many parts of the Pacific assembled for a *vaka* (canoe) pageant. Several of those taking part were sailed to their destination, using traditional navigation methods. Outside the *vaka* village a new cultural center and auditorium had been specially built for the festival, which proved to be one of the most diverse staged so far. Demonstrations were given of a wide variety of traditional arts and crafts as well as the more usual performance arts. Traditional costumes were shown, and among the skills on display were carving, canoe-making, earth-oven cooking, quilt-making, basketry, painting, tattooing and fire-walking. These took place alongside traditional story-telling, theatrical performances, music and dance displays to offer a colorful and unforgettable overview of the wide-ranging cultural and artistic richness of the Pacific.

Above A permanent memorial made of stones sent by each of the participating countries was set up in the *vaka* village. Behind this arrangement can be seen *Waan Aelon Kein*, an outrigger canoe from the Marshall Islands. Farther back stand the horned masts of Polynesian double-hulled voyaging canoes. The two closer masts belong to the celebrated modern Hawaiian canoe *Hokule'a*.

Below Musical performances are an important part of the festivals. The guitar and ukelele have long been part of Pacific music, but the most widespread of traditional instruments are different forms of drum and wind instrument, including the conch-shell trumpet and many kinds of flute.

Below A choir from Tokelau performs traditional action songs: their headbands, bodices and the mat by which they identify themselves also display their skill as fine weavers. This small New Zealand dependency was well represented at the Rarotonga festival. Members of their contingent also played traditional games, told stories and demonstrated cooking and craft skills. Participation in the Arts Festival is an excellent chance for the smaller island countries to display their unique heritage on a Pacific and wider international stage. Even tiny Pitcairn was represented in 1992, displaying its crafts and stamps.

Below Both their head wreaths and the participants themselves look in danger of wilting in the heat as a Cook Islands choir waits its turn to take part in the closing ceremonies. The Cook Islands have a rich heritage of song ranging from traditional chants and action songs to a complex multipart hymn-singing style that was developed in the last century, as well as the popular songs of today. Great energy will go into their performance once it gets under way.

Bottom The art of the woodcarver is practiced widely throughout the Pacific Islands. Here a carver works in the distinctive style of the Kanak people of New Caledonia. With modern tools he carves patterns that, topped with an abstract face, have traditionally been used on the door jambs that decorate chiefs' houses.

Tourism may prove to be a mixed blessing. Only a small part of the industry's earnings remain in the islands; the rest leaks out to foreign tour and hotel companies, and to overseas investors. The heavy costs of maintaining the infrastructure that tourists have come to expect – from airports to fresh water supplies – are burdensome to the host governments. There are concerns, too, about the undesirable social and environmental effects of tourism. Many feel that it promotes materialist values; it changes local peoples' views of their own lifestyles and creates an ever-spiraling demand for imported goods. There is a very real risk that aspects of local culture will be debased by being turned into "performances" for tourists. Governments are well aware of these dangers. Some hope to move away from the package holiday trade toward encouraging more environmentally and culturally sensitive forms of tourism. But the short-term economic benefits derived from hotel and resort development often prove too great to resist.

Aid and remittances

Aid from individual governments and international bodies such as the United Nations Development Program or the European Union plays a crucial part in offsetting the imbalances of the island economies. The South Pacific receives some of the highest per capita payments of aid in the world, and limited resources and the heavy investment costs of economic development make it difficult for most island governments to see ahead to a time when such aid will not be needed. Aid, however, is unevenly distributed across the region; the highest per capita funding tends to be in countries that still have strong metropolitan ties – the former American Trust Territories, the French territories, and the countries with links to New Zealand. Australia is also a major donor of aid, much of it going to Papua New Guinea, while Japan and Britain also make significant payments.

Aid is given in a variety of ways. It may be directed toward a specific project (sometimes with clauses committing the recipient government to contract work to companies from the donor nation), or a direct contribution may be made to government budgets. The European Union operates a scheme of price stabilization that protects participating governments from drops in the price of particular export commodities. For the small state of Tuvalu an innovative scheme was developed – a national Trust Fund from which it receives an annual income.

Remittances, the money sent back to their home countries by islanders living and working abroad, have considerable impact on the island economies. In the 1980s, remittances sent back to Tonga accounted for over a third of total foreign exchange earnings, more than the combined revenue from exports and tourism. Such remittances mostly come from those living in the countries of the Pacific rim that have former colonial ties with the islands, and so depend on the degree of access that is granted to islanders to come and go between them.

Regional organizations

One important development in economic planning has been the growth in regional cooperation, much of it through newly created regional bodies such as the Forum Fisheries Agency that provide information and make it possible to concentrate expertise where it is most needed. The Pacific Forum Line represents a joint

Left Dancers in French Polynesia put on a spectacular performance for tourists. Cultural displays like this have become part of the image by which the Pacific is sold to potential visitors, but many question the longterm benefits of tourism to Pacific cultures. There are dangers that local arts become shaped by tourist demand. Some carvers in Tonga, for example, are now producing Hawaiian-style figures because these are more saleable. Dances and songs may lose their true meaning when repeatedly performed for a tourist audience. On the other hand, in some areas tourist interest is said to have provided both the stimulus and the financial resources to have brought about a revival of interest in traditional culture.

shipping venture to 10 island countries. The Pacific Island Development program offers research, advice and training in areas such as energy policy, disaster preparedness and local private-sector development. These ventures are only one aspect of regional cooperation: the modern Pacific has a complex network of organizations and conferences, under a dazzling array of acronyms, that cover a vast range of interests. At the heart of this web are two major organizations – the South Pacific Commission, founded in 1947, and the South Pacific Forum, founded in 1971.

The South Pacific Commission was set up with the aim of promoting regional economic and social development. Its membership includes island states and territories together with outside countries that have territorial interests in the region – 27 in all, though in 1993 Britain announced its intention of withdrawing for reasons of economy. The Commission has ongoing programs in areas such as rural development and technology, food, marine resources, community health and education and environmental management. It provides technical advice and assistance, and runs projects. Its funding comes from its members and as grants from aid-providers. The South Pacific Conference meets annually to consider the Commission's work program and budget.

Largely at the insistence of France, politically sensitive issues such as nuclear testing were kept off the Commission's agenda. Dissatisfaction with this situation was instrumental in bringing about the creation of the South Pacific Forum, which provides a setting in which the independent and self-governing countries of the South Pacific (including Australia and New Zealand) can meet annually to discuss matters of mutual importance. The Forum Secretariat (formerly known as the South Pacific Bureau for Economic Cooperation, or SPEC) is also involved in the promotion of cooperative projects. It has recently been involved in telecommunications development. Intergovernmental organizations, particularly those linked to the South Pacific Commission or the Forum, proliferated to such an extent that in 1988 the South Pacific Organizations Coordinating Committee (SPOCC) came into being to try to rationalize their relations and defuse possible tensions.

A nuclear-free zone

Through no will of the island peoples, the Pacific has played a significant role in the development of nuclear weaponry. Between 1946 and 1958 a series of nuclear devices, including the first hydrogen bombs, were exploded at Enewetak and Bikini atolls in the Micronesian territories placed under the trusteeship of the United States. The United States and Britain carried out further bomb tests at other sites in the Pacific, in particular Christmas Island, now in Kiribati, and Maralinga in Australia, in the 1950s and early 1960s. Questions continue to be asked about the effects of these early tests and the responsibilities of the nuclear powers involved towards those who may have been affected by their testing programs.

Perhaps the strongest feelings of recent years have been directed toward French nuclear policy in the region. After losing control of test sites in its former colony of Algeria in 1962, France shifted its testing program to French Polynesia. Strong protests from governments of the region eventually brought an end to atmospheric tests, but underground testing continued, as did the protests. In 1985 the *Rainbow Warrior* incident marked a low point in France's relations with many Pacific nations. With changing international conditions, the French placed a moratorium on testing in French Polynesia in 1992, but the decision to embark on a new series of underground tests in 1995 brought a fierce renewal of the controversy.

Hopes for an end to the use of Pacific test sites depend upon the broader prospects for a general test ban. In 1986 the majority of South Pacific Forum countries agreed a nuclear-free zone treaty, the Treaty of Rarotonga. Of the five established nuclear-weapons-owning states, only China and the former Soviet Union complied with the invitation to sign protocols to the treaty; France, the United States and Britain held back. Nuclear weapons do not present the only cause for concern about radiation in the region. Nuclear-powered ships and submarines have jettisoned their reactors in the Pacific on several occasions, while there is perennial anxiety that the ocean may at a future date be used for storing nuclear waste. Nuclear issues provided an early focus for environmental concern in the Pacific, both for governments

Global climate change
The whole of the Island Pacific will be affected by the broader effects of global warming. As the map indicates, countries made up of low-lying atolls, such as Kiribati and Tuvalu, will be especially vulnerable to the rise in the average sea-level caused by the warming and expansion of seawater and melting of the icecaps. But even the larger and higher islands can expect impacts in their coastal areas – with potential threats to agricultural land and fisheries as well as to areas of settlement and to infrastructure. The rate and extent of the rise remain uncertain, but the International Panel on Climate Change predicts that the average sea-level will increase between 3 and 10 centimeters per decade. The impact of a continuing rise on island countries has to be viewed in conjunction with the effects of storm surges and cyclones, which may themselves be intensified by climatic change. In the early 1990s the highest tides almost reached the urban area on Majuro in the Marshall Islands. At the same time, it is possible that changing climatic patterns will intensify the problems of islands already prone to droughts, such as some of those in Kiribati.

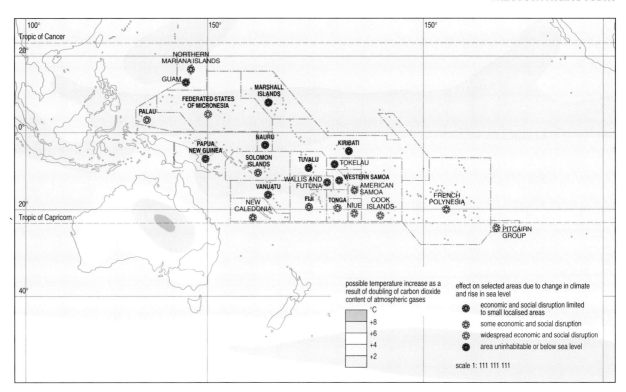

possible temperature increase as a result of doubling of carbon dioxide content of atmospheric gases

°C
+8
+6
+4
+2

effect on selected areas due to change in climate and rise in sea level

⚙ economic and social disruption limited to small localised areas

⚙ some economic and social disruption

⚙ widespread economic and social disruption

⚙ area uninhabitable or below sea level

scale 1: 111 111 111

and for international and regional organizations such as Greenpeace or the Nuclear-Free and Independent Pacific Movement. The region's churches have also been active in the antinuclear debate.

Environmental issues

Effective conservation strategies are urgently required to protect the Pacific's vulnerable island habitats. Management of coastal areas is a vital issue in the Pacific islands – shorelines, reefs and lagoons are the breeding grounds of many plant and animal species, but they are threatened by the fertilizer and pesticide run-offs from agriculture and by sewage and other wastes from urban and tourist developments. Coral reefs are particularly sensitive to pollution, which clouds seawater, inhibiting the growth of corals by depriving them of sunlight. Growing human populations create pressure to expand agricultural production onto marginal land and to intensify cropping, bringing increased risks of soil degradation. Marine resources need to be conserved by the sensible management of fish stocks, with the avoidance of overfishing. Here the Forum Fisheries Agency makes an important contribution to conservation through its information gathering and advisory service.

The pace of deforestation has been rapid in the Melanesian islands, and the need for foreign exchange in countries with few or no exports to rival the value of timber makes it difficult to resist pressure from powerful multinational interests to continue logging. Nevertheless, governments are increasingly aware of the need for greater knowledge and protection of forest resources, and for the development of sustainable forestry practices. Replanting schemes exist in a number of countries, but are unlikely to keep pace with the rate of destruction and cannot hope to replace the species diversity that has already been lost. Proposed strategies include the development of forest reserves and of plantation-grown timber resources. There are moves to improve environmental education at the local level. One interesting innovation has been the use in Papua New Guinea and the Solomon Islands of the *wokabout somil* (walkabout sawmill). These small

portable sawmills allow local people to cut timber from their own lands selectively, rather than signing away timber rights to large companies for more extensive and destructive operations.

In recent years the threat to the environment from the effects of global warming have raised particular concern in Oceania. Scientists have predicted that if emissions of carbon dioxide and other greenhouse gases into the atmosphere continue at present rates, global temperatures will heat up, causing the thermal expansion of seawater. The consequent rise in the sea-level would have serious implications for the low-lying countries of the region, especially those including the Marshall Islands, Tuvalu, Tokelau and Kiribati – that are largely made up of atolls. There is disagreement about the likely pace and extent of the climatic changes caused by global warming, but even moderate rises would have damaging effects for islands lying only a few meters above current mean sea-level. One of the first things to happen will be that groundwater is displaced by rising salt water, threatening wells and crops. Global warming may also bring about changes in weather systems, with more frequent and more damaging cyclones. As minor energy users and minor producers of greenhouse gases, the Pacific states have done little to contribute to the problem of global warming, but they are likely to be one of the major sufferers from its effects. It is an issue that they are understandably keen to bring to the forefront of international debate and policy-making.

In the last 10 to 15 years Pacific island governments have become increasingly aware of the need to take an integrated view of development and environmental issues. National environmental management programs are under consideration. The South Pacific Regional Environmental Program (SPREP) has been in existence since 1980 and has developed its own action plan and work program. The Convention for the Protection of the Natural Resources and Environment of the South Pacific Region (SPREP Convention) came into force in 1990, with protocols prohibiting nuclear testing and radioactive waste dumping at sea. The work to protect the Pacific environment has only

just begun, and there are immediate economic pressures working against the drive for greater sustainability. Nevertheless, the activities of SPREP, of some governments and of certain nongovernmental organizations such as the Solomon Islands Development Trust do hold out hope for the future. Grassroots environmental education is seen as one area of great importance. There is a growing willingness to learn from traditional environmental knowledge, especially in areas such as fishing and agriculture. Yet on fundamental issues such as the nuclear presence and global warming, action is limited to the degree of persuasive pressure that Pacific governments can exert on states outside the region.

Toward the Pacific Way

Outside the region, particularly in the industrialized nations of the northern hemisphere, the dominant image of the Pacific islands still emphasizes their supposed "timelessness". Tourist brochures and travel literature contrast the qualities of island village life, cultural continuity and unspoilt natural beauty with the problems of the industrialized world. But as much as any other region of the world in the late 20th century, the islands of the Pacific are linked into a world economy and a network of regional and global political influences, with all the pressure for social change that entails. Throughout their history the peoples of the Pacific have been the active explorers of new geographical worlds and new ideas. They have drawn on their cultural reserves to adapt to new circumstances, whether these resulted from a move to new lands, changes within their own societies, or the appearance

of new peoples. During the colonial period, they showed an ability to incorporate aspects of other cultures in ways that were relevant to their own. In the modern world external pressures and influences are growing. The issues that have to be confronted lie beyond the scope of national governments, let alone local communities, to deal with.

The slogan "the Pacific Way" was first heard in 1970 in a speech by the then Prime Minister of Fiji, Ratu Sir Kamisese Mara. Since then it has been frequently used to convey the qualities and aims common to Pacific island societies. It was the title chosen for the report submitted on behalf of 14 Pacific island countries to the United Nations Conference on Environment and Development (the Rio Conference) of 1992; this spoke of the value placed on cooperation and consensus as part of the traditional approach to problem-solving in the region and went on to say that a consensus approach was now being developed to confront the common environmental challenges facing the Pacific island societies. In the political life of the region, the slogan has inevitably been molded to particular contexts, and those who have looked for constant elements have sometimes been disappointed. Political events such as the Fiji coups or the conflict on Bougainville have seemed to threaten the ideas of tolerance and decision-making by consensus that lie behind its intent. Yet, whatever the limitations of the slogan, the Pacific Way does represent something important about the modern Pacific – a growing sense of interconnectedness and the wish for a regional identity that grows out of the social experience of the Pacific peoples themselves.

Above A supermarket at Tari in the Highlands of Papua New Guinea. For thousands of years the Highland peoples have obtained goods from other parts of New Guinea by means of personal trading networks. They are now part of an impersonal global economy that supplies new goods and services, changes perceived needs and encourages the expansion of cash-generating enterprise. Few Pacific people would wish to deny themselves the benefits of these connections to a global market. But how to balance their uptake against the pressures of the system – toward export money-earning, toward social change in many forms – is part of the challenge that currently confronts all the island nations.

GLOSSARY

Aboriginal/Aborigines A term used of indigenous peoples, specifically applied to the first inhabitants of Australia. Estimates of the number of Aboriginal peoples living in Australia before British colonization range from 500,000 to 3 million. They were divided into 500 tribal groups speaking more than 250 languages. The term Aboriginal/Aborigine, therefore, is generic. Today an Aboriginal person is defined as "someone of Aboriginal descent who identifies as such and is recognized by their Aboriginal community to be so". Having once comprised 100 percent of the continent's population, Aborigines today make up about 2 percent of the peoples of Australia.

ahu On Easter Island, a temple or place of worship, in particular the large stone platform on which ancestral statues stand. The term is also applied elsewhere in Eastern POLYNESIA to the platforms that form part of *MARAE,* or temple complexes.

antipodes Literally, with feet opposite; persons dwelling on the other side of the world. Commonly used as a synonym for Australia and New Zealand.

Anzac Acronym for the Australian and New Zealand Army Corps, which was formed in 1914 in response to Britain's appeal to its colonies for troops to fight in the war against Germany. The Anzacs' first campaign was fought against the Turks at Gallipoli in 1915. The date of the landing, 25 April, is unofficially observed as Australia's national day.

ANZUS Pact A security treaty made between Australia, New Zealand and the United States in 1951. It was the first external relations agreement signed by Australia and New Zealand that did not involve Britain. Its guarantees have greater symbolic than actual force. Each of the signing countries acknowledges that "an armed attack in the Pacific Area on any of the Parties would be dangerous to its own peace and safety and declares that it would act to meet the common danger in accordance with its constitutional processes." New Zealand withdrew from the treaty in 1984 after denying docking facilities to US nuclear ships.

Aotearoa The MAORI name for New Zealand, commonly translated as "land of the long white cloud". Another translation renders it as "long daylight". It is proposed as an alternative title for the nation.

Aranda (*also* **Arrernte**) The name given to the ABORIGINAL people of central Australia.

ariki The term for a paramount chief among the MAORI and a number of other POLYNESIAN societies.

Arnhem Land The area of northern Australia running from Rose River in the south to Wessel Island in the north and from the South Alligator River in the west to Groote Eylandt in the east. It is rich in ABORIGINAL culture, religion and art.

assisted migration/passage Refers to subsidies and other sponsorship schemes that encouraged immigration to Australia and New Zealand; first used to send "free" (that is, non-convict) settlers to Swan River in Western Australia (1829).

atoll CORAL REEFS that break the surface of the water as a circular chain of low-lying islands and enclose a shallow lagoon.

Australian Capital Territory (ACT) A federal territory in which Canberra, Australia's national capital, is situated. The site was acquired from NEW SOUTH WALES in 1911.

Australoid A term first used in the 19th century to define the original peoples of Australia, once held to be a distinct racial group but now believed to be related to other indigenous groups in south Asia and the Pacific region.

Austronesian A language family of more than 800 related languages found largely in Southeast Asia and the Pacific. They include the languages of POLYNESIA and MICRONESIA as well as some 400 languages in MELANESIA. Seafaring skills assisted the Austronesian-speaking ancestral peoples in their dispersion across the Pacific, a process that began c. 4000–3000 BC.

Batavia The Dutch trading port on Java, founded in 1619, which served as the commercial and administrative headquarters of the powerful Dutch East India Company in Southeast Asia. Today, as Jakarta, it is the capital city of Indonesia.

"big man" A term often applied to MELANESIAN leaders who attain their position by their achievements, skills and the manipulation of wealth rather than simply as a result of inherited status.

blackbirding Used popularly in the late 19th century to describe the illegal capture and indenture of MELANESIAN for work on the cane fields of northern Queensland, Australia. See also INDENTURED LABOR.

boomerang A V-shaped ABORIGINAL throwing stick used for hunting, ceremony and sport. Some, but not all, were aerodynamically designed to return to the thrower.

Botany Bay An inlet on the eastern coast of Australia, about 8 kilometers south of present-day Sydney, where James Cook first landed in Australia. It was recommended by Cook and Joseph Banks as the site for the first penal settlement, but proved unsuitable. PORT JACKSON was chosen instead. Botany Bay remained the popular name in British and Australian vernacular for the colony of New South Wales; more specifically, the place of exile for transported felons.

bushrangers Criminals living in the Australian bush, from where they raided settlements. Originally used of escaped convicts, but by the 1850s bushrangers were more akin to highwaymen, by-products of the southeastern Australian goldrushes. The agrarian unrest of the 1870s and 1880s bred further bushrangers. Ned Kelly's gang are the best-known examples of this later type of rural bandit.

cargo cult The name given to movements, religious and often millenarian in nature, formed among indigenous peoples in response to colonization. Used specifically of religious cults in New Guinea and other parts of MELANESIA whose followers believed that their ritual observances would result in the arrival of western consumer goods, or cargo, the overturning of the colonial social order, and the end of the world.

Chamorros The indigenous people of the Mariana Islands. Their culture was virtually eradicated during the Spanish occupation of the islands between 1565 and 1898.

Commonwealth of Australia The official title of the federation of Australian states (formerly self-governing colonies) that came into being on 1 January 1901.

coral reef A barrier of limestone rock formed by the accumulation of the skeletons of millions of coral polyps. Reefs grow as polyps build on the shells of dead generations.

corroboree A meeting of tribal ABORIGINAl groups held to discuss important matters and to participate in ceremonial and other rituals.

cultural cringe A term first used in the 1950s to describe the colonial tendency to defer to the larger metropolitan cultures of Europe.

didgeridoo (*also* **didjeridu**) An ABORIGINAL wind instrument made out of a hollowed branch.

digger A popular name for an Australian male, an informal term of address between Australian men. Its origins are unclear, though it was probably first used of miners on the Australian goldfields. During World War I it became the generic label for any Australian soldier.

dreaming The commonly accepted term used to describe the creation myths of the ABORIGINES. According to the dreaming, the world existed in a mundane form until given features and significance during the creation period. The land became sacred, totems were formed, and animals and plants came into being.

emancipist In the transportation period, originally described a convict who had been pardoned by the governor but was later extended to any convict whose terms of sentence had expired.

exchange system A structured and repeated reciprocal transfer of valuables and commodities between individuals or groups. Some Pacific exchange systems have a strong element of ceremonial.

Extended Economic Zone (EEZ) A zone of up to 200 nautical miles around their shores within which, under the international Law of the Sea, states can claim sovereign rights to explore, exploit, conserve and manage natural resources.

fae The "stone money" of Yap. Large stone disks with a central hole that were items of wealth used in ceremonial EXCHANGE.

First Fleet The name given to the 11 ships that carried the first white settlers (convicts, marines and civilians) to Australia in 1788.

FLNKS (*Front de Libération Nationale, Kanak et Socialiste*) The major pro-independence grouping of New Caledonia, an umbrella organization incorporating a number of smaller groups.

free association A form of voluntary political linkage between a country and a former colonial power; a political status involving extensive self-government but falling short of full independence, within which the former colonial power has certain limited and defined continuing rights and responsibilities.

godhouse A structure formerly found in a number of POLYNESIAN societies that acted as a repository for images of gods and objects associated with them.

Gondwanaland The ancient southern supercontinent that incorporated the present-day landmasses of South America, Africa, the Indian Subcontinent, parts of Southeast Asia, Australia and Antarctica. It began to break up about 200 million years ago. The last parts to break away were Antarctica and Australia about 95 million years ago. Some ABORIGINAL groups choose to call Australia Gondwanaland.

Gubber ABORIGINAL creole for a white person that may derive from "governor", normally restricted to the eastern seaboard of Australia.

Gunwinggu One of the ABORIGINAL peoples of Arnhem Land, whose area is defined by the Liverpool and East Alligator rivers.

hapu A MAORI tribal section or sub-tribe; a descent group lying between the tribe and the extended family, traditionally occupying a specific area of tribal territory and cooperating more regularly in a wider range of activities than the tribe as a whole.

Heidelberg school A group of Australian artists of the late 19th century who experimented with impressionism and painting *en plain air* and are credited with being the first distinctive school of Australian art.

indentured labor A system of recruiting workers by indenturing them to a person or industry and arranging their transportation, usually in rudimentary conditions, to the place of work. Convictism is sometimes referred to as a form of indentured labor.

iron gangs Convict labor gangs sent to work on open-air public works. They were restrained by leg irons.

kainga An undefended MAORI village or settlement.

Kanak An indigenous MELANESIAN inhabitant of New Caledonia.

kava A drink made from the pounded or chewed roots of the plant *Piper methysticum* infused in water, which produces relaxation and mild euphoria. Particularly in western POLYNESIA, its ceremonial consumption is part of the rituals of status and chieftainship.

kula A ceremonial EXCHANGE SYSTEM of the d'Entrecasteaux archipelago of southeastern Papua New Guinea. Armshells and necklace valuables pass between partners in a ring of exchange relationships.

kurdaitcha Sorcerer figures in ABORIGINAL society. They possessed the power to "sing" to death people who had been identified as wrongdoers or were punished as part of retribution for wrongdoing by clansmen and women.

Lapita ware A pottery tradition that, from around 1600 BC, spread through the island chains of MELANESIA, reaching Fiji, Tonga and Samoa. It has importance in establishing the migrations of the peoples thought to be the ancestors of the POLYNESIANS.

latte Parallel rows of capped standing stones found in the Mariana Islands, believed to have been supports for houses.

London Missionary Society A pentecostal evangelical movement founded in 1795 to send missionaries to the Pacific.

malanggan ceremonies Ceremonies honoring the recent dead and ancestors held in New Ireland, Papua New

Guinea. Intricate painted carvings representing ancestors and spirits are produced for these occasions.
mana A POLYNESIAN concept of power and prestige. To have *mana* is to have authority and to be able to show effective power. *Mana* can be inherited and is related to social rank, but can be enhanced or lost through one's actions. It can be seen as having supernatural dimensions.
maneaba An open-sided community meeting house in Kiribati.
Mangaasi ware A pottery tradition of central Vanuatu existing from around 700 BC to between 1200 and 1600 AD. Decoration of the earlier examples include relief work and incised patterns.
Maori The indigenous POLYNESIAN people of AOTEAROA-New Zealand whose ancestors settled the country between 800 and 1000 AD. *Maori* is an eastern Polynesian word meaning "native" or "of this place". Cook Islanders also describe themselves as *Maori,* while Tahitians use the similar *Ma'ohi.*
Marianas Red A thin red-slipped pottery, sometimes with incised lime-filled patterns, found in the archaeological record of the Mariana Islands, probably dating between 1500 BC and 800 AD.
marae In the islands of central eastern POLYNESIA, a traditional ceremonial center, an open-air place of worship for the former gods. Among the MAORI, a local ceremonial center, normally with an open space in front of a meeting house, where a range of social rituals, weddings, funerals and public meetings are carried out.
matai The titled head of an extended family in Samoa.
mateship A creed, almost an article of faith, among Australian males, based on egalitarian and socialist principles, that those in any need whatever will always be helped out.
Maui POLYNESIAN culture hero and trickster, stories of whom are found in many Polynesian societies. Exploits attributed to him include fishing up land from the sea and procuring fire for humankind. In MAORI myth he dies trying to overcome the death goddess.
Melanesia One of three major cultural regions of the Pacific (see also MICRONESIA and POLYNESIA) lying in the western Pacific. It includes the island of New Guinea (Papua New Guinea and Irian Jaya), Solomon Islands, Vanuatu, New Caledonia and Fiji.
merino A breed of sheep, originating in Spain, that produces a heavy fleece of exceptional quality. Introduced into Australia in 1797, merinos were the foundation of the Australian fine wool industry.
Micronesia One of the three major cultural regions of the Pacific (see also MELANESIA and POLYNESIA). Its many small islands lie in the western Pacific north of Melanesia and include Kiribati, Nauru, Guam, Palau, Federated States of Micronesia, Marshall Islands, and Northern Mariana Islands.
Miglew A name given to white people by the ABORIGINES of the eastern seaboard.
moa The name given by the MAORI to a group of large flightless birds their ancestors found living in AOTEAROA that ranged from the turkey-sized *Anomalopteryx* to the huge *Dinornis maximus*, well over 3 meters tall. Extensive hunting by the Maori was almost certainly an important factor in the extinction of all *moa* species.
moko The art of tattooing among the MAORI. Traditionally, patterns were cut deeply with a tattooing comb or chisel.

New Holland The name given to the western part of the Australian landmass by 17th-century Dutch mariners. Later extended to the whole continent, its use did not finally disappear until about the 1820s, by which time the name Australia had replaced it.
New South Wales One of the constituent states of the COMMONWEALTH OF AUSTRALIA. It was under this name that James Cook took possession of the eastern half of the Australian continent for Britain in 1770, reaffirmed by Arthur Phillip in 1788. New South Wales originally comprised the entire British colony of Australia. Van Diemen's Land (Tasmania) was separated from it in 1825, Victoria in 1851 and Queensland in 1859. Western Australia was annexed as a separate colony in 1829, South Australia in 1836. The Northern Territory, part of New South Wales from 1824, was annexed to South Australia in 1863, and land for the AUSTRALIAN CAPITAL TERRITORY was transferred to the Commonwealth in 1911.
New South Wales Corps An army unit raised in Britain in 1789 specifically for policing duties in the convict colony.
New Zealand Company Active in the 1830s in promoting ASSISTED MIGRATION from Britain to New Zealand. The Company purchased large tracts of land for settlement from the MAORI tribes in the Cook Strait area, often by dubious means.
Nyoongar (also **Nungar**) The name, literally meaning "human being", applied to the ABORIGINAL peoples of southwestern Australia.

pa Fortified settlements of the MAORI with a variety of defensive features, including earthworks, ditches, palisades and fighting stages, that made use of natural features such as ridges and promontories. They include both permanent settlements and strongholds used in time of danger.
pakeha The MAORI name for white people.
Panaramittee A type of ABORIGINAL rock engraving from South Australia found in extensive galleries, usually consisting of abstract maze-like designs.
payback A system of ABORIGINAL tribal retribution for the punishing of wrongdoing.
Polynesia The largest of the three major cultural regions of the Pacific (see also MELANESIA and MICRONESIA). With the exception of some outlier islands, the area of Polynesian settlement falls within a great triangle, its corners lying at Hawaii, Easter Island and AOTEAROA-New Zealand.
Port Jackson An inlet on the southeastern coast of Australia first sighted and named by Captain Cook. Today part of Sydney, it was chosen as the site of the first British settlement in Australia after BOTANY BAY was found to be unsuitable.
Proto-Polynesian The presumed language of the ancestral POLYNESIANS, for which some vocabulary has been constructed through the comparison of existing Polynesian languages.

rangatira Those of chiefly status in MAORI society, sometimes loosely described as "aristocrats", likely to be closely related to the chief of their *HAPU* and outranking commoners. Similar terms are found elsewhere in eastern POLYNESIA.
rongorongo A script from Easter Island, of uncertain age. The symbols that make up the script are found carved in rows on wooden *rongorongo* tablets. They have not been certainly translated and possibly the symbols do not represent true writing but acted as memory aids in the chanting of oral traditions and genealogy.

sawei An EXCHANGE SYSTEM of the Caroline Islands, involving canoe voyaging to bring tribute to the island of Yap from other islands of the chain.
sennit Cordage produced from the fiber of the outer husk of coconuts.
Scottish Martyrs The popular name for five political prisoners found guilty of sedition in Edinburgh in 1793 and 1794 and transported to Australia.
secondary punishment A system instituted to punish convicts who had reoffended after transportation to Australia.
selectors Small farmers who took up parcels of land in the wake of a series of Land Acts in the second half of the 19th century aimed at breaking up the power of the SQUATTERS. Many failed, often because the land they were given was unsuitable for farming.
South Pacific Commission A nonpolitical consultative agency, established in 1947, that provides advice, training and assistance to promote economic, social, cultural and environmental improvements in the 22 Pacific states and territories that make up its member countries.
South Pacific Forum An intergovernmental forum for the independent and self-governing countries of the Pacific, established in 1971. It holds regular meetings and the Forum Secretariat (formerly the South Pacific Bureau for Economic Cooperation) coordinates projects and provides a basis for cooperation among its members.
squatters Originally former convicts who occupied land without authority, the term was later applied to pastoralists who built up large properties of grazing land by occupying them before they had been officially gazetted. By the 1860s the squatters were the most influential economic and social group in Australia, particularly NEW SOUTH WALES and Victoria.
swagmen, swaggies Itinerant rural laborers who traveled from property to property in Australia. Their rugged individualism and practical ways made them a symbol of national identity.

***tambaran* cults** Spirit cults of the Sepik region of northern Papua New Guinea. Representations of spirits may be stored in a village *haus tambaran,* sometimes described as a "spirit house" or "men's house".
tapa Barkcloth, made by beating together strips of the fibrous inner bark of the paper mulberry and other trees.
tapu A POLYNESIAN term for that which is sacred or ritually restricted. *Tapu* offers supernatural protection for prestigious people, places, events and objects. The source of the English word "taboo".
terra australis incognita The Latin name, meaning "unknown southern land", marked on European maps before the discovery of Australia denoting the presence of an imaginary southern continent.
terra nullius A Latin term meaning "land belonging to no one" that was applied by the British to Australia, thereby legalizing British possession and depriving the ABORIGINES of rightful claim to their traditional tribal lands. *Terra nullius* was overturned in 1992 when native title was recognized.
terretoires d'outre-mer **(TOMS)** French overseas territories, regarded as integral parts of France, though with special arrangements that allow some degree of self-government. French Polynesia, New Caledonia and Wallis and Futuna have this status in the Pacific.
ticket of leave A system of reward and release that licensed convicts to secure work independent of the public works programs.
tohunga Among the MAORI, an expert or specialist. This may be in artistic or craft skills such as those of the carver or tattooist, but the term is strongly linked with priestly or ritual expertise. Similar titles (eg. *ta'unga, kahuna)* are found elsewhere in POLYNESIA.
Torres Strait Islanders The indigenous MELANESIAN inhabitants of the approximately 70 Torres Strait Islands. Different in culture and society from the ABORIGINES, they are classified as indigenous Australians because the islands are politically part of Australia.
trust territory A territory administered by another country under the supervision of the United Nations Trusteeship Council. A trusteeship agreement between the UN and the United States created the Trust Territory of the Pacific Islands in 1947. This took in most of MICRONESIA (with the exception of Nauru and what is now Kiribati). By the mid 1990s all the states of the former Trust Territory of the Pacific Islands had emerged to new political statuses.
Tu'i Tonga The title, from about the 10th century, of the paramount ruler of Tonga. It was abolished after its last holder died in 1865, its dignity passing to the continuing title of King or Queen of Tonga.
tutua The commoner group in traditional MAORI society.

Uluru The ABORIGINAL (Matijula) and, since 1985, official name of the giant monolith, 2.5 kilometers long and 1.5 wide, that emerges out of the deserts of central Australia, formerly known as Ayers Rock.

waddi (or **waddy**) A club-like wooden weapon used by Australian ABORIGINES.
Wadjella (also **Wadjulla**) The NYOONGAR name for a white person, probably a creole form of "white fella". It has become widespread throughout Australia but is not universally found.
Weipa An ABORIGINAL community on the west coast of the Cape York Peninsula.
White Australia Policy The euphemistic name for the policy deriving from Australia's Restrictive Immigration Act that, from 1901, excluded non-European migrants, chiefly by means of a dictation test. It ceased to be enforced in practice in the 1940s and 1950s but was not officially abandoned until the 1970s, when it was replaced by non-discriminatory immigration legislation.
Wik An ABORIGINAL people indigenous to western Cape York Peninsula.
woomera An ABORIGINAL throwing stick used for hunting and in ceremonies.

yaqona The Fijian term for *KAVA*. Sometimes given as *yanggona*, which more closely reflects pronunciation.

BIBLIOGRAPHY

AUSTRALIA AND NEW ZEALAND

Indigenous culture: Australia
Geoffrey Blainey, *The Triumph of the Nomads*, Melbourne, 1975.
G. Bardon, *Papanyu Tula: Art of the Western Desert*, Ringwood, Victoria, 1991.
R.M. and C.H. Berndt, *The World of the First Australians: Aboriginal Tradition Life – Past and Present*, Canberra, 1988.
Noel Butlin, *Our Original Aggression: Aboriginal Populations in South Eastern Australia 1788–1850*, Sydney, 1983.
Noel Butlin, *The Economics of the Dreaming*, Sydney, 1994.
Michael Cannon, *Who Killed the Koories*, Melbourne, 1990.
Max Charlesworth, Howard Morphy, Dianne Bell, Kenneth Maddock (eds), *Religion in Aboriginal Australia: An Anthology*, St Lucia, Queensland, 1984.
J. D. Clark, *Aboriginal Languages and Clans: An Historical Atlas of Western and Central Victoria*, Clayton, South Australia, 1988.
R. W. M. Dixon, *Languages of Australia*, Cambridge, UK, 1980.
R. W. M. Dixon, *Words of our Country*, St Lucia, Queensland, 1991.
J. Dodson (ed), *Native Lands: Prehistory and Environmental Usage in Australia and the South-West Pacific*, Melbourne, 1992.
Josephine Flood, *The Moth Hunters: Aboriginal Prehistory of the Australian Alps*, Canberra, 1980.
Josephine Flood, *Archaeology of the Dreamtime*, Sydney, 1983.
M. Lands, *Mayi: Some Bush Fruits of Dampierland*, Broome, Western Australia, 1987.
Robert Layton, *Australian Rock Art: A New Synthesis*, Melbourne, 1992.
Kenneth Maddock, *The Australian Aborigines: A Portrait of their Society*, Ringwood, Victoria, 1982.
A. M. Moyle, *Aboriginal Sound Instruments*, Canberra, 1985.
D. J. Mulvaney, *The Prehistory of Australia*, Ringwood, Victoria, 1975.
D. J. Mulvaney and J. P. White (eds), *Australians to 1788*, Sydney, 1987.
N. Peterson (ed), *Tribes and Boundaries*, Canberra, 1976.
Peter Read, *A Hundred Years War: The Wiradjuri People and the State*, Canberra, 1988.
N. B. Tindale, *Aboriginal Tribes of Australia: Their Terrain, Environmental Controls and Proper Names*, Canberra, 1974.
Peter Ucko (ed), *Form in Indigenous Art: Schematisation in the Art of Aboriginal Australia and Prehistoric Europe*, Canberra, 1977.

Colonial history
Peter Adams, *Fatal Necessity: British Intervention in New Zealand*, Auckland, 1977.
James Belich, *The New Zealand Wars and the Victorian Interpretation of Racial Conflict*, Auckland, 1986.
Geoffrey Bolton (ed), *The Oxford History of Australia*, Melbourne, 1994.
Tim Bonyhady, *Burke and Wills: from Melbourne to Myth*, Sydney, 1991.
Richard Broome, *Aboriginal Australians: Black Responses to White Dominance*, Sydney, 1982.
K. S. Inglis, *The Australian Colonists*, Melbourne, 1974.
Noel Loos, *Invasion and Resistance: Aboriginal-European Relations on the North Queensland Frontier*, Canberra, 1982.
D. F. McKenzie, *Oral Culture, Literacy and Print in Early New Zealand: the Treaty of Waitangi*, Wellington, 1985.
Stephen Nicholas (ed), *Convict Workers: Reinterpreting Australian History*, Cambridge, UK, 1988.
W. H. Oliver and B. R. Williams, *The Oxford History of New Zealand*, Wellington, 1981.
Claudia Orange, *The Treaty of Waitangi*, Wellington, 1981.

Jock Phillips, *A Man's Country: The Image of the Pakeha Male, a History*, Auckland 1990.
Ian Pool, *The Maori Population of New Zealand 1769–1971*, Auckland, 1977.
Peter Read, *A Hundred Years War: the Wiradjuri People and the State*, Canberra, 1982.
Henry Reynolds (ed), *Dispossession: Black Australians and White Invaders*, Sydney, 1989.
Henry Reynolds, *Frontier: Aborigines, Settlers and the Land*, Sydney, 1987.
Henry Reynolds, *The Law of the Land*, Ringwood, Victoria, 1987.
Henry Reynolds, *The Other Side of the Frontier*, Ringwood, Victoria, 1982.
Tom Ryan and Bill Parham, *The Colonial New Zealand Wars*, Wellington, 1986.
Graham Seal, *Ned Kelly in Popular Tradition*, Melbourne, 1980.
Keith Sinclair, *A History of New Zealand*, Auckland, 1988.
Keith Sinclair (ed), *The Oxford Illustrated History of New Zealand*, Auckland, 1990.

Twentieth-century history
Roderick Alley (ed), *New Zealand and the Pacific*, Boulder, Western Australia, 1984.
Stephen Alomes, *A Nation At Last?* Sydney, 1988.
Paul Baker, *King and Country Call: New Zealanders, Conscription and the Great War*, Auckland, 1988.
Angela Ballara, *Proud to be White?: A Survey of Pakeha Prejudice in New Zealand*, Wellington, 1986.
C.E.W. Bean, *Anzac to Amiens*, Canberra, 1946.
David Bedggood, *Rich and Poor in New Zealand: A Critique of Class and Politics and Ideology in New Zealand*, Wellington, 1980.
Boyak, *Behind the Lines: the Lives of New Zealand Soldiers in the First World War*, Auckland, 1990.
Verity Burgman and Jenny Lee (eds), *The People's History of Australia since 1788*, Melbourne, 1988.
Peter Cochrane, *Simpson and the Donkey: the Making of a Legend*, Melbourne, 1992.
Peter Cleave, *The Sovereignty Game: Power, Knowledge and Reading the Treaty*, Wellington, 1989.
Ron Crocombe, *Pacific Neighbours: New Zealand's Relations with Other Pacific Islands: Aotearoa me Nga Moutere o te Moana Nui a Kiwa*, Christchurch, 1992.
Frank Crowley, *New History of Australia*, Melbourne, 1974.
David Day, *Reluctant Nation: Australia and the Allied Defeat of Japan 1942-1945*, Melbourne, 1992.
B. Easton, *Social Policy and the Welfare State in New Zealand*, Auckland, 1980.
Peter Firkins, *The Australians in Nine Wars: Waikato to Long Tan*, Adelaide, 1971.
Bill Gammage, *The Broken Years*, Ringwood, Victoria, 1987.
Robin Gerster, *Big Noting: the Heroic Theme in Australian War Writing*, Melbourne, 1987.
H. Gold, *New Zealand Politics in Perspective*, Auckland, 1985.
John Gould, *The Rake's Progress: the New Zealand Economy Since 1945*, Auckland, 1982.
Patricia Grimshaw, Marilyn Lake, Ann McGrath, Marion Quartly, *Creating a Nation*, Melbourne, 1994.
Kayleen M. Hazelhurst, *Political Expression and Ethnicity: Statecraft and Mobilization in the Maori World*, Westport, NZ, 1993.
Donald Horne, *The Australian People, Biography of a Nation*, Sydney, 1972.
Colin James, *New Territory: the Transformation of New Zealand, 1984–1992*, Wellington, 1993.
John Malony, *History of Australia*, Ringwood, Victoria, 1987.
Noel McLachlan, *Waiting for the Revolution*, Ringwood, Victoria, 1989.
Humphrey McQueen, *Gallipoli to Petrov: Arguing with Australian History*, Sydney, 1984.
Humphrey McQueen, *A New Britannia: Arguments Concerning the Social Origins of Australian Radicalism and Nationalism*, Ringwood, Victoria, 1986.

Richard Mulgan, *Democracy and Power in New Zealand*, Auckland, 1984.
Richard Mulgan, *Maori, Pakeha and Democracy*, Auckland, 1989.
Geoffrey Pemberton, *All the Way: Australia's Road to Vietnam*, Sydney, 1987.
Christopher Pugsley, *Gallipoli: The New Zealand Story*, Auckland, 1984.
John Rickard, *Australia: A Cultural History*, Melbourne, 1988.
Jane Ross, *The Myth of the Digger: Australian Soldiers in Two World Wars*, Sydney, 1985.
Paul Spoonley, *The Politics of Nostalgia: Racism and the Extreme Right in New Zealand*, Palmerston North, 1987.
Ranginui Walker, *Nga Tau Tohetohe: Years of Anger*, Auckland, 1988.
Ranginui Walker, *Ka Whawhai Tonu Matau: Struggle Without End*, Auckland, 1990.
Richard White, *Inventing Australia*, Sydney, 1981.
Dennis Winter, *25 April 1915: The Inevitable Tragedy*, St Lucia, Queensland, 1994.
A.T. Yarwood and M.J. Knowling, *Race Relations in Australia*, Sydney, 1982.

Contemporary society
Alan Atkinson, *The Muddleheaded Republic*, Melbourne, 1993.
Scott Bennett, *Aborigines and Political Power*, Sydney, London and Boston, 1989.
Gill Bottomley and Marie de Lepervanche (eds), *Ethnicity, Class and Gender in Australia*, Sydney, 1991.
Frank Brennan, *Sharing the Country: The Case for an Agreement between Black and White Australians*, 1991.
Council for Aboriginal Reconciliation, *Addressing Key Issues of Reconciliation*, Canberra, 1994.
Sarah Ferber, Chris Healy, Chris McAuliffe, *Beasts of Suburbia: Reinterpreting Cultures in the Australian Suburbs*, Melbourne, 1994.
David Headon *et al*, *Crown or Country: The Tradition of Australian Republicanism*, St Leonards, NSW, 1994.
Brian Hocking (ed), *Australia Towards 2000*, London, 1990.
Wayne Hudson and David Carter, *The Republicanism Debate*, Kensington, NSW, 1993.
Michael Gilding, *The Making and Breaking of the Australian Family*, Sydney, 1993.
Ann Gollan (ed), *Questions for the Nineties*, Sydney, 1990.
David Goodman, Dinny A'Hearn, Chris Wallace-Crabbe, *Multicultural Australia*, Melbourne, 1991.
Al Grassby, *Australian Republic*, Sydney, 1993.
Sneja Gunew, *Culture, Difference and the Arts*, St Leonards, NSW, 1994.
Philip Hayward (ed) *From Pop to Punk to Post Modernism: Popular Music and Australian Culture from the 1960s to the 1990s*, Sydney, 1992.
Colin James, *The Quiet Revolution: Turbulence and Transition in Contemporary New Zealand*, Wellington, 1986.
I. H. Kawharu (ed), *Waitangi: Maori and Pakeha Perspectives on the Treaty of Waitangi*, Auckland, 1989.
M. King, *Being Pakeha: An Encounter with New Zealand and the Maori Renaissance*, Auckland, 1986.
Stephen Levine and Vasil Raj, *Maori Political Perspectives: He Whakaaro Mari Mo Nga Ti Kanga Kawantanga*, Auckland, 1985.
Stuart Macintyre and Susan Janson, *Through White Eyes*, Sydney, 1990.
Hugh MacKay, *Reinventing Australia*, Sydney, 1993.
Andrew Markus, *Australian Race Relations*, St Leonards, NSW, 1994.
Ian Marsh, *Governing in the 1990s: An Agenda for the Decade*, Melbourne, 1993.
Peter McKinlay (ed), *Redistribution of Power? Devolution in New Zealand*, Wellington, 1990.
Joan Metge, *In and Out of Touch: Whakamaa in Cross Cultural Context*, Wellington, 1986.
Richard Nile (ed), *Australian Civilisation*, Melbourne, 1994.

Richard Nile (ed), *Immigration and the Politics of Ethnicity and Race in Australia and Britain*, London, 1991.
Richard Nile (ed), *Indigenous Rights in the Pacific and North America*, London, 1992.
Gay Ochiltree, *Children in Australian Families*, Melbourne, 1990.
Tim Rowse, *After Mabo*, Melbourne, 1994.
D. T. Rowland, *Ageing in Australia*, Melbourne 1991.
Andrew Sharp, *Justice and the Maori: Maori Claims in New Zealand Political Argument in the 1980s*, Auckland, 1991.

Art, culture and literature
Bill Ashcroft, Gareth Griffiths, Helen Tiffin, *The Empire Writes Back*, London, 1989.
Leigh Atsbury, *Sunlight and Shadow: Australian Impressionist Painters 1880–1900*, Sydney, 1989.
Michael Cannon, *Australia: Spirit of a Nation*, Melbourne, 1985.
John Carroll (ed), *Intruders in the Bush: The Australian Quest for Identity*, Melbourne, 1992.
Manning Clark, *The Quest for an Australian Identity*, St Lucia, Queensland, 1980.
Terry Colling, *Beyond Mateship: Understanding Australian Men*, Sydney, 1992.
Ronald Conway, *The Great Australian Stupor: An Interpretation of the Australian Way of Life*, Melbourne, 1985.
Ian Craven (ed), *Australian Popular Culture*, Cambridge, UK, 1994.
Geoffrey Dutton (ed), *The Literature of Australia*, Ringwood, Victoria, 1976.
Geoffrey Dutton, *Sun, Sea, Surf and Sand: The Myth of the Beach*, Melbourne, 1985.
John Fiske, Bob Hodge and Graeme Turner, *Myths of Oz - Readings in Australian Popular Culture*, Sydney, 1987.
Paul Foss, *Islands in the Stream: Myths of Place in Australian Culture*, Sydney, 1988.
Richard Haese, *Rebels and Precursors: The Revolutionary Years of Australian Art*, Ringwood, Victoria, 1988.
F. A. Hanson and L. Hanson, *Counterpoint in Maori Culture*, London, 1983.
Brian Head and James Walter (eds), *Intellectual Movements and Australian Society*, Melbourne, 1988.
Lauri Hergenhan (ed), *Penguin History of Australian Literature*, Ringwood, Victoria, 1988.
Witi Ihimaera, *Te Ao Marama: Regaining Aotearoa – Maori Writers Speak Out*, Auckland, 1993.
S. Jones, *Early Painters of Australia: 1788–1880*, Sydney, 1988.
Susan Magarey, Sue Rowley and Susan Sheridan, *Debutante Nation: Feminism Contests the 1890s*, Sydney, 1993.
Drusilla Modjeska, *Exiles at Home: Australian Women Writers 1925–1935*, Sydney, 1981.
David Myers, *The Bleeding Battlers from Ironbark: Australian Myths in Fiction and Film 1890s–1980s*, Rockhampton, Queensland, 1992.
David Novitz and Bill Willmott (eds), *Culture and Identity in New Zealand*, Wellington, 1989.
Kent Pearson, *Surfing Subcultures of Australia and New Zealand*, St Lucia, Queensland, 1979.
A. A. Phillips, *The Australian Tradition*, Melbourne, 1958.
Ian Reid, *Fiction and the Great Depression in Australia and New Zealand*, Sydney, 1981.
Ken Scarlett, *Australian Sculptors*, Melbourne, 1980.
Kay Schaffer, *Women and the Bush: Forces of Desire in the Australian Cultural Tradition*, Cambridge UK, 1988.
Graham Seal, *The Hidden Culture: Folklore in Australian Society*, Melbourne, 1989.
Geoffrey Serle, *From Deserts the Prophets Come*, Melbourne, 1973.
Adam Shoemaker, *Black Words, White Pages: Aboriginal Literature 1929–1988*, St Lucia, Queensland, 1990.
Keith Sinclair, *A Destiny Apart: New Zealand's Search for National Identity*, Wellington, 1986.
Bernard Smith and F. B. Smith, *Australian Painting*, Sydney, 1992.
F. B. Smith and S.L. Goldberg (eds), *Australian Cultural History*, Cambridge, UK, 1991.
G. Sturgeon, *The Development of Australian Sculpture*, London, 1978.

Elaine Thompson, *Fair Enough: The Politics of Egalitarianism in Australia*, Kensington, NSW, 1994.
Russel Ward, *The Australian Legend*, Melbourne, 1958 and subsequent edns.
Gillian Whitlock and David Carter (eds), *Images of Australia*, St Lucia, Queensland, 1992.
William H. Wilde, Joy Hooton, Barry Andrews, *The Oxford Companion to Australian Literature*, Melbourne, 1995.

THE PACIFIC ISLANDS
Archaeology and indigenous culture
W.H. Alkire, *An Introduction to the Peoples and Cultures of Micronesia*, California, 1977.
W.H. Alkire, *Coral Islanders*, Arlington Heights, Illinois, 1978
J. Allen, J. Golson and R. Jones (eds), *Sunda and Sahul: Prehistoric Studies in Southeast Asia, Melanesia and Australia*, London, 1977.
T. Bataua Batiri et al, *Kiribati: A Changing Atoll Culture*, Suva, Fiji, 1985.
T. Barrow, *The Art of Tahiti: and Neighbouring Society, Austral and Cook Islands*, London, 1979.
B. Brake, J. McNeish and D. Simmons, *Art of the Pacific*, Oxford, 1979.
P. Bellwood, *Man's Conquest of the Pacific*, Auckland, 1978.
P. Bellwood, *The Polynesians*, London, 1987.
J.M. Davidson, *The Prehistory of New Zealand*, Auckland 1984.
D.K. Feil, *The Evolution of Highland Papua New Guinea Societies*, Cambridge, UK, 1987.
B.R. Finney (ed), *Pacific Navigation and Voyaging*, Wellington, 1976.
R. Firth, *We, the Tikopia*, 1936, reprinted Boston, 1963.
T. Gladwin, *East is a Big Bird: Navigation and Logic on Pulawat Atoll*, Cambridge, Mass., 1970.
J. Golson (ed), *Polynesian Navigation*, Wellington, 1963.
M. Gondolier and M. Strathern (eds), *Big Men and Great Men: Personification of Power in Melanesia*, Cambridge, UK, 1991.
A.V.S. Hill and S.W. Serjeantson (eds), *The Colonisation of the Pacific: A Genetic Trail*, Oxford, 1989.
A. Howard and R. Borofsky (eds), *Developments in Polynesian Ethnology*, Honolulu, 1989.
G. Irwin, *The Prehistoric Exploration and Colonisation of the Pacific*, Cambridge, UK, 1992.
J.D. Jennings (ed), *The Prehistory of Polynesia*, Cambridge, Mass., 1979.
P.V. Kirch, *The Evolution of the Polynesian Chiefdoms*, Cambridge, UK, 1984.
P.V. Kirch (ed), *Island Societies: Archaeological Approaches to Evolution and Transformation*, Cambridge, UK, 1986.
D. Lewis, *We, the Navigators: The Ancient Art of Land-finding in the Pacific*, Canberra, 1972.
B. Malinowski, *Argonauts of the Western Pacific: An Account of Native Enterprise and Adventure in the Archipelagos of Melanesian New Guinea*, New York, 1922, reprinted London 1978.
J. Metge, *The Maoris of New Zealand: Rautahi*, London, 1976.
W.N. Morgan, *Prehistoric Architecture in Micronesia*, Austin, Texas, 1988.
D.L. Oliver, *Oceania: The Native Cultures of Australia and the Pacific Islands*, Honolulu, 1989.
A.J. Strathern, *The Rope of Moka: Big-men and Ceremonial Exchange in Mount Hagen, New Guinea*, Cambridge, UK, 1971.
J. Terrell, *Prehistory in the Pacific Islands*, Cambridge, UK, 1986.
J.P. White and J.F. O'Connell, *A Prehistory of Australia, New Guinea, and Sahul*, Sydney, 1982.

European visions of the Pacific
Charles R. Anderson, *Melville in the South Seas*, New York, 1939.
J. C. Beaglehole (ed), *The Journals of Captain James Cook on his Voyages of Discovery*, 4 vols, Cambridge, UK, 1955–1974.
Paul Carter, *Road to Botany Bay: An Essay in Spacial History*, Ringwood, Victoria, 1987.
Gavan Daws, *A Dream of Islands*, London, 1980.

A. Grove Day, *Adventurers of the Pacific*, New York, 1969.
A. Grove Day, *Jack London in the South Seas*, Boston, 1979.
A. Grove Day, *James A. Mitchener*, Boston, 1977.
A. Grove Day (ed), *Melville's South Seas: An Anthology*, New York, 1970.
A. Grove Day, *Pacific Islands Literature: One Hundred Basic Books*, Hawaii, 1971.
William Everson, *Archetype West: The Pacific Coast as a Literary Region*, Berkeley, 1976.
John McLaren, *New Pacific Literatures: Culture and Environment in the European Pacific*, New York, 1993.
Bill Pearson, *Rifled Sactuaries: Some Views of the Pacific Islands in Western Literature to 1900*, Auckland, 1984.
Bernard Smith, *European Vision and the South Pacific*, New Haven, 1992.
O.H.K. Spate, *The Pacific Since Magellan*, Canberra, 1988; published in 3 volumes as *The Spanish Lake (1979)*, *Monopolists and Freebooters (1983)*, *Paradise Found and Lost (1988)*.

The South Pacific Today
Fanaaafi Le Tagaloa Aiono et al (R. Crocombe et al, eds), *Culture and Democracy in the South Pacific*, Suva, Fiji, 1992.
R. Crocombe, *The South Pacific: An Introduction*, Suva, Fiji, 1983 (revised 1989).
N. Douglas and N. Douglas (eds), *The Pacific Islands Yearbook*, NSW (17th edn, 1995).
Te'o I.J. Fairburn et al, *The Pacific Islands: Politics, Economics and International Relations*, Honolulu, 1991.
D.B. Gewertz and F.K. Errington, *Twisted Histories, Altered Contexts: Representing the Chambri in a World System*, Cambridge UK, 1991.
E. Hau'ofa et al, *Class and Culture in the South*, Suva, Fiji, 1987.
S. Henningham, *France and the South Pacific*, Sydney, 1992.
V. Hereniko, *Art in the New Pacific*, Suva, Fiji, 1979.
S. Hoadley, *The South Pacific Foreign Affairs Handbook*, Sydney, 1992.
M. Jolly and M. MacIntyre (eds), *Family and Gender in the Pacific: Domestic Contradictions and the Colonial Impact*, Cambridge UK, 1989.
G. McCall, *Rapanui: Tradition and Survival on Easter Island*, Sydney, revised edn 1994.
T. O'Meara, *Samoan Planters: Tradition and Economic Development in Polynesia*, Fort Worth, Texas, 1990.
A. Ravuvu, *Development or Dependence: The Pattern of Change in a Fijian Village*, Suva, Fiji, 1988.
D. Robie, *Blood on their Banner: Nationalist Struggles in the South Pacific*, London, 1989.
A.D. Robillard (ed), *Social Change in the Pacific Islands*, London, 1992.
South Pacific Regional Environment Programme, *The Pacific Way: Pacific Island Developing Countries' Report to the United Nations Conference on Environment and Development*, prepared by the South Pacific Regional Environment Program, South Pacific Commission, 1992.
E. Weingartner, *The Pacific: Nuclear Testing and Minorities* (Minority Rights Group Report), London, 1991.

Literature
V. Eri, *The Crocodile*, Harlow UK, 1970 (Papua New Guinea).
P. Grace, *Waiariki and Other Stories*, Auckland, 1986 (Aotearoa).
E. Hau'ofa, *Tales from the Tikongs*, Auckland, 1983 (Tonga).
K. Hulme, *The Bone People*, London, 1983 (Aotearoa).
W. Ihimaera, *Tangi*, Auckland, 1973 (Aotearoa).
Subramani, *South Pacific Literature*, Suva, Fiji, 1985 (revised 1992).
A. Wendt, *Lali: A Pacific Anthology*, Auckland, 1980.
A. Wendt, *Leaves of the Banyan Tree*, London, 1980 (Western Samoa).

LIST OF ILLUSTRATIONS

Cartographical data on pages 131 and 135 based on information from the *New Zealand Historic Atlas* (1996)

GAZETTEER

An entry includes a descriptive term if it is a physical feature and the modern country name Abaiang *(atoll)*, *(Kiribati)*. An entry followed by an asterisk* indicates a territorial unit eg a province, kingdom or region.

Abaiang *(atoll)*, *(Kiribati)*, 1°43´N 173°00´E, 218
Abemama *(atoll)*, *(Kiribati)*, 0°20´N 173°50´E, 218
Acapulco *(Mexico)*, 16°51´N 99°56´W, 99
Actaeon Group (Las Cuatro Coronadas) *(atolls)*, *(French Polynesia)*, 22°00´S 136°00´W, 98
Adamstown *(Pitcairn Group)*, 25°04´S 130°05´W, 13, 201
Adelaide *(Australia)*, 34°56´S 138°36´E,12, 48, 124, 142, 144, 152, 175, 176, 185, 194, 200
Adelgong *(Australia)*, 35°21´S 148°04´E, 176
Admiralty Bay *(New Zealand)*, 40°55´S 173°53´E,115
Admiralty Islands *(Papua New Guinea)*, 2°30´S 147°20´E, 12, 58, 104
Adventure Bay *(Australia)*, 43°07´S 147°00´E, 114
Agana *(Guam)*, 13°28´N 144°45´E, 12, 200
Ahé (Waterlandt) *(atoll)*, *(French Polynesia)*, 14°30´S 146°19´W, 100
Ahioma *(Papua New Guinea)*, 10°20´S 150°35´E, 89
Ahuriri *see* Napier
Ahu Vinapu No1 *(Easter Island)*, 27°10´S 109°24´W, 81
Aitutaki *(isl)*, *(Cook Islands)*, 18°52´S 159°46´W, 141
Akaroa *(New Zealand)*, 43°50´S 172°59´E, 135
Albany *(Australia)*, 34°57´S 115°54´E, 48, 142, 144, 152, 175, 185, 194
Albury *(Australia)*, 36°03´S 146°53´E, 142, 185
Alcester *(isl)*, *(Papua New Guinea)*, 9°34´S 152°25´E, 89
Alice Springs *(Australia)*, 23°42´S 133°52´E, 12, 48, 142, 175, 185, 194, 200
Allen´s Cave *(Australia)*, 31°00´S 128°07´E, 35
Aloa *(Solomon Islands)*, 9°30´S 160°30´E, 212
Alofi *(Niue)*, 19°03´S 169°55´W, 13, 201
Alotau *(Papua New Guinea)*, 10°20´S 150°23´E, 89
Alu *(isl)*, *(Solomon Islands)*, 7°06´S 155°30´E, 212
Ambon *(isl)*, *(Indonesia)*, 4°50´S 128°10´E, 124
American Samoa *(United States)*, 13, 124, 201, 210, 221
Amsterdam *see* Tongatapu
Anakena *(Easter Island)*, 27°04´S 109°19´W, 81
Antipodes Islands *(New Zealand)*, 49°42´S 178°50´E, 12
Anuta *(isl)*, *(Solomon Islands)*, 11°43´S 170°00´E, 58
Aotearoa *see* New Zealand
Apia *(Western Samoa)*, 13°48´S 171°45´W, 13, 201, 217
Apo, Mt, *(Philippines)*, 6°50´N 125°24´E, 16
Apolima *(isl)*, *(Western Samoa)*, 13°48´S 172°06´W, 217
Apolima Strait *(Western Samoa)*, 217
Araluen *(Australia)*, 35°29´S 149°38´E, 176
Aranuka *(atoll)*, *(Kiribati)*, 0°10´N 173°35´E, 218
Ararat *(Australia)*, 37°20´S 143°00´E, 176
Arawe Islands *(Papua New Guinea)*, 6°10´S 148°56´E, 58
Argentina, 196
Arnhem Land *(Australia)*, 13°10´S 134°30´E, 175
Arorae *(isl)*, *(Kiribati)*, 2°39´N 176°54´E, 218
Asau *(Western Samoa)*, 13°26´S 172°35´W, 217
Ashburton *(New Zealand)*, 43°54´S 171°46´E,135
Ashburton *(r)*, *(Australia)*, 43°54´S 171°46´E, 48, 142, 175, 185
Asia, 16, 18, 98, 100, 114
Atafu *(atoll)*, *(Tokelau)*, 8°40´S 172°40´W, 218
´Atele *(Tonga)*, 21°12´S 175°12´W, 73
Atori *(Solomon Islands)*, 8°42´S 160°57´E, 212
Auckland *(New Zealand)*, 36°55´S 174°45´E, 12, 61, 124, 131, 135, 144, 194, 200, 210
Auckland Islands *(New Zealand)*, 50°35´S 166°00´E, 12, 194, 200
Auki *(Solomon Islands)*, 8°45´S 160°44´E, 212
Aurukun *(Australia)*, 13°12´S 141°47´E, 144
Australia (New Holland, Terra Australis), 12, 16, 18, 36, 48, 58, 98, 100, 104, 114, 124, 141, 142, 144, 152, 175, 176, 185, 192, 194, 196, 200, 210
Austral Islands *see* Tubuai Islands
Austral Seamounts *(Pacific Ocean)*, 13
Avarua *(Cook Islands)*, 21°12´S 159°46´W, 13, 201
Awamoa *(New Zealand)*, 45°06´S 170°57´E, 61
Ayers Rock (Uluru) *(mt)*, *(Australia)*, 25°18´S 131°18´E, 36
Ba *(Fiji)*, 17°34´S 177°40´E, 215
Babau *(Indonesia)*, 10°08´S 123°47´E, 100
Babelthuap *(isl)*, *(Palau)*, 6°40´N 134°39´E, 12, 94, 192
Bairiki *(Kiribati)*, 1°25´N 173°00´E, 12, 200
Baker Island *(atoll)*, *(United States)*, 0°12´N 176°28´W, 218
Balclutha *(New Zealand)*, 46°16´S 169°48´E, 135
Ballalae *(isl)*, *(Solomon Islands)*, 7°05´S 155°39´E, 212
Ballarat *(Australia)*, 37°36´S 143°58´E, 176, 185
Balof 2 *(Papua New Guinea)*, 2°59´S 151°28´E, 52
Banaba *(isl)*, *(Kiribati)*, 0°52´S 169°35´E, 218
Bangka *(isl)*, *(Indonesia)*, 2°20´S 106°10´E, 12
Baniara *(Papua New Guinea)*, 9°46´S 149°51´E, 89
Banjarmasin *(Indonesia)*, 3°22´S 114°33´E, 124
Barambah *(Australia)*, 25°09´S 151°43´E, 144
Barbados, 196
Barcoo *(r)*, *(Australia)*, 175
Bass, Iles de *see* Marotiri
Bass Point *(Australia)*, 33°40´S 151°07´E, 35
Bass Strait *(Australia)*, 12, 48, 152, 175, 210
Batavia *see* Jakarta
Bathurst *(Australia)*, 33°27´S 149°35´E, 142, 144, 175, 176, 185
Batiki *(isl)*, *(Fiji)*, 17°47´S 179°10´E, 215
Beaconsfield *(Australia)*, 41°11´S 146°46´E, 176
Beagle Bay *(Australia)*, 17°13´S 122°22´E, 144
Begawan *(Brunei)*, 4°54´N 114°57´E, 2, 200
Beginners Luck Cave *(Australia)*, 42°30´S 146°40´E, 35
Bellona *(isl)*, *(Solomon Islands)*, 11°20´S 159°47´E, 58, 212
Bendigo *(Australia)*, 36°48´S 144°21´E, 142, 176, 185
Beqa *(isl)*, *(Fiji)*, 18°24´S 178°09´E, 215
Beru *(atoll)*, *(Kiribati)*, 1°15´S 176°00´E, 218
Biak *(isl)*, *(Indonesia)*, 1°10´S 136°05´S, 192
Bikini *(atoll)*, *(Marshall Islands)*, 11°35´N 165°20´E, 200
Birnie *(isl)*, *(Kiribati)*, 3°40´S 171°50´W, 218
Bishop of Osnaburgh´s Island *see* Tematangi
Bismarck Archipelago *(isls)*, *(Papua New Guinea)*, 4°32´S 152°25´E, 144
Blenheim *(New Zealand)*, 41°32´S 173°58´E, 135
Bloomfield River *(Australia)*, 15°56´S 145°21´E, 144
Bluff *(New Zealand)*, 46°38´S 168°21´E, 131, 135
Boeroe *see* Buru
Bolubolu *(Papua New Guinea)*, 9°22´S 150°22´E, 89
Bomaderry *(Australia)*, 34°21´S 150°34´E, 144
Bonin Islands (Ogasawara Gunto), *(Japan)*, 27°00´N 142°10´E, 12, 18, 192
Bora Bora *(isl)*, *(French Polynesia)*, 16°30´S 151°45´W, 100
Borneo *(isl)*, *(Indonesia, Malaysia)*, 1°30´N 115°00´E, 12, 16, 18, 98, 100, 124, 185, 192
Boscawen *see* Tafahi
Botany Bay *(Australia)*, 34°04´S 151°08´E, 114
Bottomless Islands *see* Takaroa and Takapoto
Bougainville *(isl)*, *(Papua New Guinea)*, 6°00´S 155°00´E, 12, 52, 104, 124, 212
Bougainville Strait *(Vanuatu)*, 104
Bouman´s Islands *see* Samoa Islands
Bounty Islands *(New Zealand)*, 48°00´S 178°30´E, 12, 141, 194
Bourke *(Australia)*, 30°09´S 145°59´E, 142, 185
Bowen *(Australia)*, 20°00´S 148°15´E, 144
Brazil, 196
Brisbane *(Australia)*, 27°30´S 153°00´E, 12, 48, 124, 142, 144, 175, 185, 194, 200, 210
British New Guinea *see* Papua, Territory of
British North Borneo *(Britain)*, 124
Broken Hill *(Australia)*, 31°57´S 141°30´E, 142, 185, 194
Broome *(Australia)*, 17°58´S 122°15´E, 142, 144, 185, 192
Brunei, 98, 124, 200
Bua *(Fiji)*, 16°48´S 178°38´E, 215
Buala *(Solomon Islands)*, 8°11´S 159°37´E, 212
Buang Marabak *(Papua New Guinea)*, 3°17´S 151°55´E, 52
Buca *(Fiji)*, 16°38´S 179°51´E, 215
Buka *(isl)*, *(Papua New Guinea)*, 5°10´S 154°30´E, 52, 104, 124, 212
Buller *(r)*, *(New Zealand)*, 131, 135
Buna *(Papua New Guinea)*, 8°40´S 148°25´E, 192
Bunbury *(Australia)*, 33°20´S 115°34´E, 142, 152, 185
Bundaberg *(Australia)*, 24°50´S 152°21´E, 185
Buntingdale *(Australia)*, 38°20´S 143°37´E, 144
Burketown *(Australia)*, 17°44´S 139°22´E, 142, 185
Burrill Lake *(Australia)*, 35°26´S 150°22´E, 35
Buru (Boeroe) *(isl)*, *(Indonesia)*, 3°30´S 126°30´E, 12, 104
Busselton *(Australia)*, 33°43´S 115°15´E, 152
Bustard Bay *(Australia)*, 24°02´S 151°48´E, 114
Bwagaoia *(Papua New Guinea)*, 10°39´S 152°48´E, 89
Bwasiaiai *(Papua New Guinea)* , 10°06´S 150°48´E, 89
Cagalai *(isl)*, *(Fiji)*, 17°56´S 178°48´E, 215
Cairns *(Australia)*, 16°51´S 145°43´E, 142, 185, 194
Callao *(Peru)*, 12°05´S 77°08´W, 99
Campbell Island *(New Zealand)*, 52°30´S 169°02´E, 12
Canada, 196
Canberra *(Australia)*, 35°18´S 149°08´E, 12, 194, 200
Cannac *(isl)*, *(Papua New Guinea)*, 9°14´S 153°28´E, 89
Canton *(China)*, 23°08´N 113°20´E, 124
Carnavon *(Australia)*, 24°51´S 113°45´E, 142
Caroline Island *(atoll)*, *(Kiribati)*, 10°00´S 150°15´W, 98, 219
Caroline Islands *(Federated States of Micronesia)*, 7°50´N 145°00´E, 12, 16, 18, 58, 94, 100, 104, 124, 144, 192
Carondelet Reef *(Kiribati)*, 5°33´S 173°50´W, 218
Carpentaria, Gulf of *(Australia)*, 12, 48, 142, 152, 175, 185, 192, 194
Carteret *see* Malaita
Castlemaine *(Australia)*, 37°05´S 144°19´E, 176
Castlepoint *(New Zealand)*, 40°54´S 176°15´E, 131, 135
Cave Bay Cave *(Australia)*, 40°53´S 144°49´E, 35
Ceduna *(Australia)*, 32°07´S 133°42´E, 142
Celebes *see* Sulawesi
Ceram *(isl)*, *(Indonesia)*, 3°10´S 129°30´E, 12
Changsha *(China)*, 28°10´N 113°00´E, 192
Channel Country *(Australia)*, 22°52´S 143°20´E, 175
Charleville *(Australia)*, 26°25´S 146°13´E, 142, 185
Chatham Islands *(New Zealand)*, 44°00´S 176°35´W, 13, 58, 61, 194, 201
Chile, 196
China, 12, 124, 192, 196, 200
Chirovanga *(Solomon Islands)*, 6°40´S 156°38´E, 212
Choiseul *(isl)*, *(Solomon Islands)*, 7°00´S 157°00´E, 104, 212
Christchurch *(New Zealand)*, 43°33´S 172°40´E, 12, 131, 135, 194, 200
Christmas Island *see* Kiritimati
Chuuk *(isl)*, *(Federated States of Micronesia)*, 7°12´N 151°53´E, 210
Chuuk Islands (Truk Islands), *(Federated States of Micronesia)*, 7°12´N 151°53´E, 94, 192
Cicia *(isl)*, *(Fiji)*, 17°46´S 179°16´W, 215
Cikobia *(isl)*, *(Fiji)*, 15°43´S 179°52´W, 215
Cipangu *see* Japan
Clarence *(r)*, *(New Zealand)*, 61, 75, 135
Clarence River Mouth *(New Zealand)*, 42°10´S 173°56´E, 61
Clogg´s Cave *(Australia)*, 37°21´S 148°31´E, 35
Cloncurry *(Australia)*, 20°41´S 140°30´E, 142
Cloudy Bay *(Australia)*, 42°08´S 145°21´E, 100
Clunes *(Australia)*, 37°20´S 143°51´E, 176
Clutha *(r)*, *(New Zealand)*, 61, 75, 131, 135
Clyde *(New Zealand)*, 45°11´S 169°22´E, 135
Cobar *(Australia)*, 31°32´S 145°51´E, 176
Cocos *see* Tafahi
Cohuna *(Australia)*, 35°47´S 144°15´E, 35
Colless Creek *(Australia)*, 18°37´S 138°50´E, 35
Collingwood (Gibbstown), *(New Zealand)*, 40°41´S 172°41´E, 131, 135
Conversion de San Pablo *see* Hao
Cook Islands *(New Zealand)*, 13, 16, 18, 58, 124, 144, 196, 201, 211, 219, 223
Cook, Mt *(New Zealand)*, 43°45´S 170°12´E, 12
Cook Strait *(New Zealand)*, 12, 115, 135, 210
Cooktown *(Australia)*, 15°29´S 145°15´E, 185, 194
Cooper Creek *(r)*, *(Australia)*, 142, 185
Copang *see* Kupang
Coral Sea Islands Territory *(Australia)*, 16°20´S 150°21´E, 12
Coral Coast *(Fiji)*, 18°18´S 177°40´E, 215
Coromandel Peninsula *(New Zealand)*, 36°45´S 175°30´E, 131
Cromwell *(New Zealand)*, 45°03´S 169°14´E, 135
Croydon *(Australia)*, 18°12´S 142°14´E, 185
Cunnamulla *(Australia)*, 28°04´S 145°40´E, 185
Dala *(Solomon Islands)*, 8°36´S 160°41´E, 212
Dalap-Uliga-Darrit *(Marshall Islands)*, 7°09´S 171°12´E, 12, 200
Daly River *(Australia)*, 13°50´S 130°40´E, 144
Dampier *(Australia)*, 20°45´S 114°48´E, 100, 194
Dampier Archipelago *(isls)*, *(Australia)*, 20°43´S 114°45´E, 100
Dampier Strait *(Papua New Guinea)*, 100
Dangerous Archipelago *see* Tuamotu Archipelago
Dargaville *(New Zealand)*, 35°57´S 173°53´E, 131, 135
Daria *(Fiji)*, 16°49´S 179°50´E, 215
Darling *(r)*, *(Australia)*, 12, 16, 18, 36, 48, 58, 142, 175, 176, 185, 194, 200, 210
Darwin *(Australia)*, 12°23´S 130°44´E, 12, 48, 142, 144, 152, 175, 185, 192, 194, 200, 210
Deliverance, Cape of *(pen)*, *(Papua New Guinea)*, 11°25´S 154°26´E, 104
D´Entrecasteaux Islands *(Papua New Guinea)*, 9°30´S 150°40´E, 89
Devil´s Lair *(Australia)*, 33°40´S 115°46´E, 35
Diamantina Trench *(Indian Ocean)*, 12, 16
Dog Island *see* Pukapuka
Drue *(Fiji)*, 19°00´S 178°11´E, 215
Dubbo *(Australia)*, 32°16´S 148°41´E, 185
Duc de Gloucester, Iles (Duke of Gloucester Islands) *(isls)*, *(French Polynesia)*, 20°37´S 143°05´W, 104
Ducie Island (La Encarnacion), *(Pitcairn Group)*, 24°40´S 124°48´W, 98
Duff Islands (Our Lady of Succour, Taumako), *(Solomon Islands)*, 9°53´S 167°08´E, 98, 213
Duke of Gloucester Islands *see* Duc de Gloucester, Iles
Duke of York Islands *(Papua New Guinea)*, 4°12´S 152°28´E, 58
Dunedin (Otago), *(New Zealand)*, 45°52´S 170°30´E, 131, 135, 144, 194
Dusky Bay *(New Zealand)*, 45°46´S 166°31´E, 115
Dusky Sound *(New Zealand)*, 45°46´S 166°31´E, 131
Dutch New Guinea *(Netherlands)*, 185
Dutch East Indies *see* Indonesia
Early Man Shelter *(Australia)*, 14°49´S 144°31´E, 35
East Cape *(pen)*, *(New Zealand)*, 37°42´S 178°35´E, 131
Easter Island (Isla de Pascua, Paasch, Rapa Nui), *(Chile)*, 27°05´S 109°20´W, 13, 19, 81, 100, 104, 114, 125, 144, 201
Eastern Pacific Rise *(Pacific Ocean)*, 13
East Timor *(Portugal)*, 8°35´S 125°34´E, 185
Eauripik *(atoll)*, *(Federated States of Micronesia)*, 6°42´N 143°04´E, 94
Echunga *(Australia)*, 35°00´S 138°46´E, 176
Efaté *(isl)*, *(Vanuatu)*, 17°40´S 168°25´E, 12, 58, 210
Egmont, Cape *(pen)*, *(New Zealand)*, 39°17´S 173°45´E, 131
Egmont, Mt *(New Zealand)*, 39°20´S 174°05´E, 115
Egypt, 196
Elato *(atoll)*, *(Federated States of Micronesia)*, 7°52´N 145°06´E, 94
Elietoga *(mt)*, *(Western Samoa)*, 13°36´S 172°37´W, 217
Ellice Islands *see* Tuvalu
Elouae Island *(Papua New Guinea)*, 1°47´S 150°00´E, 58
Emerald *(Australia)*, 23°30´S 148°08´E, 185
Emu *(Australia)*, 32°13´S 119°29´E, 200
Encounter Bay *(Australia)*, 35°35´S 138°44´E, 175
Enderbury *(atoll)*, *(Kiribati)*, 3°08´S 171°05´W, 218
Enewetak (Eniwetok) *(atoll)*, *(Marshall Islands)*, 11°30´S 162°15´E, 12, 192, 200
Engineer Group *(isls)*, *(Papua New Guinea)*, 10°43´S 151°23´E, 89
Eniwetok *see* Enewetak
Eretoka *(isl)*, *(Vanuatu)*, 17°24´S 168°13´E, 58
Esa-ala *(Papua New Guinea)*, 9°45´S 150°47´E, 89
Esperance *(Australia)*, 33°49´S 121°52´E, 142, 175, 194
Espiritu Santo *(isl)*, *(Vanuatu)*, 15°50´S 166°50´E, 12, 98, 114, 210
´Eua *(isl)*, *(Tonga)*, 21°23´S 174°55´W, 73
Eurasian Plate, 16
Eyre, Lake *(Australia)*, 28°30´S 137°25´E, 12, 36, 175
Fagafau *(Western Samoa)*, 13°37´S 172°41´W, 217
Fagamalo *(Western Samoa)*, 13°27´S 172°24´W, 217
Fais *(isl)*, *(Federated States of Micronesia)*, 9°45´N 140°31´E, 94
Fakaofo *(atoll)*, *(Tokelau)*, 9°30´S 171°15´W, 218
Falealupo Peninsula *(Western Samoa)*, 13°25´S 172°45´W, 217
Falealupo-tai *(Western Samoa)*, 13°25´S 172°45´W, 217
Faleasi´u *(Western Samoa)*, 13°48´S 171°56´W, 73, 217
Falelima *(Western Samoa)*, 13°30´S 172°41´W, 217
Fale´ula *(Western Samoa)*, 13°46´S 171°48´W, 217
Falevao *(Western Samoa)*, 13°53´S 171°31´W, 217
False Island *(New Zealand)*, 46°21´S 169°48´E, 61
Fangataufa *(atoll)*, *(French Polynesia)*, 22°11´S 138°17´W, 201
Faraulep *(atoll)*, *(Federated States of Micronesia)*, 8°36´N 144°33´E, 94
Farewell, Cape *(pen)*, *(New Zealand)*, 40°30´S 172°43´E, 131
Fatuosofia, Cape *(pen)*, *(Western Samoa)*, 13°52´S 172°03´W, 217
Federated States of Micronesia,12, 200, 210, 223
Feni Islands *(Papua New Guinea)*, 4°06´S 154°05´E, 58
Fergusson Island *(Papua New Guinea)*, 9°27´S 150°37´E, 89
Fiji, 12, 100, 124, 194, 200, 210, 215, 223
Fiji Islands *(Fiji)*, 18°00´S 178°00´E, 16, 18, 58, 73, 144, 193, 196
Fito *(mt)*, *(Western Samoa)*, 13°54´S 171°43´W, 217
Fitzroy *(r)*, *(Australia)*, 48, 142, 185
Flinders *(r)*, *(Australia)*, 48, 142, 175, 185
Flint *(isl)*, *(Kiribati)*, 11°25´S 151°48´W, 219
Flores *(isl)*, *(Indonesia)*, 8°40´S 121°20´E, 12
Florida Islands *(Solomon Islands)*, 8°53´S 160°00´E, 212
Fly Island *see* Rangiroa
Fly *(r)*, *(Papua New Guinea)*, 194
Fongafale *(Tuvalu)*, 7°27´S 179°10´E, 12, 200
Forbes *(Australia)*, 33°24´S 148°03´E, 176
Formosa *see* Taiwan
Fouia *(Solomon Islands)*, 8°26´S 160°51´E, 212
Framlingham *(Australia)*, 38°00´S 144°29´E, 144
France, 196
Fraser Cave *(Australia)*, 43°15´S 146°40´E, 35
Fraser Island *(Australia)*, 25°15´S 153°10´E, 144
Fremantle (Swan River), *(Australia)*, 32°07´S 115°44´E, 48, 142, 144, 152, 185, 194
French Polynesia *(France)*, 13, 196, 201, 211, 223
Friendly Islands *see* Tonga
Fulaga *(isl)*, *(Fiji)*, 19°10´S 178°39´W, 73, 215
Funafuti *(atoll)*, *(Tuvalu)*, 8°30´S 179°12´E, 12, 210, 218
Futuna *(isl)*, *(Wallis and Futuna)*, 14°25´S 178°20´W, 58, 124
Gadaisu *(Papua New Guinea)*, 10°19´S 149°45´E, 89
Galoa *(isl)*, *(Fiji)*, 19°05´S 178°13´E, 215
Gambier, Iles *(isls)*, *(French Polynesia)*, 23°10´S 135°00´W, 13, 58, 144
Gascoyne *(Australia)*, 25°02´S 115°15´E, 144
Gatavai *(Western Samoa)*, 13°46´S 172°22´W, 217
Gau *(isl)*, *(Fiji)*, 18°00´S 179°16´E, 215
Gaua (Virgen Maria) *(isl)*, *(Vanuatu)*, 13°34´S 167°24´E, 98
Gawa *(isl)*, *(Papua New Guinea)*, 9°00´S 151°58´E, 89
Geelong *(Australia)*, 38°10´S 144°26´E, 194
Gente Hermosa *see* Swains
George Sound *(New Zealand)*, 44°50´S 167°21´E, 131
Geraldton *(Australia)*, 28°49´S 114°36´E, 142, 152, 175, 185, 194
German New Guinea, 124, 185

Mexico,13, 196
Mexico City *(Mexico)*, 19°25′N 99°10′W, 13
Mid-Pacific Seamounts *(Pacific Ocean)*, 12
Midway Islands *(United States)*, 28°12′N 177°24′W, 12, 193, 200
Milne Bay *(Papua New Guinea)*, 10°24′S 150°24′E, 89
Milton *(New Zealand)*, 46°08′S 169°59′E, 135
Minami-Tori-Shima (Marcus) *(isl)*, *(Japan)*, 24°18′N 153°58′E, 192
Mindanao *(isl)*, *(Philippines)*, 7°30′N 125°00′E, 12, 16, 18, 192
Mindoro *(isl)*, *(Philippines)*, 13°00′N 121°00′E, 12
Miriwun *(Australia)*, 15°52′S 128°28′E, 35
Misima *(isl)*, *(Papua New Guinea)*, 10°38′S 152°45′E, 89
Misisil *(Papua New Guinea)*, 6°07′S 150°00′E, 52
Mitchell River *(Australia)*, 15°12′S 141°35′E, 144
Moa-Bone Point Cave *(New Zealand)*, 43°36′S 172°43′E, 61
Moala *(isl)*, *(Fiji)*, 18°34′S 179°53′E, 215
Moce *(isl)*, *(Fiji)*, 18°38′S 178°32′W, 215
Moeraki *(New Zealand)*, 44°46′S 170°50′E, 131, 144
Moikau *(New Zealand)*, 41°19′S 175°14′E, 61
Mokau *(New Zealand)*, 38°41′S 174°37′E, 144
Momi Bay *(Fiji)*, 17°55′S 177°17′E, 215
Mono *(isl)*, *(Solomon Islands)*, 7°23′S, 155°32′E, 212
Monte Bello Islands *(Australia)*, 20°30′S 115°30′E, 200
Moreton Bay *(Australia)*, 27°10′S 153°25′E, 144, 152, 175
Morotai *(isl)*, *(Indonesia)*, 2°10′N 128°30′E, 192
Mortlock Islands *(Federated States of Micronesia)*, 5°12′N 153°46′E, 94
Mossgiel *(Australia)*, 33°18′S 144°05′E, 35
Motiti Island *(New Zealand)*, 37°39′S 176°22′E, 131
Motuhora *(isl)*, *(New Zealand)*, 37°46′S 176°53′E, 131
Motu Marotiri *(isl)*, *(Easter Island)*, 27°07′S 109°15′W, 81
Motu Nui *(isl)*, *(Easter Island)*, 27°12′S 109°28′W, 81
Motutapu Island *(New Zealand)*, 36°47′S 174°52′E, 61
Mount Camel *(New Zealand)*, 34°50′S 173°09′E, 61
Mount Isa *(Australia)*, 20°50′S 139°29′E, 142, 194
Mount Magnet *(Australia)*, 28°06′S 115°50′E, 142, 185
Mount Morgan *(Australia)*, 23°40′S 150°25′E, 185
Mount Newman *(Australia)*, 23°20′S 119°39′E, 35
Mu′a (Lapaha), *(Tonga)*, 21°11′S 175°07′W, 73
Mulifanua *(Western Samoa)*, 13°50′S 172°02′W, 73, 217
Munda *(Solomon Islands)*, 8°18′S 157°15′E, 212
Mungo, Lake *see* Willandra Lakes
Munia *(isl)*, *(Fiji)*, 17°20′S 178°53′W, 215
Murchison *(r)*, *(Australia)*, 48, 142, 175, 185
Murderers′ Bay *(New Zealand)*, 41°05′S 173°14′E, 100
Murray *(r)*, *(Australia)*, 12, 16, 18, 36, 48, 58, 142, 175, 176, 185, 194, 200
Murrumbidgee *(r)*, *(Australia)*, 175
Mururoa *(atoll)*, *(French Polynesia)*, 22°00′S 140°00′W, 201
Nabouwalu *(Fiji)*, 17°00′S 178°43′E, 215
Nacula *(isl)*, *(Fiji)*, 16°54′S 177°25′E, 215
Nadarivatu *(Fiji)*, 17°34′S 177°59′E, 215
Nadi *(Fiji)*, 17°48′S 177°25′E, 215
Nadi *(r)*, *(Fiji)*, 215
Naduri *(Fiji)*, 16°26′S 179°08′E, 215
Nagasaki *(Japan)*, 32°45′N 129°52′E, 192
Nagoya *(Japan)*, 35°08′N 136°53′E, 192
Naigani *(isl)*, *(Fiji)*, 17°36′S 178°40′E, 215
Nairai *(isl)*, *(Fiji)*, 17°52′S 179°26′E, 215
Naitaba *(isl)*, *(Fiji)*, 17°01′S 179°19′W, 215
Nakabuta *(Fiji)*, 18°05′S 177°31′E, 215
Namenalala *(isl)*, *(Fiji)*, 17°08′S 179°06′E, 215
Namonuito *(atoll)*, *(Federated States of Micronesia)*, 8°42′N 150°09′E, 94
Namu *(atoll)*, *(Marshall Islands)*, 8°00′N 168°08′E, 98
Namuka-i-Lau *(atoll)*, *(Fiji)*, 18°50′S 178°41′W, 215
Nanukuloa *(Fiji)*, 17°29′S 178°14′E, 215
Nanumanga *(isl)*, *(Tuvalu)*, 6°20′S 176°25′E, 218
Nanumea (Isle of Jesus) *(atoll)*, *(Tuvalu)*, 5°40′S 176°10′E, 98, 218
Napier (Ahuriri), *(New Zealand)*, 39°30′S 176°54′E, 131, 135, 144, 194
Nasau *(Fiji)*, 17°18′S 179°27′E, 215
Nasorolevu *(mt)*, *(Fiji)*, 16°44′S 179°23′E, 215
Nassau *(isl)*, *(Cook Islands)*, 11°05′S 165°25′W, 13, 219
Natadola Beach *(Fiji)*, 18°07′S 177°21′E, 215
Natewa Bay *(Fiji)*, 16°36′S 179°40′E, 215
Natovi *(Fiji)*, 17°40′S 178°35′E, 215
Natunuku *(Fiji)*, 17°27′S 177°51′E, 73
Naulabila *(Australia)*, 13°06′S 132°42′E, 35
Nauru, 12, 194, 200, 210, 223
Nauru *(isl)*, *(Nauru)*, 0°31′S 166°56′E, 12, 124, 144, 192, 210
Nausori *(Fiji)*, 18°01′S 178°33′E, 215
Navatu *(Fiji)*, 17°23′S 178°04′E, 73
Navigator Islands *see* Samoa Islands
Naviti *(isl)*, *(Fiji)*, 17°07′S 177°14′E, 215
Navolivoli *(Fiji)*, 17°00′S 179°55′E, 73
Navua *(Fiji)*, 18°11′S 178°12′E, 215
Navua *(r)*, *(Fiji)*, 215
Navuga *(Fiji)*, 16°50′S 179°54′W, 73
Navunievu *(Fiji)*, 16°48′S 178°33′E, 215
Nawa *(Fiji)*, 16°56′S 179°55′E, 73
Nawamoyn *(Australia)*, 12°25′S 133°16′E, 35
Nayala Yala *(Fiji)*, 16°48′S 179°58′W, 73
Nayau *(isl)*, *(Fiji)*, 18°00′S 179°05′W, 215
Ndai (Gower) *(isl)*, *(Solomon Islands)*, 7°54′S 160°36′E, 104
Negros *(isl)*, *(Philippines)*, 10°00′N 123°00′E, 12
Nelson *(New Zealand)*, 41°18′S 173°17′E, 131, 135, 144, 194
Nendo *(isl)*, *(Solomon Islands)*, 10°42′S 166°03′E, 213
Netherlands, 196
Newark *(New Zealand)*, 35°37′S 172°56′E, 144
New Britain *(isl)*, *(Papua New Guinea)*, 6°00′S 150°00′E, 12, 52, 58, 100, 104, 185, 192, 210
New Caledonia *(France)*, 12, 18, 124, 144, 194, 200, 210, 223
New Caledonia *(isl)*, *(New Caledonia)*, 21°30′S 165°30′E, 12, 16, 58, 114, 192, 210
Newcastle *(Australia)*, 32°55′S 151°46′E, 142, 152, 176, 185, 194
New Georgia *(isl)*, *(Solomon Islands)*, 8°15′S 157°35′E, 212
New Georgia Islands *(Solomon Islands)*, 8°45′S 156°15′E, 212
New Guinea (Magna Margarita) *(isl)*, *(Indonesia, Papua New Guinea)*, 5°00′S 142°00′E, 12, 16, 18, 36, 48, 52, 58, 89, 98, 100, 104, 114, 141, 142, 144, 152, 192
New Hebrides *see* Vanuatu
New Hebrides Trench *(Pacific Ocean)*, 16
New Holland *see* Australia
New Ireland *(isl)*, *(Papua New Guinea)*, 2°30′S 151°30′E, 12, 52, 58, 100, 104, 185, 192
New Leinster *see* Stewart Island
New Munster *see* South Island
New Norcia *(Australia)*, 30°58′S 114°15′E, 144
New Plymouth (Ngamotu Beach), *(New Zealand)*, 39°03′S 174°04′E, 131, 135, 194
New South Wales* *(Australia)*, 142, 152, 185
New Ulster *see* North Island
New Zealand (Aotearoa, Nieuw Zeeland), 12, 16, 18, 58, 61, 75, 100, 104, 115, 124, 131, 135, 141, 144, 152, 194, 196, 200, 210, 223
Ngamotu *(New Zealand)*, 39°02′S 174°17′E, 75
Ngamotu Beach *see* New Plymouth
Ngaroto *(New Zealand)*, 37°42′S 175°11′E, 61
Nggela Pile *(isl)*, *(Solomon Islands)*, 9°10′S 160°20′E, 212
Nggela Sule *(isl)*, *(Solomon Islands)*, 9°05′S 160°15′E, 212
Ngulu *(atoll)*, *(Federated States of Micronesia)*, 8°30′N 137°30′E, 94
Nieuw Zeeland *see* New Zealand
Niihau *(isl)*, *(Hawaii)*, 21°50′N 160°11′W, 114
Nikumaroro *(atoll)*, *(Kiribati)*, 4°42′S 174°33′W, 218
Nikunau *(atoll)*, *(Kiribati)*, 1°20′S 176°25′E, 218
Niuatoputapu (Keppel′s Island) *(isl)*, *(Tonga)*, 15°59′S 173°58′W, 58, 73, 104
Niue *(New Zealand)*, 13, 201, 210, 223
Niue (Savage Island) *(isl)*, *(Niue)*, 19°02′S 169°55′W, 13, 114, 124, 144
Niutao *(isl)*, *(Tuvalu)*, 6°06′S 177°16′E, 218
Nomuka (Rotterdam) *(isl)*, *(Tonga)*, 20°15′S 174°46′W, 100, 114, 141
Nonouti *(atoll)*, *(Kiribati)*, 0°44′S 174°28′E, 218
Noola *(Australia)*, 33°14′S 150°00′E, 35
Norfolk Island *(Australia)*, 29°02′S 167°57′E, 12, 114, 124, 144, 152, 194, 200, 210
Normanby Island *(Papua New Guinea)*, 10°05′S 151°05′E, 58, 89
Normanton *(Australia)*, 17°40′S 141°05′E, 142, 185, 194
Noro *(Solomon Islands)*, 8°15′S 157°11′E, 212
Northam *(Australia)*, 31°40′S 114°40′E, 185
North America, 19, 99, 114
North Cape *(pen)*, *(New Zealand)*, 34°28′S 173°00′E, 12, 131
Northern Mariana Islands *(United States)*, 12, 200, 210, 223
Northern Territory* *(Australia)*, 185
North Island (New Ulster, Te Ika a Maui), *(New Zealand)*, 12, 61, 75, 131, 135, 144
North West Cape *(pen)*, *(Australia)*, 21°48′S 114°10′E, 12
Nouméa *(New Caledonia)*, 22°16′S 166°27′E, 12, 200, 210
Nui *(atoll)*, *(Tuvalu)*, 7°12′S 177°10′E, 218
Nuku′alofa *(Tonga)*, 21°07′S 175°12′W, 13, 201
Nukubasaga *(isl)*, *(Fiji)*, 16°20′S 179°15′W, 215
Nukufetau *(atoll)*, *(Tuvalu)*, 8°00′S 178°30′E, 218
Nuku Hiva *(isl)*, *(French Polynesia)*, 8°56′S 140°00′W, 211
Nukulaelae *(atoll)*, *(Tuvalu)*, 9°20′S 179°50′E, 218
Nukunono *(atoll)*, *(Tokelau)*, 9°10′S 171°55′W, 218
Nukutavaké (Queen Charlotte Island) *(isl)*, *(French Polynesia)*, 19°11′S 138°42′W, 104
Nullarbor Plain *(Australia)*, 31°30′S 128°00′E, 12, 36, 48, 175
Nu′ulua *(isl)*, *(Western Samoa)*, 14°05′S 171°24′W, 217
Nu′utele *(isl)*, *(Western Samoa)*, 14°04′S 171°25′W, 217
Oahu *(isl)*, *(Hawaii)*, 21°30′N 158°00′W, 13, 211
Oamaru *(New Zealand)*, 45°07′S 170°58′E, 135
Ogasawara Gunto *see* Bonin Islands
Ogea Driki *(isl)*, *(Fiji)*, 19°11′S 178°26′W, 215
Ogea Levu *(isl)*, *(Fiji)*, 19°07′S 178°24′W, 215
Ohawe *(New Zealand)*, 39°32′S 174°16′E, 61
Ohinemutu *(New Zealand)*, 38°06′S 176°16′E, 61
Okiato *see* Russell
Okinawa *(isl)*, *(Japan)*, 26°30′N 128°00′E, 192
Olorua *(isl)*, *(Fiji)*, 18°35′S 178°46′E, 215
Omeo *(Australia)*, 37°09′S 147°38′E, 176
Oneata *(isl)*, *(Fiji)*, 18°27′S 178°30′W, 215
Ono *(isl)*, *(Fiji)*, 18°53′S 178°30′E, 215
Ono-i-Lau *(isl)*, *(Fiji)*, 20°48′S 178°45′W, 215
Onotoa *(atoll)*, *(Kiribati)*, 1°55′S 175°34′E, 218
Ontong Java *(atoll)*, *(Solomon Islands)*, 5°18′S 159°20′E, 98, 100, 212
Oodnadatta *(Australia)*, 27°30′S 135°27′E, 142, 175, 185
Open Bay Islands *(New Zealand)*, 43°46′S 169°05′E, 131
Opito *(New Zealand)*, 36°41′S 175°47′E, 61
Opotiki *(New Zealand)*, 38°00′S 177°18′E, 131, 135, 144
Orona *(atoll)*, *(Kiribati)*, 4°35′S 172°20′W, 218
Orongo *(Easter Island)*, 27°11′S 109°27′W, 81
Oruarangi *(New Zealand)*, 37°13′S 175°41′E, 61
Otago *see* Dunedin
Otago Peninsula *(New Zealand)*, 45°48′S 170°45′E, 131, 135
Otaheite *see* Tahiti
Otakanini *(New Zealand)*, 36°34′S 174°19′E, 61
Otaki *(New Zealand)*, 40°45′S 175°08′E 131, 144
Otatara *(New Zealand)*, 39°30′S 176°46′E, 61
Otawhao *(New Zealand)*, 38°17′S 175°20′E, 144
Oturehua *(New Zealand)*, 45°00′S 170°00′E, 61
Our Lady of Succour *see* Duff Islands
Outer Arumpo, Lake *see* Willandra Lakes
Ovalau *(isl)*, *(Fiji)*, 17°40′S 178°47′E, 215
Ovens *(Australia)*, 36°20′S 146°18′E, 176
Owhyhee *see* Hawaii
Paasch *see* Easter Island
Pacific Plate, 16
Pago Pago *(American Samoa)*, 14°16′S 170°42′W, 13, 201
Palau, 5°00′N 135°00′E, 12, 124, 192, 200, 210, 223
Palawan *(isl)*, *(Philippines)*, 9°30′N 118°30′E, 12, 98
Palikir *(Federated States of Micronesia)*, 6°40′N 158°27′E, 12, 200
Palliser Islands *(atolls)*, *(French Polynesia)*, 15°05′S 146°22′W, 114
Palmerston Island *(atoll)*, *(Cook Islands)*, 18°04′S 163°10′W, 114
Palmerston North *(New Zealand)*, 40°20′S 175°39′E, 35
Palmyra Island *(atoll)*, *(United States)*, 5°52′N 162°05′W, 219
Panaete *(isl)*, *(Papua New Guinea)*, 10°40′S 152°22′E, 89
Panakiwuk *(Papua New Guinea)*, 2°51′S 151°09′E, 52
Panay *(isl)*, *(Philippines)*, 13°58′N 124°20′E, 12
Papakura *(New Zealand)*, 37°04′S 174°59′E, 144
Papatowai *(New Zealand)*, 46°30′S 169°34′E, 61
Papeete *(French Polynesia)*, 17°32′S 149°34′W, 13, 201
Papua, Territory of (British New Guinea), 124, 185
Papua New Guinea, 12, 194, 200, 210, 223
Parasi *(Solomon Islands)*, 9°41′S 161°27′E, 212
Parece Vela *(isl)*, *(Japan)*, 20°24′N 136°02′E, 192
Pariwhakatau *(New Zealand)*, 42°39′S 173°20′E, 61
Parramatta *(Australia)*, 33°37′S 151°02′E, 144
Pascua, Isla de *see* Easter Island
Patea *(New Zealand)*, 39°45′S 174°29′E, 75, 135, 144
Patutiva *(Solomon Islands)*, 8°34′S 157°53′E, 212
Pavuvu *(isl)*, *(Solomon Islands)*, 9°10′S 159°07′E, 212
Pea *(Tonga)*, 21°10′S 175°13′W, 73
Pearce Point *(Australia)*, 14°22′S 129°20′E, 175
Peleliu *(isl)*, *(Palau)*, 7°02′N 134°15′E, 192
Penrhyn *(atoll)*, *(Cook Islands)*, 9°00′S 158°00′W, 219
Peregrina *see* Swains
Perth *(Australia)*, 31°58′S 115°49′E, 12, 48, 142, 144, 152, 175, 185, 194, 200
Peru, 196
Peterborough *(Australia)*, 33°00′S 138°51′E, 185
Petre *see* Wanganui
Philippines, 12, 196, 200
Philippine Islands *(Philippines)*, 11°00′N 123°00′E, 98, 100, 124, 192
Philippine Plate, 16
Philippine Trench *(Pacific Ocean)*, 12, 16
Phoenix Islands *(atolls)*, *(Kiribati)*, 3°30′S 172°00′W, 13, 16, 18, 58, 124, 210, 218
Pinaki (Whitsun Island) *(isl)*, *(French Polynesia)*, 19°20′S 138°40′W, 104
Pinatubo, Mt *(Philippines)*, 15°25′N 120°15′E, 16
Pins, Ile des *(isl)*, *(New Caledonia)*, 22°37′S 167°30′E, 58
Pitcairn Group *(Britain)*, 13, 201, 211, 223
Pitcairn Island *(Pitcairn Group)*, 25°04′S 130°06′W, 13, 19, 104, 125, 141, 144
Pohnpei *(isl)*, *(Federated States of Micronesia)*, 6°40′N 158°27′E, 12, 210
Poike Ditch *(Easter Island)*, 27°06′S 109°17′W, 81
Point Mcleay *(Australia)*, 36°58′S 139°39′E, 144
Point Pearce *(Australia)*, 35°18′S 136°53′E, 144
Poonindie *(Australia)*, 33°53′S 136°33′E, 144
Porirua *(New Zealand)*, 41°08′S 174°52′E, 131
Port Arthur *(Australia)*, 43°08′S 147°50′E, 152
Port Augusta *(Australia)*, 32°30′S 137°27′E, 142, 175, 185
Port Cooper *see* Lyttleton
Port Curtis *(Australia)*, 23°50′S 151°13′E, 175
Port Dalrymple *(Australia)*, 41°04′S 146°48′E, 152
Port Essington *(Australia)*, 11°30′S 132°32′E, 144, 175
Port Hedland *(Australia)*, 20°24′S 118°36′E, 142, 175, 185, 194
Port Jackson *see* Sydney
Portland *(Australia)*, 38°21′S 141°38′E, 185
Portland Bay *(Australia)*, 38°20′S 141°40′E, 175
Port Lincoln *(Australia)*, 34°43′S 135°49′E, 142, 144, 175
Port Macquarie *(Australia)*, 31°28′S 152°25′E, 48, 142, 152, 175
Port Molyneux *(New Zealand)*, 46°14′S 169°59′E, 131
Port Moresby *(Papua New Guinea)*, 9°30′S 147°07′E, 12, 185, 192, 200, 210
Port Pegasus *(New Zealand)*, 47°17′S 167°35′E, 131
Port Phillip *(Australia)*, 38°05′S 144°50′E, 152
Port Pirie *(Australia)*, 33°11′S 138°01′E, 142, 185
Port Stephens *(Australia)*, 32°43′S 152°08′E, 152
Port-Vila *(Vanuatu)*, 17°45′S 168°18′E, 12, 200
Port William *(New Zealand)*, 46°56′S 168°02′E, 131
Posarae *(Solomon Islands)*, 7°20′S 157°09′E, 212
Possession Island *(Australia)*, 10°40′S 142°10′E, 114
Pounawea *(New Zealand)*, 46°17′S 169°58′E, 61
Poutasi *(Western Samoa)*, 14°00′S 171°43′W, 217
Poverty Bay *(New Zealand)*, 38°39′S 178°01′E, 115
Preservation Bay *(New Zealand)*, 46°07′S 166°46′E, 131
Providence, Cape *(pen)*, *(New Zealand)*, 46°01′S 166°28′E, 131
Pu′apu′a *(Western Samoa)*, 13°34′S 172°12′W, 217
Pukapuka (Dog Island, Honden) *(atoll)*, *(French Polynesia)*, 14°50′S 138°50′W, 100
Pukapuka *(atoll)*, *(Cook Islands)*, 10°53′S 165°49′W, 219
Pulap *(atoll)*, *(Federated States of Micronesia)*, 7°38′N 149°25′E, 94
Pulusuk *(atoll)*, *(Federated States of Micronesia)*, 6°05′N 149°30′E, 94
Puluwat *(atoll)*, *(Federated States of Micronesia)*, 7°21′N 149°11′E, 94
Puna Pau *(Easter Island)*, 27°08′S 109°24′W, 81
Puntutjarpa *(Australia)*, 25°10′S 125°40′E, 35
Purakanui *(New Zealand)*, 45°43′S 170°41′E, 61
Puriri *(New Zealand)*, 37°12′S 175°38′E, 144
Qalau *(Fiji)*, 16°58′S 179°54′E, 73
Qamea *(isl)*, *(Fiji)*, 16°46′S 179°46′W, 215
Qele Levu *(isl)*, *(Fiji)*, 16°05′S 179°10′W, 215
Queen Charlotte Island *see* Nukutavaké
Queen Charlotte′s Islands *see* Santa Cruz Islands
Queen Charlotte′s Sound *(New Zealand)*, 41°15′S 174°09′E, 115
Queensland* *(Australia)*, 142, 185
Queenstown *(New Zealand)*, 45°02′S 168°40′E, 135
Rabaraba *(Papua New Guinea)*, 10°00′S 149°50′E, 89
Rabi *(isl)*, *(Fiji)*, 16°30′S 179°57′W, 215
Rakahanga *(atoll)*, *(Cook Islands)*, 10°03′S 161°06′W, 219
Rakaia *(r)*, *(New Zealand)*, 61, 75, 131, 135
Rakaia River Mouth *(New Zealand)*, 43°54′S 172°13′E, 61
Rakiraki *(Fiji)*, 17°18′S 178°12′E, 215
Ralik Chain *(atolls)*, *(Marshall Islands)*, 8°00′N 168°00′E, 12
Ramos, Isla de *see* Malaita
Rangiaowhia *(New Zealand)*, 38°00′S 175°31′E, 144
Rangiroa (Fly Island) *(atoll)*, *(French Polynesia)*, 15°00′S 147°40′W, 100
Rangitaiki *(r)*, *(New Zealand)*, 75, 131
Rangitoto Island *(New Zealand)*, 36°47′S 174°52′E, 135
Rano Kao *(mt)*, *(Easter Island)*, 27°11′S 109°26′W, 81
Ranongga *(isl)*, *(Solomon Islands)*, 8°01′S 156°35′E, 212
Rano Raraku *(Easter Island)*, 27°07′S 109°18′W, 81
Rapa Nui *see* Easter Island
Raroia (La Sagitaria) *(atoll)*, *(French Polynesia)*, 16°00′S 142°25′W, 98
Rarotonga *(isl)*, *(Cook Islands)*, 21°15′S 159°45′W, 13, 141, 211
Ratak Chain *(atolls)*, *(Marshall Islands)*, 8°20′N 171°10′E, 12
Rawaki *(isl)*, *(Kiribati)*, 3°43′S 171°25′W, 218
Reef Islands *(Solomon Islands)*, 10°15′S 166°18′E, 213
Reefton (Reef Town), *(New Zealand)*, 42°07′S 171°52′E, 135
Reef Town *see* Reefton
Refreshment *see* Makatéa
Rendova *(isl)*, *(Solomon Islands)*, 8°30′S 157°16′E, 212
Rennell *(atoll)*, *(Solomon Islands)*, 11°45′S 160°15′E, 58, 212
Restoration Island *(Australia)*, 13°20′S 144°49′E, 141
Rewa *(r)*, *(Fiji)*, 215
Rewa Delta *(Fiji)*, 18°08′S 178°35′E, 215
Rio Grande *(r)* *(United States)*, 13
Riverton (Jacobs River), *(New Zealand)*, 46°21′S 168°01′E, 131, 135
Rockhampton *(Australia)*, 23°22′S 150°32′E, 48, 142, 185
Rocks Point *(New Zealand)*, 40°53′S 172°08′E, 131
Roebourne *(Australia)*, 20°48′S 115°10′E, 175
Roebuck Bay *(Australia)*, 19°04′S 122°17′E, 100
Roncador Reef *(Solomon Islands)*, 6°15′S 159°23′E, 212
Roonka *(Australia)*, 34°07′S 139°26′E, 35
Roper River *(Australia)*, 14°40′S 135°30′E, 144
Ross *(New Zealand)*, 42°54′S 170°49′E, 135
Rossel Island *(Papua New Guinea)*, 11°23′S 154°12′E, 89
Rota *(isl)*, *(Northern Mariana Islands)*, 14°10′N 145°15′E, 94
Rotorua *(New Zealand)*, 38°07′S 176°17′E, 144
Rotterdam *see* Nomuka
Ruapehu, Mt *(New Zealand)*, 39°18′S 175°36′E, 12, 16
Ruapuke Island *(New Zealand)*, 46°46′S 168°31′E, 75, 131, 135, 144
Russell (Okiato), *(New Zealand)*, 35°16′S 174°08′E, 131, 135
Russell Islands *(Solomon Islands)*, 8°53′S 158°30′E, 212
Russia, 196
Ryukyu Islands *(Japan)*, 26°30′N 125°00′E, 12, 16
Ryukyu Trench *(Pacific Ocean)*, 12, 16
Safotu *(Western Samoa)*, 13°26′S 172°24′W, 217
Sahul, 35
St Elmo *see* Marutéa
Saipan *(isl)*, *(Northern Mariana Islands)*, 15°12′N 145°43′E, 12, 192, 200, 210
Sala′ilua *(Western Samoa)*, 13°42′S 172°35′W, 217
Salelesi *(Western Samoa)*, 13°51′S 171°38′W, 217
Salelologa *(Western Samoa)*, 13°43′S 172°13′W, 217
Salialevu *(Fiji)*, 16°58′S 180°00, 215

INDEX